THE COLLECTED ESSAYS OF
# Robert Creeley

# THE COLLECTED ESSAYS OF
# Robert Creeley

UNIVERSITY OF CALIFORNIA PRESS

*Berkeley    Los Angeles    London*

University of California Press
Berkeley and Los Angeles, California
University of California Press, Ltd.
London, England
© 1989 by
The Regents of the University of California
Printed in the United States of America
1   2   3   4   5   6   7   8   9

Library of Congress Cataloging-in-Publication Data

Creeley, Robert, 1926–
    The collected essays of Robert Creeley.

    Includes index.
    I. Title.
PS3505.R43A16   1989      814'.54      88-27865
ISBN 0-520-06150-0 (alk. paper)

*What thou lovest well remains,*
*the rest is dross . . .*

EZRA POUND, Canto LXXXI

# Contents

# Introduction

On my eighteenth birthday my brother-in-law gave me a copy of the Yale edition of Pound's essays, *Make It New*. That, together with *Polite Essays* and *Pavannes and Divisions* (which last I had bought for myself in Gordon Cairnie's Grolier Bookshop), became a tacit measure for the practice of such writing as is here collected. Or—better—it made very clear to me the rhetorical possibilities, and, even more, the factually passionate engagement that was, so I felt, a necessity in any such discussion.

It was Pound, of course, who so scathingly qualified "books about books," and spoke of critics "busily measuring the Venus de Milo," etc. His energetic contempt for almost all of that critical writing which had been my reference in college was, to put it mildly, bemusing. Finally, his insistent sense was that one must depend upon oneself to learn whatever proved requisite. There was no one else to do it for you.

Although I hadn't the least sense of how to proceed, writing was my concern and commitment early on. I worked at it intently and almost incrementally began to gather a company who were met, for the most part, in the pages of the little magazines to which I applied with my own work. Given the time, and the enclosing orthodoxy with respect to either poetry or prose, there seems little wonder in the fact my early essays have an embattled manner. I was quite certain that we faced an indefatigable army of resistance, a sense I've never really been able to persuade otherwise. Clearly, a good deal of my critical disposition had to do with an imagination of moral context, that there were those who furthered the light and those who did not, and I was hardly objective, nor had thought to be, in my proposals of value. Yet, as Edith Piaf said, "*Je ne regrette rien . . .*"

In addition to Pound there were a number of others significant, as Williams certainly. To this day I deeply resent the bowdlerized edition of his *Selected Essays,* in which he was persuaded, as he then told me, to avoid complicating reference to Eliot and to attempt a comfortably generalizing context of 'subjects,' e.g., Dylan Thomas. He had hoped that his publication by a major house would make him more known but whatever the fact, it seems now a sad detour with such essays as "Letter to an Australian Editor" or "With Rude Fingers Forced" still without place. In any case, I so emphasize it because there can be no such discretion finally, of the author or of anyone else.

Then D. H. Lawrence was immensely important to me in the intensely affective disposition of his various arguments and demonstrations. I was much impressed that he would stop a novel's action cold in order to discuss his own imagination of a proper marriage. Edward Dahlberg had an even more impassioned rhetoric, a prodigiously self-wrought language of judgment. My imagination of the active context of critical proposition would make a foursquare 'table' of Lawrence's *Studies in Classic American Literature,* Dahlberg's *Can These Bones Live,* Williams' *In the American Grain*— and the classic work of my own contemporary, Charles Olson's *Call Me Ishmael.* The so-called common denominator would be the articulately generative nature of the writing itself, in each case a formal authority equal to that in other engagements of prose, or in poetry.

Still I had or have no belief such as the late forties or early fifties entertained, i.e., that criticism constituted the active literary accomplishment of this century in American literature. I think that was said in the *New York Times Book Review* around 1950, but it seems a very long time ago. Rather I felt with Pound that the active critical work would come from those defined in the arts relating, and that their criticism, so to speak, would follow their writing otherwise as 'the two feet of one biped.' Such has seemed the case.

Reading back now over what I've written, the only regret seems an obvious one. I wish that far more might have been made apparent, noted, simply proposed. Again Pound's quotation of de Gourmont has the same abiding clarity as when I first read it all those years ago: *Franchement d'écrire ce qu'on pense, seul plaisir d'un écrivain . . .* It has been mine here.

Finally I thank all who so generously contributed to this book's occasion, and none more than Donald M. Allen whose editing of two collections of my essays previously gave me an absolute model for this present one. Whatever coherence is here comes from his advice and example. Michael Davidson proved once again an excellent friend with his useful suggestions. His sense of possible materials was especially helpful. William McClung, Marilyn Schwartz, Jeanne Sugiyama, and especially Barbara Ras were classic 'friends of the family' all along and their exceptional editorial capability makes the Press a singular one in all respects. Then there is Holly Hall, Head of Special Collections at Washington University, St. Louis, and her patient staff. Much here was located by fact of their care. Closer to home, Michael Boughn of the State University of New York at Buffalo has managed to find things I long ago had forgotten existed and has been impeccably patient with all my demands. The real pleasure is that it was and remains a common world.

Robert Creeley

*Buffalo, New York*
*January 14, 1988*

# I Heroes/Elders

# Introduction to
# Penguin *Selected Whitman*

One of the most lovely insistences in Whitman's poems seems to me his instruction that one speak for oneself. Assumedly that would be the person most involved in saying anything, and yet a habit of 'objective' statement argues the contrary, noting the biases and distortions and tediums of the personal that are thereby invited into the writing. Surely there is some measure possible, such would say, that can make statement a clearly defined and impersonal instance of reality, of white clouds in a blue sky, or things and feelings not distorted by any fact of one man or woman's intensive possession of them. Then there would truly be a common possibility, that all might share, and that no one would have use of more than another.

Yet if Whitman has taught me anything, and he has taught me a great deal, often against my own will, it is that the common *is* personal, intensely so, in that having no one thus to invest it, the sea becomes a curious mixture of water and table salt and the sky the chemical formula for air. It is, paradoxically, the personal which makes the common insofar as it recognizes the existence of the many in the one. In my own joy or despair, I am brought to that which others have also experienced.

My own senses of Whitman were curiously numb until I was thirty. In the forties, when I was in college, it was considered literally bad taste to have an active interest in his writing. In that sense he suffered the same fate as Wordsworth, also condemned as overly

*Whitman, Selected by Robert Creeley,* Poet to Poet series (Harmondsworth, England: Penguin Books, 1973).

prolix and generalizing. There was a persistent embarrassment that this naively affirmative poet might affect one's own somewhat cynical wisdoms. Too, insofar as this was a time of intensively didactic criticism, what was one to do with Whitman, even if one read him? He went on and on, he seemed to lack 'structure,' he yielded to no 'critical apparatus' then to hand. So, as students, we were herded past him as quickly as possible, and our teachers used him only as an example of 'the America of that period' which, we were told, was a vast swamp of idealistic expansion and corruption. Whitman, the dupe, the dumbbell, the pathetically regrettable instance of this country's dream and despair, the self-taught man.

The summation of Whitman and his work was a very comfortable one for all concerned. If I felt at times awkward with it, I had only to turn to Ezra Pound, whom the university also condemned, to find that he too disapproved despite the begrudging 'Pact.' At least he spoke of having 'detested' Whitman, only publicly altering the implications of that opinion in a series of BBC interviews made in the late fifties. William Carlos Williams also seemed to dislike him, decrying the looseness of the writing, as he felt it, and the lack of a coherent prosody. He as well seemed to change his mind in age insofar as he referred to Whitman as the greatest of American poets in a public lecture on American poetry for college students. Eliot also changes his mind, as did James before him, but the point is that the heroes of my youth as well as my teachers were almost without exception extremely critical of Whitman and his influence and wanted as little as possible to do with him.

Two men, however, most dear to me, felt otherwise. The first of these was D. H. Lawrence, whose *Studies in Classic American Literature* remains the most extraordinary apprehension of the nature of American experience and writing that I know. His piece on Whitman in that book is fundamental in that he, in a decisively personal manner, first castigates Whitman for what he considers a muddling assumption of 'oneness,' citing "I am he that aches with amorous love . . ." as particularly offensive, and then, with equal intensity, applauds that Whitman who is, as he puts it, "a great charger of the blood in men," a truly heroic poet whose vision and will make a place of absolute communion for others.

The second, Hart Crane, shared with Whitman my own teachers' disapproval. I remember a course which I took with F. O. Matthiessen, surely a man of deep commitment and care for his students, from which Crane had been absented. I asked for permission to give a paper on Crane, which he gave me, but I had over-

looked what I should have realized would be the response of the
class itself, understandably intent upon its own sophistications.
How would they accept these lines, for example?

yes, Walt,

Afoot again, and onward without halt,—
Not soon, nor suddenly,—no, never to let go
    My hand
        in yours,
            Walt Whitman—
                so—

If they did not laugh outright at what must have seemed to them
the awkwardly stressed rhymes and sentimental camaraderie, then
they tittered at Crane's will to be one with his fellow *homosexual*. But
didn't they hear, I wanted to insist, the pacing of the rhythms of
those lines, the syntax, the intently human tone, or simply the
punctuation? Couldn't they read? Was Crane to be simply another
'crudity' they could so glibly be rid of? But still I myself didn't read
Whitman, more than the few poems of his that were 'dealt with' in
classes or that some friend asked me to. No doubt I too was embarrassed by my aunt's and my grandmother's ability to recite that
terrible poem, "O Captain! My Captain!," banal as I felt it to be,
and yet what was that specious taste which could so distract any attention and could righteously dismiss so much possibility, just because it didn't 'like' it? Sadly, it was too much my own.

So I didn't really read Whitman for some years although from
time to time I realized that the disposition toward his work must be
changing. Increasing numbers of articles began to appear as, for
one example, Randall Jarrell's "Whitman Revisited." But the im-
port of this writing had primarily to do with Whitman's work as instance of social history or else with its philosophical basis or, in
short, with all that did not attempt to respect the technical aspects
of his writing, his prosody and the characteristic method of his organization within the specific poems.

It was, finally, the respect accorded Whitman by three of my fellow poets that began to impress me as not only significant to their
various concepts of poetry but as unmistakable evidence of his basic
use to any estimation of the nature of poetry itself. I had grown up,
so to speak, habituated to the use of poetry as compact, epiphanal
instance of emotion or insight. I valued its intensive compression,
its ability to 'get through' a maze of conflict and confusion to some
center of clear 'point.' But what did one do if the emotion or terms

of thought could not be so focused upon or isolated in such singularity? Assuming a context in which the statement was of necessity multiphasic, a circumstance the components of which were multiple, or, literally, a day in which various things *did* occur, not simply one thing—what did one do with that? Allen Ginsberg was quick to see that Whitman's line was of very specific use. As he says in "Notes Written on Finally Recording Howl," "No attempt's been made to use it in the light of early XX Century organization of new speech-rhythm prosody to *build up* large organic structures." The structure of "Howl" itself and of subsequent poems such as "Kaddish" demonstrates to my own mind how much technically Ginsberg had learned from Whitman's method of taking the poem as a 'field,' in Charles Olson's sense, rather than as a discrete line through alternatives to some adamant point of conclusion.

In the work of Robert Duncan the *imagination* of the poem is very coincident with Whitman's. For example, in a contribution to *Poets on Poetry* (1966) Duncan writes:

> We begin to imagine a cosmos in which the poet and the poem are one in a moving process, not only here the given Creation and the Exodus or Fall, but also here the immanence of the Creator in Creation. The most real is given and we have fallen away, but the most real is in the falling revealing itself in what is happening. Between the god *in* the story and the god *of* the story, the form, the realization of what is happening, stirs the poet. To answer that call, to become the poet, means to be aware of creation, creature and creator coinherent in the one event . . .

If one reads the 1855 Preface to *Leaves of Grass* in the context here defined, the seeming largenesses of act which Whitman grants to the poet find actual place in that "immanence of the Creator in Creation" which Duncan notes. More, the singular presence of Whitman in Duncan's "A Poem Beginning with a Line by Pindar" is an extraordinary realization of the *measure* Whitman has given us:

> There is no continuity then. Only a few
>      posts of the good remain. I too
> that am a nation sustain the damage
>      where smokes of continual ravage
> obscure the flame.
>                     It is across great scars of wrong
>      I reach toward the song of kindred men
>      and strike again the naked string
> old Whitman sang from. Glorious mistake!
>      that cried:

"The theme is creative and has vista."
"He is the president of regulation."

I see always the under side turning,
fumes that injure the tender landscape.
    From which up break
lilac blossoms of courage in daily act
    striving to meet a natural measure.

Louis Zukofsky, the third friend thus to instruct me, recalls and transforms Whitman's *Leaves* again and again, as here:

The music is in the flower,
Leaf around leaf ranged around the center;
Profuse but clear outer leaf breaking on space,
There is space to step to the central heart:
The music is in the flower,
It is not the sea but hyaline cushions the flower—
Liveforever, everlasting.
The leaves never topple from each other,
Each leaf a buttress flung for the other.

                                        (from *"A"* 2, 1928)

I have no way of knowing if those lines directly refer to Whitman's *Leaves of Grass* and yet, intuitively, I have no doubt of it whatsoever. Zukofsky once told me that, for him, the eleventh section of "Song of Myself" constituted the American *Shih King*, which is to say, it taught the possibilities of what might be said or sung in poetry with that grace of technical agency, or mode, thereby to accomplish those possibilities. *It presents*. It does not talk about or refer to—in the subtlety of its realization, it becomes real.

It is also Zukofsky who made me aware of Whitman's power in an emotion I had not associated with him—a deeply passionate anger. Zukofsky includes an essay called "Poetry" in the first edition of *"A" 1-12*, at the end of which he quotes the entire text of "Respondez!," a poem which Whitman finally took out of *Leaves of Grass* in 1881 but which I have put in this selection, as singular instance of that power and in respect to the man who made me aware of it.

Then, in the late fifties, I found myself embarrassed for proper academic credentials although I was teaching at the time, and so went back to graduate school, to get the appropriate degree. One of the first courses I took in that situation was called "Twain and Whitman," taught by John Gerber, who was a visiting professor at the University of New Mexico from Iowa State. One thing he did with us I remember very well—he asked us to do a so-called thematic outline of "Song of Myself." The room in which we met had large blackboards on all four walls and on the day they were due, we were told to copy our various outlines on to the blackboards. So we all got up and did so. When we finally got back to our seats, we noticed one very striking fact. No two of the outlines were the same—which was Professor Gerber's very instructive point. Whitman did not write with a systematized logic of 'subject' nor did he 'organize' his materials with a logically set schedule for their occurrence in the poem. Again the situation of a 'field' of activity, rather than some didactic imposition of a 'line' of order, was very clear.

At that same time I became interested in the nature of Whitman's prosody and looked through as many scholarly articles concerning it as I could find in the university library. None were really of much use to me, simply that the usual academic measure of such activity depends upon the rigid presumption of a standardized metrical system, which is, at best, the hindsight gained from a practice far more fluid in its own occasion. Sculley Bradley (co-editor with Harold W. Blodgett of the best text for Whitman's poems available to my knowledge: *Leaves of Grass*, Comprehensive Reader's Edition, New York University Press, 1965) did speak of a *variable stress* or *foot*, that is, a hovering accent, or accents, within clusters of words in the line, that did not fall in a statically determined pattern but rather shifted with the impulse of the statement itself. This sense of the stress pattern in Whitman's poems was interestingly parallel to William Carlos Williams' use of what he also called "the variable foot" in his later poems, so that the periodicity of the line, its duration in time, so to speak, stayed in the general pattern constant but the stress or stresses within the unit of the line itself were free to move with the condition of the literal things being said, both as units of semantic information, e.g., "I am the chanter . . . ," or as units of sound and rhythm, e.g., "I chant copious the islands beyond . . ." It is, of course, impossible ever to separate these two terms in their actual function, but it is possible that one will be more or less concerned with each in turn in the activity of writing. More simply, I remember one occasion in high school when I turned a 'unit' primarily involved with sounds and rhythm into a 'unit' particularly involved with semantic statement, to wit: "Inebriate of air am I . . ." altered in my memory to read, "I am an inebriate of air . . ." My teacher told me I had the most unpoetic ear he'd yet encountered.

Remember that what we call 'rhyming' is the recurrence of a sound sufficiently similar to one preceding it to catch in the ear and mind as being the 'same' and that such sounds can be modified in a great diversity of ways. In the sounding of words themselves the extension seems almost endless: *maid, made, may, mad, mate, wait, say,* etc. Given the initial vowel with its accompanying consonants and also its own condition, i.e., whether it is 'long' or 'short,' one can then play upon that sound as long as one's energy *and* the initial word's own ability to stay in the ear as 'residue' can survive. In verse the weaving and play of such sound is far more complex than any observation of the rhymes at the ends of lines can tabulate.

This kind of rhyming is instance of what one can call *parallelism,* and the parallelism which similarity of sounds can effect is only one of the many alternate sources of 'rhyming' which verse has at hand. For example, there is a great deal of syntactic 'rhyming' in Whitman's poetry, insistently parallel syntactic structures which themselves make a strong web of coherence. There is also the possibility of parallelism in the nature of what is being thought and/or felt as emotion, and this too can serve to increase the experience of coherence in the statement the poem is working to accomplish.

The constantly recurring structures in Whitman's writing, the insistently parallel sounds and rhythms, recall the patterns of waves as I now see them daily. How can I point to *this* wave, or *that* one, and announce that it is *the* one? Rather Whitman's method seems to me a process of sometimes seemingly endless gathering, moving in the energy of his own attention and impulse. There are obviously occasions to the contrary to be found in his work but the basic pattern does seem of this order. I am struck by the fact that William Michael Rossetti in the introduction to his *Poems of Walt Whitman* (1868) speaks of the style as being occasionally "agglomerative," a word which can mean "having the state of a confused or jumbled mass" but which, more literally, describes the circumstance of something "made or formed into a rounded mass or ball." A few days ago here, walking along the beach, a friend showed me such a ball, primarily of clay but equally compacted of shells and pebbles which the action of the waves had caused the clay to pick up, all of which would, in time, become stone. That meaning of "agglomerate" I think particularly relevant to the activity of Whitman's composition, and I like too that sense of the spherical, which does not locate itself upon a point nor have the strict condition of the linear but rather is at all 'points' the possibility of all that it is. Whitman's constant habit of revisions and additions would concur, I think, with this notion of his process, in that there is not 'one thing' to be said and, that done, then 'another.' Rather the process permits the material ('myself' in the world) to extend until literal death intercedes. Again, it is interesting to think of Zukofsky's sense that any of us as poets "write one poem all our lives," remembering that Whitman does not think of his work as a series of discrete collections or books but instead adds to the initial work, *Leaves of Grass*, thinking of it as a "single poem."

The implications of such a stance have a very contemporary bearing for American poets—who can no longer assume either their world or themselves in it as discrete occasion. Not only does Whitman anticipate the American affection for the pragmatic, but he equally emphasizes that it is space and process which are unremittingly our condition. If Pound found the manner of his poems objectionable, he nonetheless comes to a form curiously like *Leaves of Grass* in the *Cantos*, in that he uses them as the literal possibility of a life. Much the same situation occurs in Williams' writing with *Paterson*, although it comes at a markedly later time in his own life. Charles Olson's *Maximus Poems* and Louis Zukofsky's *"A"* are also instances of this form which proposes to 'go on' in distinction to one that assumes its own containment as a singular case.

Another objection Rossetti had concerned what he called "absurd or ill-constructed words" in Whitman's writing. One distinct power a poet may be blessed with is that of *naming* and Whitman's appetite in this respect was large and unembarrassed. One should read a posthumously published collection of notes he wrote on his own sense of words called *An American Primer* (City Lights, 1970), wherein he makes clear his commitment to their power of transformation. Whitman's vocabulary moves freely among an extraordinarily wide range of occupational terminologies and kinds of diction found in divers social groupings. Frequently there are juxtapositions of terms appropriate to markedly different social or occupational habits, slang sided with words of an alternate derivation:

> I chant the chant of dilation or pride,
> We have had ducking and deprecating about enough . . .

Whatever the reader's response, such language permits Whitman to gain an actively useful diversity of context and tone. The toughness of his verse—what Charles Olson referred to as its *muscularity*, giving as instance "Trickle Drops"—can sustain the tensions created in its movement by these seeming disparities in diction. It is, moreover, a marked characteristic of American poetry since Whitman, and certainly of the contemporary, to have no single source for its language in the sense that it does not depend upon a 'poetic' or literary vocabulary. In contrast, a German friend once told me that even a novelist as committed to a commonly shared situation of life as Günter Grass could not be easily understood by the workers whose circumstances so moved him. His language was too literary in its structure and vocabulary, not by fact of his own choice but because such language was adamantly that in which novels were to be written in German. An American may choose, as John Ashbery once did, to write a group of poems whose words come entirely from the diction of the *Wall Street Journal,* but it is his own necessity, not that put upon him by some rigidity of literary taste.

Comparable to this flexibility of diction in Whitman's writing is the tone or mood in which his poems speak. It is very open, familiar, at times very casual and yet able to be, on the instant, intensive, intimate, charged with complexly diverse emotion. This manner of address invites, as it were, the person reading to 'come into' the activity and experience of the poems, to share with Whitman in a paradoxically unsentimental manner the actual texture and force of the emotions involved. When he speaks directly to the reader, there is an uncanny feeling of his literal presence physically.

I have avoided discussion of Whitman's life simply because I am not competent to add anything to the information of any simple biography, for example, Gay Wilson Allen's *Walt Whitman* (Evergreen Books, London, 1961). I am charmed by some of the details got from that book. Apparently Mrs. Gilchrist, the widow of Blake's biographer, Alexander Gilchrist, was very smitten upon reading Whitman's poems and wrote accordingly:

> Even in this first letter (3 September, 1871) Mrs. Gilchrist made it plain that she was proposing marriage. She hoped, she said, to hear, "My Mate. The one I so much want. Bride, Wife, indissoluble eternal!" And, "Dear Walt. It is a sweet & precious thing, this love: it clings so close, so close to the Soul and Body, all so tenderly dear, so beautiful, so sacred . . ."

It is simple enough to make fun of this lady and yet her response, despite Whitman's very careful demurring, is one that his poems are unequivocally capable of producing. It would be sad indeed if books could not be felt as entirely human and possible occasion.

More to the point, Whitman's life is a very discreet one, really. John Addington Symonds so pestered him concerning "the meaning of the 'Calamus' poems," that Whitman finally answered, "Though unmarried, I have six children." But whether or not that was true, or untrue, or whether Whitman was homosexual, bisexual, or heterosexual, has not primarily concerned me. In other words, I have been intent upon the writing and what there took place and that, literally, is what any of us have now as a possibility. We cannot haul him back any more than we can Shakespeare, just to tell us who he was. It would seem that he *had*, with such magnificent articulation one is almost persuaded there can be no end to him just as there is none to the genius of his writing.

Nor have I been able to do more than gloss the multiplicity of uses I find in the work itself. I wish there were time to think of Whitman as instance of what Allen Ginsberg pointed out as a great tradition of American poets, that of the *crank* or true eccentric. Surely his contemporaries often felt him to be. There is a lovely letter which Gerard Manley Hopkins wrote Bridges, in which he says that Whitman is closer to him in technical concerns than any other poet then writing—but also, that he is a veritable madman. So what does that make poor Hopkins? Or I would like to consider a suggestion of Duncan's, that possibly Williams' uneasiness with Whitman's writing had in part to do with the fact that Williams uses *enjambment*, or 'run-over' lines, very frequently whereas Whitman uses it not at all—wherein he is very like Ezra Pound. Or to trace more carefully the nature of Whitman's influence on American poetry—an influence I find as clearly in Frank O'Hara's poems as I do in Crane's or Ginsberg's.

Undertaking any of this, I felt a sudden giddiness—not at all self-humbling. This man is a *great* poet, our first, and it is unlikely indeed that his contribution to what it literally means to be an *American* poet will ever be equaled. But I do not want to end this note with such blatant emphasis. As Duncan says, Whitman is a deeply gentle man and, humanly, of great, great reassurance. If our America now is a petty shambles of disillusion and violence, the dreams of its possibility stay actual in Whitman's words. It is not 'democracy' that, of itself, can realize or even recognize the common need. It is only, and literally, people themselves who have that choice. So then, as Lawrence said: "Ahead of all poets, pioneering into the wilderness of unopened life, Whitman . . ."

*Bolinas, California*
*January 30, 1972*

# Hart Crane and the Private Judgment

In the July 1932 issue of *Poetry* there is an essay by Allen Tate called
"Hart Crane and the American Mind." Hart Crane had committed
suicide on April 28, 1932. Tate's judgment certainly was affected by
the fact, and by the friendship he had held for Crane, and yet the
matter of his comments on Crane's life and value as a poet continues very much the same as what we deal with today, facing a like
problem of judgment.

What Tate there gives to Crane is this:

> Sometime in May, 1922, I received a letter from Hart Crane saying he
> liked a poem of mine which he had seen in the May number of *The
> Double Dealer*. It was my first printed poem, and Hart's letter was not
> only an introduction to him; it was the first communication I ever re-
> ceived from another writer.[1] In that same issue of *The Double Dealer*
> appeared some translations by him of Laforgue, which seemed to me
> very fine; I looked up previous numbers of the magazine, and found
> "Black Tambourine," an early poem that contained some of the char-
> acteristic features of this later and mature style. I had seen nothing
> like it in Anglo-American poetry. From that time until his death one
> could trace the development of a poetry which, though similar in
> some technical respects to French Symbolism, is now a distinct contri-
> bution to American literature. It is a poetry that could have been writ-
> ten only in this country and in this age.

*The Free Lance*, vol. 5, no. 1, 1960 (Wilberforce University).

1. This letter is not in Brom Weber's selection (*The Letters of Hart Crane* [New
York, 1952]), but the one following (May 16, 1922) is to be found on p. 87.

Hart Crane has now become a kind of 'symbol,' for many, of the irresponsible in poetry, the disordered intelligence that creates a chaos only as a refuge from its own inabilities. Grover Smith, for example, calls him "that pitiable anarch . . . ," continuing, "It should be patent to the student of both [Crane's life and work], however, that Crane as man and poet was grievously disordered, that the neurotic irresponsibility of his private life and loves was directly synchronous with the undisciplined fancy manifest in his poetic images. Crane's inner world was a fluxion in which neither personal relations nor traditional thought and utterance were coherent enough to form laws even for themselves."[2] This is, of course, a very personal judgment, and one made completely as a contention—the only quotations from the book in question are taken from Brom Weber's introduction to *The Letters of Hart Crane*. Smith says, of the letters themselves: "There is no concentration of alert feelings; there is no style." But Tate had felt them to be "always written in a pure and lucid prose." Whatever our own opinion may arrive at, at least we must see that we can accept neither of these two as given, until we have found our own proof.

The 'failures,' 'mistakes,' 'flaws,' etc., of Hart Crane's poetry have seemed to me intimate with the successes equally demonstrable. I think that a reader must judge for himself, at last, which quality is the more sustained. Crane *was* 'disordered' to the extent that he conceived his responsibility as a poet to transcend even the obligations he felt as a man. Perhaps there is no direct proof of this fact, i.e., a statement unequivocally supporting it. But—"It is a new feeling, and a glorious one, to have one's inmost delicate intentions so fully recognized as your last letter to me attested. I can feel a calmness on the sidewalk—where before I felt a defiance only. And better than all—I am certain that a number of us at last have some kind of community of interest. And with this communion will come something better than a mere clique. It is a consciousness of something more vital than stylistic questions and 'taste,' it is vision, and a vision alone that not only America needs, but the whole world. . . . What delights me almost beyond words is that my natu-

2. Grover Smith, "On Poets and Poetry," *New Mexico Quarterly*, Autumn 1953, p. 319. The article is an omnibus review, which may explain the briefness of Smith's discussion of the Weber collection, but hardly excuses the unsupported statements involved concerning not only Crane's letters and poetry, but his "private life and loves" as well. Cf. Weber's edition of *The Letters*, pp. 298 ff.

ral idiom . . . has reached and carried to you so completely the very blood and bone of me."[3]

The nature of this "vision" concerned an alternative to the negativistic position which Eliot, and to a lesser degree (though ultimately even more final) Joyce, had provided for their work. The genius of both men made the position attractive almost 'per se'— at least the question of its implications does not seem to have been recognized at first by very many. But one of those who did, William Carlos Williams, speaks of it (in retrospect) as follows: "These were the years just before the great catastrophe to our letters—the appearance of T. S. Eliot's *The Waste Land*. There was heat in us, a core and a drive that was gathering headway upon the theme of a rediscovery of a primary impetus, the elementary principle of all art, in the local conditions. Our work staggered to a halt for a moment under the blast of Eliot's genius which gave the poem back to the academics. We did not know how to answer him."[4]

Hart Crane's answer was *The Bridge*—now discredited as a total poem, which is to say, a failure in terms of its literal writing, and the problems involved in that writing. But the conception? We know that the 'failure' in some sense caused Crane to doubt all of his abilities as a poet. Tate writes, "I think he knew that the framework of *The Bridge* was finally incoherent, and for that reason—as I have said—he could no longer believe in even his lyrical powers; he could not return to the early work and take it up from where he had left off." But Crane himself had written to Tate: "Perhaps it can serve as at least the function of a link connecting certain chains of the past to certain chains and tendencies of the future. In other words, a diagram or 'process.'"[5] It is here, I think, that the conception of the poem is most significantly stated, and since it has to do with problems of the 'scientific method,' there is that reason for a brief digression.

Attitudes in the 'social sciences,' even as late as the twenties, con-

3. Weber, ed., *The Letters of Hart Crane*, p. 127. Crane is twenty-four years old. Tate believes the conception of the "idea" and "leading symbolism" of *The Bridge* to date from the year following, i.e., "probably early in 1924."

4. W. C. Williams, *Autobiography* (New York, 1951). It is relevant to point out the coincidence of materials in Williams' *In the American Grain* and Crane's *The Bridge*. Cf. Weber, ed., *The Letters of Hart Crane*, pp. 277–78.

5. Weber, ed., *The Letters of Hart Crane*, p. 353. This is the letter of which Tate writes: "He had an extraordinary insight into the foundations of his work, and I think this judgment of it will never be refuted."

tinued to maintain that world view which held that a system of knowledge was extensible to a point where the world's ills might, reasonably, be done away with. Perhaps the attitudes were never quite so barely expressed, or even realized, but their content was nonetheless predicated on such a system of thought. Moreover, this way of thinking was involved in many of the other sciences, and was also, very clearly, the base idea or opinion held by many, many laymen.

A recent book, *Modern Science and Modern Man*, by James B. Conant,[6] reviews these attitudes, and, more particularly, shows why they can no longer be quite so easily held. But the most interesting thing, in connection with Crane's comment on *The Bridge*, is Conant's discussion of "the philosophic implications of the new physics," wherein he quotes from J. J. Thomson's *The Corpuscular Theory of Matter* (1907)[7] as follows: "From the point of view of the physicist, a theory of matter is a policy rather than a creed; its object is to connect or coordinate apparently diverse phenomena and above all to suggest, stimulate, and direct experiment."[8] *The Waste Land* was a 'creed' (how much of a creed we can now show, by

6. James B. Conant, *Modern Science and Modern Man* (New York: Anchor Books, 1953).

7. Ibid., p. 91. The reorientation which Thomson had literally accomplished in 1907 is one which many men have even yet to consider in 1953. In the art of poetry, above all, there is great need to recognize the problem inherent in any such reorientation of an entire basis for the *use* of knowledge.

8. "The poet's concern must be, as always, self-discipline toward a formal integration of experience. For poetry is an architectural art, based not on Evolution or the idea of progress, but on the articulation of the contemporary human consciousness *sub specie aeternitas*, and inclusive of all readjustments incident to science and other shifting factors related to that consciousness." Hart Crane, *Collected Poems*, Appendix B, "Modern Poetry" (New York, 1933). This was first published in 1929—but must have been an active concept in his work long before. For comparison: "We can no longer say, The World is like this, or the World is like that. We can only say, Our experience up to the present is best represented by a world of this character; I do not know what model will best represent the world of tomorrow, but I do know that it will coordinate a greater range of experience than that of today." Herbert Dingle, "The Scientific Outlook in 1851 and in 1951," *British Journal for the Philosophy of Science*, II (1951), p. 86; quoted by Conant, *Modern Science and Modern Man*, p. 89. Crane's problem was not one of conception—but of means (though not at all in Smith's sense of a criticism). The essay first cited ("Modern Poetry") includes comments on a "terminology of poetic reference," etc., which indicates that, although Crane could conceive of a necessary shift in substantive qualifications, he continued to depend on nominative qualifications, when it came to the actual means. (This problem of the substantive vs. the nominative was pointed out to me by Charles Olson.)

means of Eliot's later work), depending on the *finality* of knowledge. But *The Bridge*, 'failure' though it was and still may seem to us, was a 'process' or 'policy,' an attempt to direct attention to a *significant* content in the American corpus, both historical and mythic, and to posit juxtapositions and methods of dealing with this material which *might* prove fruitful.

Perhaps that is all too simply opinion, mainly my own.[9] But we have damned *The Bridge* much too simply on the grounds of its having failed as a poem. Certainly we are allowed to do that, and finally we must. And yet it seems to me wasteful to ignore the other implications involved. It is not even a question of giving credit where credit is due, though I should like to consider that part of it. The several questions remaining are: (1) who has answered Eliot? (2) isn't that answer even more called for *now*, than it was then? (3) doesn't the present 'picture' of our world (again 'now') have a great, great deal to do with it?

Let me leave those as questions only. Crane's position as 'prophet,' if you will, is one which I cannot discuss very competently here. Moreover, until he is again read, as he deserves to be, any discussion must, of necessity, be meaningless. But to suggest, as Smith has done, that Crane was committed to "rebellion for its own sake" is neither helpful nor true. Further, his sense of the poems as a "jumble of images thrown up by the poet's unconscious" which leave the reader to perform "the 'plastic' task proper to the poet himself" does not strike me as very adequate—granted that there are reasonable alternatives to his opinion.[10]

As his critics have remarked, Crane learned a great deal from the French Symbolists, and much of his early work is dominated by what he learned. For example, Tate (speaking "logically") notes that Crane "became so dissatisfied, not only with the style of the poem ["For the Marriage of Faustus and Helen"], which is heavily influenced by Eliot and Laforgue, but with the 'literary' character of the symbolism, that he set about the greater task of writing *The Bridge*." The point is that Crane had become at first a poet by way of a poetry dependent on irony, on the dissociations possible in the very surfaces of language, on a quick and nonpassive verbalism

9. Another man holding related opinions at least is M. Elath. Cf. his article "In Another Direction" published in a double number of *Intro*, New York, Winter 1951.

10. The "oddness" of Crane's vocabulary often produces this reaction—but is it valid? I think one had better examine the relevance of such language *in context*. Crane's worksheets (cf. Weber's biography) would defeat the sense which Smith is trying to suggest.

which was in direct opposition to anything then evident in English or American poetry. His 'style,' if you will, was developed in great part from this source. And this will explain much of the surface character of Crane's poetry, i.e., the rapidity of image, the disparateness, the whole sense of 'words' being used almost for their own, single character. Certainly both Eliot and Pound (as well as Stevens, Williams, et al., at home) had begun to use these same things.

But it is Crane's development away from the Symbolists, and their dependence on irony in particular, that leads to the later style, and of course to the character of language usage which Grover Smith dislikes. In fairness to both him and myself—not to mention Crane—it should be stated that a poem is an asserted unit of meaning, among other things. And that our appreciation of it, or disapproval of it, depends, again partially, on whether or not we can allow that the means used to effect that end provide a meaning apprehensible by us. Once having allowed that, we then take upon ourselves the act of judging whether or not the means used seem the most effective possible, i.e., the most proper, etc. Smith, then, is suggesting that Crane's "jumble of images" does not properly provide for an effect of *meaning*—and that it depends on our sympathy for resolution. In any case (because a poem will be given shortly) a few lines, here, may show the nature of the difficulty, at least insofar as Smith has been thinking of it.

> Yes, tall, inseparably our days
> Pass sunward. We have walked the kindled skies
> Inexorable and girded with your praise,
>
> By the dove filled, and bees of Paradise.

Briefly the line of the sense can be given as this: that Crane and the one he speaks to share a time together which is passing, and that this time has been, to put it very simply, happy. I don't think that belies the base meaning involved, insofar as its 'action' character is concerned. So—the images, etc. The first, "our days pass[ing] sunward" with the further sense of "tall, inseparably," engenders in my mind an effect of dignity (from the "tall"), of a close love (from the whole complex of "our days pass sunward," with the echo of "sun" as life-giving, high, a source of nobility and godhead). To bypass, the next sentence comes to me as a statement of fulfillment, that they have, together, come to a sense of complete fulfillment. And that, in any case, can serve as a description, if nothing else, of how the lines begin to attain to an effect of *meaning* for me.

Now one might argue, how can he talk about walking up in the sky if he has just said that his days (an apparent possession) pass sunward? How can they do that, if he is up there, etc.? And—who is "inexorable" and "girded," etc.? But doesn't that really come to quibbling—if an effect is achieved and sustained in rereading? And isn't this latter just what each reader must decide for himself? I suggest that Crane's use of language (i.e., such words as "inexorable," "tall," and such image complexes as in the first three lines) will invariably be attached to an *emotion* which can and will sustain them in a total pattern of *meaning.* That line of *meaning* can be determined in all of his active poems (which will serve, for a beginning, to belie Smith's "jumble of images"), and that this line will depend, precisely, on the assumedly disconnected images which some readers have balked at. Remember that an association existing between images need not be 'logical.' That term is most usually an a priori designation for an assumptional rationality of progression. The fact is that we do not know what we know before we know it. And a poem's line, or what to call it, of *meaning* need not be 'logical,' if it can effect its meaning by virtue of another sense of possible sequence. And, at that, Crane is really no great instance of the uses of theoretic dissociation in sequence. One might argue, in fact, that an apparent 'excess' in language was the only irony that Crane finally permitted himself.

To allow discussion to end there, however, ignores all of Crane's metrics, and all of his sense of structure in the shorter poems—particularly the latter. I have seen no comment on Crane's sense of rhythm, although it is, for me, one of the most dominant aspects of his work.[11] But the reader can judge both that, and the "jumbled images," for himself:

*Island Quarry*

Square sheets—they saw the marble into
Flat slabs there at the marble quarry
At the turning of the road around the roots of the mountain
Where the straight road would seem to ply below the stone,
    that fierce
Profile of marble spiked with yonder
Palms against the sunset's towering sea, and maybe
Against mankind. It is at times—

11. All Crane's work is best read aloud. The reader can't pick up the sounds or the rhythms sufficiently otherwise. A recording of a half dozen of his poems by a competent reader would do much more than any "criticism" ever will. He is one of the most *verbal* poets in the English language.

In dusk it is at times as though this island lifted, floated
In Indian baths. At Cuban dusk the eyes
Walking the straight road toward thunder—
This dry road silvering toward the shadow of the quarry
—It is at times as though the eyes burned hard and glad
And did not take the goat path quivering to the right,
Wide of the mountain—thence to tears and sleep—
But went on into marble that does not weep.

It is very possible to argue that this is an almost perfect instance
of form—technically. Actually, our own ears have arrived at that
conclusion upon hearing it, and our perception of the content involved makes it not at all necessary to revert to questions purely of
sentiment. The poem is a good one because of its very skillful alteration and development of the two rhythms involved (i.e., those
contained in words like "marble," "mountain," "maybe," etc., and
those contained in "sheets," "fierce," "dusk," "weep," etc.). The
hard opening of the poem, like a double stroke, falls then off to the
softer rhythms, then reasserts itself in the opening of the second
line—and so on to the final, broken close. This, of course, is the
usual method of 'analysis.' We may also point out that the vowel
leadings in this poem are quite equal to anything done by Yeats—
although we have never heard of them being mentioned either in
this poem, or any other by Crane. Nor has there been comment on
the very effective handling of line—as this poem, again, shows it,
with the undulation of the lines, almost opening and closing like
actual breathing, to end with the line pulling in, stumbling, unmistakable in its emphases.

All that can be said, defended—and much more can be said and
defended, concerning both this one poem and at least a dozen
others. My own preferences in the first book, *White Buildings*, are:
"Praise for an Urn," "Lachrymae Christi," "The Wine Menagerie,"
"For the Marriage of Faustus and Helen," "At Melville's Tomb,"
and perhaps one or two others, i.e., these are only evidences of my
*own* taste, and what I think I could defend as 'good poetry.' In the
later book, *Key West:* the quoted poem, "The Mermen," "A Name
for All," "Imperator Victus," "The Hurricane," "And Bees of Paradise," "Moment Fugue," "The Broken Tower," "The Phantom
Bark," and, again, perhaps a few more, because my taste is hardly
invariable.[12] But do people still read these poems, and, if they
don't—how can we discuss them all so glibly, or say, so glibly, that
they are this thing or that?

12. Hart Crane, *Collected Poems* (New York, 1933).

For an ending: the reader who saw Crane survive Weber's first book on him may have noticed this particular account, in Weber's preface to *The Letters*, concerning the death of Hart Crane's mother:

> The last chapter in the Crane biography occurred in 1947. On July 30th of that year, Mrs. Grace Hart Crane, the poet's mother, died in Teaneck, New Jersey. Before her death, she told Samuel Loveman that she wished to be cremated and her ashes to be cast into the East River from the Brooklyn Bridge. The necessary arrangements were made, and the editor was one of a small party which proceeded along Brooklyn Bridge on a windy, sunlit afternoon in Fall 1947. At intervals on the Bridge, there are signs warning pedestrians not to throw anything from the structure. By the time the party reached the center of the Bridge, considerable trepidation existed about the feasibility of respecting Mrs. Crane's last wishes. It remained at last for the editor to grasp the small, undecorated tin can and shake the ashes into the air, where they swirled about for a few moments and then fell mistily into the water below. Thus Crane's mother joined him in the element which had claimed him fifteen years earlier.

But this is Smith's hero, not mine. The reader who can trust a 'character analysis' of Hart Crane coming from the same source is welcome to, but he has no reason, here, to read further.

The men who knew Hart Crane, with the authority of friendship, have said many things about him, each from the particulars of their own life. Allen Tate ends his essay, written that short time after Crane's death, by saying: "After he had lost the instinct for self-definition, and later, after the exploration of his symbol of the will had brought him back upon himself, he might have continued to breathe, but he would no longer have been alive." That whole question of will, of "the will gone all teeth" (as Charles Olson has called it in another reference), will, someday, have to be examined, and closely. Poetry, the whole art of it, had failed Crane, and that is why he could not live—even if it is not why he died.

Other men speak of him as the friend which no other man has ever quite taken the place of. Against the public that sees him as homosexual, drunkard, and all the rest, for them he was an incredible man, whom they knew. For Robert Graves, he was a "lovely man," however much he seemed a tragic one. For Slater Brown, the best friend he ever had.

What else is there to be said. Except that we can read the poems, and see what they are, for ourselves.

*1953*

# The Letters of Hart Crane, Edited by Brom Weber

*The Letters of Hart Crane,* edited by Brom Weber. New York: Hermitage House, 1952.

If there is a ghost, or unquiet spirit, of a man ever left to us, it may well be that Hart Crane is not dead—or not in our comfortable sense of that word. I note that Brom Weber brings this up, unintentionally, in his ridiculous preface and chronology for the book in question: "Three days later, on the 27th, he [Crane] either jumped or fell into the Caribbean Sea and was drowned. His body was not recovered" (p. xvi). Perhaps we have our own fears of the sea, and also of a man not actually 'laid to rest,' not finally put under as we are accustomed to do with the dead.

But lacking the body, an age of critics can still sustain its necrophilia on the body of the work itself. Hart Crane "was admittedly not a thinker," Weber says (p. x), ignoring, for one thing, Williams' premise that "the poet thinks with his poem, in that lies his thought, and that is the profundity." To prepare us, Weber speaks of Crane's "acquisitive need for sympathy, pity, understanding, affection," of a man "tyrannically governed by a chronic need to love and be loved" (pp. vi, viii). One might well say the same of *any* human being.

In any case some anger can be righteous, and some usage cannot be put up with. Lacking a present means to deal with Weber, finally—the reader is advised to bypass his comments altogether. (Or better, to judge for himself the man writing "The last chapter of the Crane biography" [p. x].) He is not helpful.

*Origin,* Summer 1954.

Crane is, however, and we have, at last, a reasonable addendum to the poetry itself which may serve as the gauge we had lacked. What was Crane's conception of poetry? "Poetry, in so far as the metaphysics of any absolute knowledge extends, is simply the concrete *evidence* of the *experience* of a recognition (*knowledge* if you like). It can give you a *ratio* of fact and experience, and in this sense it is both perception and thing perceived, according as it approaches a significant articulation or not. This is its reality, its fact, *being*" (p. 237).

More than that, what was Crane's summation of his own position—the cause back of all Weber's inanities, not to mention his biography of Crane or Waldo Frank's fantastic introduction to the *Collected Poems*? Was it absolutely this fact of "Crane's tender friendships . . . with boys who followed the Sea" and "drink" as "the Sea's coadjutor"? So says Frank—but does it matter?

> I have a certain code of ethics. I have not as yet attempted to reduce it to any exact formula, and if I did I should probably embark on an endless tome with monthly additions and digressions every year. It seems obvious that a certain decent carriage and action is a paramount requirement in any poet, deacon or carpenter. And though I reserve myself the pleasant right to define these standards in a somewhat individual way, and to shout and complain when circumstances against me seem to warrant it, on the other hand I believe myself to be speaking honestly when I say that I have never been able to regret— for long—whatever has happened to me, more especially those decisions which at times have been permitted a free will. . . . And I am as completely out of sympathy with the familiar whimpering caricature of the artist and his "divine rights" as you seem to be. I am not a Stoic, though I think I could lean more in that direction if I came to (as I may sometime) appreciate more highly the imaginative profits of such a course. (pp. 299–300)

Back of this, there are the poems, forgotten for the most part— but if this book can do anything, and one hopes at least, it may bring us back to them somewhat sobered. We know, we know, we know, etc., that *The Bridge* was a 'failure'—though why, and how, we are not at all quite so sure of. Crane wrote to Allen Tate: "I shall be humbly grateful if *The Bridge* can fulfill simply the metaphorical inference of its title. . . . You will admit our age (at least our predicament) to be one of transition" (p. 353). It has done that, I think.

The shorter poems, those found in *White Buildings* and *Key West*, have escaped the 'failure' of *The Bridge,* but they have also been affected, i.e., they seem to be thought less 'significant.' And there again we have the critic's help. "One is appalled, on reading his

[Crane's] explication of 'At Melville's Tomb' to realize that while he could associatively justify the chain of metaphors comprising the poem, he was oblivious of the difference between a random and logical mode of association." (Which is Grover Smith, from within his own oblivion.) But the poem?

*At Melville's Tomb*

Often beneath the wave, wide from this ledge
The dice of drowned men's bones he saw bequeath
An embassy. Their numbers as he watched,
Beat on the dusty shore and were obscured.

And wrecks passed without sound of bells,
The calyx of death's bounty giving back
A scattered chapter, livid hieroglyph,
The portent wound in corridors of shells.

Then in the circuit calm of one vast coil,
Its lashings charmed and malice reconciled,
Frosted eyes there were that lifted altars;
And silent answers crept across the stars.

Compass, quadrant and sextant contrive
No farther tides. . . . High in the azure steeps
Monody shall not wake the mariner.
This fabulous shadow only the sea keeps.

This is the GREATEST summation of Melville I have ever read. O well. . . .

"I don't know whether you want to hear from me or not—since you have never written—but here's my love anyway. . . ." He did all anyone could.

# A Note on Ezra Pound

For my generation the fact of Ezra Pound and his work is inescapable, no matter what the particular reaction may be. But it should equally be remembered that during the forties, that time in which we came of age, Pound's situation was, in all senses, most depressed. To the young of that period he was often simply a traitor, an anti-Semite, an obscurantist, a money crank—and such courses in universities and colleges as dealt with modern poetry frequently avoided all mention of the *Cantos*. For example, I remember in my shyness going to F. O. Mathiessen at Harvard, to ask why we had not used the *Cantos* in his own course on contemporary poetry. His answer was that he understood Pound's work too poorly, that he felt Pound's political attitudes most suspect, and that he could not finally see the value of the work in a course such as ours was.

It is hard to see, in one sense, how we were not frightened away from Pound—there was so much to persuade us of his difficulties and of those he would surely involve us with. But who else could responsibly teach us that "nothing matters but the quality of the affection," that "only emotion endures"? The work we were otherwise given was, on the one hand, Auden—wherein a socially based use of irony became the uselessly exact rigor of repetitive verse patterns—or perhaps Stevens, whose mind one respected, in the questions it realized, but again whose use of poetry had fallen to the questionable fact of a device.

Pound, on the other hand, brought us immediately to the con-

*Agenda*, October–November 1965.

text of how to write. It was impossible to avoid the insistence he put on *precisely* how the line *goes,* how the word *is,* in its context, what *has been* done, in the practice of verse—and what *now* seems possible to do. It was, then, a *measure* he taught—and a measure in just that sense William Carlos Williams insisted upon:

> . . . The measure itself
> has been lost
> and we suffer for it.
> We come to our deaths
> in silence. . . .

To the attacks upon Pound as bigot merely, Charles Olson—speaking in the guise of Yeats in defense of Pound, in 1946—makes the relevant answer:

> It is the passivity of you young men before Pound's work as a whole, not scripts alone, you who have taken from him, Joyce, Eliot and myself the advances we made for you. There is a court you leave silent—history present, the issue the larger concerns of authority than a state, Heraclitus and Marx called, perhaps some consideration of descents and metamorphoses, form and the elimination of intellect.*

For my own part I came first to the earlier poems, *Personae,* and to the various critical works, *Make It New, Pavannes and Divisions, ABC of Reading, Guide to Kulchur,* and *Polite Essays.* It was at that time the critical writing I could most clearly use, simply that my own limits made the *Cantos* a form intimidating to me. As a younger man, I wanted to know in a 'formal' sense where it was I was going, and had a hard time learning to admit that the variousness of life is as much its quality as its quantity. Or rather—akin to the anecdote Pound tells of Agassiz's student not really *looking* at the fish—I wanted the categories prior to the content which might in any sense inform them.

But it is again the sense of *measure,* and how actively it may be proposed, that I found insistently in Pound's work. Rather than tell me *about* some character of verse, he would give the literal instance side by side with that which gave it context. This method is, of course, an aspect of what he calls the *ideogrammic*—it *presents,* rather than comments upon. The emphasis I feel to be present in all his work, from the rationale of imagism, to the latest *Cantos.*

In the same sense he directed a real attention to characters of

---

*Charles Olson, "This Is Yeats Speaking," *Partisan Review* 13, no. 1 (Winter 1946), 139–42.

verse in the early discriminations he offered as to its nature. For example, he spoke of "three chief means" available to the man wanting to "charge language with meaning to the utmost possible degree"—in the context that "Literature is language charged with meaning":

I throwing the object (fixed or moving) on to the visual imagination.

II inducing emotional correlations by the sound and rhythm of the speech.

III inducing both of the effects by stimulating the associations (intellectual or emotional) that have remained in the receiver's consciousness in relation to the actual words or word groups employed.

(phanopoeia, melopoeia, logopoeia)

Such location of attention meant an active involvement with what was happening in the given poem—and not a continuingly vague discussion of its aesthetic 'value,' or its 'period,' or all that area of assumption which finds place in unrealized generality. Pound's discriminations were located in the poem's literal activity.

How large he was then for us, is more simply stated than described. He took the possibility of writing to involve more than descriptive aesthetics. He defined sincerity as Kung's "man standing by his word." He moved upon the active principle of intelligence, the concept of *virtu*, so that, as Charles Olson has written:

> . . . his single emotion breaks all down to his equals or inferiors (so far as I can see only two, possibly, are admitted, by him, to be his betters—Confucius, & Dante. Which assumption, that there are intelligent men whom he can outtalk, is beautiful because it destroys historical time, and
>
> thus creates the methodology of the *Cantos*, viz., a space-field where, by inversion, though the material is all time material, he has driven through it so sharply by the beak of his ego, that, he has turned time into what we now must have, space & its live air.*

Beyond that sense of principle—if such 'beyonds' can exist—there is the effect of reading Pound, of that experience of an energy, of ear and mind, which makes a language man's primary act. A sound:

> And then went down to the ship,
> Set keel to breakers, forth on the godly sea . . .

*Charles Olson, *Mayan Letters* (Bañalbufar, Mallorca: Divers Press, 1953).

# Why Pound!?!

Best done quickly, sans any 'reasons' of expected kind—for example, my first solid edition of the *Cantos* dated 1950 (still here with me), recall pondering its modes and information much as I had earlier the *Draft of XXX Cantos* in the confusions of Burmese jungle warfare. Caught now by what then held me, e.g., marks in margin apropos:

> Life to make mock of motion . . .
>
>        \*    \*    \*
>
> Shines
> in the mind of heaven God
> who made it
> more than the sun
> in our eye . . .
>
>        \*    \*    \*
>
> dawn stands there fixed and unmoving
>     only we two have moved . . .

Etc. All this noted now at random, i.e., I am not presenting a case but rather recalling how those sounds and their moving, and the insistent stance of an active (possible!) intelligence, then *moved* me (as it surely did my eventual company: Ginsberg, Blackburn, Duncan, Olson, for those immediate). Had I thought the whole world *reflective*, pondering the possible significances of what was

*Agenda* (Twenty-first Anniversary Ezra Pound Issue) 17, nos. 3–4; 18, no. 1 (Autumn-Winter-Spring 1979/80).

long gone? No doubt. I know I expected 'college' to educate me, and when it didn't, it still wasn't that simple to admit Pound's insistent demand that one must *learn* to learn what one had to. That was work!

I wrote to him, in the late 40s, and was absolutely gratified by the reply: *What have you read?* "Ogden rather dead, etc., etc." So this was an art, and not just subject matter. That fact alone changed my life.

British poet once said to me, poets in England come just after tv reviewers—this in Shakespeare's country. I couldn't at first believe it . . . Pound proposed the *power* of poetry, that it was primarily as "tales of the tribe"—what it means, collectively and as one, to use language as means to score the life of the mind *and* body. As Ginsberg says, first poet of our accessible time to reclaim poetry as sound. Also Ginsberg's emphasis, on hearing of Pound's death: that the *Cantos* are first articulate record/graph of mind/emotions continuous over fifty years. *That* is very interesting.

This side of the water we need heroes, models of active human context, call it—I mean, people who make clear a life can be lived specifically, not just drifted along with, that *choice* is crucial, certainly in mind. Pound took it all on, was not, as Olson remarked in another context, "an epicene poet"—"Like Pope." No power that finally matters, either in person or in poetry—'descriptive.'

The messy 'lives' are no doubt those who do go for broke, are possessed by the "gigantism" remarked by British reviewer of American poet's recent collection: "a poet of the widest apprehensions and comprehensions, and this without the gigantism that so haunts American poetic ambition." Of course we can have a 'place' if we're careful.

# The Release

*The Autobiography of William Carlos Williams.* New York: Random House, 1951.

Dr. Williams is 'unique' in no sense unfamiliar. There have been other men likewise of this intent: to hit ground somewhere, to anchor somehow to present. An autobiography can effect the impact of a recognition perhaps beyond the *art*—though I should look to nothing else but such art for major effect, or what can now be of essential use.

The present book is one of *many* by Dr. Williams, no reader can forget that. The material is, to some extent it must be, of lower intensity than that which we have witnessed before—he can not do it all over again, in any form, and the years here dealt with are those in which his other work first appeared. In 1925 *In the American Grain* recorded a like purpose, of "autobiography," and continues as informant:

> The strong sense of a beginning in Poe is in *no one* else before him. What he says, being thoroughly local in origin, has some chance of being universal in application, a thing they never dared conceive. Made to fit a *place* it will have that actual quality of *things* anti-metaphysical—

The prose of that earlier book has, of course, been noted but not in its particulars, i.e., the first evidence of a prose *method* we have yet to acknowledge by use. "No ideas but in things."

*Contact* (Toronto), November–January 1952–53.

# 1

A time denies itself in thinking of *time*—the *place* is a similar escape if it be left there, and not used. It is a theme of *use,* and how one can come to fix on any *thing* some signal of his own existence. Clearly, it is not in any usual sense: "What becomes of me has never seemed important, but the fates of ideas living against the grain in a nondescript world has always held me breathless." The "world" is nondescriptive, either in our hands—to speak of it so—or in its own character. A *use* is a *relation,* and these determine no adequate symbol or metaphor beyond their very *presence*—that they exist in such permanent character.

On this the poem rests, on this presence. "The poet thinks with his poem, in that lies his thought, and that in itself is the profundity." Against the half-conceived, or the recoil—the poem also a thing—equal, if you will, to Nature or to any mass conception. In this poetry has dominance, and a *form*. It is neither explanation nor description, but *actual* in such form.

> These were the years just before the great catastrophe to our letters— the appearance of T. S. Eliot's *The Waste Land.* There was heat in us, a core and a drive that was gathering headway upon the theme of a rediscovery of a primary impetus, the elementary principle of all art, in the local conditions. Our work staggered to a halt for a moment under the blast of Eliot's genius which gave the poem back to the academics. We did not know how to answer him.

A form "in the local conditions" depends on what relation is possible, and, to that end, one attacks. Particulars are relevant in their own attack on the man who wants to confront them. Released, they find form in themselves, and use any man as their declaration. It is, perhaps, that struggle is impossible against them—in this alien way. "When she died there was nothing left. In his despair he had nowhere to turn. It is the very apotheosis of the place and time."

But from that "place" or "time" there is nowhere else—either then, for Poe, or for us now. At this point we fight lacking all we might wish, or want, otherwise. In *release* from despair. The poem *begins* here. In time, if you want, and also in place. Its locus is that effect, of itself, on that corpus of the particular, the world in detail. What effect can be made is *in* the poem—not *then* alien, or strange to its locality. Our language is more uniquely ourselves than any other act, it is our marriage.

"Nothing can grow unless it taps into the soil."

2

Within my own experience I have heard Williams called "anti-poetic." This is a testament, of my own—that I oppose it. "When a man makes a poem, makes it, mind you, he takes words as he finds them interrelated about him and composes them—without distortion which would mar their exact significances—into an intense expression of his own perceptions and ardors that they may constitute a revelation in the speech that he uses." All *use* is a personal act, and I have used this *sense,* of poetry, insofar as I have been capable.

Some definitions are without meaning, lacking, as they do, a ground on which to bear. Any discussion of poetry must come to the poem itself, and take there, if anywhere, its own assumption of meaning. A theory of poetry is relevant only in what it can produce, in quite literal poems. Pound notes, "I think it will be usually found that the work outruns the formulated or at any rate the published equation, or at most they proceed as two feet of one biped."

> Outside
>                    outside myself
>                                        there is a world,
>     he rumbled, subject to my incursions
>     —a world
>                    (to me) at rest
>                         which I approach
> concretely—

("Eliot had turned his back on the possibility of reviving my world. . . . Only now, as I predicted, have we begun to catch hold again and restarted to make the line over. This is not to say that Eliot has not, indirectly, contributed much to the emergence of the next step in metrical construction, but if he had not turned away from the direct attack here, in the Western dialect, we might have gone ahead much faster.")

No man can make poetry without the ground of himself—in whatever character that should be open to him. "After it was over we rushed up—already there was a young man telling him he was more poet than doctor (shyly) and Williams saying he was simply both & the manner of his life affected his poetry very much he thought." Definition would be a man's act, and so his poetry, not so much in the character of things beyond reach, call it—but in those *things* immensely to hand, in that shape they make a "world" no matter. It is from this world a man must care *not* to escape, having *no* other of such kind.

"He sat to read, just turning the pages & looking at the people. Everybody I could hear near me responded in a way that staggered me.—Dead silence, tremendous applause—and the people who have money to go to these things don't read poetry. Common speech, and he really got to everyone. I was maudlin, with tears in my eyes—at the whole idea."

# William Carlos Williams: *Selected Essays*

*Selected Essays*, by William Carlos Williams. New York: Random House, 1954.

This is a difficult book to find one's way around in, because there are many apparent concerns. Most of these, however, make no more than a superficial continuity. For example, there is a surprising emphasis on poets whom one had not thought to associate with Dr. Williams' own work, since the latter has been so much beyond usual peripheries—even called at times 'antipoetic.' Of the various people whom he has chosen so to recommend, many strike one as, at best, parallel to his own practice, while some seem almost to confute it.

Pound has been one of these last for a long time, and in the early essays Williams gives us some hint of this:*

> But our prize poems are especially to be damned not because of superficial bad workmanship, but because they are rehash, repetition in another way of Verlaine, Baudelaire, Maeterlinck—conscious or unconscious—just as there were Pound's early paraphrases from Yeats

*Black Mountain Review*, Winter 1954.

*Williams' most interesting comment on Pound (for myself) is not here included, but to note it: "Letter to an Australian Editor," published in a Williams number of the *Briarcliff Quarterly*. There are many such omissions, and I have since learned the book represents roughly half the text originally planned by the author. Much controversial material, for example, is missing—among other things, a very succinct note on Eliot's espousal of Milton, "With Rude Fingers Forced" (printed in *Four Pages*). The resulting loss is considerable, and the reader should keep it in mind, both in reading the book itself and this review of it.

and his constant cribbing from the Renaissance, Provence and the
modern French: Men content with the connotations of their masters.

(Prologue to Kora in Hell, 1918)

True or false, this is a persistent judgment, which continues in
one character or another throughout Williams' comment. But by
1934 ("A Pound Stein") he can end a thoroughly acute perception
of what both have done, saying: "It may be added that both Gertrude Stein and Ezra Pound live in Europe." In short, Williams has
had, I think, a continual notion that men were *wrong* per se to run
away from 'local conditions'; for himself, they were all that could
generate the *forms* for which he looked. Yet there remained the dilemma of the *success* of others, come to again and again in both his
poems and criticism:

> Sometimes I envy others, fear them
> a little too, if they write well. . . .

("The Cure")

Of those closer to him, in point of geography at least, Marianne
Moore is (in this selection) the most singled out:

> Work such as Miss Moore's holds its bloom today not by using slang,
> not by its moral abandon or puritanical steadfastness, but by the aes-
> thetic pleasure engendered where pure craftsmanship joins hard sur-
> faces skillfully.

("Marianne Moore," 1931)

> Therefore Miss Moore has taken recourse to the mathematics of art.
> Picasso does no different: a portrait is a stratagem singularly related
> to a movement among the means of the craft. By making these opera-
> tive, relationships become self-apparent—the animal lives with a hu-
> man certainty. This is strangely worshipful. Nor does one always
> know against what one is defending oneself.

("Marianne Moore," 1948)

This is not a fair way of citing such things, but certain discrepancies
are clear. The first note, read in its entirety, argues a completely
relevant 'value,' e.g., "The 'useful result' is an accuracy to which
this simplicity of design greatly adds. The effect is for the effect to
remain 'true'; nothing loses its identity because of the composition,
but the parts in their assembly remain quite as 'natural' as before
they were gathered." The second (more a favor?) is not, however,

this positive in its analyses: "I don't think there is a better poet writing in America today or one who touches so deftly so great a range
of our thought."

Such matters are, of course, minimal, a man has what friends he
can have and is biased accordingly. What Williams might say of Marianne Moore's translations of La Fontaine, however interesting,
would leave us still beside the point. And this *is* important to note,
because it is so often the case that Williams says things in spite of
his 'subject.' There are, for example, essays on the work of Robert
Lowell ("It is to assert love, not to win it that the poem exists."), on
Karl Shapiro ("Shapiro speaks lovingly of his 'rime' which he defines here and there in his poem—variously, as it should [not] be
defined. It is the whole body of the management of words to the
formal purposes of expression. We express ourselves there [men]
as we might on the whole body of the various female could we ever
gain access to her [which we cannot and never shall]"), on Dylan
Thomas ("Reading over his collected poems I have thought of what
chances he had to enhance his fame by thinking again and perhaps
more profoundly of what he had in mind. But what can be more
profound than song? The only thing that can be asked is whether a
man is content with it.").

So it is a provocative book, for anyone who has either learned
from or felt sympathy for Williams' own work. Forgetting the above
for the moment (because I believe these 'occasions' to be of little
importance), the last piece in the book ("On Measure—Statement
for Cid Corman") brings to a head an issue more at root in Williams'
sense of structure than even his insistence on the 'local.' It begins:

> Verse—we'd better not speak of poetry lest we become confused—
> verse has always been associated in men's minds with "measure," i.e.,
> with mathematics. In scanning any piece of verse, you "count" the syl-
> lables. Let's not speak either of rhythm, an aimless sort of thing with-
> out precise meaning of any sort. But measure implies something that
> can be measured. Today verse has lost all measure.

(I would like to cite two other men here, whose practice and/or
belief may have less bearing than I think, but no matter. I am told
of an essay by an Elizabethan, Samuel Putman, "On Proportion,"
wherein he speaks of *numbers and measure* as being *arhythmus;* and of
that rhythm which we find in poems, as *rhythmus.* For him, rhythm
implied irregularity; he also speaks of poetic rhythm as that "regu-
larity just out of hearing." The other man is Thomas Campion,

who was both musician and poet, and who also said he paid no attention to any 'measure.' He gave his attention to the words and the
rhythms which they carried in them, to be related then as they occurred. This is very clear, of course, reading any of his poems:

*Kinde are her answeres*

    Kinde are her answeres,
    But her performance keeps no day;
Breaks time, as dancers
    From their own Musicke when they stray:
    All her free favors and smooth words,
Wing my hopes in vaine.
O did ever voice so sweet but only fain?
    Can true love yeeld such delay,
    Converting joy to pain?

    Lost is our freedome,
    When we submit to women so:
Why doe wee neede them,
    When in their best they worke our woe?
    There is no wisedome
Can alter ends, by Fate prefixt.
O why is the good of man with evill mixt?
    Never were days yet cal'd two,
    But one night went betwixt.

To 'scan' this is hardly possible, nor, more actually, at all the point.
The 'process' is literally the same as that by which Williams himself
writes, or any man who can effect such things with words. In any
case, here is Williams:

*The World Narrowed to a Point*

Liquor and love
when the mind is dull
focus the wit
on a world of form

The eye awakes
perfumes are defined
inflections
ride the quick ear

Liquor and love
rescue the cloudy sense
banish its despair
give it a home.

This is not the 'same,' granted, but see that the second verse, in particular, involves us in that same character of variation which makes Campion himself a delight.)

Williams continues:

> Most poems I see today are concerned with what they are *saying*, how profound they have been given to be. So true is this that those who write them have forgotten to make poems at all of them. Thank God we're not musicians, with our lack of structural invention we'd be ashamed to look ourselves in the face otherwise. There is nothing interesting in the construction of our poems, nothing that can jog the ear out of its boredom. I for one can't read them. There is nothing in their metrical construction to attract me, so I fall back on e. e. cummings and the disguised conventions that he presents which are at least amusing—as amusing as "Doctor Foster went to Gloucester, in a shower of rain."

The charge is reasonable enough, but for one thing—it seems to posit an either/or choice for "metrical construction" (?) versus some other means. But it is *not* metrics that are the fact in any of this, since, to compose 'metrically' would oblige one literally to an assumption of the 'foot' and the patterns then possible well before any poem could be written. This is the confusion, I think. Also— that it seems to be 'metrical construction' as against some form of 'typographical' construction (?); "It [the poem] is all over the page at the mere whim of the man who has composed it." But Stevens, for one, answered this, when he said there were those who thought of form as if it were a derivative of plastic shape. Which it is not, etc.

> Without measure we are lost. But we have lost even the ability to count. Actually we are not as bad as that. Instinctively we have continued to count as always but it has become not a conscious process and being unconscious has descended to a low level of invention. . . . I have accordingly made a few experiments which will appear in a new book shortly [*The Desert Music*]. . . . There will be other experiments but all will be directed toward the discovery of a new measure by which may be ordered our poems as well as our lives.

That, in brief, is the substance of the essay in question (here dated 1953). The first essay in the book is dated 1920. The first preoccupations are with the poem's structure—apart from content. This must be the issue of the *place* where it occurs—an answer, a disattachment, to the past. The line must be 'retaken,' reasserted, in terms of an immediate context. Against 'old forms,' congealed casts, which Williams names "the sonnet." ("To me the sonnet form is thoroughly banal because it is a word in itself whose meaning is definitely fascistic.") "Measure" is first spoken of in "Pound's Eleven New 'Cantos'" (1934):

> The line must be measured to be in measure—but this does not mean disfigurement to fit an imposed meter. It's a matter of technique or the philosophy of poetry. Difficult to find many who will agree about it. With Pound it is in itself a revolution—how difficult to comprehend: unless the term revolution be well understood.

That is part and parcel with the "*relatively* stable foot" called for in "On Measure," i.e., it is, I think, a confusion. To take literally the first of the sentence, "The line must be measured to be in measure . . . ," is to involve oneself in an obviously vicious circle. No poem was ever written "in this direction."

So, then, what does it all come to. That the words in a poem must cohere in terms of their rhythms and sound weights—this is reasonable enough. We have lost considerable ground—if one wishes to speak of it all as ground covered—by thinking too literally of 'quantitative verse,' and then, in a form of reflex, of that which we have been given by poets in our own immediate tradition. But 'measure,' bitterly enough, has most usually been that means by which lesser men made patterns from the work of better—so to perpetuate their own failure. There is even a hint of this in a review published in the *London Times Literary Supplement,* of Williams' *Collected Later Poems:* "But his forms are so irregular in outline that there is no way of measuring them. Any metrical ideas which the reader retains while reading him will be an interruption." So much for 'measure' (which has nothing to do with *rhythm,* which, as Olson reminds us, the "pedants of Alexandria made it"). But Williams no longer trusts rhythm—"an aimless sort of thing without precise meaning of any sort."

It all goes around and around. That I suppose would hold as true of the world as anything else would. Let's measure that?

# A Character for Love

*The Desert Music and Other Poems,* by William Carlos Williams. New York: Random House, 1954.

We can hope that the woman be merciful, a kind of repose (and our rejection in part) for that for which she attacks. And yet there is no woman either to be kind or to live with a kind man, and rightly. The man who would come to her comes with his own weapons, and if he is not a fool, he uses them.

That much might well be dogma—an apology only to those who have gone down before its alternative, the 'understanding.' It was this that Lawrence fought all his life, perhaps more closely (more desperately) than any man before or since. Because we can have no way to declare love, except by the act of it.

Here it is that Dr. Williams not so much rests as still persists—in that persistence which, because it knows itself (and will not understand), is love too.

> There are men
> who as they live
> fling caution to the
> wind and women praise them
> and love them for it.
> Cruel as the claws of
> a cat   .   .

*Black Mountain Review,* Summer 1954.

You do not describe this thing, neither you nor I. Married, the world becomes that act, or nothing.

> The female principle of the world
> is my appeal
> in the extremity
> to which I have come.

I think that much of this content (by no means to beg it) came from him from the first, and, to that extent, American poetry had something even Poe (whom Williams alone saw this in) could not in his own dilemma give it. It is interesting, certainly that, to read the last part of the Poe essay in *In the American Grain*—where Poe's attempt to register himself is so characterized as this persistence, this hammering at the final edge of contact.

And this is the same force of Williams' stories, the best of them I think, even that possible vagueness in the one about the returning doctor, at the friend's house (also a doctor), and of the friend's wife who comes in and sits there, in the dark, by the edge of the bed, lies down on it, because *he* cannot sleep.

> You are a woman and
> it was
> a woman's gesture . . .
> I declare it boldly
> with my heart
> in my teeth
> and my knees knocking
> together. Yet I declare
> it, and by God's word
> it is no lie.

The *Autobiography,* more than any of his other books, now, is the place where the materials of his work are given—not done, but there to be found and related, if that is the purpose, to their forms in his art. What the poem is—beyond his sense of this service as "capsule for punishable secrets" or including it—comes again and again to the fact of women. In the preface to the book he speaks of that "form" which men have given to his life, but it is women who have made for the "energy." And energy begins it.

> Of asphodel, that greeny flower,
> like a buttercup
> upon its branching stem . . .

save that it's green and wooden . . .
                I come, my sweet,
                                to sing to you.

For what reason, to sing, even to be a 'poet'?

                                        I *am* a poet! I
                am. I am. I am a poet. I reaffirmed, ashamed

                Now the music volleys through as in
                a lonely moment I hear it   Now it is all
                about me. The dance! The verb detaches itself
                seeking to become articulate

There shall be no other judge—*not* judge, but she who will take
it. And for that reason, that it begins where all things (*mind you*)
begin, the dance is the plain fact of contact, god help us.

                You seem quite normal. Can you tell me? Why
                does one want to write a poem?

                                Because it's there to be written.

                Oh. A matter of inspiration then?

                                                Of necessity.

                Oh. But what sets it off ?

                                I am that he whose brains
                                are scattered
                                        aimlessly

At this point one turns, to laugh (ha), because it is what you
wanted? Well, put it that here we are thrown out, not by Williams
but by that which he knows, perfectly. We shall get no thanks for
what we do, 'poets' or not. Nor can we lie down, asking it.

                                There is, in short,
                a counter stress,
                                born of the sexual shock,
                                        which survives it
                consonant with the moon,
                                to keep its own mind.

We have had so much hope, both in love and in poetry, that I
wonder what is or can be left. Yet put them together and you will
have nothing at all. You cannot sit in a woman's lap, however comfortable. And, despite the humiliation, the door must be shut of necessity—until you can bang it down or open it.

You understand
         I had to meet you
               after the event
and have still to meet you,
         Love
               to which you too shall bow
along with me—
         a flower
               a weakest flower
shall be our trust
         and not because
               we are too feeble
to do otherwise
         but because
               at the height of my power
I risked what I had to do,
         therefore to prove
               that we love each other
while my very bones sweated
         that I could not cry out to you
               in the act.

Let us do what we will, generally—there will be no statement beyond this. It is fantastic, to me, that Williams at such a time as now confronts him should be so incredibly clear. Yet, what else to be—

         Hear me out
               for I too am concerned
and every man
         who wants to die at peace in his bed
               besides.

# The Fact

*Pictures from Brueghel and Other Poems,* by William Carlos Williams. New York: New Directions, 1962.

There is no simple way to speak of this book. It is so singularly the work of a man, one man, that it moves thereby to involve all men, no matter what they assume to be their own preoccupations.

> What shall I say, because talk I must
> > That I have found a cure
> > > for the sick?
>
> I have found no cure
> > for the sick
> > > but this crooked flower
>
> Which only to look upon
> > all men
> > > are cured . . .
>
> ("The Yellow Flower")

The insistence in our lives has become a plethora of plans, of solutions, of, finally, a web of abstract commitments—which leave us only with confusions. Against these Dr. Williams has put the fact of his own life, and all that finds substance in it. He had earlier insisted, "No ideas but in things," meaning that all which moves to an *elsewhere* of abstractions, of specious 'reliefs,' must be seen as false. We live as and where we are. It is, for example, literally *here:*

First draft of a review published in *The Nation,* October 13, 1962.

*The World Contracted to a Recognizeable Image*
at the small end of an illness
there was a picture
probably Japanese
which filled my eye

an idiotic picture
except it was all I recognized
the wall lived for me in that picture
I clung to it as a fly

What device, means, rhythm, or form the poem can gain for its coherence are a precise issue of its occasion. The mind and ear are, in this sense, stripped to hear and organize what is given to them, and the *dance* or *music* Williams has used as a metaphor for this recognition and its use is that which sustains us, poets or men and women.

But only the dance is sure!
make it your own.
Who can tell
what is to come of it?

in the woods of your
own nature whatever
twig interposes, and bare twigs
have an actuality of their own

this flurry of the storm
that holds us,
plays with us and discards us
dancing, dancing as may be credible.

("The Dance")

It is equally that music which informs our lives with a coherence beyond their intention or apparent significance. In "The Desert Music" (the title poem of an earlier collection [1954] included in *Pictures from Brueghel,* as is also *Journey to Love* [1955]) this music is "a music of survival, subdued, distant, half heard. . . ." And against the external music of the juke-box, band, or whatever, the "nauseating prattle," Williams puts "the form of an old whore in / a cheap Mexican joint in Juárez, her bare / can waggling crazily. . . .":

What the hell
are you grinning
to yourself about? Not
at *her?*

        The music!
    I like her. She fits

    the music        .

And again, finding the form of no shape, no identity, "propped
motionless—on the bridge / between Juárez and El Paso—unrec-
ognizeable / in the semi-dark. . . .":

                    But what's THAT?
                                    the music! the
    *music!* as when Casals struck
    and held a deep cello tone
    and I am speechless        .

    The *dance,* the acts of a life, move to that *music,* the life itself, and
it is these which it is the poet's peculiar responsibility to acknowledge and recover by his art:

    Now the music volleys through as in
    a lonely moment I hear it.   Now it is all
    about me.   The dance!   The verb detaches itself
    seeking to become articulate        .

                And I could not help thinking
                of the wonders of the brain that
                hears that music and of our
                skill sometimes to record it.

Coming then to the later poems, what can be said now is that there
is all such truth, such life, in them. I cannot make that judgment
which would argue among the poems that this or that one shows
the greater mastery. I think there must come a time, granted that
one has worked as Williams to define the nature of this art, when it
all coheres, and each poem, or instance, takes its place in that life
which it works to value, to measure, to be the fact of. As here:

    *To Be Recited to Flossie on Her Birthday*

    Let him who may
    among the continuing lines
    seek out

    that tortured constancy
    affirms
    where I persist

    let me say
    across cross purposes
    that the flower bloomed

struggling to assert itself
simply under
the conflicting lights

you will believe me
a rose
to the end of time

# Foreword to *The Manuscripts and Letters of William Carlos Williams,* by Neil Baldwin and Steven L. Meyers

No simple comment suffices in an attempt to make clear the persistent and extraordinary value of William Carlos Williams' work as a writer. Public estimation came late for him, in some respects, but it is clear from the outset that his own peers, as Ezra Pound and the slightly younger Louis Zukofsky, took him as unique measure of the possibilities of the art they shared. For the then younger generation—Robert Lowell, Charles Olson, Kenneth Rexroth, Robert Duncan—he continued, as Olson put it, the one clean source in an activity often perverted by topical advantage and self-publicizing. For those of my own age, as Allen Ginsberg and Denise Levertov, he was intensely responsive and reassuring, always there to answer the endless letters we wrote to him, despite failing health in the latter years of his life. He was truly our hero, and we knew that he would hear us.

In *The Autobiography* he recollects the circumstances that resulted in the present collection of his manuscripts and related materials:

> Charles Abbott came to see us one winter's day about ten years ago. We sat in our front room all afternoon, Floss, he and I, over a highball or two, staring into a wood fire in our grate, letting the light fade. We hardly moved other than to refill our glasses. The phone didn't ring once. We thought we were in heaven.
>
> He told us of his project: to collect manuscripts of the living poets,

Neil Baldwin and Steven L. Meyers, *The Manuscripts and Letters of William Carlos Williams in the Poetry Collection of the Lockwood Memorial Library, State University of New York at Buffalo: A Descriptive Catalog* (Boston: G. K. Hall, 1978).

English and American—whatever could be had—material that as often was thrown away or lost that could be used later to piece out an understanding of their lives and methods of work. He had written asking me if I had anything of the sort lying about the house that I could give him for the Lockwood Memorial Library at the University of Buffalo where a room had been set aside for the collection.

Generously, enthusiastically, Williams accepted the invitation, very possibly a singular one for him at that time. So it was that, from time to time, bulky brown envelopes filled with his work drafts began to arrive in Buffalo for deposit at the University Library, and, as the years passed, their accumulation resulted in the most extensive collection of Williams materials that we now have.

What is their value? Williams himself, I think, makes it very evident: "material . . . that could be used later to piece out an understanding of their lives and methods of work." Whether one be literary historian or critic, or writer, or, most appropriately, a student—whose world has not as yet coalesced into professional habit—a very simple piece of paper, with words scrawled or typed in unequivocal impulse, can be wonder beyond all others. *There it literally is, that's how he did it!*

But it is not merely explanations one is after. Such are all too simple and will no doubt change too, as readers and the worlds in which they live. The virtue of what Williams wrote is equal to the virtue of the diverse flowering earth he loved. Both change endlessly, to remain the same. In that sense there will never be a finally right answer, nor will these materials yield it.

Rather, it is the intimate revelation possible, when one can so witness the issue of such words as he did write by means of an agency as movingly common as a man's own two hands. The human dimension becomes so dearly manifest, and all pretensions of formula or abstract objectification fall away.

Although many indeed did make use of the materials here catalogued previous to this present recording of them, the two young men who have finally done this painstaking and perceptive labor are to be honored and thanked. Clearly their knowledge of Williams is now intimate in the sense I have used that word. Put briefly, they cared—and, as Williams might well have told them, all you can do with caring is to make it an *act*, such as theirs.

# "paradise/our/speech . . ."

*All: The Collected Short Poems, 1923–1958,* by Louis Zukofsky. New York: Norton, 1965.

Louis Zukofsky has defined his poetics as a function, having as
lower limit, speech, and upper limit, song. It is characteristic of him
to say that a poet's "major aim is not to show himself but that order
that of itself can speak to all men." It is his belief that a poet writes
one poem all his life, a continuing *song,* so that no division of its
own existence can be thought of as being more or less than its sum.
This is to say, it *all* is.

Williams wrote of him, "The musician and the poet should be
taken as a critical unit in our effort to understand the poet Zukofsky's meaning." It was his own thought that "it was never a simple
song as it was, for instance, in my own case." But that complexity
which Williams noted can be deceptive if it proposes that something intently difficult is involved with whatever sense of purpose.
In many instances, the *song* of both men is similar, and it is necessary to isolate the character of *music* either might mean. For example, here is a poem of Zukofsky's in which the "tune" is defined
deliberately as a consequence of rhythms and sounds:

> The lines of this new song are nothing
> But a tune making the nothing full
> Stonelike become more hard than silent
> The tune's image holding in the line.

> (20, *Anew*)

Again as Williams has said, "He uses words in more or less sentence formation if not strictly in formal sentence patterns, in a wider relationship to the composition as musical entity." I had first understood this possibility by means of a poem of Williams', "The End of the Parade":

> The sentence undulates
> raising no song—
> It is too old, the
> words of it are falling
> apart. . . .

That is, I *heard* the fact of the poem's statement as well as understood its meaning. Such hearing is immediately necessary in reading Zukofsky's work insofar as meaning is an intimate relation of such sound and sense. It can be as close as—

> Crickets'
> thickets
>
> light,
> delight . . .

> (16, "29 Songs")

—or move with an apparent statement, seeming to "say" enough to satisfy that measure; but again it will be that one *hears* what is so said, not merely deciphers a "meaning":

> And so till we have died
> And grass with grass
> Lie faceless as the grass
>
> Grow sheathed with the grass
> Between our spines a hollow
> The stillest sense will pass
> Or weighted cloud will follow.

> (19, *Anew*)

> Strange
> To reach that age,
> remember
> a tide
> And full
> for a time
> be young.

> (36, *Anew*)

The consequence of such a way leads to a recognition of what is being heard at each moment of the writing, or reading, and the effect is evident in either:

> . . . Having seen the thing happen,
> There would be no intention 'to write it up,'
>
> But *all* that was happening,
> The mantis itself only an incident, *compelling any writing*
> The transitions were perforce omitted.
>
> Thoughts'—two or three or five or
> Six thoughts' reflection (pulse's witness) of what was
>     happening
> All immediate, not moved by any transition.
>
> Feeling this, what should be the form
> Which the ungainliness already suggested
> Should take? . . .
>
> ("Mantis," An Interpretation)

It leads to other distrusts of any kind of *plan* which distorts the actuality of feeling:

> Understanding:
>     I wasn't going to say
> for fear
>     You didn't want to hear.
>
> That's the worst
>     of understanding,
> a handshake
>     would be better.
>
> ("4 Other Countries")

The way of such feeling is clear in the words, as "for fear / You didn't want to hear" or "understanding, / a handshake," and trusts to that sense, "*The vowels / abide / in consonants / like / / Souls / in / bodies—*" for the life of what it says.

This life—*All: The Collected Short Poems, 1923–1958*—is evidence of Zukofsky's own, but not as some biographical record, although much detail of that kind can be taken from it. It is, rather, that by virtue of the occasion so shared each has come to live in all the diversity of either. In this respect, I can think of no man more useful to learn from than Zukofsky, in that he will not 'say' anything but that which the particulars of such a possibility require, and follows the *fact* of that occasion with unequaled sensitivity. But to *hear* it, is necessary—

That song
  is the kiss
it keeps
  is it
The
  unsaid worry
for what
  should last.

                                ("4 Other Countries")

# Louis Zukofsky: *All: The Collected Short Poems, 1923–1958*

In his preface to *A Test of Poetry* (1948) Louis Zukofsky notes at the outset, "The test of poetry is the range of pleasure it affords as sight, sound, and intellection. This is its purpose as art." In his long poem *"A"* he qualifies its occasion as *"Out of deep need . . ."* Then, continuing:

> Who had better sing and tell stories
> Before all will be abstracted.
> So goes: first, *shape*
> The creation—
> A mist from the earth,
> The whole face of the ground:
> Then *rhythm*—
> And breathed breath of life;
> Then *style*—
> That from the eye its function takes—
> "Taste" we say—a living soul.
> First, glyph; then syllabary,
> Then letters. Ratio after
> Eyes, tale in sound. First, dance. Then
> Voice. First, body—to be seen and to pulse
> Happening together.
>
> <div align="right">(<i>"A"</i> 12)</div>

It is a sense that proposes poetry to be evidence as to its own activity, apart from any other sense of description or of a conve-

*Agenda,* Summer 1966.

nience to some elsewise considered reality of things. More, it is a belief, deeply committed, that what is said says 'what-is-said'—a complexity of no simple order. For example, the first poem in *All* notes by the fact of its activity that any *said* thing exists in its saying and cannot be less than said—each time it is. It is interesting that this poem is called "Poem beginning 'The'"—which article is itself a determined emphasis upon what is defined in speech. In this case, a method as well takes form in this poem, as William Carlos Williams points out in his essay "Zukofsky," included in "A."* It is based, I feel, upon the premise that all that is, as whatever has spoken it, may occur as it is, each time it is spoken. In other words, there is nothing which anything so existent is 'about,' that will go away in time, so as to embarrass the actuality of such existence. Zukofsky makes a lovely note of *time* in the 28th of 29 Songs, which is pertinent to all such facts of *factness:* ". . . And for years it was four o'clock,—not time which would have broken the hour and placed a statue of David in history, but an ornamental herb of that name,— with flowers that grow in Peru of a great variety of color. So that for years it was four o'clock and the same as bloom from 4 P.M. till the next morning."

There is one poem which I would feel very useful for many senses of Zukofsky's poems, both in that character with which I have been concerned and also, very much, in the full complexity of their involvement with the man who is writing them. The poem is "Mantis" and there is a note as to its date of writing, November 4, 1934. At a time when so much concern has come to center on assumptions of form, and remembering also that Empson's *Seven Types of Ambiguity,* for one such instance, was published in the early thirties—this poem makes clear a context of possibility and response itself a manifest of the poem's writing. The ostensible form of the poem is a sestina, and in "'Mantis,' An Interpretation"—a close response to the poem's writing and concerns which follows in the next—Zukofsky says:

> The sestina, then, the repeated end words
> Of the lines' winding around themselves,
> Since continuous in the Head, whatever has been read,
> > whatever is heard,
> > whatever is seen

*Origin Press edition (1959).

Perhaps goes back cropping up again with
Inevitable recurrence again in the blood
Where the spaces of verse are not visual
But a movement,
With vision in the lines merely a movement . . .

One feels in fact inevitably
About the coincidence of the mantis lost in the subway,
About the growing oppression of the poor—
Which is the situation most pertinent to us—
With the fact of the sestina:
Which together fatally now crop up again
To twist themselves anew
To record not a sestina, post Dante,
Nor even a mantis.

What I am most intent to point out here is that Zukofsky feels form as an intimate presence, whether or not that form be the use or issue of other feelings in other times, or the immediate apprehension of a *way* felt in the moment of its occurrence. The distinction is, then, against what appropriates the outline sans an experience of its intimate qualities—as Zukofsky notes in this same section:

What is most significant
Perhaps is that C—and S—and X—of the 19th century
Used the "form"—not the form but a Victorian
Stuffing like upholstery
For parlor polish,
And our time takes count against them
For their blindness and their (unintended?) cruel smugness.

Again: as an experiment, the sestina would be wickerwork—
As a force, one would lie to one's feelings not to use it.

There is no reason I would credit to prevent a man's walking down a road another has made use of—unless the road, by such use, has become a 'road,' an habituated and unfelt occasion. But as "force" its possibility is timeless.

Given the briefness of these notes, I am embarrassed to deal with all that in this poem excites and informs me. It is a peculiar virtue of Zukofsky's work that it offers an extraordinary handbook for the writing of poems. His particular sensitivity to the qualities of poetry as "sight, sound, and intellection" marks the significance of his relation to Ezra Pound, who dedicated *Guide to Kulchur* "To Louis

Zukofsky and Basil Bunting, strugglers in the desert." It is Bunting who says that his own first experience of poetry as an unequivocal possibility for himself came with the recognition that the order and movement of *sound* in a poem might itself create a coherence of the emotions underlying. In this respect, the following note by Zukofsky merits much thought:

> How much what is sounded by words has to do with what is seen by them, and how much what is at once sounded and seen by them crosscuts an interplay among themselves—will naturally sustain the scientific definition of poetry we are looking for. To endure it would be compelled to integrate these functions: time, and what is seen in time (as held by a song), and an action whose words are actors or, if you will, mimes composing steps as of a dance that at proper instants calls in the vocal cords to transform it into plain speech.
>
> ("Poetry," in *"A"* [Origin Press edition, 1959])

The brilliance, then, of these poems is their grace in such a recognition, that they can move so articulately in all the variables of a life. I can make no selection because, as their author has said, one writes one poem all one's life, and there can be no significant division. But as one moment, this may stand as token of all:

> Strange
> To reach that age,
>                   remember
>         a tide
> And full
>         for a time
>                   be young.

                                                            (36, *Anew*)

# A Note

There is a possibility in reading and writing, which knows words as in the world in much the same way that men are, and that each may know that possibility which Herrick defines:

> And when all bodies meet,
>   In Lethe to be drowned,
> Then only numbers sweet
>   With endless life are crowned.

There is no presumption in the fact that Louis Zukofsky puts two poems of Herrick's together with his own song, "Little wrists," as an instance of *grace* in his comparative anthology, *A Test of Poetry*. One hears in the possibility another has articulated what may thus bring clear one's own, and though there are three hundred years intervening, the measure of grace is not variable.

Zukofsky says, one writes one poem all one's life. All that he has written may be felt as indivisible, and all *one*—which word occurs frequently in the text in this sense.

Another word found often is *leaf*, echoing, specifically at times as in the latter part of *"A"* 12, Whitman's *Leaves of Grass*. Despite what seem dissimilarities, they are like men in that both would favor— with Shakespeare as Zukofsky has proposed—the "clear physical eye" as against "the erring brain." The experience of one's life as one is given to have it, and as relationships of its nature are found, unfold, then, as *leaves*, finding home in time far past or in the instant now:

Introduction to Louis Zukofsky, *"A" 1–12* (New York: Doubleday, 1967).

> The music is in the flower,
> Leaf around leaf ranged around the center;
> Profuse but clear outer leaf breaking on space,
> There is space to step to the central heart:
> The music is in the flower,
> It is not the sea but hyaline cushions the flower—
> Liveforever, everlasting.
> The leaves never topple from each other,
> Each leaf a buttress flung for the other.

This is taken from "A" 2, written in 1928. In "A" 11, twenty-two years later:

> . . . Honor

> His voice in me, the river's turn that finds the
> Grace in you, four notes first too full for talk, leaf
> Lighting stem, stems bound to the branch that binds the
> Tree, and then as from the same root we talk, leaf
> Over leaf of his thought, sounding
> His happiness: song sounding
> The grace that comes from knowing
> Things, her love our own showing
> Her love in all her honor.

". . . His voice in me. . . ." That men do so move, one to one, here grandfather, to father, to son—but that also, as Zukofsky thinks possible, it may be that Shakespeare had read Catullus, and that men who may so read the same text may so *in time* relate. Certainly, as the outset of the work makes clear, Zukofsky *hears* Bach, and after hearing:

> I walked on Easter Sunday,
>   This is my face
>   This is my form.
> Faces and forms, I would write
>                 you down
> In a style of leaves growing.

One may well quote Pound, as Zukofsky has, to give measure for such occasion:

> Hast 'ou fashioned so airy a mood
>   To draw up the leaf from the root?
>             * * *
> and the rest as time has cleft it

The title *"A"* itself is what one might call initial, and initiating, evidence of the kind of intelligence Zukofsky has—seeing and hearing words in the world as the specific possibilities they contain. He has said, in fact, that "a case can be made out for the poet giving some of his life to the use of the words *the* and *a:* both of which are weighted with as much epos and historical destiny as one man can perhaps resolve." How much "world" can lie between *the* and *a* is hardly for either *a* or *the* grammarian to decide.

We may speak of *the* as some thing previously noted or recognized, and of *a* as that which has not been thus experienced—but think too that "from A to Z" may mean something, and that if one looks at an A, it may very possibly become a sawhorse:

> Horses: who will do it? out of manes? Words
> Will do it, out of manes, out of airs, but
> They have no manes, so there are no airs, birds
> Of words, from me to them no singing gut.
> For they have no eyes, for their legs are wood,
> For their stomachs are logs with print on them;
> Blood red, red lamps hang from necks or where could
> Be necks, two legs stand A, four together M.

*Horses* and *leaves:*

> You keep up to date
> On all fours
> That canter sometimes
> Before boughs that grace trees.
> Sparks from hoofs:
> There is horse . . .
>
> So year to year—
> Nor do the arts
> Ever end.
> How can man say
> "I am certain"
> For certain and uncertain
> Do not make certain.
> Only forever is previous
> And not a horse's forever.
> If someone stole off with its body
> Be sure that its spirits
> Canter forever.
> Blacksmith, creator, shapes his shoe
> Into substance.

Born in New York's lower east side, Zukofsky's life cannot have been simple, and the kinds of complexity one realizes do confront him here are deeply to be considered. In the opening movements there are bitter terms of death, poverty, war—

> "I beg your pardon
> I've a— "h" begins the rhyme here,
> Shall we now?"
>
>> "You misconstrue—uh
>> Men's rue—eh,
>> Anyhow!"
>
>>> The sailors in the carousel
>>> looking for a place to
>>> bury—Ricky;
>>> Seaweed, fellow voters, and
>>> spewn civic sidewalks.

> Thus one modernizes
> His lute,
> Not in one variation after another;
> Words form a new city,
> Ours is no Mozart's
> Magic Flute—
> Tho his melody made up for a century
> And, we know, from him, a melody resolves
>> to no dullness—
> But when we push up the daisies,
> The melody! the rest is accessory:
>
> My one voice. My other: is
> An objective—rays of the object brought to a focus,
> An objective—nature as creator—desire
>     for what is objectively perfect
> Inextricably the direction of historic and
>> contemporary particulars.

He was first published in *The Exile* by Ezra Pound in the twenties. The poem was "The," which is relevant, and it led subsequently to his publication in *The Dial* and other magazines of the period. In 1931 he edited an issue of *Poetry* in which he presented a number of writers, among them Carl Rakosi, Kenneth Rexroth (for whom it was his first publication), William Carlos Williams (whose poem "The Alphabet of the Trees" gained him one of his first awards), and others of like significance. Asked for some tag, whereby to identify the group, Zukofsky used the term "objectivist"—which he once spoke of in conversation as follows:

> I picked the word simply because I had something very simple in mind. You live with the things as they exist and as you sense them and think them. That's the first thing, and that I call *sincerity* in an essay that was printed at the back of that *Poetry* number. Otherwise how sincere your intentions doesn't matter. The rest is, once you do that, you do put them into a shape that, apart from your having lived it, is now on its own, and that's what goes into the world and becomes part of it.

He has been long and quietly about his work, and, in the passage of time, he has written other books which complement it significantly—*All*, the collected short poems in two volumes (1923–1958; 1956–1964), and *Bottom: On Shakespeare* (published in 1963) among them. What he has said of the latter makes a useful focus here. First, despite that it is written in prose, he calls it "a long poem on a theme for the variety of its recurrences." The theme is, "that Shakespeare's text thruout favors the clear physical eye against the erring brain" and "that this theme has historical implications." Second, a "valid skepticism, that, as 'philosophy of history' taking in the (arts and sciences) my book takes exception to all philosophies from Shakespeare's point of view, that is, the physical eye against the erring brain." Third, "a continuation of my work on prosody in my other writings. In this sense my wife's music [her setting of Shakespeare's *Pericles* is the second volume of this work] saves me a lot of words, and she did a note to every syllable of *Pericles*." Finally, it is "a poet's autobiography as involvement of twenty years in a work shows him up, or, as in the case of Shakespeare, his words show him, are his life. . . ."

About *All,* Zukofsky says: "In a sense *All* is an autobiography: the words are my life . . . Or to put it in other words, the poet's form is never an imposition of history, but the desirability of making order out of history as it is felt and conceived."

In the title story of *It was,* a collection published in 1961, the story itself having been written twenty years earlier, one finds: "This story was a story of our time. And a writer's attempts not to fathom his time amount but to sounding his mind in it. I did not want to break up my form by pointing to well-known place names and dates in the forty years that I had lived—events familiar to most of us, to some more than myself. I wanted our time to be the story, but like the thought of a place passed by once and recalled altogether: seen again as through a stereoscope blending views a little way apart into a solid—defying touch. I was saying something that had had a sequence, like the knowledge of taking a breath, and hiding it, because one breathes without pointing to it before and after. . . ." "Thanks to the Dictionary," the final piece of this same book, written in 1932, begins:

> "A." Quoting the dictionary. Remembering my sawhorses, my little a.'s abbreviated for afternoon, perhaps for years, this afternoon.

Quoting Satie, "born very young in a world already old," he has said of "A," "The idea is much as the brain does err, it will willynilly get down, and sometimes the eye sees—the form in that sense organic, or all of one's life, and this is the life, and for the rest nobody else's business. It's written in one's time and place, and it refers to other times and places as one grows, whatever way one grows. It takes in books that survive—say, well, like Bach's music it can go down, it can go up, that's the interest of it and all to come through the form of the thing. To hold it together, I don't know—a song?" From "A" 12:

> You remember
> The houses where we were born
> The first horse pulsed
> Until the evening and the morning
> Were the first day?
>
> I'll tell you.
> About my *poetics*—
>
> $$\int \begin{matrix} \text{music} \\ \text{speech} \end{matrix}$$
>
> An integral
> Lower limit speech
> Upper limit music
>
>        \* \* \*
>
> *Time qualifies the fire and spark of it*
> I can't improve *that*.
> That closed and open sounds saw
>       Things,
> See somehow everlastingly
> Out of the eye of sky.

Poetics. With constancy.

⁂

As I love:
My poetics. . . .

⁂

Better a fiddle than geiger?
With either there is so much in 1
And in one:

$$\int_{-1}^{1} \int \begin{array}{l} \text{sound} \\ \text{story—eyes: thing thought} \end{array}$$

⁂

Courses tide, and a tide
       brings back folk
       after twenty years,
A cycle a light matter or more,
So my song with an old voice is whole:
Another way of saying
You cannot take out of the circle—what was in it . . .

Thus to *hear*, as he would hear Catullus, in the translation he has made with his wife—"fact that delights as living hint and its cues" being "*facit delicias libidinesque*"—"which is much more simple in the Latin. It has to do with pleasures and desires . . ." So "*A*" 9 is an extraordinary reading of Guido Cavalcanti's *Donna me prega*, the *experience* of valuation, and of love, with Marx as he stems from Aristotle included—the form a canzone, which demands that fifty-four of the one hundred and fifty-four syllables occurring in a strophe be rhymed, extending to seventy-five lines in all. As Zukofsky notes, "it's all wound in," which impulse the sonnet form reverses. Here he has composed two distinct canzones—the first, of value, the second, of love—not a literal translation of Cavalcanti but rather an intensive experience of the intimate situation of his writing, as fact of sounds in the rhythms then relating. The second canzone repeats, almost verbatim, the rhymes of the first:

    (1)
An impulse to action sings of a semblance
Of things related as equated values,
The measure all use is time congealed labor
In which abstraction things keep no resemblance

To goods created; integrated all hues
Hide their natural use. . . .
    (2)
An eye to action sees love bear the semblance
Of things, related is equated—values
The measure all use who conceive love, labor
Men see, abstraction they feel, the resemblance
(Part, self-created, integrated) all hues
Show to natural use. . . .

To know what men say, one must hear them, and to hear them
means moving with the intimate means of their occasion—

*Out of deep need*
Four trombones and the organ in the nave
A torch surged—
Timed the theme Bach's name
Dark, larch and ridge, night:
From my body to other bodies
Angels and bastards interchangeably
Who had better sing and tell stories
Before all will be abstracted.

*Buffalo, N.Y.*
*April 2, 1967*

# All Ears Hear Here

"*A*". By Louis Zukofsky. 826 pp. Berkeley, Calif.: University of California Press, 1978.

There seems to me a very simple human longing, that life *mean* something, that there be a world *contingent*—as Louis Zukofsky might say—with that sadly meager human fact, *I'm alive!* Yet *world* itself comes from a root (*weorld*) whose own meaning might well recall to us that a human life *is*, in fact, the world, and the only one we will ever have. There is no longer an explicit order, secular or divine, which can encode us, so to speak, discover for us a collective significance of cohering and relieving order—unless one feels factually secure in the chaos of *life styles*, the persistent destructiveness of seemingly endless wars, the dereliction of any political responsibility, the outrage of *business*, the utter disjunct of literal *place* and *person*.

So it is that the heroic imagination of our time has been, of necessity, the responsibility of our artists, just that no other human conduct seemed to care that much—as long as one's own piece of the action was acknowledged and given sufficient reward. Presidents and plumbers alike *only work here* and, thanks to unions and parties, are amply paid no matter what *works* or doesn't. Yet who among them would so risk his life, as Pound, right *or* wrong; as William Carlos Williams, shaken by one stroke after another, yet insistently maintaining that life *is* a wonder; as Charles Olson, dying, continuing to claim that the "fundament," that very human *thing* we are, is

*New York Times Book Review*, May 20, 1979.

forever as real as the "firmament," all those stars overhead, which so invite us.

Louis Zukofsky's life work is *"A"*—not *the*, mind you, but *a*, for as he said, "a case can be made out for the poet giving some of his life to the use of the words *the* and *a* . . ." *The* good life is one thing, then, and *a* life quite another. The contents page of this extremely useful edition notes that the first section of the poem (there are 24 in all, which number echoes for me significantly the human measure of a day) was written in 1928, when the poet was 24 years old. The last writing is dated 1974 (*"A"* 23), so that one has the range of 46 years—without question a *life's* commitment, in all possible respects, to what does come and go, of a day, and what does stay put—as value, as measure, as possibility.

Unlike Pound's *Cantos* (whose time of composition might be seen as parallel), Zukofsky's work is grounded in a *triad*, a life lived with two intensively significant *other* people, his wife, Celia, and his son, Paul. They are presences in the poem as much as the poet's own. So there is a clear *domestic* locus, and the fact of these three is humanly vulnerable always, yet tenaciously coherent in that they are a *human* relationship, a seemingly timeless pattern of organic order: becoming, being, and ending. There is also the world, of course, and all that it proposes and/or constitutes. And the *art* of poetry, as he said:

> the whole art of poetry which "is nothing else but the completed action of writing words to be set to music"—music being the one art that more than the others aims in its reach to speak to all men.

Zukofsky's *art*, in this work, is without equal. No poet of our time can so *sound* the resources of language, so actuate *words* to become all that they might be thought otherwise to engender. So that Bach be—

> Blest
> Ardent
> Celia
>     unhurt and
> Happy

Or Marx discover himself compacted with Cavalcanti (*"A"* 9) in the demanding measure of a sestina, wherein 54 of the 154 sounds possible in the strophe must rhyme:

> An impulse to action sings of a semblance
> Of things related as equated values . . .

> An eye to action sees love bear the semblance
> Of things, related is equated,—values . . .

Or, magnificently, in the close of the poem's "single voice" (*"A"* 23):

> Of Nought—light, leaf, grief—
> lend grace wife and her
>
> son keep to life's end
> serein (horse) a full lawn.

But how begin to suggest *all* that is heard here—*all ears hear here,* one's tempted to say. For, led by Bach ("A/Round of fiddles playing Bach . . .") into this complexly various dance, there follow all this life's responses to *all:* ". . . *mathémata* / *swank* for *things* / *learned* ('like' caged / 'silence' which pulses)— / yet in each / case *what happens.* . . ." So come Homer, Aristotle, Shakespeare, J.Q. and H. Adams, Swift, among many signifying others—as Whitman or Plautus, whose *vernacular* power in Latin is matched only by Catullus. (Louis and Celia Zukofsky's translation of Catullus is, in fact, a formidable *transliteration* of this poet's *sounds*—Plautus' *Rudens,* in Zukofsky's translation, is *"A"* 21.) Then there are those, as Pound and Williams, who shared in the commitment. *"A"* 17, "A CORONAL / for Floss"(which begins with a quotation from Williams' poem of that title) is a chronological anthology of testament to the life Zukofsky found in Williams (whose own response may be felt in the fact that he gave Zukofsky the responsibility of editing and also ordering the poems collected in *The Wedge* [1944], which is dedicated "To L.Z.").

The close of the poem is a melding, "a five-part score—music, thought, drama, story, poem" (as its title says, "L.Z. Masque") in which his wife, Celia, composed "four voices" of his writings following the "one-voice" of Handel's "Harpsichord Pieces" in the order noted (from *Prepositions,* his collected essays, "Arise, Arise," a play, "It was," a story, and *"A"* itself )—to effect a polyphony of senses, simultaneously, where all had begun and now ends. In that shifting, reiterating order, no *one* is now dominant—or rather, all is now *one.* And who had been speaking to us is forever now this mingling, recollective harmony. Because—as Zukofsky once wrote in the wish to define his own commitment to this art, "For My Son When He Can Read"—the poet's "major aim is not to show himself but that order that of itself can speak to all men. . . ." Pray, friends, that we can hear.

# For L.Z.

It is an *honor* to know men and women of genius and probity, because we live, finally, in a human world and however we would dispose ourselves toward that world otherwise the case, it is the human one which makes the most intimate and significant judgment. For myself and others of my generation, our elders in the art were extraordinary example and resource. Despite a chaos of restrictive generalization, we had nonetheless the active, persistent functioning of example: Ezra Pound, William Carlos Williams, Basil Bunting, Louis Zukofsky—to note those most dear to my own heart.

My first information of Zukofsky was in the dedications of two books crucial to my senses of poetry, Ezra Pound's *Guide to Kulchur* ("To Louis Zukofsky and Basil Bunting, strugglers in the desert") and Williams' *The Wedge* ("To L.Z."). It was, however, Edward Dahlberg who gave me my first active sense of Zukofsky's situation and urged me to invite him to contribute to *The Black Mountain Review,* which happily I did, resulting in the publication of a section from *"A"* 12 (BMR #5), and "Songs of Degrees" and *"Bottom: On Shakespeare,* Part Two" (BMR #6). In the meantime Robert Duncan had arrived in Mallorca and become a close friend and mentor, and it was he who showed me Williams' review of *Anew* as well as texts by Zukofsky himself. Then, in 1955 as I recall, while teaching at Black Mountain and visiting briefly in New York, I determined to meet Zukofsky if possible, and so one evening attempted the subway out to Brooklyn with just twenty cents in my pocket. As luck would have it, I overshot my destination, spent my remaining dime

*Paideuma* 7, no. 3 (Winter, 1978).

on correcting my error, and finally arrived tentative, confused, and literally penniless.

It's to the point, I believe, that such acts be remembered, especially when they define the possibilities of human responsibility and choice. As I came into the house on Willow Street, to be met by these extraordinarily dear and tender people, I somehow determined it would be best for all concerned if I revealed my predicament immediately, and I tried to. But Louis asked a favor of me, as he put it, saying that Celia was altering an overcoat for him, and it would help the sense of fitting required if I would put it on so that he might see how it looked. I did, and immediately Louis said, "There, it's yours!" Or words to that effect, because I cannot remember clearly what literally he did say, being then so distracted by the generosity of the gift and the fact that I had still to tell them I was broke. Finally I got *that* said, and their response was the specific coin required for the subway, *and* a five dollar bill to go with it, *and* a substantial lunch for the trip back to Black Mountain next day.

*And* it never changed. Always that shy, intensive warmth, that dear, particular care. In fact, the last time I saw them together was in New York—we had met the day previous, by blessed accident, in the street—and I had come up to see them where they were now living in a residential hotel off Central Park. As luck would have it, there was a torrential thunderstorm through which I walked a considerable distance, and arrived, dripping and wet to the skin. My coat was taken from me and hung up over the bath tub to dry. I was sat down and given hot coffee to warm me up, etc., etc. When Celia asked me if I'd like cream, I said, yes, if it was simple—which it proved not to be. So she gave me a spoonful of vanilla ice cream, to act as cream for the coffee, and then a full dish of it, in the event I might enjoy it for its own sake. And *then* we talked.

If I try to isolate my senses of Louis Zukofsky from those memories now, I neither can nor can I see the reason to. He taught me so much, in so many ways. Without the least trying, so to speak, the measures of person, of conduct, of art, which he constituted, are all of a factual piece. Again I think of that frail man's walking me late at night to the subway entrance, so I wouldn't have difficulty finding it, despite the effort it must have been for him to confront those streets at that hour, and his walk back alone. I remember "raise grief to music"—"the joy that comes from knowing things"—"the more so all have it"—"upper limit music, lower limit speech"—"love lights light in like eyes"—"he got around. . . ." And if I misquote, then I do—because this is the practical, *daily* company of

Louis Zukofsky for me, the measure of his father, "everybody loved Reb Pincos because he loved everybody. Simple. . . ."

Thankfully, I was able at times to make clear my respect—in various reviews and notes, in the rather crunky introduction to *"A" 1-12* (New York: Doubleday, 1967) with its several misprints, etc. And, more privately, I could argue the case at times, as Hugh Kenner will remember, apropos "The winds / agitating / the / waters." Which certainly *looked* easy, as he said, but trying, did discover was otherwise—and then wrote the primary review of *"A" 1-12* (in its first Origin edition), in which he rightly qualifies the *art* of Zukofsky's practice as so much the more accomplished than Auden's, whose *Homage to Clio* he was also reviewing. Etc. These 'arguments' will die with us too. L.Z.—never.

# A Personal Note

I have never understood very clearly why a man of Basil Bunting's accomplishment should have so little use in his own country. We have had like situations here—in the case of Louis Zukofsky, only recently 'discovered' after many years indeed of exceptional writing, and I can remember as well how resistant the elders of my own generation were to the work of Williams and Pound. H. D. remains for the most part an obscure figure, despite the fact that she is so uniquely a major one.

But if no one shouts, or keeps the insistence active, then these things do happen. Some years ago, when *Origin* was first being published, I wrote to Bunting to ask his help with finding active people in England and especially to see if he might have poems himself to send. He answered most kindly that his life had never been 'literary,' and since much of it had been spent in Persia, he was not aware of what might be of use then (roughly 1952) in England. He said he saw few English writers, and that when Alec Waugh, for example, had visited him, they talked of the water table and of the migration of game.

I had known of his work for some time, associating it with that of Pound, in whose *Active Anthology* I had first had chance to read Bunting's poems. *Kulchur* is also dedicated to Bunting and Zukofsky, "strugglers in the desert" of all too real a fact. Then in 1950 the Cleaners' Press published his *Poems,* and we had our first chance

*Granta,* 6 November 1965.

to see the range and subtlety of what he had done. Shortly after, *Poetry* published his long poem *The Spoils* (1951).

But then the silence settled in again. When I visited last October in England, of the many literary men I saw, only two had occasion to speak of Bunting. One, George Fraser, loaned me his copy of *Poems* to take back with me to London, in hopes someone there might be interested. The other, Charles Tomlinson, was curious to know what Bunting's present circumstances might be.

So I knew as little as ever. Then, coming down from Scotland, I stopped to read in Newcastle, at the invitation of Tom Pickard, and there to my great pleasure and surprise was Bunting himself.

I value that occasion very much, simply that there are men who are measures of all possibility, in what they do literally and in how they do it. I can't report all of the conversation we had, but, again, it continues to serve me as measure both of my own circumstances and of what poetry itself can be as an active art. With respect to Eliot, he questioned the rhythms, finding them "gross" I think his word was, yet pointed out that the diction—the literal vocabulary of his work—was very clear indeed. He made a useful distinction between organizations of sound as one meets them in a lyric— where the briefness of the poem's length gives them a necessarily emphatic situation—and in a long poem, where their texture may accumulate relationships without the reader being aware of their singular condition. He talked of Pound, more parallel he felt to Spenser than to Chaucer, in that each man gives an encyclopaedia of possibilities to those who then come after.

Of his own condition he said little. We walked above the Tyne, back of the village of Wylam where he lives. When he was a boy, there were several fisheries along that river, but now industrial wastes and like circumstances made it unlikely that even a casual fisherman would find much to catch. He told me the Northumberland clans were the last to give in to the organizations of county, more implacable even than the Scots. He spoke of the reforestation program in Northumberland, and in all he said there was evidence of a deep sense of place and of his own commitment to it.

There is such a clarity to him, and in what he has written. I wonder it is not seen more simply, but happily that situation now changes. There is no one else who can help as much, both in the fact of his work—it offers, I feel, the most real occasion for the work of younger men now—and himself, of all men unique in the quiet determination of what he has valued.

Have you seen a falcon stoop
accurate, unforeseen
and absolute, between
wind-ripples over harvest? Dread
of what's to be, is and has been—
were we not better dead?
His wings churn air
to flight.
Feathers alight
with sun, he rises where
dazzle rebuts our stare,
wonder our fright.

(from *The Spoils*)

# A Note on Basil Bunting

The publication of Basil Bunting's poems in England regains a possibility that has been equivocal for some time, if not literally absent. I am not the one to write of it simply that I am not English, nor of that particular root which Bunting has such use of. R. S. Woolf, reviewing *Loquitur* and *Briggflatts* in *Stand* (8, No. 2), puts emphasis on the almost flat pessimism, the insistence of death, throughout Bunting's work. It is there without question as it is equally in Samuel Beckett's, or in Dunbar's *Lament for the Makers.* Also relevant are the tone and manner of Michael Alexander's translations, *The Earliest English Poems,* from which comes the following:

> A man who on these walls wisely looked
> who sounded deeply this dark life
> would think back to the blood spilt here,
> weigh it in his wit . . .
> Alas, proud prince! How that time has passed,
> dark under night's helm, as though it never had been!
>
> ("The Wanderer")

Beckett, translating *An Anthology of Mexican Poetry,* comes to a very like tone (which is more than the transposition of a content evident in the Spanish):

> This coloured counterfeit . . .
> is a foolish sorry labour lost,

*Agenda,* Autumn 1966.

is conquest doomed to perish and, well taken,
is corpse and dust, shadow and nothingness.

> (Juana de Asbaje, "This coloured
> counterfeit that thou beholdest . . .")

In short, I am curious to know if an implicit quality of language occurs when words are used in a situation peculiar to their own history. *History,* however, may be an awkward term, since it might well imply only a respectful attention on the part of the writer rather than the implicit rapport between words and man when both are equivalent effects of time and place. In this sense there is a lovely dense sensuousness to Bunting's poetry, and it is as much the nature of the words as the nature of the man who makes use of them. Again it is a circumstance shared.

I am caught by the sense of himself Bunting defines:

I hear Aneurin number the dead and rejoice,
being adult male of a merciless species.
Today's posts are piles to drive into the quaggy past
on which impermanent palaces balance.

> (*Briggflatts*)

It is the hierarchal situation of *poet* going deeper in time than one could borrow or assume, and hence the issue of some privileged kinship with the nature of poetry itself in one's own language. Pound's "heave," with the trochee, proved him sensitive to it and makes clear one aspect of the relation between Bunting and himself. Bunting, from the earliest poems in *Loquitur* to the greatness of *Briggflatts* itself, is closely within the peculiar nature of his given language, an English such as one rarely now hears. In the earlier poems he makes use of a Latin, call it, appropriately enough:

Narciss, my numerous cancellations prefer
slow limpness in the damp dustbins amongst the peel
tobacco-ash and ends spittoon lickings litter
of labels dry corks breakages and a great deal

of miscellaneous garbage picked over by
covetous dustmen and Salvation Army sneaks
to one review-rid month's printed ignominy,
the public detection of your decay, that reeks.

> ("To a Poet who advised me to
> preserve my fragments and false starts")

But the insistent intimate nature of his work moves in the closeness of monosyllables, with a music made of their singleness:

Mist sets lace of frost
on rock for the tide to mangle.
Day is wreathed in what summer lost.

(*Briggflatts*)

Presumptuously or not, it seems to me a long time since English verse had such an English ear—as sturdy as its words, and from the same occasion.

# Basil Bunting

There must be a way to be human that neither crouches back of the door nor barges in with some overbearing pretension of significance. Anyone can have a world, so to speak, if he or she is willing to lop off little (or big) pieces of the existing one, so as to manage a convenience for the self. "It's himself!" cried the mother in those Irish families of my youth, as said person staggered up the steps, home again.

But this is no story, much as it might entertain, of anyone at all. You must know people in your own life, who don't so much stay put as be there, for all and any to witness. There is no overwhelming claim they make, nothing has to make room for them, nor do they come and go with some shy disclaimer of their significance. Not only can you trust them, but you can *not* trust them, equally, if it's funny business you have in mind. For lack of any other better word, or way of putting it clearly, they are literally alive and inexorably human, and they have all they seemingly require therefor. It has nothing to do with being hungry or well-fed, all of which is possible for any of us, but how it all then is lived with.

Bunting is an extraordinary teacher, although I doubt that he has much thought to be, except in very specific instances. He has not even been persistent, call it, in the usual manner of the artist who overcomes great odds indeed just that his art be permitted. There are sizable gaps of time, when evidently he had other things to do. One time, years ago, I wrote him a letter asking advice of ac-

*Paideuma* 9, no. 1 (Spring 1980).

tive writing in England, and got a generous reply, from the Middle East, in which he told me he knew nothing of current doings in that world, rarely if ever saw another writer, and that, when he did, conversation had usually to do with the migration of game, and the water table. When at last I did meet him, he was working as a financial reporter for the Newcastle paper, having come from like labors in London.

Now I'm not at all interested that poets can be otherwise than the kids who couldn't play baseball, as Rexroth once said. But there is an imagination of poetry that has to do with the actual particulars of its conduct as a mode of words engendering emotion as a formal pattern:

> . . . with never a crabbed turn or congested cadence,
> never a boast or see-here; and stars and lakes
> echo him and the copse drums out his measure,
> snow peaks are lifted up in moonlight and twilight
> and the sun rises on an acknowledged land.
>
> (*Briggflatts, IV*)

In that interest so committed, there are no measures but those of the factual life one is given, the physical place in which one lives, and what others have done with like particulars. In his *Collected Poems* (Oxford, 1978)—his "Preface" to which says all, and far better, that one might think to here—the following would appear the most recent:

> *At Briggflatts meetinghouse*
>
> Boasts time mocks cumber Rome. Wren
> set up his own monument.
> Others watch fells dwindle, think
> the sun's fires sink.
>
> Stones indeed sift to sand, oak
> blends with saints' bones.
> Yet for a little longer here
> stone and oak shelter
>
> silence while we ask nothing
> but silence. Look how the clouds dance
> under the wind's wing, and leaves
> delight in transience.
>
> ("Second Book of Odes," 11)

The world which knows this is old beyond time—that time mocks our human ambitions, that only our own acts can survive in mem-

ory even for a moment. Humanly, there are so many who feel a
despair in what seems the very transformation of the world into a
dying place. All true—yet here, in this human moment of time,
asking only that silence which permits it, it *is* here, actual beyond all
else in that it will not, *cannot*, be forever.

And for the *art*—such particular sounds of human voice so tuned,
to the weaving rhythm, the *dance*-ing *transcience.* . . . What to say
*not* said by it? And what else is there ever to say.

# H. D.

I presume I must first have read her work in high school, at least (and expectably) the short "Imagist" poems for which she was primarily known. Her intense, elusive edginess displaced me because I could not follow it as "thinking"—it was curiously emotions she offered. In any case, I found no attachment and when, some years later, Pound sent me an inscribed copy of *By Avon River* from St. Elizabeth's along with a flotsam of bulletins and journals relating to economics, agriculture and politics, again I paid little attention— frankly even less than I might have, just that Pound seemed so little interested despite its personal directive.

Therefore Robert Duncan's bringing the *Trilogy* with him to Mallorca in 1954 is really an introduction in all ways, because not only was the poet of that great poem new to me, as they say, but the whole place of such power (which was also Duncan's) had never been so vividly manifest. It was revelation in such articulate, tangible measure—a pace, extraordinarily specific, of feeling in literalizing sounds. I think now of:

> I go where I love and am loved,
> into the snow;
>
> I go to the things I love
> with no thought of duty or pity;
>
> I go where I belong, inexorably. . . .

*Sagetrieb* (H. D. Special Issue) 6, no. 2 (Fall 1987).

It broke my heart with its mastery, its singular evocation of humanness.

Duncan noted the irony of the publication, the meager response, so that the first book is followed by two smaller, cheaper editions in paper only—it is wartime, no one is really hearing it, and Pound and Williams, likewise at the base of their own powers, singular, isolate, fighting for coherence and survival, seemingly have no consciousness of their heroic companion in the same place.

Then somewhat later, again thanks to Duncan, I was able to hear the recording she made for Norman Holmes Pearson (as Robert led me to understand) of parts of *Helen of Egypt* and that voice with its absolute sounding of each interval of word, each cadence, caught me entirely. She was the master of this art.

Much more recently, at a gathering committed to her honor, I was displaced by someone's proposing that we, as readers, need not finally be possessed by the visions so insistent in her work—as though we might rationally understand and yet avoid what so compelled her. I do not think so.

# Here

*What is a play.*
*A play is scenery.*
*A play is not identity or place*
*or time but it likes to feel it oh yes*
*it does wonderfully like to feel it.*
*That is what makes it a play.*

GERTRUDE STEIN, *The Geographical*
*History of America*

"A play is scenery." In a lecture ("Plays," 1934) she speaks of a play as being *a landscape*. In either case the usual process of familiarizing oneself with casual patterns of identity, or of place or time, the "progressive familiarity" one gains in reading a novel, is absent— "the actors are there they are there and they are there right away." That, as she says, has "a great deal to do with the nervousness of the theatre excitement," insofar as "the introduction to the characters on the stage has a great many different sides to it." Then there is the fact of her "early recollections . . . One which is in a way like a circus that is the general movement and light and air which any theatre has, and a great deal of glitter in the light and a great deal of height in the air, and then there are moments, a very very few moments but still moments. One must be pretty far advanced in adolescence before one realizes a whole play."

Robert Creeley, *Was That a Real Poem & Other Essays*, ed. Donald Allen (Bolinas, Calif.: Four Seasons Foundation, 1979).

A little later in the same lecture she speaks very movingly of being adolescent "and going to the theatre all the time, a great deal alone, and all of it making an outside inside existence for me, not so real as books, which were all inside me, but so real that it the theatre made real outside me which up to that time I never had been in my emotion. I had largely been so in an active daily life but not in any emotion." The problem then met with, sadly, was "the great difficulty of having my emotion accompany the scene and then moreover I became fairly consciously troubled by the things over which one stumbles over which one stumbled to such an extent that the time of one's emotions in relation to the scene was always interrupted . . . Could I see and hear and feel at the same time and did I." What then comes as solution is Sarah Bernhardt—"it was all so foreign and her voice being so varied and it all being so French I could rest in it untroubled. And I did . . . This experience curiously enough and yet perhaps it was not so curious awakened in me a desire for melodrama on the stage, because there again everything happened so quietly one did not have to get acquainted and as what the people felt was of no importance one did not have to realize what was said."

These several statements are most interesting to me, just that they locate very clearly her own preoccupations—the possible situations of *time,* specifically the nature of the *present* as interior and exterior condition—and the experiential location, so to speak, which the stage *per se* had to offer. One sturdy fact of existence would seem to me at least that whatever *happens* in the world, or can be said to have happened or to be about to happen, or eventually, is, by nature of the necessity constituted by the statement itself, happening *now.* There seemingly is no other 'place' for it to occur. Of course there are endlessly possible patterns of causality, most usefully so very often, but their reality also is dependent on this specific *now* insofar as they presume a precedent or a consequence for what it is (*now*) they are involved with.

Thinking of a "play" and "scenery" and "landscape" (and *not* of "identity" and "place" and "time," for these are abstractions which accumulate their various meanings rather than possess them by fact of activity or literal substance), all three have the common quality of being primarily a *present* event. Their significance takes root in their being 'here and now' and their history or consequence seems secondary, despite its possible relevance. In like sense, *feeling,* as one says, is insistently a present reality. It may be useless to "cry over spilt milk" but feeling will never know it, only thought.

And thought itself may be issue, finally, of feeling. Thus "it likes to feel it oh yes it does wonderfully like to feel it . . ."

In any case, a disjunct can occur in experience when the "inside" existence of any one of us confronts an existing "outside" which is not in phase or 'in time' with our own. The feeling then of dislocation is very unhappy and, understandably, we avoid such circumstance if we can. Reading, the solution is quite simple. We can put the book down despite its already having 'got into' us, and hopefully, reassert our own experiences of 'place' and 'time' and 'identity,' our so-called various 'selves.'

So there is, put mildly, extraordinary power in any *present* moment, the more so feelings have been powerfully engaged—and by "power" I mean some common sense of *energy*, presumably a basic quantity in activity of whatever order. Something's *happening*. I'm attracted by the fact that Gertrude Stein's qualification of literature was, is it or isn't it *exciting*. It's much like Pound's sense of poetry being language *charged* to the highest degree of that possibility.

Coming to the opera (physically, or in mind), it is, as an activity, *here* and also apparently dominant in relation to any one of us *here* as well. That is, if I get up and start shouting that its activity is not congruent with my own, I'll either find myself flooded with a 'present' equal to my own—thus I'll be *on stage*, intentionally or not *in the act*—or else ejected, much as food is by a preoccupied body. I don't think this has to do with a social fact, in the sense of manners. Rather, it seems the situation of reality itself, which the stage *is*, in its occupation of the common *present*, and the divers alternatives to that situation which each of us in our own particulars might constitute are not so much yielded as enclosed by the power of that event, that *present* which theater in all of its modes—music, dance, drama, or their combination—so particularly creates.

It's all a long way round to come to some rather simple point no doubt. But this *present* is such a true one, gift or given—and she spent her whole life, one might say, insistent upon the nature and condition of its reality. Words. Now. Here. In thought, at least, *there* would be so much more commodious. But, as a sister poet said, *if we're going to be here, let's be here now!*

*The Mother of Us All* is her last work, makes use of narrative (which her earlier collaboration with Virgil Thomson, *Four Saints in Three Acts*, did not), has personages anachronistically in the same 'time' and 'place,' muses, wisely, on various circumstances of this life (men, marriage, names, women), uses a lifelong acquisition of language's patterns, 'simply' 'elemental':

Where is where. In my long life of effort and strife, dear life, life is strife, in my long life, it will not come and go, I tell you so, it will stay it will pay but

(A long silence)

But do I want what we have got, has it not gone, what made it live, has it not gone because now it is had, in my long life in my long life

(Silence)

Life is strife, I was a martyr all my life not to what I won but to what was done.

(Silence)

Do you know because I tell you so, or do you know, do you know.

(Silence)

My long life, my long life.
*Curtain*

*Buffalo, N.Y.*
*September 26, 1975*

# II  THE COMPANY

# Introduction to
# *The New Writing in the USA*

Nothing will fit if we assume a place for it. To attempt to classify writing before one has had the experience of its activity will be to misplace it altogether. What can be said is something itself particular—to senses of form, to the literal nature of living in a given place, to a world momently informed by what energies inhabit it.

## 1

The forties were a hostile time for the writers here included. The colleges and universities were dominant in their insistence upon an *idea* of form extrinsic to the given instance. Poems were equivalent to cars insofar as many could occur of similar pattern—although each was, of course, 'singular.' But it was this assumption of a *mold*, of a means that could be gained beyond the literal fact of the writing *here and now*, that had authority.

It is the more ironic to think of it, remembering the incredible pressure of *feeling* also present in these years—of all that did want 'to be said,' of so much confusion and pain wanting statement in its own terms. But again, it is Karl Shapiro's *Essay on Rime* (written in the South Pacific at a military base, "without access to books," in iambic pentameter) which is successful, and Auden is the measure of competence. In contrast Ezra Pound, H. D., William Carlos Williams (despite the token interest as *Paterson* begins to be published), Hart Crane, and especially Walt Whitman are largely disregarded.

Donald Allen and Robert Creeley, eds., *The New Writing in the USA* (Harmondsworth, England: Penguin Books, 1967).

The situation of prose I remember as much the same. Despite the apparent insistence of *digression* in the work of Joyce, Faulkner, Céline, and others who are valued, there is nonetheless the attempt to shape all discussion of their 'form' to the context of an overt pattern, a symbolism, an explanation again anterior to the instance. In short, it is a period when criticism enjoys control of literary reference—so much so, that it can propose itself to be of primary value quite apart from its 'subjects.'

The sense of *form* which comes of this insistence is defined by Robert Duncan in an essay, "Ideas of the Meaning of Form":

> Form, to the mind obsessed by convention, is significant insofar as it shows control. What has nor rime nor reason is a bogie that must be dismissed from the horizons of the mind. . . . Wherever the feeling of control is lost, the feeling of form is lost. The reality of the world and men's habits must be constricted to a realm—a court or a salon or a rationale—excluding whatever is feared. . . . Metaphor must be fumigated or avoided (thought of as displaying the author's fancy or wit) to rid the mind of the poetic where metaphor had led dangerously towards Paracelsus' universe of psychic correspondences, towards a life where men and things were beginning to mix and cross boundaries of knowledge. Poets, who had once had dreams and epiphanies, now admit only to devices and ornaments. Love, that had been a passion, had best be a sentiment or a sensible affection. . . . The struggle was to have ideas and not to let ideas have one. Taste, reason, rationality rule, and rule must be absolute and enlightened, because beyond lies the chiaroscuro in which forces co-operate and sympathies and aversions mingle. The glamor of this magic haunts all reasonable men today, surrounding them with, and then protecting them from, the darkness of possibilities that controls cannot manage, the world of thought and feeling in which we may participate but not dominate, where we are used by things even as we use them.

Confronting such *rule,* men were driven back upon the particulars of their own experience, the literal *things* of an immediate environment, wherewith to acknowledge the possibilities of their own lives. This alternative must now be familiar, but at that time there were few indeed to propose it. It is first found for me in Williams' introduction to *The Wedge* (1944):

> Therefore each speech having its own character the poetry it engenders will be peculiar to that speech also in its own intrinsic form. . . . When a man makes a poem, makes it, mind you, he takes words as he finds them interrelated about him and composes them—without distortion which would mar their exact significances—into an intense ex-

pression of his perceptions and ardors that they may constitute a revelation in the speech that he uses. . . .

It is, in fact, a congruence of "the darkness of possibilities that control cannot manage" and that "revelation in the speech" that Williams emphasizes, which informs the first major work of Allen Ginsberg, *Howl*. He writes of its composition as follows:

> By 1955 I wrote poetry adapted from prose seeds, journals, scratchings, arranged by phrasing or breath groups into little short-line patterns according to ideas of measure of American speech I'd picked up from W. C. Williams' imagist preoccupations. I suddenly turned aside in San Francisco, unemployment compensation leisure, to follow my romantic inspiration—Hebraic-Melvillean bardic breath. I thought I wouldn't write a *poem*, but just write what I wanted to without fear, let my imagination go, open secrecy, and scribble magic lines from my real mind—sum up my life—something I wouldn't be able to show anybody, writ for my own soul's ear and a few other golden ears. So the first line of *Howl*. . . .

It is relevant that he says, "I thought I wouldn't write a *poem*, but just write what I wanted to without fear . . ."—as does Duncan so emphasize that it was fear that felt "The reality of the world and men's habits must be constricted to a realm . . . excluding whatever is feared. . . ." The need becomes, then, literally:

> to recreate the syntax and measure of poor human prose and stand
> before you speechless and intelligent and shaking with shame,
> rejected yet confessing out the soul to conform to the rhythm of
> thought in his naked and endless head,
> the madman bum and angel beat in Time, unknown, yet putting
> down here what might be left to say in time come after death,
> and rose reincarnate in the ghostly clothes of jazz in the goldhorn
> shadow of the band and blew the suffering of America's naked
> mind for love into an eli eli lamma lamma sabacthani saxophone
> cry that shivered the cities down to the last radio
> with the absolute heart of the poem of life butchered out of their own
> bodies good to eat a thousand years.
>
> (*Howl*, Part 1)

## 2

The usual critical vocabulary will not be of much use in trying to locate the character of writing we have now come to. If one depends on the dichotomy of *romantic* and *classical,* one is left with,

too simply, an historical description, itself a remnant from an earlier 'period.'

The question becomes, *what is real*—and what is of that nature?
The most severe argument we can offer against the 'value' of some
thing or act, is that it is *not* real, that it has no given place in what
our world has either chosen or been forced to admit. So it is the
*condition* of reality which becomes our greatest concern—in which
relation the following notes by Charles Olson are most useful:

> All things did come in again, in the 19th century. An idea shook loose,
> and energy and motion became as important a structure of things as
> that they are plural, and, by matter, mass. It was even shown that in
> the infinitely small the older concepts of space ceased to be valid at all.
> Quantity—the measurable and numerable—was suddenly as shafted
> in, to any thing, as it was also, as had been obvious, the striking char-
> acter of the external world, that all things do extend out. Nothing was
> now inert fact, all things were there for feeling, to promote it, and be
> felt; and man, in the midst of it, knowing well how he was folded in, as
> well as how suddenly and strikingly he could extend himself, spring
> or, without even moving, go, to far, the farthest—he was suddenly
> possessed or repossessed of a character of being, a thing among things,
> which I shall call his physicality. It made a reentry of or to the uni-
> verse. Reality was without interruption, and we are still in the business
> of finding out how all action, and thought, have to be refounded. . . .
>
> ("Equal, That Is, to the Real Itself")

This recognition had come primarily from scientific thinking, as
it might be called—but its evidence in the way in which the world
occurs in *Moby-Dick* (the object of Olson's discussion) is very striking. What happens to 'plot' or all such instance of 'category'—the
assumption of action as *contained*, for example—when all is continuous, "when the discrete [isn't] any longer a good enough base for
discourse. . . ."? The sentence itself—as Fenollosa had proposed in
*The Chinese Written Character as a Medium for Poetry*, and Olson reasserts—has become "an exchange of force" in no way a "completed
thought," since such "completion" is impossible in the context of
that *real* which Melville had apprehended, Olson notes, as "the absolute condition of present things . . ." Let it be stressed:

> [Melville] put it altogether accurately himself, in a single sentence of a
> letter to Hawthorne, written when he was writing *Moby-Dick* (1851):
> "By visible truth we mean the apprehension of the absolute condition
> of present things."
>
> (Ibid.)

The context so defined will include such present statement as this one taken from William Burroughs' *Naked Lunch:*

> There is only one thing a writer can write about: *what is in front of his senses at the moment of writing.* . . . I am a recording instrument. . . . I do not presume to impose "story" "plot" "continuity". . . .

What has been criticized as a loss of coherence in contemporary American prose—specifically that of Burroughs and Kerouac—has been, rather, evidence of this character of the *real* with which we are involved. In "Kerouac's Sound" Warren Tallman makes a parallel distinction:

> In conventional fiction the narrative continuity is always clearly discernible. But it is impossible to create an absorbing narrative without at the same time enriching it with images, asides, themes and variations—impulses from within. It is evident that in much recent fiction—Joyce, Kafka, Virginia Woolf, and Faulkner are obvious examples—the narrative line has tended to weaken, merge with, and be dominated by the sum of variations. Each narrative step in Faulkner's work is likely to provoke many sidewinding pages before a next narrative step is taken. More, a lot of Faulkner's power is to be found in the sidewindings. In brief, what happens in jazz when the melody merges with the improvisations and the improvisations dominate, has been happening in fiction for some time now.

Not only have the earlier senses of 'form' been rejected, but equally 'subject' as a conceptual focus or order has given place to the literal activity of the writing itself.

> The objects which occur at every given moment of composition (of recognition, we can call it) are, can be, must be treated exactly as they do occur therein and not by any ideas or preconceptions from outside the poem, must be handled as a series of objects in field in such a way that a series of tensions (which they also are) are made to *hold,* and to hold exactly inside the content and the context of the poem which has forced itself, through the poet and them, into being.
>
> (Charles Olson, *Projective Verse*)

But it is in the nature of the writing itself that this thinking finds its most active definition—as here in the final section of John Wieners' "A Poem for Painters":

> . . . At last. I come to the last defense.
>
> > My poems contain no
> > wilde beestes, no

lady of the lake, music
of the spheres, or organ chants.
Only the score of a man's
struggle to stay with
what is his own, what
lies within him to do.

Without which is nothing.
And I come to this
knowing the waste,
leaving the rest up to love
and its twisted faces,
my hands claw out at
only to draw back from the
blood already running there.

## 3

Finally, there seems so much that might be said. The American
condition has much to do with *place,* an active spatial term which
differs in that way from what has been assumed its European equivalent. Space, as physical ground, not sky, I feel to be once again politically active—as it has always been for the American from the
outset. It is useless, for example, to acknowledge the growing political weight of either Africa or China without seeing the literal
measure these *places* effect in relation to all senses of the European
continuum—in which the American takes its place, at least in part.

But more than that—since 'place' is not now more than activity—
there is the question of *all* terms of relationship, and of the possible
continuities of that relationship in a *time* which is continuous and at
all moments 'present'—else it never was.

The point seems that we cannot, as writers—or equally as readers—assume such content in our lives, that all presence is defined
as a history of categorical orders. If the nature of the writing is to
move in the field of its recognitions, the "open field" of Olson's
*Projective Verse,* for example, then the nature of the life it *is* demands a possibility which no assumption can anticipate.

In such a situation the entity of oneself becomes more than a cultural 'program' and the attempt to recognize its potential has led
to experiment with 'consciousness expanding' drugs such as mes-
caline, and writing which attempts to record such states, as Michael
McClure's "Peyote Poem."

The impulse is also clear in attempts to rediscover the viable content of terms of life which precede the 'categorical' defined by Aristotle. One does not want to go 'back,' merely. But I feel it true, as Duncan writes, "We have come so far that all the old stories / whisper once more . . ." History, as 'progress,' seems quite dead.

Otherwise—*things* as they have taken place so consistently with us in this country are relevant, both as condition and as presence. They have been, always, a basic company, and they involve, with persistence, our uses of space. Further, I do not feel that Allen Ginsberg's insistent equation of states of feeling or being with so-called 'material' things is surreal and/or a dimension of reality less present in one of its aspects than in another. There is a persistent literalness in American writing—very much so in the tradition with which we are concerned—and it has never been easily 'symbolic.' "All the accumulations of life, that wear us out—clocks, bodies, consciousness, shoe, breasts—begotten sons—your Communism—'Paranoia' into hospitals . . ." is literal reality and literally apprehended. It is—as Denise Levertov notes from Jung for the title of one of her poems—that "everything that acts is actual," and the context may be a street in broad daylight where reality is just as pervasive 'as a dream'—in fact, *is* 'the dream' equally with consciousness.

One cannot describe it, so to speak. Either one acts in an equal sense—becomes the issue of a term 'as real as real can be'—or else there is really nothing to be said. Again, the writing here collected seems to me distinct in point of its distance from the usual habit of *description*—by which I mean that practice that wants to 'accompany' the *real* but which assumes itself as 'objectively' outside that context in some way. Certainly it is possible to minimize or otherwise distort one's concern in a given matter or relation. Yet one is either there or not, and being there, cannot assume some 'not being' so as to 'talk about it.'

I feel, however, that what I am trying to say here comes clearer in Edward Dorn's discussion of Olson's *Maximus Poems* (with their center in the town of Gloucester, Massachusetts):

> when the Place is brought forward fully in form conceived entirely by the activation of a man who is under its spell it is a resurrection for us and the investigation is not extractable. And it is then the only *real* thing. I am certain without ever having been there, I would be bored to sickness walking through Gloucester. Buildings as such are not important. The wash of the sea is not interesting in itself, that is luxuria, a degrading thing, people as they stand, must be created, it doesn't matter at all they have reflexes of their own, they are casual, they do more than you could hope to know, it is useful, it is a part of industry.

It has an arrogance of intention. This is the significance of Olson's distrust of Thucydides and his care for Herodotus. It is the significance of Blake's "the practice of art is anti-christ." Which further means that if you are not capable of the non-functional striking of the World, you are not practicing art. Description, letting things lay, was reserved for not necessarily the doubtful, but the slothful, or the merely busy.*

4

To tell the story, is all one can do. What accumulates as the tradition of a craft—its means, its sophistications—must each time be reapprehended, not for 'style.' Because as Louis Zukofsky has taken care to say, of poetry:

> This does not presume that the style will be the man, but rather that the order of his syllables will define his awareness of order. For his . . . major aim is not to show himself but that order that of itself can speak to all men.
>
> ("Poetry," in "A" [Kyoto: Origin Press, 1959])

That undertaking most useful to writing as an art is, for me, the attempt to *sound* in the nature of the language those particulars of time and place of which one is a given instance, equally present. I find it here.

*1965*

*Edward Dorn, *What I See in the Maximus Poems* (Ventura, Calif./Worcester, England: Migrant Press, 1960).

# Charles Olson: *Y & X*

*Y & X*, by Charles Olson. Washington, D.C.: Black Sun Press, 1949.

Any movement poetry can now make beyond the achievement of Pound, Williams, et al., must make use of the fact of their work and, further, of what each has stressed as the main work now to be done. We can't discard either of these men by calling them 'experimentalists' or by thinking that however right their method may be for their own apprehension of *form,* we can now ignore its example in our own dilemmas. Unless we also can find for ourselves a *method* equal to our content, show some comprehension of the difficulties involved, we stay where we are.

A recent comment of Dr. Williams notes one of the headaches. "To me the battle lodges for us as poets in the poetic line, something has to be done with that line—it's got to be opened up. . . ." I cite this here, since a good many feel that it's just the opposite that should be done, that the line must be tightened, pulled in, fixed. We should by now have a clear idea as to what this kind of *tightness* implies. To begin with, it's an external *tightness,* having more to do with the poem's pattern than with the movement of its sense. And it's this same *tightness* which Stevens has damned by implication: "There is, however, a usage with respect to form as if form were a derivative of plastic shape."

The five poems in this present collection of Olson's work demonstrate a technique set squarely against this *tightness.* They mark the

*Montevallo Review,* Summer 1951.

alternatives. For Olson the line becomes a way to a movement beyond the single impact of the words which go to make it up, and brings to their logic a force of its own. Instead of the simple wagon which carries the load, he makes it that which drives too, to the common logic, the sense of the poem.

The first poem, "La Préface," is an illustration. Here the line is used to make the ground logic beyond the single 'senses' of the words. The poem can't be understood, lacking a comprehension of the work the line is doing here. What it does do, then, is give the base pattern which pulls the poem's juxtaposition of *action* and *thing* to a common center where the reader can get to bedrock. Meaning.

> Put war away with time, come into space.
> It was May, precise date, 1940. I had air my lungs could
>     breathe.
> He talked, via stones   a stick   sea rock   a hand of earth.
> It is now, precise, repeat. I talk of Bigmans organs
> he, look, the lines! are polytopes.
> And among the DPs—deathhead
>                         at the apex
>                                 of the pyramid.

The line is the means to focus, is that which says 'how' we are to weight the various *things* we are told. And as it is there, to do this work, so the words break through to their *sense*.

Perhaps enough to find this use of line in these poems, but Olson is a good deal more than a competent technician. There is a reach in these five poems, a range of subject and a depth of perception, that mark him exceptional. His language is exact, hangs tight to the move of his thought.

> Shallows and miseries shadows from the cross,
> ecco men and dull copernican sun.
> Our attention is simpler
> The salts and minerals of the earth return
> The night has a love for throwing its shadows around a man
> a bridge,   a horse,   the gun,   a grave.
>
>                                         ("The K")

Again, if poetry is to get further, develop, it will depend on those who, like Olson, make use of its present gains, push these beyond. Olson's work is the first significant advance.

# Charles Olson: *In Cold Hell, in Thicket*

*In Cold Hell, in Thicket,* by Charles Olson. *Origin,* 8. Boston/Palma, Mallorca, 1953.

Ernst Robert Curtius has described Charles Olson's talent as returning us to that same presence, of force, which is evident in a Mayan glyph. The point is that Mr. Olson's work represents a sole and major content in contemporary American poetry.

This content is most clearly demonstrated in one of the several long poems here included, "The Kingfishers." Its first line gives us the basic preoccupation: "What does not change / is the will to change. . . ."

> Not one death but many,
> not accumulation but change, the feed-back proves, the feed-
>     back is
>
> the law
>
>> Into the same river no man steps twice
>> When fire dies air dies
>> No one remains, nor is, one

It is this change, and the force which demands it, which hold the only 'continuity' possible. If a culture is to maintain itself, it can do so only by a *use* of this force, and the problem is as Mr. Olson puts it:

*New Mexico Quarterly,* Autumn 1953.

I am no Greek, hath not th'advantage.
And of course, no Roman:
he can take no risk that matters,
the risk of beauty least of all.

But I have my kin . . .

Despite the discrepancy (an ocean    courage    age)
this is also true: if I have any taste
it is only because I have interested myself
in what was slain in the sun

    I pose you your question:

shall you uncover honey / where maggots are?

    I hunt among stones

Such problems of change, and origin, are common to the American temper, but their occurrence in American poetry has become less and less frequent. Or, perhaps better, they have been absorbed in other attitudes or left as "European," i.e., relating to a past shared in effect with poets either in England or on the continent. But this is a simplification of a useless sort. The American, for example, has this reference to contend with:

(of the two who first came, each a conquistador, one
    healed, the other
tore the eastern idols down, toppled
the temple walls, which, says the excuser
were black from human gore)
hear
hear, where the dry blood talks
    where the old appetite walks

He can only quiet it, by confronting it. Similarly, the whole area of how we now live, or can live, is part of Mr. Olson's attack. The title poem is a form of 'lyricism' brought from the instant, or the single and abrupt emotion, to bear on all there is for any man, or woman—"Or, if it is me, what / he has to say. . . ." So it is that:

                    . . . hell now
is not exterior, is not to be got out of, is
the coat of your own self, the beasts
emblazoned on you   And who
can turn this total thing, invert
and let the ragged sleeves be seen
by any bitch or common character? Who

can endure it where it is, where the beasts are met,
where yourself is, your beloved is, where she
who is separate from you, is not separate, is not
goddess, is, as your core is,
the making of one hell. . . .

The value of any poem is not at all the fact of any technique, however much it is necessary to be the master of just such things. For the reader, beyond the way a poem is written or made, is the ultimate impact of its *meaning*, what it either can or does mean—to us. Mr. Olson's poetry provides for much more than delight.

# Preface to *Mayan Letters,*
# by Charles Olson

Sometime toward the end of 1950, it was in December I think, but
the letter isn't dated, I heard that Charles Olson was off to Yucatan.
A sudden "fluke"—the availability of some retirement money owed
him from past work as a mail carrier—gave him enough for the
trip, "not much but a couple of hundred, sufficient, to GO, be,
THERE. . . ." By February I had got another letter, "have just this
minute opened this machine in this house lerma. . . ." From that
time on I heard from him regularly, and so was witness to one of
the most incisive experiences ever recorded. Obviously it is very
simple to call it that, that is, what then happened, and what Olson
made of his surroundings and himself. Otherwise, it is necessary to
remember that Olson had already been moving in this direction,
back to a point of origin which would be capable of extending
"history" in a new and more usable sense. In his book on Melville,
*Call Me Ishmael,* he had made the statement, "we are the last first
people . . ."; and in his poetry, most clearly in "The Kingfishers,"
there was constant emphasis on the need to break with the too
simple westernisms of a 'greek culture.'

Yucatan made the occasion present in a way that it had not been
before. The alternative to a generalizing humanism was locked,
quite literally, in the people immediately around him, and the conception, that there had been and *could* be a civilization anterior to
that which he had come from, was no longer conjecture, it was fact.
He wrote me, then, "I have no doubt, say, that the American will

Charles Olson, *Mayan Letters* (Bañalbufar, Mallorca: Divers Press, 1953).

more and more repossess himself of the Indian past. . . . If you and I see the old deal as dead (including Confucius, say), at the same time that we admit the new is of the making of our own lives & references, yet, there is bound to be a tremendous pick-up from history other than that which has been usable as reference, the moment either that history is restored (Sumer, or, more done, Chichen or Uaxactun) or rising people (these Indians, as camposinos ripe for Communist play—as ripe as were the Chinese, date 1921, June 30). . . ." The problem was, to give form, again, to what the Maya had been—to restore the "history" which they were. For in the Maya was the looked-for content: a *reality* which is "wholly formal without loss of intimate spaces, with the ball still snarled, yet, with a light (and not stars) and a heat (not androgyne) which declares, the persistence of both organism *and* will (human). . . ."

In editing the present selection, I have tried to maintain a continuity in spite of the limits of space and the loss of some letters which it has meant. I have indicated excisions with dots (. . .), whenever such were necessary.

*February 12, 1953*

# Charles Olson:
## *The Maximus Poems, 1–10*

In poetry the attentions can come to govern, as a man might be governed by what he loves or despises, or what number of things his hands can hold. Seeing the thing, even so it remains outside him until he can give it substance in the multiple involvement—which means only that he and the thing, and the possibility which has no limit, can coexist in a form which it is his own responsibility to effect. "The thing" is an ugly word for it. But it is ugly only because we have so degraded what confronts us, that we ride in on our own isolation thinking not to see anything, and hating that which we have to.

*The Maximus Poems* are, or seem first to me, the modulation of a man's attentions, by which I mean the whole wonder of perception. They are truth because their form is that issue of what is out there, and what part of it can come into a man's own body. That much is not sentimental, nor can anything be sentimental if we make it that engagement. The local is not a place but a place in a given man— what part of it he has been compelled or else brought by love to give witness to in his own mind. And that is *the* form, that is, the whole thing, as whole as it can get.

I think we will be fools to be embarrassed by it. We know the other neatness possible, the way of the neat pattern, and the dodging which it must call for. Grace has no part in that. At some point

First published on a prospectus of *The Maximus Poems* enclosed as a loose insert in *The Maximus Poems, 1–10*, by Charles Olson (Stuttgart: Jonathan Williams, 1953).

reached by us, sooner or later, there is no longer much else but ourselves, in the place given us. To make that present, and actual for other men, is not an embarrassment, but love.

*1953*

# Olson & Others:
# Some Orts for the Sports

Where writing will go to, what comes next, or the answers to any of those profoundly speculative questions bred of Saturday afternoons in comfortable surroundings—god alone knows. Where it's all come from is another question, and a few sentences may serve as well to answer it as any more documented or descriptive account. For example, in 1950 Cid Corman, the subsequent editor of *Origin*, had a radio program in Boston called *This Is Poetry*, which by a fluke of air waves I heard one night in Littleton, N.H. The guest was Richard Wilbur, who read with such graceful accents I was filled with envious ambition to read also, although I had none of his qualifications; and some weeks later, after correspondence with Cid which that night began, I convinced him I was good enough, or he was tolerant enough, and so I read one Saturday night while I was in Boston showing chickens at the Boston Poultry Show. Literary history is like that, and this event would be altogether unnotable, were it not that a magazine which I then tried to start (with much the same motives), but could not get printed, was absorbed in the first two issues of Cid's *Origin*—and that among the contacts so contributed were Charles Olson, Paul Blackburn, and Denise Levertov.

Charles Olson is central to any description of literary 'climate' dated 1960. I don't think any of those involved knew, at the time, he had written *Call Me Ishmael;* and I remember my own dumbfounded reception of that book—from a man I had assumed to be

*Big Table*, no. 4, 1960.

sharing my own position of unpublished hopefulness. The Olson I knew, and wrote to daily if possible, was the one whose *Y & X* had been published by Caresse Crosby's Black Sun Press, who had among other poems in manuscript a long one called "The King-fishers," and whose own letters were of such energy and calculation that they constituted a practical 'college' of stimulus and information. Some of this last can be seen in an article he published at that time, partly derived from letters as it happens, which he called "Projective Verse" (*Poetry New York*, No. 3, 1950; reprinted with addenda, New York: Totem Press, 1959). He outlines there the premise of "composition by field" (the value of which William Carlos Williams was to emphasize by reprinting it in part in his own *Autobiography*); and defines a basis for structure in the poem in terms of its '*kinetics*' ("the poem itself must, at all points, be a high energy-construct and, at all points, an energy discharge"), the '*principle*' of its writing ("form is never more than an extension of content"), and the '*process*' ("ONE PERCEPTION MUST IMMEDIATELY AND DIRECTLY LEAD TO A FURTHER PERCEPTION"). Olson equally distinguishes between breathing and hearing, as these relate to the line: "And the line comes (I swear it) from the breath, from the breathing of the man who writes, at that moment that he writes. . . ."

Some distinctions are now possible. Verse practice today splits in point of several emphases, and this is reasonable enough. Most familiar are those poets who have looked at a re-informing of traditional structures, at times with great ability. It is not at all a question of falling back into the same old sofa, etc., but to manage a use of that which those back of you have given in such fashion that you will both honor them and those differences which the nature of time seems to insist upon. There are also others, most definitive in the thirties, who extend to their writing of verse concerns which haunt them, again reasonably enough, in the other areas of their living.[1] They are in this way poets of 'content,' and their poems argue images of living to which the contents of their poems point. They argue the poem as a means to recognition, a signboard as it were, not

1. Kenneth Fearing would be one man I'd think of in this connection, though that may be simply my own circumstances. Names are deceptive in any case, since they tend to develop a false chronology, granted men change. The point is that the *sociology* which the thirties develops is present in poetry also, both as methodology and sense of purpose. The methods and concern are felt later in Ciardi, Shapiro, et al. It's also in Weldon Kees. The contrast is the early work of Rexroth, Carl Rakosi, George Oppen, and very certainly Zukofsky.

in itself a structure of 'recognition' or—better—cognition itself.
Some, then, would not only not hear what Olson was saying, but
would even deny, I think, the relevance of his concerns. The great
preoccupation with symbology and levels of image in poetry insisted upon by contemporary criticism has also meant a further bias
for this not-hearing, since Olson's emphasis is put upon prosody,
not interpretation.

Those who were sympathetic, who felt as Dr. Williams did ("it is
as if the whole area lifted . . ."), were those equally concerned with
prosody. "Prosody," said Pound, "is the articulation of the total
sound of a poem." This is an obviously difficult and painstaking re-
quirement; and, again, a division of method appears between those
who make use of traditional forms, either for discipline or solution,
and those who, as Olson, go "by ear," by, in effect, the complexly
determined response to work literally in hand. Robert Duncan's
discussion precludes mine; I refer you to that ("Notes on Poetics
Regarding Olson's *Maximus," Black Mountain Review,* No. 6, 1956).
But, to suggest its relevance here, Duncan writes, using the image
of "The coming into life of the child . . .":

> . . . that the breath-blood circulation be gaind, an *interjection!* the lev-
> els of the passions and inspiration in *phrases;* second, that focus be
> gaind, a *substantive,* the level of vision; and third, the complex of mus-
> cular gains that are included in taking hold and balancing, *verbs,* but
> more, the *movement of language,* the *level* of the ear, the hand, the foot.
> All these incorporated in mea*sure.*[2]

At this point it becomes necessary to read, which is, after all, what
we are here for. The following books are, at best, a partial list of
materials—yet serve to indicate others, so that much is served:

   (1) Charles Olson, *The Maximus Poems 1–10, 11–22* (1953,
      1957). Olson's handling of the poems as an 'open field,'
      using a variable measure as concerns of content, and the
      emotional or informational character thereof, indicate,
      show what *range* can be managed.

   (2) Louis Zukofsky, *Some Time* (1956), *Barely and Widely*
      (1953), and *"A"* (1960). Zukofsky teaches *prosody*—and
      these are only three of the books which might be cited.
      One should also see his *A Test of Poetry:* "The test of
      poetry is the range of pleasure it affords as sight, sound,
      and intellection. . . ." By a complex of juxtaposed

---

2. Italics mine. Duncan has given, *in fine,* the steps of a poetic *grammar.*

> examples (following Pound's *ideogrammic* method), "a
> means for judging the values of poetic writing is
> established by the examples themselves. . . ."
> (3) Robert Duncan, *Letters* (1958), and *Selected Poems* (1959).
> The second book includes *The Venice Poem*—again a
> study in *formal* solutions, for those who will read it with
> attention. Duncan's other books are also valuable—
> *Fragments of a Disordered Devotion* (1952) and *Caesar's Gate*
> (1955). His notes and articles should be searched out as
> well.

Etc. Because the list continues, happily: to books like Denise Levertov's *Overland to the Islands* and *Here and Now;* to Paul Blackburn's
*Proensa* and *The Dissolving Fabric;* to Allen Ginsberg's *Howl;*[3] to first
books like Joel Oppenheimer's *The Dutiful Son,* and the as yet uncollected poems of Edward Dorn. All of these relate to the same
areas of technical concern, surely. Otherwise, 'content' in every man
is singular; which fact is a happy one.

Meeting Christopher Logue in Paris in 1956—an English poet
who looked so Englishly like that illustration of the Mad Hatter in
*Alice in Wonderland*—his first question, hoarsely yelled at me because the cafe whereto I had been brought by his friend Alex Trocchi, was so noisy, etc., was: "Tell me about Olson." Later we went to
Logue's room where he showed me his Pound books (which are as
much a currency in some areas as dollar bills in others) and gave
me, as I left, a carbon he had made of Pound's Cavalcanti translations. He will be amused to know that I am still trying to 'explain.'
Logue knew as much about American writing as I did, or, better,
he knew the problems shared in common—because such things are
only secondarily national these days.

You must read, then, to know what is happening. All poets seem
to suffer certain things in common, as certainly all must: difficulties
of self-support, or, if a family is involved, some means of sufficiencies in common, and the dignity any man has right to claim, granted
it has never been his purpose to ask for it. We all of us live in an
increasingly pinched world, pinched emotionally, pinched referen

---

3. Ginsberg's *Howl* has been read too simply as 'social document' and its technical concerns ignored. See his discussion in "Notes Written on Finally Recording
Howl" (*Evergreen Review,* No. 10), e.g., "So these poems are a series of experiments
with the formal organization of the long line . . . No attempt's been made to use it
(Whitman's line) in the light of early XX Century organization of new speech-
rhythm prosody to *build up* large organic structures."

tially—despite the fact that the moon comes closer. "How shall I
love you? Let me count the ways" is too often a proposed calculus
of possibilities; and that, alone, is no good. In despite, relationships, here as elsewhere, continue, serving a common need for survival and growth. The issue is the poem, a single event—to which,
as to the Battle of Gettysburg, or the Pan American Highway, many
men may well contribute—"*aperiens tibi animum.* . . ." Like, you dig
the 85th Canto? Like—that's all.

# Some Notes on Olson's *Maximus*

Eyes have a major place in this work as anyone familiar with it will know. And despite the easiness of the pun, an 'eye' here is 'I,' not the singular psychologic misfit of contemporary society—but the major term of relation to external world, in just the sense that as one *sees* a thing, one may then deal with it or be dealt with by it, in a manner to which one is a party. In that way Olson makes clear, early in the poems, that:

> polis is
> eyes . . .

And also:

> There are no hierarchies, no infinite, no such many as mass,
>     there are only
> eyes in all heads,
> to be looked out of . . .

*Polis,* at first a *town,* grows in no sense otherwise—it is never more than the aggregate of people who have so joined themselves together, and its members define it. Their perception constitutes their city.

There is another point to be made in this respect. John Burnet in his *Early Greek Philosophy* characterizes the Pythagorean concept of society in this way:

> In this life there are three kinds of men, just as there are three sorts of people who come to the Olympic Games. The lowest class is made

*Yugen,* no. 8, 1962.

up of those who come to buy and sell, and next above them are those
who come to compete. Best of all, however, are those who come to
look on . . .

Burnet then claims these last as proving the significant relation to
science—but it is most to the point to see that *seeing* here is not a
passive act akin to spectacles—it is a looking in order to see in the
place (*in situ*), and to understand in that way.


## 2

Olson's kinship with Pythagorean thought, and with the pre-Socratic
sense of world more generally, is very marked. It occurs as a reference directly in, for example, an early poem, "The Praises," wherein
are found these proposals:

> What has been lost
> is the secret of secrecy, is
> the value, viz., that the work get done, and quickly,
> without the loss of due and profound respect for
> the materials . . .

The danger he sees here is that "dispersion which follows from /
too many having too little / knowledge . . ." "What is necessary is /
containment, / that that which has been found out by work may, by
work, be passed on / (without due loss of force) / for use . . ."
Or again:

> What belongs to art and reason is
>                                  the knowledge of
>                                        consequences . . .

It is a sense of *use*, which believes knowledge to be necessarily an
*active* form of relation to term, with the corollary, that *all* exists
in such relation, itself natural to the conditions. It is not, then,
knowledge as a junk-heap, or purposeless accumulation of mere
detail—which seems to derive too frequently from the manner of
classification which follows upon the pre-Socratic world-view. It is
knowledge used as a means to relate, not separate—which senses
must, per se, prove very different. That is why the term, *use*, is to be
met with so frequently in Olson's writing.

3

The pre-Socratics had also the question of *nominalization* to deal with. Parmenides of Elea gives a good sense of it:

> The thing that can be thought and that for the sake of which the thought exists is the same; for you cannot find thought without something that is, as to which it is uttered . . .

All of "Tyrian Businesses" seems to me much involved by this question, as this quotation will illustrate:

> There may be no more names than there are objects
> There can be no more verbs than there are actions . . .

And, too, the use in this section of *Maximus* of a *particularizing* vocabulary (e.g., "futtocks, we call 'em" or "the honey in the lion, the honey / in woman . . .") forces thought to specific terms—much against a progress of easy, generalized understanding. Words, here, are forced to be seen specifically.

This character of language—and the use of language—is much to be found throughout *Maximus*, and as well in the writing before it. One such instance in earlier work is the first part of "ABC's," like this:

> b  l  a  c  k        eat a peck of storage batteries 'fore
>                      I die . . .

All meaning is local to an instance, wherefrom it derives, but also, whereto it returns. If a writer promotes a sense of language that floats in a middle way, neither here nor there, he is reasonably to be suspected. It becomes clear that this emphasis is one Olson shares with Williams ("No ideas but in things . . .") and with Pound who has given much emphasis to the problem of terminology, an aspect of nominalization. (It is Pound who tells of Santayana, that he had said, it doesn't so much matter what books they read in college, say, so long as they read the *same* books—and thereby have means for a *common* reference for terms. That we greatly lack at present, and our society tends to give prizes to those who can think up new 'terms' for old ones, not really changing anything at all but further confusing the so-called issue, a bothersome kind of euphemism.)

"Letter 5" in Olson's *Mayan Letters* is another reference for this question—and a very useful one for those who have means to check it. There Olson says the problem is "to bring any time so abreast of us that we are in this present air, going straight out, of our selves, into it . . ." In fact, that might well serve as a sense of the purpose in *The Maximus Poems* themselves, and it is no fluke that such a thing had been on his mind. He felt then (March 8, 1951) that a too simple "nomination" and/or name-reference as part of a traditional use of 'history' would fail to realize that, as he saw it, the shift had become "substantive" (i.e., he broke free of 'great men' to consider the question of maize, as in Carl Sauer's work)—a parallel to what scholars in the allied fields of anthropology, archaeology, geography, physics, etc., had already begun to document toward the end of the 19th century. I.e., the world had been *prior* to its reference in historical texts, where too often its use was simply "the passage of time & time's dreary accumulations by repetition . . ." A man writing had now to find his 'names' in terms that would free them for use *now*—not simply leave them caught in the trap of the 'past.' The reference, in that way, could no longer be a question of memory.

I find myself hammering at this for several reasons, as (1) the use of historical materials in *Maximus* will not be realized until one understands that they are being brought into a context of the *present*—no one is 'going back' to them, nor is there any question of the 'good old days'; and (2) that just as Mencius can say, how is it far if you think it, so Olson: how is it past, if you think it. All that can inhabit the present, is present. That is why, I think, such documents as John Smith's "The Sea Marke" or the list of what the fourteen men left at Stage Head had for provisions are given literally—to see as of *now*, else we see nothing sufficiently of that literal ground we occupy, a place accomplished by men. In that there may well be much of *time*, perhaps, yet those men are *there* too, and by no simple trick of language—we do not finally have to remove ourselves to a future, in which we will all be dead, to understand that fact. All is, as it is, where it is, when it is—and the dead in that respect do bury the dead, altogether.

## 4

A parallel statement is Gertrude Stein's comment: ". . . the making of a portrait of anyone is as they are existing and as they are existing has nothing to do with remembering anyone or anything . . ." In *Maximus* the "portrait" is a place, Gloucester, with all that may thereto be related—first of all, men, since "polis is / eyes . . . ," and then the 'measure' of those men and that place, as:

> I measure my song,
> measure the sources of my song,
> measure me, measure
> my forces . . .

or the literal 'mapping' of "Letter, May 2, 1959," and as well, the sense that "metric then is mapping, and so, to speak modern cant, congruent means of making a statement . . ."


## 5

Again, in an earlier poem, "Concerning Exaggeration, or How, Properly, to Heap Up," Olson has this question, "how / can you be otherwise than / a metaphor . . ." The sense of the sign that men make as, and of, themselves continues into *Maximus*, and is also an explanation of *Maximus* himself—the metaphor for a man not simply 'large' but more, the Pythagorean 'looker-on,' the measurer of terms and relationships. In that sense he stands at the apex of human activity in this same order.

(I do not propose a catalogue of all such 'metaphors' in the poems, but this way of thinking of it may help to explain the Ferrini section—where Ferrini proves token, or sign, for one kind of activity and its apparent value and the Burke section, another. People are to this extent consistently the face they wear, and the things which they do, in the place given them. Anecdotes have a like function I think, as here:

> was such a man
> he was embarrassed
> to ask for the rent . . .

They make a vocabulary of activities, which in turn are freed from category by virtue of their being *local*.)


## 6

Were the poems simply social criticism, they would not be very interesting. What they do offer, and work to provide, is just such a 'vocabulary' as I have mentioned. Williams has said with persistent desperation:

> The measure itself
> has been lost
>       and we suffer for it.
>             We come to our deaths
> in silence . . .

What does this mean? It means that we have lost control of the very terms by which we propose to live—that we can, say, argue 'limited war,' or defensive armament, for peace, which seem the most bloated instances one can quickly think of. It means that we are committed to suffering and desperation for specious reasons— since there is *no* reason except the duplicity of our reference. We fear commitment and risk of quite another kind. It is the contrary of all this I believe Olson to know:

> He left him naked
> the man said, and
> nakedness
> is what one means
>
> that all start up
> to the eye and soul
> as though it had never
> happened before

# Introduction to Charles Olson:
## *Selected Writings* I

---

There is a relevant measure of Olson's situation to be found in William Carlos Williams' notes upon a parallel figure—a man equally embarrassed by conveniences—Sam Houston. Of him Williams writes: "He wants to have the feet of his understanding on the ground, his ground, *the* ground, the only ground that he knows, that which *is* under his feet."

It is simple enough to generalize the American situation itself by reference to its pragmatism, its lack of traditional objectives, so to speak. But to turn it to use, the form of this world requires from the first an adamant recognition of *place,* of a literal geography such as John Smith could manage, so that, as Olson says, "The sort of knowledge Smith gave Hudson . . . Hudson went straight to the river." Smith is not, in Olson's context, the enlarged issue of a *hero,* but rather a primary instance of conduct, the *how* a man might demonstrate given the fact of himself in an environment that will only admit him as he *can* be there.

But I slur here too quickly into a sense of will, which is not to the point. However much a man may want something, the possibility is still not his to determine, although it is certainly his to recognize. One had much better see that no relief comes of any enlargement, or recourse to some sense of the world as *idea* merely. That "eu-

This original version of the Introduction to Olson's *Selected Writings* (New York: New Directions, 1966) was superseded by a subsequent writing (see following essay) that appeared in the Olson volume. The original Introduction was first published in Robert Creeley, *A Quick Graph: Collected Notes & Essays,* ed. Donald Allen (San Francisco: Four Seasons Foundation, 1970).

phoria" which Olson defines in "Tyrian Businesses" is the result of a kind of containment, which is not one at all—but, instead, a spilling over of the "personality," a false measure of human presence, onto all that confronts it.

There can be, then, no relief of such an order. I am most impressed that, in Olson's writing, these several measures of human term are adamant: (1) that the instant is human *time* and/or all that can be so felt must be so present, or else cannot exist; (2) that human content and possibility are the issue of acts, and are only absolute in that finiteness; and (3) that the *geography*, the complex of place—not at all the simplicity of a humanistic 'nature'—is the complement of all human condition.

So it is that the first essay of this collection insists that, for a man, "It is his body that is his answer, his body intact and fought for, the absolute of his organism in its simplest terms, this structure evolved by nature, repeated in each act of birth, the animal man; the house he is, this house that moves, breathes, acts, this house where his life is. . . ." Elsewhere he writes:

> I have this sense
> that I am one
> with my skin
>
> Plus this—plus this:
> that forever the geography
> leans in
> on me. . . .

When reality is so confronted, much occurs that is otherwise lost in the roar of good intentions. Olson's criticism of those systems of logic and classification, and of those senses of symbology inherited by our humanists from the Greeks, has as its basis his assertion "that a thing, any thing, impinges on us by a more important fact, its self-existence, without reference to any other thing, in short, the very character of it which calls our attention to it, which wants us to know more about it, its particularity. . . ." "Human Universe" is a brilliant qualification of this circumstance, and the same thinking underlies his premise in "Projective Verse":

> The objects which occur at every given moment of composition (of recognition, we can call it) are, can be, must be treated exactly as they do occur therein and not by any ideas or preconceptions from outside the poem, must be handled as a series of objects in field in such a way that a series of tensions (which they also are) are made to *hold*, and to

hold exactly inside the content and the context of the poem which has forced itself, through the poet and them, into being.

The point is that no form can exist as a possibility apart from that which informs it, the content of which it is the issue. The idealism of a sense of absolute form is answered as follows:

> Here again, as throughout experience, the law remains, form is not isolated from content. The error of all other metaphysic is descriptive, is the profound error that Heisenberg had the intelligence to admit in his principle that a thing can be measured in its mass only by arbitrarily assuming a stopping of its motion, or in its motion only by neglecting, for the moment of the measuring, its mass. And either way, you are failing to get what you are after—so far as a human being goes, his life.

This leads him to a kind of writing that is never more, nor less, than 'what it has to say.' It is primarily what he calls "language as the act of the instant" since—as he also makes clear—"the habits of thought are the habits of action," however difficult such action may prove. But at no moment may one step aside—to think *about* the world, rather than *in* it or *of* it or *as* it. Again, there can be no relief in such a generalization.

The poems themselves are, then, the issue of an engagement, of an impingement, a location that is constantly occurring. They are not a decision of forms more than such forms may be apprehended, literally gained, as possible in the actual writing. "But a field / is not a choice . . . ," however much within it may occur that sense of "choice" he takes care to qualify as *recognition*.

It is in this sense that Olson has been *given* Gloucester, which I may note briefly is a city in Massachusetts, a seaport up the coast from Boston. But that is merely what it is *for me*, which is not the point—nor is it even interesting to think of what it is *for Olson*. It is how Olson is involved with this place, that is interesting, how it is that he is "caught in Gloucester," in "The Librarian," or in another context, quite otherwise:

> It rained,
> the day we arrived.
> And I have rowed the harbor since,
> out the window of Johnny's Candy Kitchen,
> through that glass and rain through which I looked
> the first time I saw
> the sea.

These are statements, themselves their own occasion. It is relevant that Olson's discussion of Shakespeare's late plays and the character of the verse they develop provides the most useful measure of his own verse that I can offer. For example, he says "logicality persists in the syntax and image but the thinking and weighing in of the quantity stop twist and intensify the speech, thus increasing the instancy." The insisted upon 'forms' of the language and its 'subjects' are still evident, then, in the patterns of syntax and image, in these plays, but the words in their own literal occurrence, and in what they so think of, gain an *immediate* context, one momently present. "Some Good News" demonstrates a like gain, but also moves in its syntax and image free of an external limit, as here:

> . . . shoals, worse
>
> than rock because
> they do blow shift lie,
> are changing as you sound—
> on this crooked sand
> Portuguese (when?)
>
> had a fishing station.
> It wasn't new,
> what happened,
> at Cape Ann. It's where
> and when it
>
> did . . .

But it seems wisest, now, to stop such illustration, and to enter directly upon the writing. Its selection has been as arbitrary as I, or any one, must be, and much is left out—as the whole of *Call Me Ishmael*, his study of Melville, which will not admit to what were here the necessities of choice. One will, in any case, want to read more, and there is much more of Olson to read. This is a beginning, echoing what was my own, upon a way of being in the world which made clear to me and I hope now to you—

There are no hierarchies, no such many as mass, there are only eyes in all heads,
to be looked out of

*February 12, 1965*

# Introduction to Charles Olson:
## *Selected Writings* II

It is simple enough to note the main details of Charles Olson's background. Born December 27, 1910, he lived for some years in Worcester, Massachusetts, and his family spent summers while he was still quite young in Gloucester, on the coast of the same state. I once saw a picture of him, aged about eleven, taken together with the whole summer camp community at that time, some forty people who vacationed in this part of Gloucester, separated from the main town by the Cut or channel that runs in to the inner harbor. He is sitting on the edge of a roof and his legs hang down very evidently, giving a sense of the size he will later have as a man. He was to be tall indeed, roughly six foot eight or nine.

Subsequently he went first to Wesleyan, then to Yale, and Harvard, where he worked toward the Ph.D. in American studies. His jobs were various. He was a mailman for a while in Gloucester, he worked on a fishing boat, he taught at Clark and Harvard for relatively brief periods, he was chairman to foreign language groups for the Democratic Party during Roosevelt's campaign for a fourth term. Then, in the late forties, he took a job vacated by Edward Dahlberg, at that point a close and significant friend, to teach at Black Mountain College in North Carolina on the invitation of Theodore Dreier and Josef Albers, then rector of the college. Albers soon after went to Yale, and in the early fifties Olson became rector. Although it was a difficult time financially for all involved,

*Selected Writings of Charles Olson*, edited and with an Introduction by Robert Creeley (New York: New Directions, 1966).

and the college had relatively few students, nonetheless Black
Mountain proved a focal point for much significant activity in
the arts. John Cage, Robert Duncan, Merce Cunningham, Franz
Kline—all of whom were present at one time or another during
this period—show briefly the range and intensity of what was then
happening. The students—John Wieners, Robert Rauschenberg,
Edward Dorn, John Chamberlain, Michael Rumaker, Cy Twombly,
Joel Oppenheimer, Dan Rice, Fielding Dawson, to name several—
were equally notable.

Olson had come to Black Mountain following publication of a
most singular critical work on Melville, *Call Me Ishmael* (1947),
which he had written with the help of a Guggenheim Fellowship.[1]
In that book he makes clear his relation to a responsiveness and
decision in such writing to be found only in such comparable works
as D. H. Lawrence's *Studies in Classic American Literature,* W. C. Williams' *In the American Grain,* and Edward Dahlberg's *Can These
Bones Live.* In this respect, criticism is not only a system of notation
and categorization—it is an active and definitive engagement with
what a text proposes. It is not merely a descriptive process. *Call Me
Ishmael* begins:

> I take SPACE to be the central fact to man born in America, from
> Folsom cave to now. I spell it large because it comes large here. Large,
> and without mercy.
>     It is geography at bottom, a hell of wide land from the beginning.
> That made the first American story (Parkman's): exploration . . .

Olson had also been in touch with Ezra Pound, who had recently
been returned to the States to face trial on the charge of treason.
There is a very moving defense of Pound written by Olson for the
*Partisan Review,*[2] for whom he acted as a "reporter" in order to gain
admittance to Pound's first arraignment in Washington. It is called
"This Is Yeats Speaking"—the title itself a clear measure of those
circumstances Pound's accusers were preparing to ignore. As Yeats,
he says:

> We were the forerunners—Pound only the more extreme—but our
> time was out of phase and made us enders. Lawrence among us alone
> had the true mask, he lacked the critical intelligence, and was pro-
> spective. You are the antithetical men, and your time is forward, the

---

1. Shortly after, Olson received a second Guggenheim Fellowship, for a book on
the morphology of American culture.
2. Vol. XIII, no. 1, Winter 1946.

conflict is more declared, it is for you to hold the mirror up to authority, behind our respect for which lay a disrespect for democracy
as we were acquainted with it. A slogan will not suffice . . .

## 2

Olson's approach was thus twice removed from the terms of any
other critical intelligence of that period. He spoke of "geography"
and that was clearly antiliterary. He proposed a sense of the literal
nature of this country quite distinct from those critics influenced by
European traditions. If he was involved with particular European
evidences (as witness his translation of Rimbaud's last recorded
poem, "Ô saisons, ô châteaux . . . ," in "Variations Done for Gerald
van de Weile"), he so involved them that they became the American
context equally:

> I offer, in explanation, a quote:
> si j'ai du goût, ce n'est guères
> que pour la terre et les pierres . . .
>
> ("The Kingfishers")

*If I have any taste, it is only for earth and stones . . .* Or to continue with
Rimbaud's text from which this is also taken:

> Je déjeune toujours d'air
> De roc, de charbons, de fer.[3]
>
> *Daily I dine on air,*
> *rock, coal, iron . . .*

It is relevant, then, that Olson's particular nature should lead
him in Yucatan[4] to just such exploration as he values in Parkman,
or equally in Herodotus ("I would be an historian as Herodotus
was, looking / for oneself for the evidence of / what is said . . . ,"
"Letter 23," *The Maximus Poems*). In *Mayan Letters* we have unequivocal evidence of a *kind* of intelligence which cannot propose the assumption of content prior to its experience of that content, which
*looks*, out of its *own* eyes. This does not mean that conjecture is to be
absent, insofar as *jacio* means "throw" and *con*, "together"—however simply this point may note the actual process. It is a consistent

---

3. "Faim," *Délires* II.
4. Olson lived in Lerma from February to July 1951. *Mayan Letters* is a selection
made from letters written to me at that time. In 1952 he was awarded a Wenner-
Gren Foundation grant for further study of Mayan hieroglyphs.

fact with Olson that he does use his legs, and does depend on what his own instincts and intelligence can discover for him. In this way he *throws together* all he has come to possess.

But humanism, as a system of thought or ordering of persons in their relations to other things in the world, is distinctly absent. Even the most sympathetic ordering of human effects and intelligence leads to unavoidable assumptions and the test—which is the reality of one's quite literal being—denies any investment of reality prior to its fact.

> There are no hierarchies, no infinite,
> > no such many as mass, there are only
> eyes in all heads,
> to be looked out of
>
> > > > > ("Letter 6")

This commitment is further proposed and defined in "Human Universe," written, significantly, during that same period in Yucatan. We are not here involved with existentialism, despite the apparent closeness of sympathies at times. That is, Camus may speak of a world *without appeal,* but the system of discourse he makes use of is still demonstrably a closed one. What he seems most despairing about is that language cannot make sense of the world, that logic and classification do not lead to conclusions and value—but open only to the dilemma of experience itself. But *L'Étranger* is again a closed demonstration, a "fiction" proposed as example, and this, of course, is to stay within that universe of discourse which Olson distrusts.

> . . . such an analysis only accomplishes a *description,* does not come to grips with what really matters: that a thing, any thing, impinges on us by a more important fact, its self-existence, without reference to any other thing, in short, the very character of it which calls our attention to it, which wants us to know more about it, its particularity. This is what we are confronted by, not the thing's "class," any hierarchy, of quality or quantity, but the thing itself, and its *relevance* to ourselves who are the experience of it (whatever it may mean to someone else, or whatever other relations it may have).
>
> > > > ("Human Universe")

Camus despairs of his inability to fit experience to possible orders of language, whereas Olson would insist that language be returned to its place *in* experience, neither more nor less than any other act.

## 3

William Carlos Williams had said, "No ideas but in things," thereby insisting that reality was a real matter. Pound equally insisted, "Any tendency to abstract general statement is a greased slide." Both men have clearly to do with possibilities in writing of which Olson is further evidence, but his own qualifications of either man are also relevant. For example, Pound he felt limited to an "ego-system":

> Ez's epic solves problem by his ego: his single emotion breaks all down to his equals or inferiors. . . . Which assumption, that there are intelligent men whom he can outtalk, is beautiful because it destroys historical time, and thus creates the methodology of the *Cantos*, viz, a space-field where, by inversion, though the material is all time material, he has driven through it so sharply by the beak of his ego, that, he has turned time into what we must now have, space & its live air . . .
>
> (*Mayan Letters*)

The gain is that any instance of intelligence is relevant insofar as it proves so, that what was said in 500 B.C. can be actively heard in 1965—and in that sense "time" is denied as a limit of such a possibility. But the dilemma it leads to is that the ego or mind is made the sole measure of such experience.

In contrast, Olson feels that Williams offers an *emotional* system, which does not limit the context of writing to an assumption of *understanding*—or, better, it attains a way of writing that *feels* as it goes as well as *sees*. This allows the experience of writing to be more sensitive than the ego alone can admit.

In the second part of "Projective Verse,"[5] Olson makes this useful summary:

> Objectism is the getting rid of the lyrical interference of the individual as ego, of the "subject" and his soul, that peculiar presumption by which western man has interposed himself between what he is as a creature of nature (with certain instructions to carry out) and those other creations of nature which we may, with no derogation, call objects. For a man is himself an object, whatever he may take to be his advantages, the more likely to recognize himself as such the greater his advantages, particularly at that moment that he achieves an humilitas sufficient to make him of use.

---

5. "Projective Verse" was first published in *Poetry New York*, No. 3, 1950. The date is significant.

4

When Williams first read "Projective Verse," his response was immediate:

> I share your excitement, it is as if the whole area lifted. It's the sort of thing we are after and must have. . . . Everything in it leans on action, on the verb; one thing *leads* to another which is thereby activated . . .[6]

It was an excitement which many of us shared, because what confronted us in 1950 was a closed system indeed, poems patterned upon exterior and traditionally accepted models. The New Criticism of that period was dominant and would not admit the possibility of verse considered as an "open field."

But, thinking now of what else was clearly happening, that attitude was already losing ground. In Jackson Pollock's comments on his painting at that time, one finds the obvious parallel:

> When I am in my painting, I'm not aware of what I'm doing. It is only after a sort of "get acquainted" period that I see what I have been about. I have no fears about making changes, destroying the image, etc., because the painting has a life of its own. I try to let it come through. It is only when I lose contact with the painting that the result is a mess. Otherwise there is pure harmony, an easy give and take, and the painting comes out well.[7]

A like situation was clear in the work of John Cage, which involved the introduction of "chance" factors and reconsidered the whole context of a "melodic" modality in music. And similar circumstances were very clear in the sciences as well. "Formal" order, taken as a *sine qua non,* could no longer be assumed as a necessary virtue.

How, then, manage its alternatives—in such a way that the result be not random but rather the most precise discrimination and attention of which the person writing is capable? Olson's premise is this:

> A poem is energy transferred from where the poet got it (he will have some several causations), by way of the poem itself to, all the way over to, the reader . . .

                                                    ("Projective Verse")

6. I take this from a letter Williams wrote me at the time. His interest is further demonstrated by the fact that he includes a substantial section of Olson's "Projective Verse" in his *Autobiography.*
7. "Problems of Contemporary Art," *Possibilities* I, 1947–48.

This means, very literally, that a poem is some *thing,* a structure possessed of its own organization in turn derived from the circumstances of its making. Thus far, it could, of course, be a sonnet— and under given circumstances well might be, supposing that the person writing discovered that possibility as it was, in fact, written. But what one is saying has intimate relation to how one is saying it—and/or the content, in this sense, is that which qualifies the possibilities of form. Valéry, in *The Art of Poetry,* qualifies as *lyric* that mode of poetry in which the content and the form are realized simultaneously. Neither one can precede the other as a possibility. It is this sense, then, which Olson extends to all occasions of writing in verse. It is hardly a careless procedure, in that no order more than that so recognized can be gained. Apropos the syllable, "the king and pin of versification," Olson writes:

> It is by their syllables that words juxtapose in beauty, by these particles of sound as clearly as by the sense of the words which they compose. In any given instance, because there is a choice of words, the choice, if a man is in there, will be, spontaneously, the obedience of his ear to the syllables . . .
>
> ("Projective Verse")

The capabilities of that ear will have no other evidence to support them but that which they define. "Prosody," Pound said, "is the articulation of the total sound of a poem." In the note to which this serves as motto, so to speak, Olson says:

> It's as though you were hearing for the first time—who knows what a poem ought to sound like? until it's thar? And how do you get it thar except as you do—*you,* and nobody else (who's a poet
> What's
> a poem?
> It ain't dreamt until it walks    It talks    It spreads its green barrazza
> Listen closely, folks, this poem comes to you by benefit of its own Irish green bazoo. You take it, from here.
>
> ("A Foot Is to Kick With")

## 5

The range of materials here collected is not evidence of "subjects" or of some preoccupation with any such term of argument. "Letter 15" notes that clearly enough: "He sd, 'You go all around the subject.' And I sd, 'I didn't know it was a subject . . .'" It is worth some thought.

Where one lives is a complex occasion, both inside and out. What we have as *place* is defined in "The Resistance," and, again, it is not only "existential." When a man walks down a street, he walks it only *now*—whether the date be 1860, 1960, or so-called centuries ago. History is a literal story, the activity of evidence.

In short, the world is not separable, and we *are* in it. The fact of "Apollonius of Tyana" is not *then,* so to speak—at some remove in time because its person is, as we might say, historical. Each moment is evidence of its own content, and all that is met with in it, is as present as anything else. Apollonius *is* a present instance.

The most insistent concern I find in Olson's writing is the intent to gain the particular experience of any possibility in life, so that no abstraction intervenes. "In Cold Hell, in Thicket" makes clear the difficulties, and "To Gerhardt, There, Among Europe's Things," the situation of the specifically American:

> . . . Or come here
> where we will welcome you
> with nothing but what is . . .

A dream *is*—as clearly as whatever else. The circumstance of "The Librarian" or "As the Dead Prey upon Us" will not be confusing to any who admit what they *know* to be a total content, rather than one divided by assumptions of understanding. "In dreams begin responsibilities . . ." I was moved on hearing Williams use that quotation from Yeats at the outset of his acceptance speech for the National Book Award in the early fifties. But it is not only "responsibilities," but also "This very thing you are . . ."

Meaning is not importantly *referential.* Reference may well prove *relevant*—but I can make myself clearer by quoting a sense of *meaning* which Olson used at the Berkeley Poetry Conference this past summer (1965): *That which exists through itself is what is called meaning.* He also noted, as a usable context for that "mapping" or measure of how one is where one is, these four terms:

> earth
> Imago Mundi
> history
> Anima Mundi

By "earth" is meant all that literal ground we walk on and its specific character, including water and sky; by "Imago Mundi," that way of seeing or view of existence evident in any particular circumstance of life; by "history," all the condition and accumulation of human acts and effects, as these exist; by "Anima Mundi," that which informs and quickens life in its own condition, the spirit—or what we speak of in saying, "the *quick* and the dead." I offer these simply as measure, for the relevance of what follows.

*Placitas, New Mexico*
*October 3, 1965*

# "A Foot Is to Kick With"

*Human Universe and Other Essays,* by Charles Olson. San Francisco: Auerbahn Society, 1965.

*Proprioception,* by Charles Olson. San Francisco: Four Seasons Foundation, 1965.

*A Bibliography on America for Ed Dorn,* by Charles Olson. San Francisco: Four Seasons Foundation, 1964.

The work of Charles Olson is a complex and densely articulate sequence of poems and critical notes. Those familiar with his earlier study of Melville, *Call Me Ishmael* (1947), are aware of the compactness of his statement, the extraordinary manner in which the juxtaposition of terms effects a shorthand of reference, a quickness of mind not often met with in such studies. For example, here is a characterization of Melville's situation taken from the opening section of that book:

> Beginner—and interested in beginnings. Melville had a way of reaching back through time until he got history pushed back so far he turned time into space. He was like a migrant backtrailing to Asia, some Inca trying to find a lost home.
>
> We are the last "first" people. We forget that. We act big, misuse our land, ourselves. We lose our own primary.
>
> Melville went back, to discover us, to come forward. He got as far as *Moby-Dick.*
>
> Ortega y Gasset puts it that the man of antiquity, before he did any-

thing, took a step like the bullfighter who leaps back in order to deliver the mortal thrust.

(*Call Me Ishmael*, p. 14)

*Human Universe and Other Essays* is a collection written primarily since the publication of *Call Me Ishmael*, the only exception being, I think, "This Is Yeats Speaking," which Olson wrote for the *Partisan Review* on the occasion of Pound's trial. Again the quality of the intelligence is remarkable, in its speed, in its complexity of reference, in the juxtaposition of terms it can accomplish. The title piece, "Human Universe," makes evident the basic nature of Olson's qualification in all senses, which I may make clear here by a brief sequence of quotes:

We have lived long in a generalizing time, at least since 450 B.C.

\* \* \*

The distinction . . . is between language as the act of the instant and language as the act of thought about the instant.

\* \* \*

It is not sufficiently observed that logos [what Olson calls "discourse" and the promoter of abstraction and of the sense of a "UNIVERSE of discourse"—"the refuge of all metaphysicians . . ."], and the reason necessary to it, are only a stage which a man must master and not what they are taken to be, final discipline. Beyond them is direct perception, and the contraries which dispose of argument. The harmony of the universe, and I include man, is not logical, or better, is post-logical, as is the order of any created thing.

\* \* \*

Here again, as throughout experience, the law remains, form is not isolated from content.

\* \* \*

Art does not seek to describe but to enact.

\* \* \*

In other words, the proposition here is that man at his peril breaks the full circuit of object, image, action at any point. The meeting edge of man and the world is also his cutting edge. If man is active, it is exactly here where experience comes in that it is delivered back, and if he stays fresh at the coming in he will be fresh at his going out. If he does not, all that he does inside his house is stale, more and more stale as he is less and less acute at the door. And his door is where he is responsible to more than himself.

\* \* \*

It is unbearable what knowledge of the past has been allowed to be-come, what function of human memory has been dribbled out to in the hands of these learned monsters whom people are led to think "know." They know nothing in not knowing how to reify what they do know. What is worse, they do not know how to pass over to us the energy implicit in any high work of the past because they purposely destroy that energy as dangerous to the states for which they work—which it is, for any concrete thing is a danger to rhetoricians and poli-ticians, as dangerous as a hard coin is to a banker.

("Human Universe")

The fact of such loss, of a literal energy, of men's disposition to-ward their own confronting of the particular world given them, is an insistence throughout this collection. "The Gate and the Cen-ter" calls to attention primacies both of conduct and of possibility—the point that "energy is larger than man, but therefore, if he taps it as it is in himself, his uses of himself are EXTENSIBLE in human directions & degree not recently granted." "Apollonius of Tyana" enacts literally as dance and speech the classical possibility of a man so determined by himself: "Apollonius' assumption is that any im-age around which any people concentrate and commit themselves is a usable one just because it is theirs, that truth is never more than its own action, and that all that ever needs attention is the quality of the action." "The Resistance" equally states that it is a man's "body that is his answer, his body intact and fought for, the absolute of his organism in its simplest terms, this structure evolved by nature, re-peated in each act of birth, the animal man; the house he is, this house that moves, breathes, acts, this house where his life is, where he dwells against the enemy, against the beast."

The complement and extension of the materials in this first sec-tion of *Human Universe* are found in *Proprioception* wherein Olson, by means of quick notation and relevant chronology and bibliogra-phy, makes evident the content of any man as literal experience in and of his *body*—not a "psychology" (which he feels as "the surface" merely) but "the data of depth sensibility/the 'body' of us as object which spontaneously or of its own order produces experience of, 'depth' . . ." This placement, so to speak, yields a brilliant view in the discussion of grammar. The subject's agency in the middle voice (as distinguished from the active voice, and also what be-comes the "copulative" passive in present habit, although it was not so then) is qualified as follows:

1. on himself: make oneself go, proceed                    [will!
             persuade oneself, trust, obey                 [belief!
2. for himself: buy for oneself
             send for a person to come to oneself,        [grace!—
                      summon, send for                    or command
                                                          courtesy !
             to take to the field, march                   [obey!
3. on something
      belonging to oneself   loose one's own, ransom       [each takes care
                      bring one's own                      of themselves!

Such a system of discourse gained a literal function for the experience of men's recognition of themselves.

Again, it is such recognition that all three of these books insist upon. In *Human Universe* I would call particular attention to "Against Wisdom as Such," "Quantity in Verse, and Shakespeare's Late Plays," "Letter to Elaine Feinstein," "Equal, That Is, to the Real Itself," and to much of the material in the fourth section, especially that concerned with John Smith, Billy the Kid, to the review of Cyrus Gordon's *Homer and Bible,* and to the active distinctions found in the discussion of Ernst Robert Curtius. These are, to my own mind, major matters indeed.

The last essay is called "The Contours of American History" and is the review of a work by William Appleton Williams having the same title. But for the involvement it proposes I think one is better advised to go to *A Bibliography on America for Ed Dorn,* just that Olson gives here his own procedure for the recognition of such history as men in complement with place and time do make actual. He says at one point, "Best thing to do is *to dig one thing or place or man* until you yourself know more abt that than is possible to any other man. It doesn't matter whether it's Barbed Wire or Pemmican or Paterson or Iowa. But *exhaust* it . . ." In the note on Williams' book there is the lovely point about "synthesis having always that advantage, that it gives intellectual experience . . ." It's always up to each man what he makes of anything.

# "An Image of Man . . .":
# Working Notes on Charles Olson's Concept of Person

Talking to a gathering of student writers (S.U.N.Y. College at Cortland, N.Y., October 20, 1967) Olson again tried to make clear that he was not involved in some self-aggrandizement and that *The Maximus Poems* were not therefore a backdrop for himself as quondam hero. He then read "Maximus of Gloucester" (*The Maximus Poems*, Volume Three, p. 101)—the date for which he notes as "Friday November 5th/1965":

> Only my written word
>
> I've sacrificed every thing, including sex and woman
> —or lost them—to this attempt to acquire complete
> concentration . . .
>
>         . . . It is not I,
> even if the life appeared
> biographical. The only interesting thing
> is if one can be
> an image
> of man, "The nobleness, and the arete."
>
> (Later: myself (like my father, in the picture) a shadow
>         on the rock

One might expect to hear this plea from two other American poets, who are felt, I think reasonably, to be Olson's predecessors, Ezra Pound and William Carlos Williams. Paradoxically T. S. Eliot, whom Olson uses as a significant antagonist in "ABCs," is not usu-

*The Iowa Review* 2, no. 4 (Fall 1980).

ally presumed to be *personally* present in his longer poems, although he said of "The Waste Land" that it was, after all, "the relief of a personal and wholly insignificant grouse against life. . . ." In contrast, Whitman's "Song of Myself" is read as an intimate relation with the factual poet himself, although the reader discovers remarkably little about Whitman literally. What Whitman depends on is the authenticity of the personal, that the fact an 'I' 'feels' this or that emotion confounds all 'authority' of an otherwise abstract or general order. Both Pound and Williams make use of this fact. As Olson writes (*Mayan Letters*, London, Cape, 1968, pp. 26 ff.), "Ez's epic solves problem by his ego: his single emotion breaks all down to his equals or inferiors . . ." and, of Williams, "Bill HAS an emotional system which is capable of extensions and comprehensions the ego-system (the Old Deal, Ez as Cento Man, here dates) is not. . . ."

It is ironic that what I call so loosely 'the personal' is both our *subject* (which only an ego can determine as existing) and our *object*, "having to do with a material object as distinguished from a mental concept, idea, or belief. . . ." It must be that Olson's own physical size (he was six foot seven) made the latter situation of person most insistent. One of his last wry points in hospital was upon his own pleasure that 'the fundament stayed as put as the firmament. . . .' The body did not go away, in short, forever lost among the stars.

Returning to Eliot, Olson again qualifies him in the second part of "Projective Verse" (*Human Universe and Other Essays*, edited by Donald Allen, Grove, 1967)—and it is the second part of this essay he felt especially valuable, as against the first part, which proved the most read:

> —it is because Eliot has stayed inside the non-projective that he fails as a dramatist—that his root is the mind alone, and a scholastic mind at that (no high *intelletto* despite his apparent clarities)—and that, in his listenings he has stayed there where the ear and the mind are, has only gone from his fine ear outward rather than, as I say a projective poet will, down through the workings of his own throat to that place where breath comes from, where breath has its beginnings, where drama has to come from, where, the coincidence is, all act springs.

What Olson means by the statement, "down through the workings of his own throat to that place where breath comes from . . . ," can be found most clearly in his brief but remarkably helpful text, "Proprioception," for example, on the first page:

the data of depth sensibility/the 'body' of us as
object which spontaneously or of its own order
produces experience of, 'depth' Viz
SENSIBILITY WITHIN THE ORGANISM
BY MOVEMENT OF ITS OWN TISSUES

It's to the point that Olson had wanted to compose a "Book of the
Body," which would be an extensive study and report of the material, presumably, the "Proprioception" text so brilliantly graphs
and/or outlines. This preoccupation is very frequently evident in
his work, as in the short, initial statement, "The Resistance" ("It is
his body that is his answer, his body intact and fought for, the absolute of his organism in its simplest terms, this structure evolved by
nature, repeated in each act of birth, the animal man . . . ," *HU*,
p. 47) or, at more length, the proposal of human event found in
"Human Universe" (*HU*, p. 10):

What happens at the skin is more like than different from what happens within. The process of image (to be more exact about transposition than the "soul" allows or than the analysts do with their tricky
"symbol-maker") cannot be understood by separation from the stuff
it works on. Here again, as throughout experience, the law remains,
form is not isolated from content. The error of all other metaphysic is
descriptive, is the profound error that Heisenberg had the intelligence to admit in his principle that a thing can be measured in its
mass only by arbitrarily assuming a stopping of its motion, or in its
motion only by neglecting, for the moment of the measuring, its mass.
And either way, you are failing to get what you are after—so far as a
human being goes, his life. There is only one thing you can do about
the kinetic, reenact it. Which is why the man said, he who possesses
rhythm possesses the universe. And why art is the only twin life has—
its only valid metaphysic. Art does not seek to describe but to enact.
And if man is once more to possess intent in his life, and to take up
the responsibility implicit in his life, he has to comprehend his own
process as intact, from outside, by way of his skin, in, and by his own
powers of conversion, out again.

Recognize, then, that surely *one* insistent human dilemma is
lodged in the abstraction which consciousness permits, *if* that mar-
vellous function be employed only to gain an "objective correlative"
to that very existence any one of us is fact of. Olson's respect for the
mushroom, specifically for the experiments which Timothy Leary
was conducting in the early 60s, has obvious bearing. Talking to an
informal group at William Gratwick's home in Pavilion, N.Y., No-

vember 16, 1963, he emphasized the apparent fact that halluci-
nogenic agents, LSD in particular, ". . . [put] you on your own au-
tonomic nervous system—as against the motor."

> And certainly the human race has been so bereft of its autonomic sys-
> tem for so long that you can practically talk that we're green. In fact I
> would think almost that you have to talk about the species today as
> *green,* individually and socially. Not at all—how you say it—the way we
> tend to talk from our progressive or evolutionary or developmental
> past as though we've now got to take this step. It's not some step that
> you take easily, or that [it can matter] even to take the step, if you stop
> to think about it. You're just who you are; what you do, if it's any good,
> is true; and you are capable of being alive because of love. I mean it's
> about as simple—it's like those simplicities operate. And that's it. Well,
> it's not so easy to come to believe as absolutes, imperatives and univer-
> sals. In fact, on the contrary, we've been encouraged to think there is
> some universal, absolute or imperative we seem to be missing out on.
> But the autonomic thing is very crucial.
>
> (*Olson,* #3, pp. 19–20)

In the same discussion he speaks of the triad of politics, theology,
and epistemology, the three intensive-extensive patternings of human 'content,' and of how crucial it is that they be examined in
present situation. Because once there is the human belief, "the idea
that there is such a thing as knowledge . . . ("invented by a man
named Plato. *Episteme* is his invention and it's one of the most dangerous inventions in the world . . .") (*O,* #3, p. 13), the dislocation
of mind and body is immediate. George Butterick's "notes from
class, 15 September 1964" make a further clarification of Olson's
emphasis:

> Olson began his Modern Poetry course at Buffalo the following fall
> with the same triad, which he identified as "Augustinian," saying that
> it was "dogmatically true." He related the term politics, or the Greek
> *physics* 'nature,' to "necessity"; epistemology, or *nous* 'mind,' to "possi-
> bility"; and religion, or *theos* 'God,' to the "imaginable."
>
> (*O,* p. 54, n. 14)

"Soul" also can be an obvious distraction, but only if you let it get
away from you so to speak. I find, somewhat sadly, that the *OED*'s
first listing of this word's definition, "The principle of life in man or
animals; animate existence," is noted as obsolete, while the second
definition not only survives but defines our problem entirely: "The
principle of thought and action in man, commonly regarded as an

entity distinct from the body" (*OED*, p. 2927). One can make a
simple measure of the dangers inherent in abstraction by recognizing how removed the valued factor in existence, the soul, has become from that which it inhabits, the body—and, equally the life,
the process, of which it is literal instance. Nonetheless the dilemma
is clear, apart from this particular resolution: how is that which we
are, as "thought," "action," "soul," what we also are as in Olson's
phrase, "what gets 'buried,' like, the flesh . . . bones, muscles, liga-
ments, etc., what one uses, literally, to get about etc. . . . ." But, he
says, "the soul is proprioceptive . . . the 'body' itself as, by movement of its own tissues, giving the data of, depth . . . that one's life
is informed from and by one's own literal body. . . . that this mid-
thing between . . . that this is 'central,' that is—in this 1/2 of the picture—what they call the SOUL, the intermediary, the intervening
thing, the interruptor, the resistor. The self."

| | |
|---|---|
| The gain: | to have a third term, so that *movement* or *action* is 'home.' Neither the Unconscious nor Projection (here used to remove the false opposition of 'Conscious'; 'consciousness' is self) have a home unless the DEPTH implicit in physical being—built-in space-time specifics, and moving (by movement of 'its own')—is asserted, or found-out as such. Thus the advantage of the value 'proprioception.' As such. |
| its own perception | The 'soul' then is equally 'physical.' Is the self.* Is such, 'corpus.' Or—to levy the gain psychology from 1900, or 1885, did supply until it didn't (date? 1948?)—the three terms wld be: |
| | surface (senses) projection cavity (organs—here read 'archtypes') unconscious the body itself—consciousness: implicit accuracy, from its own energy as a state of implicit motion. |
| Identity, | therefore (the universe is one) is supplied; and the abstract-primitive character of the real (asserted) is 'placed': projection is discrimina- tion (of the object from the subject) and the unconscious is the universe flowing-in, inside. |

(*Additional Prose*, pp. 18–19)

*See "The Soul is a body as long as God's" in *Olson*, #4, p. 7.

Again and again one finds in Olson's thinking an insistence upon the *authority* of one's own life as initial. Whether it be "that all start up / to the eye and soul / as though it had never / happened before" or "That a man's life / (his, anyway) is what there is / that tradition is / / at least is where I find it, / how I got to / what I say" (Letter 11, p. 48), there is no otherwise, or where.

It would be of point, clearly, to consider the way in which "history" is present in *The Maximus Poems,* and to say again, as he did constantly, that Olson

> . . . would be an historian as Herodotus was, looking
> for oneself for the evidence of
> what is said: Altham says
> Winslow
> was at Cape Ann in April,
> 1624
>
> > (*MP,* p. 101)

Characteristically, one is tempted to type, in the third line, "was" for "is," and "said" for "says"—but it is as much to the point that the present *is* "historical," as that there is, therefore, an "historical present." Or as answer to the question I had then asked, literally, "what is 'history'?" Olson's answer, the poem "Place; & Names":

> a place as term in the order of creation
> & thus useful as a function of that equation
> example, that the "Place Where the Horse-Sacrificers Go"
> of the Brihadaranyaka Upanishad is worth more than
> a metropolis—or, for that matter, any moral
> concept, even a metaphysical one
>                         and that this is so
> for physical & experimental reasons of
> the *philosophia perennis,* or Isness
> of cosmos beyond those philosophies
> or religious or moral systems of
> rule, thus giving factors of naming
> —nominative power—& landschaft
> experience (geography) which stay truer
> to space-time than personalities
> or biographies of such terms as specific
> cities or persons, as well as the inadequacy
> to the order of creation of anything except
> names—including possibly mathematics (?)

the crucialness being that these places or names
be as parts of the body, common, & capable
therefore of having cells which can decant
total experience—no selection
other than one which is capable
of this commonness (permanently
duplicating) will work

"Story" in other words as if not superior
at least equal to ultimate mathematical
language—perhaps superior because of
cell-ness (?) In any case history
(as to be understood by Duncan's Law
to mean a) histology & b) story)
applies here, in this equational way
& severely at the complementarity of
cosmos (complementary to individual
or private) and not to cities or
events in the way it has, in
a mistaken secondary way, been
understood

Duncan had written him (18 Dec. '61):

> But "history"?—couldn't we throw that word out and establish histol-
> ogy: the tissue and structure, weaving, of what [it] is we know.
>
> story: what we know from the questions we asked. This thing is made-
> up, or an answer—but is, also, the only thing we knew to answer:
> oracle or sphinx-demand
>
> That: we *do* hold by histology and story having to do with one *gnosis.*
> And the art, the story, seeks out histology or lapses into the cult-
> sure . . ."
>
> (*O*, 4, p. 45, n. 2)

It's also to the point to remember, that Olson's favorite definition
of the word "history" was, finally, John Smith's (despite, as he remarked, its curious faintness): "History is the memory of time . . ."
In an autobiographical note ("The Present Is Prologue"), published 1955, he writes:

> There are only two live pasts—your own (and that hugely included
> your parents), and the one other which we don't yet have the vocabu-
> lary for, because the West has stayed so ignorant, and the East has
> lived off the old fat too long. I can invoke it by saying, the mythological,
> but it's too soft. What I mean is that foundling which lies as surely in the
> phenomenological 'raging apart' as these queer parents rage in us.
>
> I have spent most of my life seeking out and putting down the

'Laws' of these two pasts, to the degree I am permitted to see them (instead of the boring historical and evolutionary one which the West has been so busy about since Thucydides) simply because I have found them in the present, my own and yours, and believe that they are the sign of a delightful new civilization of man ahead.

(*AP*, pp. 39–40)

There is a sweetness, in that last phrase, and a 'progressivism'—a sense that one is going to get somewhere 'ahead'—one does not find usually in Olson. But again, it's of use to recognize that the 'history' of *The Maximus Poems* is initial tracking ("mapping," as he would call it) and is as much the form of the *agent* (the person acquiring the 'history,' in this case Olson) as it is the events and/or persons so examined. Lest one presume that is an extraordinary distortion of 'the facts,' that is, some body of information that might be 'objectively' the case, remember that any response to and/ or statement of such data will presume a context and a meaning. It is the false face of the 'objective' or the 'general' or the 'abstract' that Olson finds contemptible, as in "Letter for Melville"—"written to be read AWAY FROM the Melville Society's "One Hundredth Birthday Party" for MOBY-DICK at Williams College, Labor Day Weekend, Sept. 2–4, 1951":

> Timed in such a way to avoid him, to see
> he gets a lot of lip (who hung in a huge jaw)
> and no service at all (none of this chicken, he
> who is beyond that sort of recall, beyond
> any modern highway (which would have saved him
> from sciatica? well, that
> we cannot do for him but we can
> we now know so much, we can make clear
> how he erred, how, in other ways
> —we have made such studies and
> we permit ourselves to think—they
> allow us to tell each other how wise
> he was
>
> (*Archaeologist of Morning*, n. p.)

As though one could tidy up the *real*, or find another place for it, or understand it apart from its enactment. . . .

Possibly the most active rehearsal of Olson's "methodology" is "A Bibliography on America for Ed Dorn" (*AP*, pp. 3–14), which George Butterick has called "a fusion of Whitehead's notion of *process* with a Herodotean sense of *history*. . . . [It] was written in January 1955 as a letter—actually two letters—to the poet Edward

Dorn, then a student at Black Mountain College. . . ." (*AP*, p. 81,
n.). The qualification there of *person* is very useful. In fact, the
"Working premises" given at the outset should make much clear:

I That *millennia:*

&                                          are not the same as either
                                           time as history or as the
                                           individual as single
II *person*

(AP, p. 3)

And a little later, same page:

> *Results,* as of historical study:
>         (a) it is not how much one knows but in what field of
> context it is retained, and used (*millennia, & quantity*)
>         (b) how, as yourself as individual, you are acquiring &
> using same in acts of form—what use you are making of
> acquired information (*person, & process*)

It's Olson's intent in these letters to define both the *nature* of that
attention he values, and the *method* which most proves its use. Because he feels it absolutely required that one move beyond any
humanistic evaluation of data "BECAUSE THE LOCAL AND
THE SENTIMENTAL IS HOW HUMANISM COMES HOME
TO ROOST IN AMERICA" (*AP*, p. 5)—as instance, "*sociology*, without exception, is a lot of shit—produced by people who are the
most dead of all, history as politics or economics each being at
least events and laws, not this dreadful beast, some average and sta-
tistic . . ." (*AP*, p. 3).
    In contrast, his proposal is as follows:

*millennia*  ⟍     *person*
*process*    ⟋     *quantity*

Continuing:

> Applying all four of these at once (which is what I mean by *attention*),
> the local loses quaintness by the test of person (how good is it for you
> as you have to be a work of your lifetime?); itself as crutch of am-
> bience, by test of millennia [to which one might add as plaintive paral-
> lel, "how long, oh Lord, how long . . ."]; its only interest is as process
> (say barbed wire, as attack on Plains husbandry) or as it may be a sig-
> nificant locus of quantity (in America how, say, prairie village called
> Chicago is still, despite itself, a prairie village. . . .

(AP, p. 4)

If, in fact, by *person* one means "what, in fact, the critter, homo sap, is, as we take it, now . . ." (*AP*, p. 6), then, as Olson says, "our own 'life' is too serious a concern for us to be parlayed forward by literary antecedence. In other words, 'culture,' no matter how great . . ." "So far as 'scholarship' might, it will disclose the intimate connection between person-as-continuation-of-millennia-by-acts-of-imagination-as-arising-directly-from-fierce-penetration-of-all-past-persons, places, things and actions-as-data (objects)—not by fiction to fiction" (*AP*, p. 7). There follows, at this point, a lovely homage to Alfred North Whitehead, who is then used to define the principle at work here—"we should start from the notion of actuality as in its essence a process" (Whitehead, *Adventures of Ideas*, p. 355, as quoted in *AP*, p. 8).

I think I might, more responsibly, now enter this discussion as a person, literally—and not as a commentator, editor, scholar, or however one may care to qualify my role thus far. Just as Olson had said to Ed Dorn, "Best thing to do is *to dig one thing or place or man* until you yourself know more about that than is possible to any other man . . . ," for me the crux was to be "the NARRATOR IN, the total IN to the above total OUT ["what I call DOCUMENT simply to emphasize that the events alone do the work"], total speculation as against the half management, half interpretation, the narrator taking on himself the job of making clear by way of his own person that life *is* preoccupation with itself, taking up the push of his own single intelligence to make it, to be—by his conjectures—so powerful inside the story that he makes the story swing on him, his eye the eye of nature INSIDE (as is the same eye, outside) a light-maker" (*HU*, p. 127). Always in my own situation, there was tacit fear some essential information was lacking, that one was dumb, in some crucial sense, left out of the 'larger picture.' So that this possibility, as a *method*, was extraordinarily moving to me insofar as it exchanged a concept of social limit (again 'culture,' in its most pernicious sense) for the active potential and authority of a human life, *lives*, literally being lived. I had known, certainly, what Olson elsewhere proposes as "There are no hierarchies, no infinite, no such many as mass, there are only / eyes in all heads, / to be looked out of" (*MP*, p. 29). So too, in somewhat parallel sense, Pound's insistence: "What thou lov'st well shall not be reft from thee / What thou lov'st well is thy true heritage . . ." (*Pisan Cantos*, p. 99). But the condition, the law, so to speak, of this situation I took time to trust.

Why? That question seems to me intimately involved with all the familiar senses of enclosure and self-limit, what Louis Zukofsky wryly put as "born very young into a world already very old. . . ." It is hard to change the system, like they say—the more so, paradoxically, when it is, by virtue of consciousness, so very simple to. Think of what's become of the various significant patterns of "history" even in our own lifetime. But my point is really that significant aspects of Charles Olson's thought and work have been confusing to its critics insofar as the *model* of 'world' in mind, in each case, was very different, if not altogether antithetical. In short, there is often a disposition to read *The Maximus Poems* as if they were a symbolic representation of the forces of history, in the abstract, and that the unremitting emphasis upon "the facts," as he would say, whether of dreams or Gloucester records or his own daily existence, are somehow there to 'describe' or otherwise 'stand for' a 'reality' of general kind. They are not. Let me, in fact, make an absolute emphasis: *they are not.*

No, the "cause" is otherwise: "It is the cause the cause, still, it is (and she, still / even though the method be / new, be / the rods and cones of a pigeon's or, a rabbit's / eye, or be / who, man, is that woman you now dream of, who / woman, is that man. . . ." ("by 3/6/51," *AM*, n.p.). In his lecture at the Berkeley Poetry Conference (July 20, 1965), Olson makes the point very flatly, "You're simply stuck with the original visionary experience of having been *you,* which is a hell of a thing. [Laughter] And, in fact, I assume that the epigraph that I've offered today is my only way of supporting that, which is [he writes on the board]: *that which exists through itself is what is called meaning. . . .*" (*CM*, p. 11).

> I believe there's simply ourselves, and where we are has a particularity which we'd better use because that's about all we got. Otherwise we're running around looking for somebody else's stuff. But that particularity is as great as numbers are in arithmetic. The literal is the same as the numeral to me. I mean the literal is an invention of language and power the same as numbers. And so there is no other culture. There is simply the literal essence and exactitude of your own . . . Truth lies solely in what you do with it. And that means *you.* I don't think there's any such thing as a creature of culture . . . The radical of action lies in finding out how organized things are genuine, are initial, to come back to that statement I hope I succeeded in making about the *imago mundi.* That *that's* initial in any of us. We have our picture of the world and *that's* the creation.
>
> (*CM*, p. 36)

There is, finally, a late text ("Gloucester, 28 Fort Square Feb. 15th (LXIX)," *AP*, p. 76) which makes an intensive compact of a great range of Olson's thinking, and since one cannot, responsibly, undertake all the materials and situations of his work in such "working notes" as these, let it serve as center for our own ending here. (Regretfully, in some respects, since much dear to my own heart, "Apollonius of Tyana," for example, or the specific relations with Jung, Corbin, and that primary man, Alfred North Whitehead, have barely been touched upon, if at all. But one takes heart in Whitehead's insistence, dear indeed to Olson: "There is nothing in the real world which is merely an inert fact. Every reality is there for feeling: it promotes feeling; and it is felt" [Whitehead, *Process and Reality*, p. 439]. So we won't miss 'it' insofar as it is 'here.')

The text, then, is "The Animate Versus the Mechanical, and Thought" (*AP*, pp. 74ff.). He begins, "Gravity, in fact, but pre- or post-mechanics. That is, not effect (Newtonian) nor proof (Recent) but experiential: phenomenological, perceptional, actionable" (*AP*, p. 74). In short, that this fact of being, in any given instance, not be taken *outside*, so to speak, but be recognized as the "Dogmatic Nature of Experience" (cf. *P&T*, p. 44), which it is. He notes the situation of a plant, which "has at the tips of its leaves and the ends of its roots 'standing-growing-responding' actions . . . and has, if and as 'weight,' gravitational 'history.'"

> In fact 'history,' as, in that sense, difference from "astronomy" [which relies, perforce, on 'mechanical' measure]: that event (in Merleau-Ponty's sense [cf. *O*, pp. 3, 44–50]—narrative) is a perceptual—that wld be *primordial*—element of experience so much so that it 'carries' throughout the system—the system being 'Creation'—as 'element' (or 'weight') as profound as any mechanically measurable or demonstrable 'truth'; that even in short—or here decisively 'history'—as *must* [as necessity, as what has to happen]—is a condition of organism. (Above 'Animate.') . . . now I am proposing an even more fundamental 'tropism' ["Tropism, I think, is actually the riddler of the lot. Or it's the management, or it's the maneuverer, or it's then . . . it's ourselves." *P&T*, p. 43]: that one cannot 'think' even—because one cannot 'act' even—without such limits as the 'lines' of being, both in the plant and the animal 'meaning,' 'animate' . . . So I am back to animate, plant-or-animal—'perception' sense—of the freshness in time of the narrative or history as a tone or mode and so activeness of, for a human being, 'Creation': that there is no 'knowledge' of the crucial (axial-tropistic) sense of *anything*, including the "Universe" or the

"Self," except by this 'Time' phenomenon of freshness which Animateness [is], *in and by itself,* as initial *of* experience.

(*AP,* p. 74)

You will recall the frequency with which Olson quoted Heraclitus, "Man stands estranged from that with which he is most familiar"— literally, that fact, that living organism, of him/herself, and the crisis, persistently, in the situation is that all else is affected by such a powerful 'unit of meaning' so intensively awry. It is as if we have entered the 'inside' of this animate 'content' with the same terms of measure and their related agency, the mechanical, with which we had presumed our mastery over the 'outside,' that "geography" also so insistently present and which "forever . . . leans in/on me . . ." (*MP,* IV, V, VI, n.p.). In contradiction, Olson proposes:

> The animate—plant or animal—is the aboriginal instance of our occurrence and is therefore the aboriginal condition which qualifies— defines both in fact and act, including the form-making usefulness of—our action.

* * *

> The import of this can quickly be stated: man as Love (plant, heliogeotropic) grows up and down, man as separateness (animal) disposes of himself by *sitio*—chooses his place but which even though it gives him freedom disposes him likewise by gravity (statolith)—starch, turgor—'weight'-of-mass)—equal tropistically. Heaven and Earth.

(*AP,* pp. 75–76)*

What's to be made of that, with that, is all that any human life or the acts that make it life can constitute:

> an actual earth of value to
> construct one, from rhythm to
> image, and image is knowing, and
> knowing, Confucius says, brings one
> to the goal: nothing is possible without
> doing it. It is where the test lies, malgre
> all the thought and all the pell-mell of
> proposing it. Or thinking it out or living it
> ahead of time.

(*MP,* Vol. 3, p. 190)

---

* *Turgor:* "The normal fullness or tension produced by the fluid content of blood vessels, capillaries, and plant or animal cells." *Statolith:* "A small, moveable concretion of calcium carbonate, found in statocysts." *Statocyst:* "A small organ of balance in many invertebrates, consisting of a fluid-filled sac containing statoliths that help indicate position when the animal moves." (*American Heritage Dictionary*)

# Charles Olson's Masterwork

*The Maximus Poems,* by Charles Olson. Berkeley, Calif.:
University of California Press, 1983.

*A Guide to* The Maximus Poems *of Charles Olson* by
George F. Butterick. Berkeley, Calif.: University of
California Press, 1978.

Charles Olson's immediate poetic elders make a context for *The Maximus Poems,* but they do not help to explain this remarkable work, nor do they define sufficiently the conceptual shift here accomplished. Ezra Pound and William Carlos Williams each imagined a New World that derived, however antagonistically, from European habits, in the arts particularly but also in forms of history and epistemology. Unlike them, Olson's background was classic American: working-class, mill town, immigrant. However aristocratic, so to speak, his subsequent education, his habits are here defined and his resources located. "Back," as the poem reads, "is no direction." But here is a more specific instance of the place of "An American," so that one may avoid any misunderstanding:

> No Greek will be able
> to discriminate my body.
> > An American
> is a complex of occasions,
> themselves a geometry
> of spatial nature.

*Washington Post Book World,* November 13, 1983.

I have this sense,
that I am one
with my skin.

Plus this—plus this:
that forever the geography
which leans in
on me I compell
backwards I compell Gloucester
to yield, to
change
            Polis
is this

Clearly the insistence of any long poem argues a need to make a composition of the disjunctive factors of the present "world"—"this present life," as the dictionary says. The epic not only permits such existence—being "one with my skin"—but discovers the actual *body* itself, inside and out. Such poems of our own time—Pound's *Cantos*, Williams' *Paterson*, Zukofsky's *"A"*—are heroically intent upon this possibility, as in Pound's great effort to measure the capacity and resource of intellect; or Williams' heartbreaking labor in age to make a place for feeling in the common commitment of that human need; or, finally, Zukofsky's intense and binding evocation of family, of our lives in relation, which must serve of necessity as their only possibility of value.

*The Maximus Poems* began as letters to an old friend of Olson's, Vincent Ferrini, a fellow poet in the city of Gloucester, Massachusetts, which itself serves as definition of human potential and consequence. But far better that one apply to the editor of this very usefully revised and established text of the poem, George Butterick, whose *A Guide to 'The Maximus Poems' of Charles Olson* includes a solid introduction with detailed information on the background of the poem's writing. One may note here, simply, that what begins as a social and politically determined address, in large part, with history a factor of pedagogic intent, soon moves far beyond that enclosure of information, despite its use and significance. In fact, this wider disposition is always present, as here:

( . . . metric then is mapping, and so,
to speak modern cant, congruent means of
making a statement), I, as Mr. Foster, went
to Gloucester, thus:

> "And past-I-go
> Gloucester—insides
> being Fosterwise of
> Charley-once-boy
> insides"

The paradigm "Gloucester" yields much more than detail, data for
the clothing of preoccupations. One needs turn to the earned emotional size of its "place" in a later poem, "I have been an ability—a
machine—up to now . . . ," to have any sense of the variousness of
its presence in the poem, because it is a place of primary, of primordial, recognitions. Just as Herman Melville had made the industry
of whaling imaginative ground for a mythos of the will, so Olson
makes of Maximus, as George Butterick aptly puts it in the *Guide*'s
introduction, an "Ahab come 'full stop.' He is Western man at the
limit of himself, who no longer has a frontier other than himself
and his extricable past, no farther west to go but to dig in deeper
where he stands, with the result that Gloucester is taken back, 'compelled' to its founding in 1623 by migrating European man, back to
the old Norse and the Algonquins, even farther back to the ice and
Pleistocene man."

One might well cite the persistent beauty of the verse. It has been
a constant wonder to me how various and particular was Olson's
genius in the literal practice of his craft. His formal invention is
constant and inevitably particular to the factors of statement. In
short, he says *things*. But even that extraordinary grace might prove
fragile were it not that he shares with D. H. Lawrence a prescient
information, a power of intuition but, more accurately, of perception that can "see" as feeling, that knows it *knows*. In an early characterization, he dubbed himself an "archaeologist of morning"
(which phrase became the title of his posthumously collected poems,
not including the *Maximus* sequence).

> He left him naked,
> the man said, and
> nakedness
> is what one means
>
> that all start up
> to the eye and soul
> as though it had never
> happened before . . .

That is the measure we are here offered.

# "A light, a glory, a fair luminous cloud"

*Letters,* by Robert Duncan. Jargon Fourteen. Highlands, N.C.: Jonathan Williams, 1958.

We are made by what we make, the poet (*makar*) also. Robert Duncan makes clear, "It is not expression nor creation that I seek; but my inventions are addressed to an adventure. The medium of words." This *medium* is both path and declaration, for it is the way by which the poet moves and the way, also, by which all moves to him. It is:

> a word giving up its ghost
> memorized as the flavor
>   from the vowels (the bowels)
>   of meaning
> (BE STILL THY BRATHE AND HEAR THEM SPEAK . . .)
>                     ("For A Muse Meant")

> The image of what I am talking about begins to come: it is a fair land, a life, a language. And we, poets, are made up by it—it is a maker— and we in turn making ourselves up are of it.
>
>                     ("With Bells Shaking")

The *Letters* then make a character for the initial communication, serve as communicants here, as everywhere and always. We know that what we see finds "images more powerful than our own power of sight." This is the truth of "the full splendour of poetry in which we blindly see."

*Poetry,* April 1960.

It were a good thing to begin a book with Blake's beginning: HEAR THE VOICE OF THE BARD! for it is the imagination who listens then—but the Bard is the voice of the listener, who hears, sees, the ancient trees, the Holy Word walking there, crying.

("Figures of Speech")

In finding this, as we read, we find ourselves discovered, by the writer, as ourselves discover him.

An imaginary woman reads by her lamplight, inclining her head slightly, listening to the words as I write them: we are there, as the poem comes into existence—she and I—losing ourselves in the otherness of what is written. I too then am imaginary.

("At the End of a Period")

Relationships derive from this ground, read or unread. The forms which sustain us are those devices of conjecture, force, or need, making ourselves the device of their forms. They wear us as their sign.

But—"Cezanne restored the destroyed mountain . . ." So Coleridge may write, "O Lady! we receive but what we give, / And in our life alone does Nature live . . ."

> Is there another altar than the fact we make,
> the form, fate, future dared
>     desired in the act?

("Upon Taking Hold")

Loss may well live here:

> the reaching out, risk of the touch,
> rhymes that mimic much of loss, ghost goings,
>     words lost in passing, echoed
> where they fall, againnesses of sound only.

("Words Open Out upon Grief")

Yet how else should we live, despite that "Never to this fullness I came, that fills me"? Such risk defines the poet, makes him as the poem.

Then with that triumph of assertion, that dear courage in which the creature addresses the creator—for we have in faith to take our stand with God, and say IT IS GOOD—I sign my name, I, Robert Duncan, made this, as best I know.

("Preface: L'Oeuvre de Vivant L'Oeuvre de fantôme")

*. . . now I, who did not see, see.*
*Friend, you have given your hand to me.*

# "To disclose that vision particular to dreams"

*Roots and Branches,* by Robert Duncan. New York: Charles Scribner's Sons, 1964.

*Roots and Branches* is characteristic in its title, as in all other respects, of a continuing work which no brief note can report with much accuracy. For one thing, Robert Duncan is of that most rare order of poets for whom the work is not an occasional exercise, nor a demonstration of metrical abilities, nor any other term of partial commitment, however interesting. This book is the eleventh of a sequence, of a life, in fact, which can only be admitted or experienced in that totality.

But I can note, albeit briefly, some of the major insistences of his work as one meets with them in this book as well as in every other which he has written. Most primary is the assertion that what one *can* say, in any circumstance of poetry, is informed by a "voice" not ours to intend or to decide. So Eve (who is first Erda, "the earth daughter," then Eve, "Imagination's child . . . Womb-man of Adam's life") in answer to Adam's "Now in your eyes I see the tree is fair / in which I lose myself thru you"—

> There's a way of speaking that's most like this
> where thought and feeling is not our own
> but belongs to a voice that would transmute
> into a music joy and grief, into one living tree
> in which beyond our selves we find release.

*Humanist,* January–February 1966.

> "Rime" the demon calld it and made a wry face
> as if it were wrong
> where words are obedient to song's measure
>         beyond our will.
> But the daimon calld it "Melody"
> and spoke, again, of our Author's delight
>         in various Truth.
>
> (Adam's Way)

Equally, Eve as "Womb-man" and "earth daughter" figures in part a sense of earth met with in "Apprehensions," an extraordinary poem indeed which I would place with those others equally notable in his earlier books, *The Venice Poem* and "A Poem Beginning with a Line by Pindar." Here the earth is sensed complexly as the occasion of births, "pitted with young," "a chain of caves," in a dream which is instruction. Then the last poem in the book, "The Continent," plays variations on the recurring theme:

>         A diary poem
> to Day, Gaia, Earth
> —murther, murmurer, demurrer.

And this "murther" elsewhere echoes as "But, of that other Great Mother / or metre, of the matter . . ." in "Two Presentations" which confront the circumstances of his own birth and relation to his mother with a deeply moving intimacy.

I am also most interested in Duncan's sense of Adam, who is wakened to Eve by the angel Michael:

> The Night is done. From your base elements
> you are removed, and Day's your bride . . .
>
> (Adam's Way)

I read a curious parallel then in the opening line of "Apprehensions": "To open Night's eye that sleeps in what we know by Day . . ." Here the need is to disclose that vision particular to dreams so that its orders may take part in that waking life otherwise given to us.

Again, might one manage it in such short space, it would be of great use, and interest, to make explicit the changes rung on these divers themes—and I have by no means noted all those which seem to me relevant. But apropos that sense of "Night's eye," for example, here is the opening verse of "A New Poem (for Jack Spicer)":

You are right. What we call Poetry is the boat.
The first boat, the body—but it was a bed.
        The bed, but it was a car.
And the driver or sandman, the boatman,
        the familiar stranger, first lover,
is not with me.

Or to follow the circumstance of false instructions, as contest of those to be honored, that he makes the issue of in "What Happened: Prelude":

                Betrayd,
    the structures of the poem or play of mind
                (angelic instructions)
                broken,
    the genii come to life,
        touch fire to ice in the living bone
                and waken
    fearful consequence. They take
        offense who'd promised happiness.

Or to find the various person, Isis, Helen, Eve, Erda, in all her presence here. But there can be no end to it here.

    Feeling and motion, impression and expression,
            contend. Drama
    is the shape of us. We are
            ourselves tears and gestures of Isis
    as she searches for what we are ourselves,

    Osiris-Kadmon into many men shatterd,
            torn by passion. She-That-Is,
    our Mother, revives ever   His legend.
            She remembers. She puts it all together.
    So that, in rapture, there is no longer
            the sensory-motor-homunculus
    subduing the forces of Nature, Horus contending with Set,

                but the sistrum

                sounds through us.

        The Will wherein the gods ride

            goes forward.

                                    ("Osiris and Set")

# Preface to *Robert Duncan: A Descriptive Bibliography*, by Robert J. Bertholf

Insofar as the world of poetry is an insistently human one—or, better, one in which the human lives at the edges of its own perception, in the common event of all else—there can be that disparity of response and use which must often make us recognize with a bitter disappointment how meager our responsibility has proved. There is no leader of this world, in the political sense of authority. But if one can hear Blake's proposal, "The authors are in eternity . . . ," then that which has been so given, having no content in possessional time, will find place in person, as agency or instrument, so that he or she becomes voice for and of many, however single in fact.

Poetry is primary community, primarily communal. It does nothing, so to speak, because it is issue of all, and cannot be constrained to any one facet or preferred disposition of circumstance, because it moves and is moved with all. That is why one cannot be by definition a "good" poet, unless one speaks of the limited factor of performance—which, though practiced with brilliant intent and consummate resourcefulness, is still a given, found only by chance, never bought, sold, or bargained for. In this world, both timeless and only this very moment, there is a seemingly endless polyphony of voices, of all ages, places, times, and situations—all pleasure, all despair. It is as vulnerable as a hallucination, because it and all the world that keeps it a very literal physical company have, paradoxically, no defense against thought, especially that which has lost its

Robert J. Bertholf, *Robert Duncan: A Descriptive Bibliography* (Santa Rosa, Calif.: Black Sparrow Press, 1986).

feeling for the human, the music specific to a body which the mind might still recognize.

I must therefore put as simple testament not only my own deep respect for Robert Duncan, my own dependence on him as a brother in this art and as a teacher, as that person of my own imagination who *is* what a poet might be—but also make clear in this manner of emphasis that Robert Duncan has been that poet of my generation who brought the communal world of this art forward again, who broke down the specious and often hostile habits of those uses of a poetry which would turn it to profit, to personal law and order, to investments of self-approval, while denying it any power of initiating wonder, and final value that might matter. The reader now considering by means of this immensely useful listing of publications, together with some clear history of their circumstance of printing, what has been the practical pattern of Robert Duncan's life as a poet will very soon discover it has only that of the *practice* of a poetry, but not simply his own—as might be said of something bought and paid for—nor another's, if that one were to be only its prior owner. He has long insisted that language and the poetry it sustains, of all human things, are common, demand a common ground. As he says in respect of Whitman:

> Speech itself, nowhere other than common, every where the source from which we derive our individuality.
>
> ("The Adventure of Whitman's Line,"
> *Convivio,* ed. John Thorpe, 1983)

It is now, happily, a common information that his use as source, as primary connection, for the poets of his world makes a geography far more ample than any of their particular intents, habits, or even accomplishments might describe. For example, only in the world of his generative and abiding transcendence of mundane literary categories could Henry Miller, Charles Olson, Kenneth Rexroth, Jack Spicer, Anaïs Nin, Louis Zukofsky, Denise Levertov, William Everson, myself and many, *many* others even begin to find room. As Whitman, he is originally and definitively American, defines a continuing person so *here.* But just as a science will engage a univ se from a single instance of its manifest presence, so this poet reads the particular sounding syllable, the suddenly discovered congruence or discord, as expanding of all relation:

> From the seed of first light the galaxies move out to the extremities of imagined time and space; Lucifer "falling" is the circumference or boundary of the need of Creation.
>
> ("Introduction," *Bending the Bow,* 1968)

The characteristic release of such power is an extraordinary intellectual energy, which can make of the *seeing* of the world, or, more aptly, its apprehension by whatever means we humanly can recognize, a vast and yet particularizing place of our lives with all else relating, a factual living tissue of those bounds/bonds.

So one may speak of him, however ineptly. One wants to make clear the *size* he constitutes, both in thinking and in practice, the parallels, variously, with Whitman, Dante, to an imagination which can bear, in birth and death, such human scale and occasion, go with it to whatever end. Therefore I cannot believe that he has ever once turned from this art and its commitments, however difficult its demands have proved. Yet to emphasize such a Puritan measure is also beside the point. No delights could ever have been more, as any reader or hearer of his poems well knows. Because such work as his is all a life, a world, and in it, miraculously, all opens, is possible, is there, or not there, meets with limit, breaks apart—to live.

*Buffalo, N.Y.*
*February 28, 1984*

# "An intensely singular art"

*Here and Now,* by Denise Levertov. The Pocket Poets Series, no. 6. San Francisco: City Lights Pocket Bookshop, 1957.

*The Dutiful Son,* by Joel Oppenheimer. Jargon Sixteen. Highlands, N.C.: Jonathan Williams, 1956.

*Some Time,* by Louis Zukofsky. Stuttgart: Jonathan Williams, 1956.

Poetry for the American has been an intensely singular art. Poe fights early for a separation from European attachments; and Whitman provides the example, basing himself on an ultimate personalism. We have, equally, Emily Dickinson, whose minutiae of personality and perception in effect pick out a world from the four walls of one small room. It is the *me* and *you* which have concerned us—the interstices of human relationships brought home, so to speak. It is there that we have most constantly begun.

This character of placement continues in contemporary verse. Sometimes the sound is belligerently self-assertive, revelatory and painful. The *I* is worn as a merit in itself; all forms break to it, and what hope of relationship to others there may once have been, is lost. This is, of course, the isolation which the American so often carries like a sore, marking him as lonely, lost, and a little pathetic.

The counter to this is the attempt to move into form, again, with others, with one's wife, husband, children—the sudden instances

*New Mexico Quarterly,* Spring–Summer 1957.

of relationship, the worn ones, all of it. How hard that seems. We cannot speak, now, of any very large aggregate of things to hold us together; and our sociality has become a business maneuver, or else (most hopefully) that the garageman does remember us, the postman smiles! We want so much to be liked.

All three of these books relate to this one center: how to live. It is not, how to stay alive, because that is something else again, almost now beyond our determination. But—in the time we have, what shall we do? Do you love me? Where are we? These are interesting questions.

The youngest of these poets, Joel Oppenheimer, came of age at the end of the second World War: a shocked time, with "love" a kind of down payment, it seemed, on a house, or perhaps a refrigerator. One didn't know. One tries, however:

*The Couples*

if i dont bring you
flowers. if i dont have any
flowers. delicate grubby violets.
chrysanthemums for your coat.
only children. what has that got
to do with it.

any child is isaac.
brushwood and sticks.
the burning bush in the hill's side.
jesus strung from a dogwood.

if it is not fair
where is fairness. if she is not
fair where is fairness. if flowers.
apples. peaches and pears
for the summer. an edible potato.

the stain of the dogwood
is in you. what now.
mushrooms. or underground
truffles. a pig with a ring
in his snout. he is hungry.
the stain of the dogwood.

who cries for another's
pain hasnt enough of his own.
where are my children they
leave me here knocking wood.

what is there i havent invented
contrived cut out of the

whole cloth. some day to
make it easier, with more
pleasure. that is a pleasure.

how else to be fecund if not
to put up with a man.

It is a sturdy defense, I think, written in like manner. But the
women know too, what there is to know. God knows they feel it—
no kindnesses, or expectancies, or money. It is different. Denise
Levertov is English, but that doesn't matter. One says (grandly!) she
knows:

*The Bird*

That crazy bird
always laughing—
he sits on the wall they are building,
the wall
which will hide the horizon,
and laughs like mad every time
we open our mouths to say
I love you I hate you etc.
He came only since
the green rain came and
softened everything, making
mud of the cracked
selfrespecting earth and rotting
the red flowers from their stems. Yes,
the rain, the trucks full
of pink bricks, that crazy
eavesdropping bird, came
together and finished
the days of burning,
and silence, and distance.

Thank God for the relief of it all. Personalism is of course only
interesting insofar as it does contain "That crazy bird . . ." One begins with oneself perhaps, and to that entity one joins one other;
and from that it may well be that a third is conceived. And so on—
because this is what the world is all about. And the birds laugh. It is
a good thing. Men and women grow whole in this image.

There is also wear, certainly, and the time that passes. But the
determination, to live with others, holds true, once chosen. And a
poet, like any other, thoughtfully enough arrives at the choice common to all. Louis Zukofsky is older than either Denise Levertov or

Joel Oppenheimer, and has been alive consistently. He has a family
much in evidence in his poems, a wife and son. His book is, in fact,
a complexly woven evidence of this basic relationship, so that I cannot, by quoting, make it all clear. But the substance of it can be
made so, and the craftsmanship whereby it is given form—and,
again, the world in which it obtains.

> *Sequence 1944–6 (4)*
>
> Having outlived self-offense
> And that of my friends
> I became brother to loneliness
> And love the fact more than the word.
>
> All that is human is
> Alien and not alien.
> All carefully chosen words
> Are here—fairly shadows.
>
> You have music to accord.
> A child
> At a remove from love
> Holds leaves in my hand.
>
> Where the world is headed
> We do not say
> As stars
> Sun and surf
>
> Flash in the sky. Were it said
> Among twigs
> "And then the world went
> And then—"
>
> Only our thoughts
> Might seek it
> In further woods.

It was never easy—but there was what there was to do. It may
well be a simplification to posit ways at all, this or that. I don't know.
Who is to say who is known? Each of these three poets knows the
isolation of being alive, and of that counter will, to move to someone, to move with someone. They celebrate *family*—America's ar-
chaic institution, but America will not decide it this time. Let it be
simple as Zukofsky:

> *Lights (8)*
>
>         See:
> My nose feels better in the air.

# Edward Dorn in the News

*The Newly Fallen,* by Edward Dorn. New York: Totem Press, 1961.

The publication of Edward Dorn's *The Newly Fallen* makes at last possible a *place* to read him simply, and in that way, ought not to be missed. The 'news' is the *line,* as in the very first poem, like this:

> I know that peace is soon coming, and love of common
>     object,
> and of woman and all the natural things I groom, in my
>     mind, of
> faint rememberable patterns, the great geography of my
>     lunacy.

If "lunacy," it is gracefully apropos—and moves with the neat light-foot way of quick sense and specific commitment. He takes hold of things, common as the "red Geranium" Indian woman of this first poem, and makes no mistake—nor invites you to any, who are so often smothered with confidences that prove bullshit. Partly the book is a 'making peace,' a necessary and valuable operation, with the old places, as "oh, mother / I remember your year-long stare / across plowed flat prairielands . . ."

Place is even more absolute in "Sousa," and in the variations of "A Country Song"—as the last lines:

> Then in front of the fire
> We talk of Spring

*The Floating Bear,* no. 6, 1961.

An obscure slight offering . . .

the beauty of the thought, and *line,* throwing back upon the melody as it fades and ends here. So "If it should ever come . . ."

> And we are all there together
> time will wave as willows do
> and adios will be truly, yes . . .

Shy in love, he is accurate and final in his condemnations, hardly to be denied:

> Will Fidel feed his people before his own stomach
> is filled? Can Jack
> hold up his grimy hands and shade us
> from that vileness falling in particles . . .

The *line* is, after all, the *measure* of the man writing, his term, peculiarly, as he writes, weighing, in the silence to follow, the particular word sense, necessary to his own apprehension of the melody, the tune—that he *hears,* to write. So, of secondhand clothing sold by charity:

> Of wearing secretly a burden,
> clothes fitting as casually as though
> they were stolen,
> from the wealth
> of the nation.

It is an anger that *must* make its terms understood, and so makes them a music no man can deign (wow!) to avoid.

# Edward Dorn's *Geography*

*Geography,* by Edward Dorn. London: Fulcrum Press, 1965.

This book returns to the orders of feeling and response a kind of intelligence that has been long absent from poetry written in America and England. There have certainly been 'political' poems in abundance, but these (with specific exception of the work of Allen Ginsberg, Robert Duncan, and Charles Olson—from each of whom Edward Dorn remains singularly distinct) have largely argued a *use* of existing evils in a way that seemed too simply satisfied with the fact of such circumstance, just that it provoked the poems in question. In short, such writing tended to promulgate the very attitudes and situations it seemed most to condemn, in a convenience of 'description'—in a luxury of hate and dissatisfaction that was otherwise not to be enjoyed.

But here—much as an anger is evident—there is a ranging knowledge of literal terms, a *geography* of actual location and of the space it has been forced to accept as a kind of time measured in miles and days and persons and things of an endless debris and confusion. Movement becomes "A modern group in cars . . ."

> In the bitterness of the great desert
> they tried to get comfortable in car seats.
> Utterly left behind was
> a mixed past, of friends and a comfortable house.

*Stand* 8, no. 2, 1966.

> They felt sorry for themselves perhaps
> for no real reason, there had never
> been in their baggage more than a few stars
> and a couple of moons, you've seen their surfaces
> in pictures.
>
> ("West of Moab")

Edward Dorn speaks literally, so that the experience of these poems, both for himself and the readers of them, is neither a symbolism nor an imaginative transfer of reality into some relieving change. It is, rather, the dry, tough, drawn, harsh, *unrelieved* experience of the world as the mind and senses are permitted to disclose it, if they *will* stay unremittingly attentive to the specific qualities *and* quantities it manifests. There is the undistracted fact, then, of Mr. Dorn's belief that "the poem is an instrument of intellection / thus a condition / of the simultaneous . . ." Thus it is issue of what perception can afford in the instant of time when things are, as they are, met by nothing more than their recognition.

One might well note the relevance of this condition to much that has preceded it in America—for example, the *dryness* of Poe's intelligence and yet the sensuality of his experience; or what another poem of Mr. Dorn's from an earlier collection, *Hands Up!*, makes so evident:

> Insofar as life can be lived
> and can be *stated*, H  D  T
> did well to write about it.
> Became more than living, that hapless verb.
> Became a survey of more than a hubbub
> of the days in which axes & bread,
> ponds, window with bars out of which
> to look and be disobedient, mere tools
> of distraction. Altho I don't
> say much for the crabby writing.
> I like the clarity. Nor have much use
> for the temper, but he was alive.
> Knowing we can't be forever waiting for the appraisor.
> In america every art has to reach toward some
> clarity. That is our hope from the start.
>
> ("The Land Below")

That Thoreau gained *particularity* in writing is much to the point here—and that Edward Dorn shares with him in that particularity the fact that—

My desire is to be
a classical poet
my gods have been men . . .
and women.

("Idaho Out")

Or also:

Thus a window
is that seemingly clear opening our tested knowledges
pass through and the world shakes not at all
before the weight of our disappointments, you will
and would be part of the new hemisphere
until it dies of the same old loosely wrought manifestoes.
All those sounds from the broken washing machine
are trying to tell you something sweetheart don't laugh
one day it will speak and not stop
all things have an insistence of their own.

("Six Views from the Same Window
of the Northside Grocery")

There is so much that instructs in this book—not as an aggression
or cheap privacy, but as the intensity of such careful thought and
weighed insight at times it is heartbreaking to realize how much
the possibilities of speech mean to this man. He is possessed of a
*lovely* ear:

If the world
or a life
or all of this
love,
all the pleasures
we do not sow
and those we do
love,
sometime end . . .

("Song")

These are poems of a deeply articulate beauty, and, at moments, of
such a catch of fragmented relief—

*Daffodil Song*

The horns of yellow
        on this plain resound
        and the twist on the air
of their brilliance

>            Say where
> say where I will find
> a love
>            or an arabesque
> of such rash fortune.

# Preface to *Selected Poems,* by Edward Dorn

There are a few people always in the world to stand for—to stand *up* for, I'd wanted to say—the possibilities of being human. If you look up the word *poetry*, in a usual dictionary, you'll find it's something written by a poet. If you look up *poet,* you'll find it's someone who writes poetry. Mr. Dorn is such a poet, and his poems are so much the definition of what a poet can do, humanly, that my proposals here will be both brief and simple.

First of all, Charles Olson used to speak of Edward Dorn's *Elizabethan* care for the sound of syllables. That is, he was very respectful of this poet's ability to make every edge of the sound in words articulate. He didn't just go pounding along on the vowels, *o sole mio*, etc.; he obviously enjoyed all the specific quality of sound that one could also make sing, e.g.,

> . . . I don't
> want a rick of green wood, I told him
> I want cherry or alder or something strong
> and thin, or thick if dry, but I don't
> want the green wood, my wife would die . . .

It's not easy to make "or alder" feel so comfortable a thing to say, and you'll see, or rather, hear, how he goes on playing this sound in the next line of this first poem here, an early one indeed.

Second, Mr. Dorn has always taken himself seriously, by which I mean he thought he, like all humans, counted for something. Years

Edward Dorn, *Selected Poems,* ed. Donald Allen (Bolinas, Calif.: Greyfox Press, 1978).

ago he told me a very moving story of how, the night of the gradua-
tion dance at the high school he'd gone to in Villa Grove, Illinois,
he and his date—she was wearing the classic white prom dress—
climbed to the top of the local water tower, and looked out on the
world, literally, on the lights of the town, the flatness, the unrelieved real life that somehow still had to be hopeful. He has never
lost that care, or humor, or anger, at what the world wants at times
to do to itself. No poet has been more painfully, movingly, *political*—because he has been as all humans only one, yet one of many.
He will not yield his specific humanness to God or anyone else.

And last—recalling Ezra Pound's notion, that *only emotion endures*—the range and explicit register of Edward Dorn's ability to
*feel* how it actually is to be human, in a given place and time, is phenomenal. So many people will tell you what you're *supposed* to feel,
and what a drear bore that is. But in reading these poems, you will
hear and feel another human's life as closely and as intimately as
that will ever be possible. And that *is* the power of this art.

That said, I can now confess to how intimidating this occasion
has been for me. A "preface" for Ed Dorn's poems? Not even a sunrise could quite manage that.

*Placitas, N.M.*
*May 28, 1978*

# The New World

*Riprap,* by Gary Snyder. Ashland, Mass.: Origin Press, 1959.

*Hymns to St. Geryon and Other Poems,* by Michael McClure. San Francisco: Auerbahn Press, 1959.

*Memoirs of an Interglacial Age,* by Philip Whalen. San Francisco: Auerbahn Press, 1960.

*Watermelons,* by Ron Loewinsohn. New York: Totem Press, 1959.

We describe our time as one in which relationships, rather than the hierarchies to which these might refer, are dominant. What is meant by politics, marriage, education, religion, or love itself, becomes modalities, terms between, people, the *you* and *me* of the subjective universe. If it is not *my* hat, then possibly it is *yours;* or if not yours, *his,* or *hers*—or *theirs,* a collective enterprise, yet one (as religion or philosophy, at present) given meaning by a *possessional* insistence. The hat itself is an occasion.

It is clear that poetry will reflect this sense of emphasis, and, if the given instance be sensitive, it will succeed in forcing a passage between individual sensibility and shared commitments (to live, to endure, and the like). Poems themselves are peculiarly suited to the present environment, because they are basically relational. In this way Charles Olson defines "A poem [as] energy transferred from where the poet got it (he will have some several causations), by way

*Yugen,* no. 7, 1961.

of the poem itself to, all the way over to, the reader . . ." The poem
is not a signboard, pointing to a content ultimately to be regarded;
but is, on the contrary, a form inhabited by intelligence and feeling.
It is the way a poem speaks, not the matter, that proves its effect,
and although this is an old insistence, it is one hard at times to remember when a great variety of desperations want a solution, a
content capable of relief.

Gary Snyder's first book, *Riprap*, calls for a ground-sense of place,
a world of substantial place, even primeval. Its manner is quiet,
low-keyed like they say, with much solidity and peace—and that is a
pleasure, offered as it is by a working intelligence and care:

> No paradise, no fall,
> Only the weathering land,
> The wheeling sky,
> Man, with his Satan
> Scouring the chaos of the mind.
> Oh Hell!

So that if we cannot escape, at least we can know, as Stendhal:

> The pleasure brought by the cessation of pain consists:
> 1. In conquering all the successive obstacles that one erects for
>    one's self.
> 2. In visualizing all the advantages of which one was about to be
>    deprived.

From specific images of work-lines, farmhouses, intensities of physical life, the poem may come to:

> Thinking about a poem I'll never write.
> With gut on wood and hide, a plucking thumb,
> Grope and stutter for the words, invent a tune,
> In any tongue, this moment one time true
> Be wine or blood or rhythm drives it through—
> A leap of words to things and there it stops.

But if it does *not* stop—if there the relation shatters, or, rather,
shivers, oscillates, flips back and forth in an ecstasy of qualification.
Ah well. It is again only an old enough irresolution—"no ideas but
in things"—*things?* What are things but ideas, until we bump our
heads finally, and that's an end to it:

> Allowing such distinctions to the mind:
> A formal garden made by fire and time.

Arrived at such peace, then, all the landscape changes, and men walk quietly, enhanced by their relationships, defined by them, as women also. It is a beautiful and painstaking world which Snyder wants to live in, has by his poems made to live in—a successful relation of hope.

But the fires burn elsewhere, in other characters, and "No man can purify another."

> Evil is done by the self alone, by the self alone
> is evil left undone, by self alone is one purified.
> Purity and impurity depend on one's own self.
>
> *(Dhammapada)*

Perhaps the present attraction of the *Dhammapada*, or other Buddhist texts, is just this emphasis—that the self is a self-isolated event, yet one which must find relationships. When contact is broken, becomes the touch of the mind, then hell becomes particular, and not at all a place where bad people go, etc. When the imagination projects for itself a world more real than that which it literally experiences, this is hell, a forfeit, as Dante said, of the goods of the intellect. Because such 'goods' are relational, *joiners*, describe a method of being-with, otherwise impossible.

The self grown huge is a common aspect of the Romantic, but it might be remembered that its size is one of *sensation*, of what is felt, and is not otherwise of magnitude. The danger inherent is what Lawrence called *sensationalism*, i.e., the repetition of a known sensation is sensationalism. This is what happens when all qualification exists as a method of feeling rather than as a posited consequence of actions.

Michael McClure describes the hair-edge of feeling *qua* sensation and feeling *qua* effect:

> The poem
>
> is confusion. Love, Sex, Death, are within
> us and we give them many names. Naming only
>
> ———————————————————————
>
> the heads, when the bodies are wound, woven
>     together. Making
>
> ———————————————————————
>
> the parts of us abstractions, Knees unreal
> their qualities are vagaries

It is McClure's virtue as a poet, that he gives to his language a space, a flux in language, held by a structure of *words*—not a program of predetermined measures, either metrical or ideological. It is, in this way, as much his risk, in writing, as it is ours, in reading— to undertake a composition.

McClure, reading aloud, speaks flatly, without color, so that the words fall into relationships which they themselves, almost alone, seem to determine. In the poems capitalization is used for divers lines as a point of enlargement, a center and/or focus for the movement. Like this:

> Sleepwalkers . . . Ghosts! Voices
> like bodies coming through the mists of sleep,
>     we float about each other—
>
>     bare feet not touching the floor.
>     Talking in our lover's voice
> NAMING THE OBJECTS OF LOVE . . .

The movement of the poems makes clear an insistent disattachment, or better, a recognition of distance qualified as separation, perhaps forever. There is a vacuum all but unentered by purpose, form, consequence—wherein events relay between a shifting possibility of relation, to come to:

> I am sure of my movements I am a bulk
>     in the air.

This center of *self* (rather than 'we' or 'they') has become a mark of the new poetry, to my own mind not unreasonably since it depends on real crises in real homes. It is very hard to make one's self understood, most of all by another—sadly, truly, etc. If culture now derives from mass orientation—and it seems that it does—kitchens and bedrooms and ultimately bathrooms house, god knows, the shaken egos of our time. Poetry, beginning with the protest of the thirties (a self-centered evaluation), moving through the chaos of the forties, loss of meaning and the huge arrival of apparently nonhuman activity (the atom, then hydrogen and cobalt, bombs, and too, such devices as the blowing up of an airliner to kill a mother-in-law, i.e., the new potential seen as property of the individual, also) comes through the fifties finding a language in a common hysteria, a nervously singular presence of mind, in which feelings are dominant as they are felt, are registered as static blurring the voice of ordinary explanation, which says that everything is all right (when it is patently not all right). At times it will, as parody, take on, in grotesque approximations, the 'walk, don't run' character of current political and social jargon. Death, love, hope, and other qualities of attitude, will appear then as crudely erected statues in vacant lots, i.e., vacant states of mind aroused by a scarecrow of desire. From all this, this vacant density, appear to come many crowded voices—as if each 'I' wanted to believe it was to be, in some miraculous way, taken away from all this, and was to wake up to a warm familiar bed, in which its place was assured.

In this situation the intelligence becomes primary, is itself the contact with the real. But being so used, it is almost necessarily suspect, and so must be itself examined—as a possible last ditch of the deception suspected. *Self-Portrait, from Another Direction* is an instance of "Philip Whalen," a series of mentally approximate images of this man's activity. One day it may be, as Norbert Wiener suggests, "that one might conceivably travel by telegraph, in addition to traveling by train or airplane." States of mind seem to show relay points in the complex which, admittedly with an overweight of emphasis, we call *self*. Whalen is not engaged in vindicating, or in revealing, himself, but in thinking himself: "I think what is thinking . . ." He presents, then, all the dilemma, and all the gain, of a man wandering around in a battle area with the constant question, *what's happening:*

> Now it is here.
> Now it is falling.
> Now it is there.
>                  which we agree upon . . .
> What comes next?
>
>                 * * *
>
> Any word you see here defies all fear doubt destruction
>    ignorance & hatefulness
> All the impossibilities unfavorable chance or luck . . .

Whalen's formal invention develops as the range of his intelligence increases, not wisdom-wise but methodologically, to contain those relationships overtly, which mentality in itself seems to involve. It is hard to suggest, much more to say, where such an emphasis may lead. Yet the areas of consciousness which are related (as in Whalen's poem) by such attention are argument enough. Conditions of thought are now too volatile, too open to a variety of persuasion, not to be examined; and Whalen makes a good lighthouse.


In *The Human Use of Human Beings* (quoted previously) Norbert Wiener says also: "The individuality of the body is that of a flame rather than of a stone, of a form rather than of a bit of substance." The human entity, person or self, depends on its environment as a context for its reality. Such proves the modulation of its own reality, felt more than known or determined. What is so new about this—except that time has entered space, and place itself is insubstantial. So both poems and people rely upon an act of thought.

It is hard to live, yet by use of the resources given, and responsible consciousness, one may find a sudden reassurance—as Loewinsohn's:

> The thing made real by
> a sudden twist of the mind:
> relate the darkness to a face
> rather than
> impose a face on the darkness
> which has no face, in reality.

("The Thing Made Real")

Ron Loewinsohn knows the common institutions of marriage, working, and friends, and in that way his poems are common too. The intelligence is, however, very specific, again an instance of *self* determination and need.

> The stillness of the poem
> a moment full of silence &
> portent, like
> the sudden halt of great machines.
> Silence that becomes a fabric
> to clothe the consciousness . . .

("The Stillness of the Poem")

What do we want from it? I don't know, but think that the poem is a form, derives its nature from the language of which it is made, is "charged" by the emotion(s) of its writer. But into that then comes the great modality of the occasion, the where and when—on some time-screen with blurred and shadowy presences. A man cannot live without the use of his intelligence. There may be, now, no common union except in the attempt to survive that intelligence, the

risk of all writing or thought. Snyder, McClure, Whalen, and Loewinsohn each make their own form *qua* poem, and the world whereto
these relate comes after, or at the same time:

> . . . A small room
> without windows & only one door;
> its acoustics make even laughter dissonant.
> Every ocean, orchard, city, speech,
> sin, book & body I've ever known
> lie scattered all over the place.
>
> (Loewinsohn, "The Occasional Room")

# For Michael

Homage to Michael McClure is both pleasure and duty, in that his work has been a provocation and delight, lo! these (almost) twenty years. First meeting recalled now effortlessly, like they say. I'd crashed on the Dorns in San Francisco circa March 1956, and soon after was taken over to the McClure household, shared in commune manner with divers others, including Jim Harmon and Ronald Bladen. Intensive, physically articulate young man, level voice, eyes remarkably clear and crystalline, viz. as with diamonds a cool *light*. Already *going about his business* with undistracted singularity. At one point asks me, generously, if I'd like to go with him to Vic Tanney's (where he worked as an instructor) to *work out*—which scared me, first, that I'd have to *expose* my distraught carcass to possibly pitiless glares and, second, that I might get hurt! Ah well . . .

Fact is Michael's attention is *merciless*, in the sense nothing distracts his mind from body signals pulsing that complicated grey pulp to insights truly *in there*. Talking with him this summer about painting and all in the fifties, he made an interesting emphasis on *value* of "action as an extension of the individual," not otherwise important in itself—in short, a "meatly" *process*. Unlike contemporaries interested in cleaning up the dump, I think his persistent involvement with *meat package* context of persons is to figure the instruction and wherewithal to bring by-product mind-thought abstractions back home to initial flesh and blood. He's not ransacking biology, say, for metaphors, nor is he trying to dream a dream, etc.

*Margins,* no. 18, 1975.

He's practical, and, artist that is he, he wants it all, and so "The function of art is not pleasure or education but to make an extension—a means toward hugeness and liberation for the man, the Beast, that invents it . . ." (*Dark Brown*, 1961).

Fascinating early continuities, i.e., preoccupation with *gesture* begins, as he told me, in high school, where first concerns were natural history and anthropology, moving (with significant buddy Bruce Connor) then to Dada and Surrealist art—and then to poetry. Struck by painters of the Kootz Gallery, the Intrasubjectivists, as they were then called: Tomlin, Motherwell, Stamos, Baziotes, Gottlieb—"biomorphic"—and Toby and Graves, out of Surrealism. Motherwell particularly useful—"an intellective kinship," as he called it. Then Pollock—"so integral that his work began immersing my way of thinking in such a subtle way so early I can't tell you when . . ." "Totally bought Abstract Expressionist spiritual autobiography . . ." Still and Rothko—with whom he hoped to study at the San Francisco Art Institute, but on arrival found they'd just left, so goes to S. F. State (where daughter Jane has just this fall begun as student: "Biology/French I/Dance/Blake").

I've been fascinated by the *range* of his statement, i.e., the diversity of modes in which he gains means of language. Sitting with him in empty Fillmore Ballroom watching dress rehearsal of *The Beard* mid-sixties, just dazzled. Ask him how he *wrote* this extraordinary play—answer is he copied down words of the two people speaking in his head, conjoining to make poles positive: "Meat/Spirit." Wow. Or his novels, e.g., *The Adept*—where he defines mind-flash subjective state of *invisibility*, just like that. One time when visiting in New Mexico, he got me to read some of the *Ghost Tantras* so that I could *feel* the body resonances and not just skate on the 'meaning.' Poem on postcard he thoughtfully sent another time when my 'world' was 'demonic' beyond belief. (He and Joanna would come out for visit, we'd go down to beach where J/ would wisely go swimming— while the 'gang' packed into Gossip's Corner would be well on way to Ultimate Energy for the evening. As my own eye would begin to glitter, Mike would back off and gracefully split for the city. Just too much too minded too destructively zapped head-tripping wanted the world to narrow to a match flare.)

*For Bob*

EACH
MAMMAL
does

a
small perfect
thing
like
to be himself
or herself
and to hold a new creation
on a shining platter
as he
(or she)
steps toward
the waiting car

"Or how we got drunk & rolled down hills in San Diego or the vision of Spider Rabbit at Kent State . . ." *Dear Friend, this is only the
beginning . . .*

# Preface to *Against the Silences,* by Paul Blackburn

I'd like to speak personally of this extraordinary poet, and take that license insofar as these poems are personal, often bitterly so. I wonder if any of us have escaped the painful, self-pitying and meager defenses of person so many of them invoke. What we had hoped might be, even in inept manner worked to accomplish, has come to nothing—and whose fault is that, we ask. Certainly not mine? Having known both of these dear people, and myself, I have to feel that there will never be a human answer, never one human enough.

When Paul Blackburn died in the fall of 1971, all of his company, young and old, felt a sickening, an impact of blank, gray loss. I don't know what we hoped for, because the cancer which killed him was already irreversibly evident—and he knew it far more literally than we. But his life had finally come to a heartfelt peace, a wife and son so dear to him, that his death seemed so bitterly ironic.

Recalling now, it seems we must have first written to one another in the late forties, at the suggestion of Ezra Pound, then in St. Elizabeth's Hospital. We shared the same hopes for poetry, the same angers at what we considered its slack misuses. Paul was without question a far more accomplished craftsman than I and one day, hopefully, the evidence of his careful readings of the poems I sent him then will be common information. We finally met at his place in New York in the late spring of 1951, just prior to my moving with my family to France. He was the first poet of my generation

Paul Blackburn, *Against the Silences* (London and New York: The Permanent Press, 1981).

and commitment I was to know, and we talked non-stop, literally, for two and a half days. I remember his showing me his edition of Yeats' *Collected Poems* with his extraordinary marginal notes, tracking rhythms, patterns of sounds, in short the whole tonal construct of the writing. He had respect then for Auden, which I did not particularly share, just that he could use him also as an information of this same intensive concern. He was already well into his study of Provençal poetry, which he'd begun as a student in Wisconsin, following Pound's direction and, equally, his insistence that we were responsible for our own education.

As it happened, we shared some roots in New England, Paul having lived there for a time with his mother's relatives when young. But the Puritanism he had to suffer was far harsher than what I had known. For example, his grandmother seems to have been classically repressed (her husband, a railroad man, was away from home for long periods) and sublimated her tensions by repeated whippings of Paul. He told me of one such time, when he'd been sent to the store with the money put in his mitten, on returning he'd stopped out front and the change, a nickel, somehow slipped out into a snowdrift. And as he scrabbled with bare hands trying to find it, he realized his grandmother was watching him from behind the curtains in the front room—then beat him when he came in. Those bleak Vermont winters and world are rarely present directly in his poems, but the feelings often are, particularly in his imagination of the South and the generous permission of an unabashed sensuality. At one point during his childhood, a new relationship of his mother's took him out of all the gray bleakness to a veritable tropic isle off the coast of the Carolinas. I know that his mother, the poet Frances Frost, meant a great deal to him—and that her own painful vulnerabilities, the alcoholism, the obvious insecurities of bohemian existence in the Greenwich Village of her time, pervade the experience of his own sense of himself. His sister's resolution was to become a nun.

Paul's first marriage was finally a sad shock to me, just that I could never accept the fact of the person to whom he'd committed himself. She is the "lady he had known for years" in "The Decisions," and one hopes she did find the "new life" that cost him so much. The antagonisms felt by her and my own wife provoked an awful physical battle between Paul and me one night, when we were all living in Mallorca (he was about to spend a year in Toulouse on a Fulbright), and for some years thereafter we didn't see each other, although we had wit enough, thankfully, to keep the faith sufficient to let me publish Paul's first book of poems, *The Dissolving Fabric* (1955).

During the sixties I was able to see Paul quite frequently, although he lived in New York and I was usually a very long way away. He and his wife, Sara, were good friends to us, providing refuge for our daughter Kirsten on her passages through the big city, and much else. Sara, characteristically, was able to get publication for another close friend's writing (Fielding Dawson, *An Emotional Memoir of Franz Kline*, Pantheon, 1967) thanks to her job with its publisher. Elsewise Paul certainly did drink, did smoke those Gauloises and Picayunes, did work at exhausting editing and proofing jobs for Funk & Wagnalls, etc., etc. It's a very real life.

The honor, then, is that one live it. And tell the old-time truth. Of course there will be human sides to it, but Paul would never argue that one wins. To make such paradoxic human music of despair is what makes us human to begin with. Or so one would hope.

*Buffalo, New York*
*November 25, 1979*

# "How Is It Far If You Think It?"

*Selected Poems, 1958–1984,* by John Wieners. Edited by Raymond Foye. Foreword by Allen Ginsberg. Illustrated. 317 pp. Santa Barbara, Calif.: Black Sparrow Press, 1986.

The poetry of John Wieners has an exceptionally human beauty—as if there ever were any other. There is in it such a commonness of phrase and term, such a substantial fact of a daily life transformed by the articulateness of his feelings and the intensity of the inexorable world that is forever out there waiting for any one of us. Charles Olson spoke of it as "a poetry of affect," by which I took him to mean a poetry that is the process of a life being lived, literally, as Keats's was, or Hart Crane's, or Olson's own. In other words, the art becomes the complex act of "making real" all that one is given to live, and whatever in them may be style or fashion, the poems are so otherwise committed, so intensely a gesture of primary need and recognition, that their survival becomes the singular value, and their immense beauty.

Yet Raymond Foye, the editor of Mr. Wieners's "Selected Poems," gives apt warning to those who would try to reduce them to the life all too simply. Two interviews with Mr. Wieners, given as "appendices . . . in lieu of an introduction," are very moving in their detailing of what happened, so to speak—of relations with mother and father and peers, of homosexuality and mental hospitals. Yet the poems are neither explained nor contained by such information:

> Five hours later and
> I come into a room
> where a clock ticks.
> I find a pillow to
> muffle the sounds I make.
> I am engaged in taking away
> from God his sound.

Those lines were written by a 24-year-old man from Boston, living in a classic residential hotel, the Hotel Wentley in San Francisco, on June 15, 1958. "The Hotel Wentley Poems," published that year, is a work of consummate power, terrifying in the complex clarity with which it defines the so-called facts of life, or of love:

> And I come to this,
> knowing the waste, leaving
>
> the rest up to love
> and its twisted faces
> my hands claw out at
> only to draw back from the
> blood already running there.

Allen Ginsberg, whose perceptive foreword to the *Selected Poems* is a very useful qualification of Mr. Wieners's authority, had published *Howl* in 1956. Jack Kerouac's landmark *On the Road* came out the next year and in 1958, along with John Wieners's first book, came books by Lawrence Ferlinghetti, Michael McClure, and Gregory Corso. By 1960 primary texts by virtually every crucial poet of the period had appeared, including Frank O'Hara, Robert Duncan, Paul Blackburn, Gary Snyder, Denise Levertov, Philip Whalen and Charles Olson (whose significant call to order, "Projective Verse," was issued as a pamphlet in 1960 by LeRoi Jones's Totem Press). The change effected in the audience for poetry by Donald M. Allen's anthology, *The New American Poetry* (1960), had already taken place in the writing, and one of its most emblematic heroes (as James Dean might invest such a term, or Bob Dylan) is John Wieners, "pure poet," as Mr. Ginsberg says, "a man reduced to loneness in poetry, without worldly distractions—and a man become one with his poetry." In the brutal outrage of the late 1950s, when one could pick up a government bulletin at the post office on the home manufacture of a bomb shelter, Mr. Wieners's painful survival in words became our own: "At last. I come to the last defense." There was nothing else to shelter or protect him.

Time and again during the sixties one wondered, worried, whether he could make it. How specious such simply charitable impulse looks in retrospect. He *was* there, he *stayed* there—as Olson once said, "he's *elemental*." His writing of this time is various, often magnificent, in poems such as "Act #2," "A Poem for Trapped Things," "Strange," and in those poems—"Ode on a Common Fountain" and "For Marion" among them—that ring curious changes on Augustan patterns. But whatever one would hope so to qualify becomes unequivocally clear in "The Ages of Youth," a great poem of life's implacable realities and the will committed to suffer them:

> Give me the strength
> to bear it, to enter those places where the
> great animals are caged.

The parallel to that is "My Mother," "talking to strange men on the subway," with its wry caring, its subtle commonness:

> She says in an artificial
> voice: Oh, for Heaven's sake!
> as if heaven cared.

If poetry might be taken as a distance, some space from the action, relief from the crowd, or if its discretions, what it managed to leave out, avoid, get rid of, were its virtue, then all these poems would be in one way or another suspect. They are far closer to a purported Chinese apothegm I read years ago and continue to muse on: "How is it far if you think it?" I don't truly know. It doesn't seem to be far at all. Nor do these poems, any of them, seem ever some place else, or where they move apart from an agent, either of feeling or thinking. They're here, as we are—certainly a hopeful convention in all respects, but where else to meet?

One continues, therefore, with all the complexity evident, into the seventies, the eighties. Mr. Ginsberg summarizes: "Parallel with *State Capitol* [*Behind the State Capitol or Cincinnati Pike*, a Wieners volume published in 1975] a number of poems of complete loneliness emerge, with various definitions of poetic friendship, rejection of false fame, estimates of the condition of middle and old age occupied by solitary art. . . . Then Wieners fell into eight years of relative silence, curtly telling his friends 'Poetry is not on my calendar' and 'I am living out the logical conclusion of my books.' And these were out of print." Paradoxically he is never gone, not the poet of "With Meaning":

Rise, shining martyrs
over the multitudes
for the season of migration
between earth and heaven.

Rise shining martyrs
cut down in fire
and darkness,
speeding past light
straight through imagination's park.

Nor is the harsh clarity of "Two Years Later" ever forgotten:

The hollow eyes of shock remain
Electric sockets burnt out in the
            skull.

The beauty of men never disappears
But drives a blue car through the
            stars.

We read together years ago at the 92nd Street Y in New York, with its great velvet curtain, raised stage. John remembered hearing Auden read there and was moved that now we would. He was thrilled that one might so follow, and so we did. But now, in these times so bitterly without human presence, risk, care, response, he becomes the consummate artist of our common voice, and his battered, singular presence our own.

# III THE WRITING LIFE

# Kenneth Patchen:
## *Fables & Other Little Tales*

*Fables & Other Little Tales,* by Kenneth Patchen. Karls-
ruhe/Baden: Jonathan Williams, 1953.

Another prose book by Kenneth Patchen brings up all kinds of
memories—dull as that occupation often is. But Patchen was always unclassifiable, his earlier books were an excitement altogether
separate from what, say, Henry Miller amounted to. There was a
wild kind of *purity* to them, and a conception few would have dared
to attempt.

All this is too simple to say. The old gimmick of breathing heavily
about a man's past performance is too often an excuse for ignoring
him all the same. In Patchen's case this has been so much the fact,
that it is tantamount to insult, finally, to invoke these older things at
the expense of what he is now doing.

The new work is not a simple matter. For once, I think, it is legitimate to speak of Patchen himself, i.e., the man writing this
book, and the particular problems with which he has been damned
through no fault, certainly, of his own. Various appeals for medical
help for him have of course appeared from time to time in almost
all the magazines—though the response to them has been hardly
enough. For a long time Patchen was thought to be suffering from
a form of arthritis, until finally it was found that the cause of all the
hell he had gone through with his back came from an 'exploded'
disc, in the spinal column. An operation partially helped this—but

*Black Mountain Review,* Spring 1954.

he is far from done with it. And the same need for money, for medical expenses, continues.

What that has to do with this present book may be vague—though I doubt it. We ask a man to tell us what he knows, and what Patchen knows must be pain, constant pain, pain moving, sitting up or trying to, pain walking. Every single day of his life. It's not a question of 'excusing' the flaws, call them, of this book—or even of feeling that, after all, the man we had known, with his incredible tenderness, and gentleness, is at last a victim even of that world he believed in. He still is there, very much there. And if it is, or seems, by inversion—a care turned inside out—I hardly think this can be called the end of it.

The tone in the book is neither very 'funny' nor anything else. It seems to me almost ugly, and almost necessarily so. What else? The punning, the discontinuous sequence, etc.—he is not the first man to call attention to horror, to the horror now on us, by the use of its own methods. It is that things *don't* 'follow,' not now—that you begin saying this, you end saying that. And who knows why, in time? Perhaps that is very far from either Patchen's intention, or, better, the book's actual point, but it is a sense that comes very strongly from it.

> "Never mind that," interjected the impatient Kraken. "Those pleasant little minnows there—" indicating the orphans, who were now contentedly belting one another with planks their steaks had come on, "I know damn well that their shoes will fit me. Only thing is, I wouldn't want to hurt their feelings . . . so I guess I'll have to eat them first."

In defiance of the jacket blurb, the book is anything but "sad, beautiful gaiety." But it may well be the beginning of, and the reasons for, an attack. Toward the end of the book he writes "Every stick points two ways, and people like you and me have either got to get an easy, knowing grip on the dirty end or else let go altogether . . ."

# A Note on Canadian Poetry

The first Canadian poet was probably the Frenchman who came over with Champlain, and had intelligence a good deal beyond the ordinary in that he saw the new world even as Champlain did. Before leaving, and almost on the dock, he had written his "Farewell to France," and by that act intended a new life, one might say; at least it was his own decision. There is an account in Parkman of how Champlain came back to Port Royal (I think it was) after a miserable voyage down the Atlantic coast. Putting in for water, he had been attacked by Indians, and off Mount Desert he had almost lost his ship in the heavy seas. In any case, he came back bitter and tired out, and was utterly dumbfounded to find himself met by men in strange costumes chanting alexandrines—a true poetic homage to himself.

As Parkman has it, the Frenchman was not lazy, and if the old world could not be translated quite so literally to the new, it was an honest sense that had made the attempt. The masque was the old form, but the context was altogether a new one.

Canadian poetry might always be this attempt, not so much to fit, say, into an environment but to act in the given place. If there is no 'major' poet in Canada, if there never was one, etc., I think it is a part of this same problem. A theoretic embarrassment of 'culture,' all the tenuosities of trying to be local and international at the same time, etc., take an energy otherwise of use in the making of an idiom peculiar to the given circumstances. In this way Canadian poetry, in its earlier forms, has much in common with the Ameri-

*Contact* (Toronto), no. 8, 1953.

can poetry of Lowell, Longfellow, et al. The model is English, and it is precisely the English which is of no use whatsoever. "Like some grey warder who, with mien sedate, etc." comes too late, and too borrowed, to be helpful. It is incredible to think of the man writing it, even then, being where he must have been. The impact of the place is dulled in the overlay of the English rhythms, and the politenesses which couldn't have been actual.

The Frenchman with Champlain was, finally, a poet in a much, much deeper sense, and it was he who catalogued a good many of the plants around their camp, and also made a garden which kept them all in vegetables. There is that sense of it, of where, particularly, one is. I think that is more 'poetic vision,' call it, than any other sense could be. The Frenchman has size in his intention, and more than that, what he intends he does, i.e., the garden, and the masque in the dead of winter, completely improvised and successful.

I don't see any other way to do it. The problems of form and content, and all the other contentions of poets, are utterly intimate with each one writing, and where he is writing, and what he tries with what's around him. Canadian poetry becomes, in each instance, which man or woman it is, and what their work can effect.

# Canadian Poetry 1954

*Contact* (An International Magazine of Poetry), nos. 4–8 (1953), edited by Raymond Souster.

*Cerberus*, by Louis Dudek, Irving Layton, Raymond Souster (1952); *Twenty-four Poems*, by Louis Dudek (1952); *The Black Huntsmen*, by Irving Layton (1951); *Love the Conqueror Worm*, by Irving Layton (1953); *Canadian Poems 1850–1952* (1953). Toronto: Contact Press.

A roundup of Canadian poetry, A.D. 1954, would probably bring in little else but these. The American reader is, or may well be, familiar enough with the work of A. M. Klein, P. K. Page, and perhaps one or two others—but I think that Irving Layton, for one example, may well have escaped attention, despite the fact that he is a better poet than either of the two noted. Why this is so, like they say, is of course simple enough to guess. Local conditions, and a prevailing provincialism, have kept the Canadians wedged between England on the one hand, and the United States on the other, and it takes a somewhat trusting soul to stick his nose out.

Contact Press, however, has broken out of this usual dilemma by way of both books and a magazine, and if a reader wants to see where actual conditions for a healthy literature can be found, he might well look here. For example, *Contact* (the magazine) is nothing very much to look at, nor does it have many of those great names well calculated to keep the reader buying. But it is, in spite of itself, *international*—insofar as its tone is open, its critical sense

*Black Mountain Review*, Spring 1954.

almost sufficient, and because it prints in each issue four or five good poems, demonstrably good poems, by poets writing all the way from Freiburg to Mexico City. Not to mention Montreal.

That, in itself, is something—and with the canons of good taste, and good business, so well set in the States, one can do worse than subscribe to such a magazine—if only for the fine sense of air, and openness, it does have.

To maintain such a thing is not of course simple, either for those writing, or the editors thereof. It is a considerable scramble to get together enough material and enough money for a decent issue of any magazine, of any length, coming out four times a year. And the Canadians, in spite of ingenuousness and an almost sticky goodwill toward Literature, are by no means apt to run out and buy something by people who are not quite acceptable. Raymond Souster, in *Cerberus*, is eloquent enough.

> Turning the crank of a mimeograph
> In a basement cellar to produce the typical
> "Little magazine" perhaps fifty will read,
> Twenty remember (and with luck) five will learn from.

The delights of the literary salon, etc., are by no means what these men know:

> Engaged through the week at Usura,
> Loaning the rich the poor man's money,
> And kidding yourself it does not leave
> The marks of its uselessness upon you.

So that to say something, *anything*, in protest, has been of necessity their payment.

Back of that is the problem of how to say it, if one is writing poetry, and this is much the same headache, for Canadians, that it is for anyone else. And they have no all-pervading tone, to sneak by with, no Great Men for a shield. Dudek, in both *Cerberus* and *Twenty-four Poems*, founders, I think, on this lack of patent authority. Or else he has not yet got to his own idiom—and too much resembles, at present, a very desperate man in a very crowded store, trying on thousands of hats, coats, and gloves, in hopes to find something to fit, before the clock strikes five-thirty. On the other hand, more relaxed, he can be very graceful:

> *An Air by Sammartini*
>
> It was something you did not know
>                 had existed—by a dead Italian.

>            Neither words nor a shape of flesh
>                          but of air;
>                               whose love it celebrated
>                               and "cold passion"
>  *Amoroso Canto*, a crystal
>                          that fell from musical fingers—
>  As a cloud comes into the eye's arena,
>                          a certain new tree
>                                  where the road turns,
>                  or love, or a child, is born,
>                               or death comes:
>  Whatever is found or is done
>                          that cannot be lost or changed.

Which, in defiance, really, of the 'love,' 'death,' etc., ends with as hard and simple a statement as any man might ask for. Because 'general statement' is Dudek's *bête noire*, on other occasions, and no matter all the goodwill in the world, his preface in *Cerberus* (with its "The way to freedom and order in the future will lie through art and poetry . . .") is incredibly naive.

Layton seems to have sprung from somewhat more hardened stock. One can imagine him biting nickels, etc., at a much earlier date. His poetry is tougher, and at the same time more gentle. His idiom, to call it that, is much of the old and even 'traditional' way of it, except that he has a very sharp ear, and a hard, clear head for rhythms:

*Mrs. Fornheim, Refugee*

Very merciful was the cancer
Which first blinding you altogether
Afterwards stopped up your hearing;
At the end when Death was nearing,
Black-gloved, to gather you in
You did not demur, or fear
One you could not see or hear.

I taught you Shakespeare's tongue, not knowing
The time and manner of your going;
Certainly if with ghosts to dwell,
German would have served as well;
Voyaging lady, I wish for you
An Englishwoman to talk to,
An unruffled listener,
And green words to say to her

Layton may well be, for the historian of literature at any rate, the first Great Canadian Poet—he has his bid in at least, not that it is not, in some of these poems, too brief and too random. But Canadian, English, American, or whatever, his poetry can be very good.

And *how* good can well be judged, thanks again to Layton, together with Dudek this time, by means of an anthology of Canadian verse which they have edited—as Pound would say, "an anthology based on terrible knowledge," if one remembers how many poems both must have read in order to produce what they come up with here. It may well be that any anthology is terrifying, not just this one. I should hate to see the same job done on American verse, all put together like this, 1850–1952. And yet one can see the use—if only to settle, once and for all, that there was and is a Canadian poetry, however dark some of its 'periods' may now seem.

Some of it is by no means as bad as all that; we have written much worse. Robert W. Service is much the same pleasure:

> I dreamed I saw three demi-gods who in a cafe sat,
> And one was small and crapulous, and one was large and fat;
> And one was eaten up with vice and verminous at that.

The editors do not rate him strictly as a poet, i.e., "a roughhouse rhymester whom everybody welcomes but no one rates strictly as a poet." I would, I think. At least he is much more of a poet than, say, F. R. Scott?

> This is our gardening
> And this our hardening,
> There is no pardoning:
> We cannot be forgiven
> For what we have not striven.

Some of it may come from an idea of 'poetry' (not the act, but the noun) which is, after all, a matter almost apart from what Dr. Williams, for one, calls, the poem. Canadians, if any of these people are evidence, or if Souster has not been beating his head on stone, are writing more and more poems.

# D. H. Lawrence:
## *Studies in Classic American Literature*

It's an odd feeling now to read a book like Cooper's *Deerslayer.* There is hardly much left of that place, and I wonder how far one would have to look, in the United States, to find timber still standing in its first growth. It must have been a fantastic world. We are, of course, the heirs to it.

So Lawrence says: ". . . it seems to me that the things in Cooper that make one so savage, when one compares them with actuality, are perhaps, when one considers them as presentations of a deep subjective desire, real in their way, and almost prophetic." Beyond the prose, heavy as it now seems, a man like Natty Bumppo is familiar enough: "This is Natty, the white forerunner. A killer."

Cooper was one root, or evidence, of the 'classic' American literature which Lawrence, and few others, had eyes to see. Even a present reclamation of Hawthorne will not judge, clearly enough, that the "prettiest of all sensations [is] the sensation of UNDERSTANDING."

> *The Scarlet Letter* gives the show away.
> You have the pure-pure young parson Dimmesdale.
> You have the beautiful Puritan Hester at his feet.
> And the first thing she does is to seduce him.
> And the first thing he does is to be seduced.
> And the second thing they do is to hug their sin in secret, and gloat over it, and try to understand.
> Which is the myth of New England.
> Deerslayer refused to be seduced by Judith Hutter. At least the Sodom apple of sin didn't fetch him.

*Origin,* Summer 1954.

But Dimmesdale was seduced gloatingly. O, luscious Sin!
He was such a pure young man.
That he had to make a fool of purity.
The American psyche.

For Lawrence *The Scarlet Letter* was ". . . perhaps, the most co-
lossal satire ever penned." It is not a comfortable implication for
any of us, but there it is.

You have the pure-pure young parson Dimmesdale.
You have the beautiful Puritan Hester at his feet.

Not one of Lawrence's implications can give us very much peace,
if that, in fact, is what we are after. The "great grey poet" (and/or
Whitman) is given the roughest ride ever accorded him. And yet it
is incredibly right, all of it. The "I AM HE THAT ACHES WITH AMO-
ROUS LOVE . . ." is a bore of immense proportions—or no one ever
indulged himself so emphatically at such length. But Crane's Whitman is also seen, again clearly, without innuendo or tenuousness:
"Now Whitman was a great moralist. He was a great leader. He was
a great changer of the blood in the veins of men." That is fact.

And Franklin: "Benjamin had no concern, really, with the immortal soul. He was too busy with social man." Crèvecoeur: "NA-
TURE. I wish I could write it larger than that. N A T U R E."

Franklin is the real practical prototype of the American. Crèvecoeur
is the emotional. To the European, the American is first and foremost
a dollar fiend. We tend to forget the emotional heritage of Hector St.
John de Crèvecoeur. We tend to disbelieve, for example, in Woodrow
Wilson's wrung heart and wet hanky. Yet surely these are real enough.
Aren't they?

At a time when so much 'revaluation' and 'revisiting' are the
practice, Lawrence can serve the very actual function of showing
how it might be done. We have valued, foolishly, the perspective of
time alone. And lost the very thing we claim to have gained, namely,
understanding of *any* of these men Lawrence cites for a classic
American literature. For one example, Melville. God knows there
has been enough talk around and about him to satisfy any of his
admirers. But—how many come up with such a simple statement
as this: "Melville knew. He knew his race was doomed. His white
soul, doomed. His great white epoch, doomed. Himself, doomed.
The idealist, doomed. The spirit, doomed."

To have a literature Lawrence adjudged it necessary to have a soul. And so we have laughed at him—how funny. How funny is it now?

"The old American literature. Franklin, Cooper, Hawthorne & Co.? All that mass of words! all so unreal!" cries the live American.

Heaven knows what we mean by reality.

# Witter Bynner: *Journey with Genius*

*Journey with Genius*, by Witter Bynner. New York: J. Day
& Co., 1951.

Witter Bynner comes late to that distinguished group who *knew*
D. H. Lawrence as opposed to those who have read him. His book
is based on a slighter acquaintance than that, say, of Aldington, but
the thirty-odd years which have since passed allow him considerable cud. And he was also the 'American' in the beginning of *The
Plumed Serpent*—which probably seemed motive enough.

Perhaps it is time, in any case, to say to hell with all such as Witter
Bynner, and to grant him, certainly, his friendship but also to insist
it was apparently misused. At least the account of it makes very dull
reading now.

As it is, we have another champion of Frieda—and why, always,
do these men go so female in their causes? Aldington wailed of
ragged undies, and the beast who let his wife go so clothed. Bynner
proclaims a conspiracy, to wit, his sage advice that she fight back
and the almost nauseous insistence that she then did, all because
*he* said to.

It is in this character that Bynner becomes precisely the has-
been, the would-be, in short, the fake which a good many good-
tempered men must have been putting up with for years. I recently
read a review of his on the biographers of Willa Cather (also a
'friend'), and that was more amiable. But nonetheless Bynner is still
one who *knew* others, and it is a dreary, dreary occupation.

*Black Mountain Review*, Summer 1954.

The loss here is that the bulk of the comment on Lawrence is always this personalism and/or the attempt so much more ragged than any underwear, to hang on to a man who had all this complexity of effect. And who was, it seems, not very simple to forget.

But all such statement is a bore. It gives us at best, as Bynner does, a kind of lover's album of a few faded flowers—because both Aldington and Bynner did aspire, as did Murray, Carswell, 'E. T.' even, who was I think the most justified. But there it is, books about a man as opposed to those books he himself wrote. Or much more important, an actual levy on what Lawrence himself was after— simply things like his pick-up on Frobenius, on American writing, on the political set of Europe, and so forth.

And that *is* what matters. In England he is still for the most part sunk in the old social fix. By which I mean, people still worry that he was a miner's son. But that is only counterpart to Bynner's remarkable insight, viz., that he spoke like 'all' British men-of-letters, with a 'high' voice, etc. Or that he took his wife swimming at the far end of the beach, because he was embarrassed by his own body. Or that he got angry, unreasonably angry, and had little boys put in jail.

No matter the middle chapters—with their ridiculous headings—this is what Bynner is talking about. And this is the extent of his contribution. He wants, I think, to posit a "while I was doing this, Lawrence was doing that," and that of course is the end of him. There is no equivalence between them, either as men, as poets, or as anything else. And this is clear, very clear, from what each has written—the *work*. It is much too late now for Bynner to work, to do what another man was doing all the time.

# Louis-Ferdinand Céline:
# *Guignol's Band* & John Hawkes:
# *The Goose on the Grave*

*Guignol's Band*, by Louis-Ferdinand Céline. Translated by Bernard Frechtman and Jack T. Nile. New York: New Directions, 1954.

*The Goose on the Grave*, by John Hawkes. New York: New Directions, 1954.

Guignol's Band lies so vulnerable to attack, like they say, that only a man with a penchant for beating carpets can really take much pleasure in working it over. But it can serve as occasion for several comments, among them, (1) that following the war a number of American 'violence' novels were published in French translation, and (2) that the reason for this was due, at least partially, to the fact that French writing had at that time no 'vocabulary' for that character of apparently gratuitous violence which they had just experienced.

So there is something strangely an insult in the publication of this particular novel in America, i.e., it is much too much like sending out some drugstore cowboy to help with the branding and all that. Because Céline is very much the dude, spit and froth as he will. And the basis of his novel, an implied attack on the conditions that make for a man like this "young French veteran now turned spiv" and his milieu, is both too late (the first World War) and too general in outline (these are types, not people). More than that, the novel's manner stays very static: "I got to know Clodo well later on. It's true that he was obliging, eager, you might say even zealous, only he'd falter for a moment, he was vague with words, had to tell him right away what you wanted, to put it on the line . . . had to know how to handle him . . ." I don't think Céline has considered the necessary mess involved in writing a novel in which it is impossible to give a damn about *any* of the characters. If this is the point (and/or Life's Forgotten Men, etc.), then he makes his statement of it the weakest yet on record. Which is a considerable come-down for the author of *Journey to the End of the Night*.

John Hawkes' *The Goose on the Grave* gives us a little of the same dilemma, backwards, since the title novel (one of two) proves he can cut the Italians, at least as we have had them in English translation. Hence the Italian campo, given Hawkes, becomes:

> The eyes were upon the body in the clay beyond them. Only Adeppi glanced up to see the crow flying. The silent figure turned in the white mud. Dragging itself, slowly animated, hardly visible, bones of the fingers resting upon the rot of the helmet filled with mud, its bare head lifted and was unable to catch breath in the rain.

Hawkes has a genius for the singularly unpleasant, and his use of it seems sometimes too simple, by which I mean, to no evident purpose but that of being unpleasant, etc. But it would be a literal distortion to put him off with that. Whereas Céline's fantasy has gone old-maidish, Hawkes' world rides in with a deep and careful terror, best used and best seen, I think, in the first of the two novels, *The Owl*. Admittedly, it is a dream-structure, a *place* which is more real, as one says, in its capacity to suggest than in the literal elements of which it is composed. And the hangman is the Hangman, Il Gufo, the Owl. People fade, eyes divorce from faces, peering out, a field tilts, men whisper. There are great heights, and wind.

> The prisoner, delivered into altitude where there was time and silence to devour him, was the hangman's. The fortress which kept him safe was cleft in two parts on the pinnacle of the city, high tower and low tower, and from either battlement there was an iron-edged view of the world, its cliff, the tilted slopes at the bottom, the sunrise and sunset, and, not so far off, the border itself of a definite black and white. To the east it was possible to find a thin white horizon, the sea. If any in Sasso Fetore saw out there a Venetian sail, they pretended it was a dream.

Disaster has only to declare its form; its premises, barrenness, despair, have already been accomplished. In that way the novel is an 'allegory,' and much of Hawkes' writing, even most of it, has been that. In this book, authority in its absolute form, the Hangman, moves with an inexorable rigidity—like those movie shots of locusts covering a field. Except that this is one man, rather one face, two hands, one mind, etc. The town, the women, the men, the Prisoner—actually they take the forms of characters, virtues and vices (though hardly that unshaded) which are met in the old morality plays. But Hawkes puts these things against the final character of a landscape, his own mind, I think, in point of the moods it takes on.

# "By God, Pomeroy, you here!"

## A Note on Francis Parkman

The problem of 'history' is a peculiar one for the American, involving as it does, "where do we come from," or better, how shall we come from where we came. It is just that apparently nonsensical statement of the dilemma which may relieve it. And there are other clues, if you will, like: skyscrapers could not have been built if it weren't for the Indians, since they are the only men in America having the nerve-set for balance at such heights. Too, what would the United States be like, if it had a king? To relieve the President for actually administrative duties, as opposed to egg-rolling, etc.

It all relates, like it or not, to a backdoor which stays shut for us, faced as we are with no past which we will recognize but that of Europe. This we will not accept, and turn in upon ourselves, to be 'better'—which is a horror, in its effects, a kind of restless continual battle to override the English, or the French, or whoever it may be we choose for the moment as our predecessors.

Parkman, Edward Dahlberg has said, had the mind of a twelve-year-old child; and *The Oregon Trail*, for him, reads like any Rover Boys story. We are so grown-up, it seems, that stories have lost all point, and in our maturity, anecdote, that which stays in the mouth and heart—however 'romantically'—is a trivial way of passing time, of killing it. Dahlberg himself is by no means so quick about these things, and has used such material with sometimes admirable ingenuity. He is as concerned as anyone to find a place to live in. In any case, it comes to, where can we begin, and Parkman, I think, is our only 'historian' in the deep tradition of the spoken.

*Black Mountain Review*, Winter 1954.

But all that can stay beside the point for the moment. Francis Parkman's *Works* (in twelve volumes) are as follows: *Pioneers of France in the New World, The Jesuits in North America, La Salle and the Discovery of the Great West, The Old Regime in Canada, Count Frontenac and New France under Louis XIV, A Half Century of Conflict, Montcalm and Wolfe, The Conspiracy of Pontiac and the Indian War after the Conquest of Canada,* and *The Oregon Trail.* The first book in the series has this for a dedication:

> To The Memory
> Of
> THEODORE PARKMAN, ROBERT GOULD SHAW, And HENRY
> WARE HALL
> Slain In Battle
> This Volume Is Dedicated By Their Kinsman
> The Author

You may take that as the *tone,* the ground-sense, of all Parkman's writings, not in point of the 'battle' so much as the 'kin.' Parkman was a New Englander, he wrote roughly between the dates 1847–1892, and in his Preface to *A Half Century of Conflict* he says:

> This book . . . fills the gap between Part V., "Count Frontenac," and Part VII., "Montcalm and Wolfe": so that the series now forms a continuous history of the efforts of France to occupy and control this continent . . . The collection was begun forty-five years ago, and its formation has been exceedingly slow, having been retarded by difficulties which seemed insurmountable,* and for years were so in fact.

The last complete edition of the books was published in 1898–1899, by Macmillan & Company, and since that time *The Oregon Trail* has been the only one to remain in print.

Parkman's idea as to how to write 'history' is happily simple, and is most concerned, I think, with getting it straight. This comes itself, if you will, from a tradition wherein a man can simply look you

---

*The difficulties in question were poor health and, particularly, bad eyesight. In the introduction to *Pioneers of France in the New World* he mentions these difficulties more explicitly: "During the past eighteen years, the state of his [the author's] health has exacted throughout an extreme caution in regard to mental application, reducing it at best within narrow and precarious limits, and often precluding it. Indeed, for two periods, each of several years, any attempt at bookish occupation would have been merely suicidal. A condition of sight arising from kindred sources has also retarded the work, since it has never permitted reading or writing continuously for much more than five minutes, and often has not permitted them at all." (January 1, 1865.)

in the eye and say, I don't think so. People from Maine are apt to be good liars, but that is almost from an excess of virtue and a cold climate. But from the beginning Massachusetts and those outlying places of a like nature took such responsibilities as 'history' with a very great seriousness, and Parkman comes, very much, from there.

His materials were not to his liking in many instances. For example, only La Salle could have distrusted Jesuits more than he does. But he is honest with, at times, wit, and always with a determined patience. He is quick to judge how deeply the Jesuit character held to its own determination, and how much these men were not only prepared to suffer, but did. "France aimed to subdue, not by the sword, but by the cross; not to overwhelm and crush the nations she invaded, but to convert, civilize, and embrace them among her children."

> . . . Who can define the Jesuits? The story of their missions is marvellous as a tale of chivalry, or legends of the lives of the saints. For many years, it was the history of New France and of the wild communities of her desert empire.

To the north, then, Jesuits, a rank breed of 'gentleman,' and a race of fur-traders, the *coureurs de bois*—of which last Parkman writes:

> . . . At least, he is picturesque, and with his red-skin companion serves to animate forest scenery. Perhaps he could sometimes feel, without knowing that he felt them, the charms of the savage nature that had adopted him.

Then follows a description of these 'haunts'—"deep recesses where, veiled in foliage, some wild shy rivulet steals with timid music . . ." Typical of Parkman is the footnote he adds to this, in justifiable irritation:

> An adverse French critic gives his opinion that the sketch of the primeval wilderness on the preceding page is drawn from fancy, and not from observation. It is, however, copied in every particular, without exception, from a virgin forest in a deep moist valley by the upper waters of the little river Pemigewasset in northern New Hampshire, where I spent a summer afternoon a few days before the passage was written.

It is, of course, impossible to outline all of the work in question, but think of it as, first, the *place*. Spanish to the South (Ponce de León, Pánphilo de Narváez, Hernando de Soto), to the North the French (Cartier, Pontgravé, Champlain)—and then, of course,

New England. There is nothing really more to it than that, except 'history,' what then followed. And like it or not, it was hardly a process of much clarity, certainly not to those whose fortunes (much more than their lives) were the issue. As far as I know, Parkman is the first American historian (and perhaps the last?) to pay such careful attention to the *ground*. For example:

> It has been a matter of debate on which side of the Niagara the first vessel on the Upper Lakes was built [the *Griffin*, which La Salle and his followers built in the spring of 1679]. A close study of Hennepin and a careful examination of the localities, have convinced me that the spot was that indicated above [Cayuga Creek, which enters the Niagara "two leagues above the cataract"]. Hennepin repeatedly alludes to a large detached rock, rising out of the water at the foot of the rapids above Lewiston, on the west side of the river. This rock may be seen immediately under the western end of the Lewiston suspension-bridge, etc., etc.

However irrelevant this may seem, it is by a like care that all 'history' is written, and from a like 'place.' To analyze comes, finally, to a presumption that no man careful of his materials cares to show. It is simple to talk about something, as if it were a convenience for the mind—whereas the mind is 'history' long before it knows that this particular problem exists.

Be that as it may, Parkman is careful to leave 'history' in the two places where it can endure; and one is, I think, in its own 'present,' i.e., where the rock has since washed away, where the foundations of the fort still show, and the other, in the letters, sayings, stories, and so on, that maintain 'history' much more actually than the supposed 'records' and commentaries.

Though his most complete success is La Salle—by which I mean, the fact of this man, given plainly, and with care—for myself, it is also in the countless anecdotes and (finally) flavors of a place I of course am too 'old' to know as he must have, because *The Oregon Trail* was written from a journal no man can ever keep again. For me, he returns 'history' to the only place which it has, in an actual continuity—hardly ours because we are its issue, but because we can perhaps recognize that we are. (At this point, surely, all the worry about 'europeanism' and so forth must become beside the point.) He stays at that one sure root, anecdote. "So they say." Men, if you will, are raised from the dead by just this:

> On board one of the transports was Seth Pomeroy, gunsmith at Northampton, and now major of Williard's Massachusetts regiment. He had

a turn for soldiering, and fought, ten years later, in the battle of Lake George. Again, twenty years later still, when Northampton was astir with rumors of war from Boston, he borrowed a neighbour's horse, rode a hundred miles, reached Cambridge on the morning of the battle of Bunker Hill, left his borrowed horse out of the way of harm, walked over Charlestown Neck, then swept by the fire of the ships-of-war, and reached the scene of action as the British were forming for the attack. When Israel Putnam, his comrade in the last war, saw from the rebel breastwork the old man striding, gun in hand, up the hill, he shouted, "By God, Pomeroy, you here! A cannon-shot would waken you out of your grave!"

Parkman continues:

But Pomeroy, with other landsmen, crowded in the small and malodorous fishing-vessels that were made to serve as transports, was now in the gripe of the most unheroic of maladies. "A terrible northeast storm" had fallen upon them, and, he says, "we lay rolling in the seas, with our sails furled, among prodigious waves." "Sick, day and night," writes the miserable gunsmith, "so bad that I have not words to set it forth."

It is never a question of 'making it real,' but rather of allowing it, whatever it is, to *stay* real. Perhaps this is simply a matter of wit, of necessity—but this character, of telling 'history,' has the proper quality of effacing even the man who records it, until it becomes all 'story,' and so, all true. It's hard to take any of it out of its place—because there are no morals to be conveyed, unless the whole substance which contains them is also to be recognized. When Parkman separates, becomes the nineteenth-century Democrat, then he is also 'history'—also a good story. But, at his best, he leaves it as it was, and so is:

Among the numerous war-parties which were now ravaging the borders, none was more destructive than a band, about sixty in number, which ascended the Kanawha, and pursued its desolating course among the settlements about the sources of that river. They passed valley after valley, sometimes attacking the inhabitants by surprise, and sometimes murdering them under the mask of friendship, until they came to the little settlement of Greenbriar, where nearly a hundred of the people were assembled at the fortified house of Archibald Glendenning. Seeing two or three of the Indians approach, whom they recognized as former acquaintances, they suffered them to enter without distrust; but the new-comers were soon joined by others, until the entire party were gathered in and around the buildings. Some suspicion was now awakened; and, in order to propitiate the dangerous guests, they were presented with the carcass of an elk lately brought in by the hunters. They immediately cut it up, and began to feast upon it. The backwoodsmen, with their families, were assembled in one large room; and finding themselves mingled among the Indians, and embarrassed by the presence of the women and children, they remained indecisive and irresolute. Meanwhile, an old woman who sat in a corner of the room, and who had lately received some slight accidental injury, asked one of the warriors if he could cure the wound. He replied that he thought he could, and, to make good his words, killed her with his tomahawk. This was the signal for a scene of general butchery. A few persons made their escape; the rest were killed or captured.

Parkman believed himself to be engaged in something, perhaps, more notable; in one of his prefaces (*Pioneers of France in the New World*), he says, "The springs of American civilization, unlike those of the older world, lie revealed in the clear light of History." That was a very hopeful surmise. But Archibald Glendenning's wife escaped—having first been captured "with her infant child" and forced to march, "guarded before and behind by the Indians."

As they defiled along a narrow path which led through a gap in the mountains, she handed the child to the woman behind her, and, leaving it to its fate, slipped into the bushes and escaped. Being well acquainted with the woods, she succeeded, before nightfall, in reaching the spot where the ruins of her dwelling had not ceased to burn. Here she sought out the body of her husband and covered it with fence-rails, to protect it from the wolves. When her task was complete, and when night closed around her, the bold spirit which had hitherto borne her up suddenly gave way. The recollection of the horrors she had witnessed, the presence of the dead, the darkness, the solitude, and the gloom of the surrounding forest, wrought upon her till her terror rose to an ecstasy; and she remained until daybreak, crouched among the bushes, haunted by the threatening apparition of an armed man, who, to her heated imagination, seemed constantly approaching to murder her.

# Waiting for Godot

*Waiting for Godot,* by Samuel Beckett. New York: Grove
Press, 1954.

Waiting for anyone is a usual problem these days, particularly
in America. It is, for one example, the army's, "Hurry up and
wait." Or when will you be through with the bathroom. Or when—
anything.

But to deal with this, as one says, in a play is not at all simple.
Granted the obvious difficulty of having nothing happen, in fact of
having nothing happen what happens—how not to release the audience just by that, i.e., how far can one go with this? A friend tells
me of a problem she had been given as a dancer, wherein she was
to effect movements which would, in turn, effect an intolerable
boredom. First the audience would shift a bit, then writhe more
openly, until, at last, something would snap. And that would be the
point.

It's point enough, frankly. As it is, we live on the edge of it all too
often, and one can say that Beckett is aware of this—of a deep,
deep pointlessness, which maims people far more than they are
willing to acknowledge. Certainly far more than they are able to repair. His play, then, is an abstraction of this awareness. Two men,
indiscriminate, waiting for a third, who will prove something not
only for them, but equally of them. It will effect something. Otherwise they have been there for they are by no means sure how long.
Other things happen—activity of a kind—but what does this mean?

*Black Mountain Review,* Winter 1954.

VLADIMIR:    We can still part, if you think it would be better.
ESTRAGON:   It's not worth while now.
                         *Silence*
VLADIMIR:    No, it's not worth while now.
                         *Silence*
ESTRAGON:   Well, shall we go?
VLADIMIR:    Yes, let's go.
                    *They do not move.*
                         *Curtain*

There are three other 'characters' in the play (Lucky, a liberal slave; Pozzo, the landowner who 'owns' him; and A Boy, the absent Godot's perpetual messenger), but they are frosting of a kind. And literally enough, the play is that which I have just quoted. Some parts are better than other parts but they are all the same thing. It is a play of 'the same thing,' taken as far as Beckett has thought practicable.

It's here, in this question of practicability, that one can, I think, argue at least the obvious difficulties. One is, for example, how effect variations upon this *monotony*, which will appear to relieve it, but which will, in fact, only contribute to it. It is the particular tightrope on which the play must balance. To let this monotony slack— that's no good; but without some relief, the man watching (remembering that he has both chosen and paid to watch) shudders and leaves. So Beckett chooses to make it a 'ballet' of sorts, by which I mean, a very formal and mannered interplay.

ESTRAGON:   A relaxation.
VLADIMIR:    A recreation.
ESTRAGON:   A relaxation.
VLADIMIR:    Try.
ESTRAGON:   You'll help me?
VLADIMIR:    I will of course.
ESTRAGON:   We don't manage too badly, eh Didi, between the
                    two of us?
VLADIMIR:    Yes, yes. Come on, we'll try the left first.
ESTRAGON:   We always find something, eh Didi, to give us the
                    impression we exist?

But it stays a *spectacle*—and that in itself is too much a relief from it. I think Beckett has, finally, solved the dilemma elsewhere, i.e., in a story called "The End" (printed in *Merlin,* Vol. II, No. 3). The hero of this is an old man from anywhere one cares to think of, for himself. Let out of a hospital, sanatorium, or whatever, he begins to stagger. "I am greatly obliged to you for these clothes, I said, and for this money, is there a law which prevents you from throwing me out naked and penniless?" He turns to begging.

There are those to be sure, who stoop, but generally speaking, people who give alms much prefer to do so without having to stoop. What they prefer above all is to espy the wretch from afar, get ready their penny, drop it in their stride, with an innocent air, and hear the God bless you dying in the distance. Personally, I never said that, nor anything like it, but I did make a noise with my mouth. So I got a kind of board, and tied it to my neck and waist. It jutted out just at the right height, pocket height, and its edge was far enough from my person for the mite to be bestowed without fear of contagion.

One day I was present at a strange scene. Normally I did not see much. I did not hear much either. But on this particular day the intrusion was too marked. For some time I had thought I heard an unwonted sound. I did not investigate the cause. For I said to myself, It's going to stop. But as it did not stop I had no choice but to find out the cause, and so be rid of it. Its cause was a man perched on the roof of a car, haranguing the passers-by, of whom many stopped, the better to see and hear. That at least was the way I looked at it. He was bellowing so loud that snatches of his oration reached my ears: injustice . . . union . . . brothers . . . Marx . . . capital . . . bread . . . love . . . right to live. It was all Greek to me. The car was drawn up against the curb, just in front of me, and I saw the orator, from behind. All of a sudden he turned around towards me, as to a specimen. Look at this down and out, he vociferated, this leftover. If he doesn't go down on four paws, it's for fear of being impounded. Old, lousy, rotten, in the garbage heap. And there are a thousand like him, worse than him, ten thousand, twenty thousand. A voice. Thirty thousand. In your plutocratic Sodom, resumed the orator, every day of your life you pass them by, and when you have won at the races you fling them a farthing. Do you ever think? The voice, No. No, indeed, resumed the orator, you find that normal, the way of the world. A penny, tuppence. The voice. Thruppence. It never enters your head, resumed the orator, that your charity is a crime, that you are subscribing to enslavement, stultification and organized murder. Take a good look at this living corpse. You may tell me it's his own fault. The voice, After you. Then he bent down towards me and flung me a phrase I did not understand. I had perfected my board. It now consisted of two boards hinged together, which enabled me, when my work was done, to fold it and carry it under my arm. So I took off the rag, as I always did when my work was done, pocketed the few coins remaining on the board, untied the board, folded it and put it under my arm. Do you hear me, you crucified bastard! the orator cried. Then I went away, although it was still light . . .

# Ramón Sender: Two Novels

*The Sphere*, by Ramón Sender. Translated by F. Giova-
nelli. New York: Hellman, Williams, 1949.

*The Affable Hangman*, by Ramón Sender. Translated by
Florence Hall. London: Cape, 1954.

There are many questions on which any piece of writing can take
off—not glibly, or one hopes not, but because these 'questions' stay
the one 'given,' in a context otherwise constantly in process of re-
formation. So—what does one believe in? Is the real real because
one admits it? Tastes it. Feels it. Knows it? Or because it is?

> We are ringed with filters attenuating all the impressions pouring in
> on us from outside . . . Those filters which are acting through all the
> forms of our sensibility constantly guard us against attack by light,
> sound forms. But the best of these filters is the mind. We have minds
> not primarily to understand but rather not to understand too much.
> What horrible or transcendent truths repair to our understanding
> and remain outside? Against what terrible revelations or evidence
> does our mind protect us?

This is quoted from the first of a series of 'mottos,' placed at the
beginning of each chapter, which form an anterior 'novel' to the
one otherwise occurring. The writing, or rather what the writing
resolves as, is a continuing displacement of a man already beyond
the character of a 'natural' reality in that (1) it is a question as to

*Black Mountain Review*, Summer 1955.

whether or not he is dead, yet he has not found death, so he is not; and (2) the book is placed on a boat, i.e., it is the geography of no geography but that which human disposition can arrive at.

More aptly, it is the journey to death, to a death realized, which is impossible—but which is *necessary,* when all calls to life have become so rotted, and ambiguous, that nothing remains outside the mind, not enough. Or, as Lawrence says it:

> Oh build your ship of death, oh build it!
> for you will need it.
> For the voyage of oblivion awaits you.

Sender says: "I am closer to my death than yesterday . . ." The progression of the novel is through circumstances, trails perhaps, or again and again questions—of the body: "And Saila came back to his mental constructions: 'I've told myself time and again that love is a "reintegration" and that it is both necessary and impossible . . .'" Of the mind: "There is a perfection upon which we all rest when we wish: reality." Of that complex, belief: "Faith was born before miracle."

And all of this comment decries, despairs, and distorts—what is being said, by this book. The form it takes, the 'mottos' juxtaposed against the 'action' and/or the literal events which form its sequence, are, also, the 'how it is, as it is,' which the mind, damned (is it), feels itself so obliged to repair to. To repair, to in fact be, also, present to—as 'it' happens. So in this instance Sender records in one man, Saila, this complex, this man with his hands, on the woman, yet un-on, or un-relieved. For example:

> With her look she asked him: "Still? In the situation we are in? What for?" But Saila said to himself: "When every road has been blocked to us there remains the absurd feminine, the great chaos over which we can place our hand in order to feel the infinite accessible."

For the moment—there is no injustice, I hope, in *using* this novel as a means to suggest the world, the literal time, which encompasses it, and also, which it hopes to encompass. A wise man asks only questions. Because the answers to them, granted they have in fact been asked, lie in the man to whom they are asked. Sender is unlike, or rather differs from, most writers of so-called 'fiction' in that he is not so eager to persuade as to demonstrate (first to himself) the complexity of the *idea* of the world which he has been brought, of necessity, to consider—whether or not that 'world' is

in fact of a real kind, or, more literally, is the real world. We know—
as we say in that now familiar tone of reassurance—that a world
does exist, beyond our minds; yet we do not.

> The person, child of experience—the return of reflection upon ac-
> tion—holds to a lineal or superficial idea of everything. It is born,
> grows and develops with that primitive tumour of the ganglia we call
> the brain.

* * *

> And what is spirit? Is it flight? I sense that force which impels every-
> thing to disintegration, reflecting perhaps the very centrifugal impul-
> sion of the planet. Gravity prevents or conditions our disintegration.
> The feeling of escape which disintegration communicates to every-
> thing we ourselves find in the tendency of our spirit first to self-
> sufficiency, and then to departure and detachment from self. This
> possibility of separation from, and even action against, the very self
> we recognize as a 'need to flee.' But at the very moment this need
> seems most imperious, a curious thing happens. That is, we return
> to the ganglia, and instead of fleeing, strengthen the unity of being;
> a reciprocal movement—it might be said—between the notion of es-
> sential being and the feeling of elemental being.

This is a resolution—a 'melting,' a 'separating into parts.' Yet—
"Miriflor looked at him confused: 'You, you Spaniards . . .' he said,
unable to finish."

## 2

The world of Sender's most recent novel, *The Affable Hangman*, is
one assembled, stumbled upon—as a man will stumble—again of
necessity. We cannot call Ramiro "the affable hangman" until we
have also stumbled, willynilly, into or upon, that thread of *occasional* purpose by which a man directs himself, given eyes and
mouth, hands and legs, and a mind, and also a heart. Diotima tells
Socrates, in Plato's *Symposium*, that:

> On the day that Aphrodite was born the gods were feasting, among
> them Contrivance, the son of Invention; and after dinner, seeing that
> a party was in progress, Poverty came to beg and stood at the door.
> Now Contrivance was drunk with nectar—wine, I may say, had not
> yet been discovered—and went out into the garden of Zeus, and was
> overcome by sleep. So Poverty, thinking to alleviate her wretched con-
> dition by bearing a child to Contrivance, lay with him and conceived

Love. Since Love was begotten on Aphrodite's birthday, and since he has also an innate passion for the beautiful, and so for the beauty of Aphrodite herself, he became her follower and servant. Again, having Contrivance for his father and Poverty for his mother, he bears the following character. He is always poor, and, far from being sensitive and beautiful, as most people imagine, he is hard and weather-beaten, shoeless and homeless, always sleeping out for want of a bed, on the ground, on doorsteps, and in the street. So far he takes after his mother and lives in want. But, being also his father's son, he schemes to get for himself whatever is beautiful and good; he is bold and forward and strenuous, always devising tricks like a cunning huntsman; he yearns after knowledge and is full of resource and is a lover of wisdom all his life, a skilful magician, an alchemist, a true sophist. He is neither mortal nor immortal; but on one and the same day he will live and flourish (when things go well for him), and also meet his death; and then come to life again through the vigour that he inherits from his father. What he wins he always loses, and is neither rich nor poor, neither wise nor ignorant.

An account of Love is, loosely enough, what later commentators have called the 'picaresque novel,' i.e., a story of a man who travels much, who becomes involved in untoward events for singular reasons, and who 'distills' (as the book jacket in the case of Sender's novel puts it) an 'idiosyncratic' philosophy.

Yet Ramiro is a hangman: "He felt real gratitude toward me [the story's narrator] because I had offered him my hand, knowing that he was a hangman . . ."; and Love would do no less.

But why does a man become a hangman—these days? Or, better, how is it that a man—in whom love moves, or else he is not—arrives at that 'authority' which allows, as Ramiro's instructor does: "It is not that one is ashamed of one's work. Someone has to do it, and nowadays they don't mistreat the *pobreto*—poor wretch—as before, but dispatch him neatly and rapidly . . ." And is not this, also, a rather *familiar* 'man's world'?

Faced with a loyalty to this or that idea, he finds himself on either 'side,' on the one hand witness of the killing of men and women with whom he has sided, and, later, on the side of those who have killed them, at another like incident, where men are forced to jump into a well and then sticks of dynamite are thrown in after them.

On the way back Ramiro was thinking: "This is more cruel than what they did to Chino and Curro Cruz and the peasants of Benalup. And the Duke, the priests of my town, the mayor, the judges know it or take it for granted. Everyone knows it and no one does anything

about it." They returned in silence. It suddenly occurred to Ramiro
that it had been a good thing for him to make himself responsible for
all that. To accept the responsibility that everyone shunned. With his
presence he was already responsible. He wanted to be even more so.
The word responsibility rang out inside him in an urgent way and
with tremendous force. It was an obsession.

Sender's method, in this book, is a constantly shifting character
of 'reality,' i.e., of fable, of naturalistic detail—of the supposed
'real' put against the hyper- or also-real. And in the narrative occur
other 'stories,' for example, of Lucia, who is in love with her sister's
husband, whom she denounces, whereupon he is killed. Ramiro
thinks:

> "I would like to make myself responsible for all the crimes in the
> world," he muttered to himself. "But how?" Then he remembered
> Lucia naked amidst the snow and he found her appealing. He liked
> not only her body but the disorder of her mind. He really believed
> that she had denounced Joaquina's husband and yet he regarded her
> as innocent. "She got into the game," he said to himself, "and had to
> do what she did, and now she is paying for it."

When Ramiro was a little boy, his mother "told tales that made
[him] cry with pain, and then she would tell everybody how tender-
hearted [he] was . . ." What is the man who will witness, and thereby
'do' what all others imply, but will not do—as, for example, we all
know that this or that has to be done, yet wait for someone to do it.
Is that why we have armies, etc. At the close of the book Ramiro
and the narrator are sitting in a cafe, talking. Noise is heard, outside. A fiesta of some kind seems to be starting.

> "But why all this?" I [the narrator] repeated, sensing an immense
> scandal in it all.
> "I don't know. In any case it concerns me alone. Don't you worry, it's
> only because of me. It apparently has nothing to do with you."
> He was more afraid than I. He looked at the cars lined up, at the
> patient crowd, and said very nervously:
> "There is no doubt about it. It is the end. This is the end. Or the
> beginning. Who knows?"

People are all around the cafe, the building; the two men are 'pris-
oners,' and then going out, Ramiro asks "questions to the right and
left of him, but no one seemed to give a satisfactory answer."

> The procession was formed. The bands continued playing. Ramiro
> started marching under the canopy . . .

So that is the end of it. Thinking of the first book, *The Sphere*—why will we not believe, or try to, until the mind itself *is* broken, breaks back, forcing the world to declare itself. Finally? Or at least 'occasionally.' And of the second, *The Affable Hangman*—the sacrifice we make is a witness, of course, to that act; and is our authority for it.

# On Love

*Self Condemned,* by Wyndham Lewis. London: Methuen, 1954.

One has been trying, for weeks, to compose oneself in terms of, or rather in relation to, a given instance. For example:

> Your letter came in a moment when my heart was limping. A star had come and I couldn't receive it for I was repenting pride. And though you were expressing the world you know in Plato's *Symposium*, the nature of love, Socrates' conversation with Diotima, "and that one's disappointment finally becomes expectant . . . ," I knew the chastisement. I'd provided the mantle of my personal size . . . Love is the world and Logos the word but Life demands that Love know itself and when Love isn't in Grace it is testy and bitter . . .

I know this lady is a fine one, and was grateful for her reassurance. For an instant—I did not, I think, wish to laugh at either one of us, but how not to. I was afraid that I was I, and she was she. Writing is private, I thought. Later I read in Stein's *Everybody's Autobiography:*

> . . . when you say what you do say [these were lectures] you say it in public but when you write it in private if you do not write it, that is what writing is, and in private you are you and in public you are in public and everybody knows that . . .

My heart has been limping, for months now. In that way, I tend to forget the lady, a little. Without glibness, Wyatt must have known it, very exactly, and he was then much older: "They flee from me who sometimes did me seek." For an instant, no matter more—there are these several juxtapositions possible, e.g., H.D.'s saying, *I go where I love and am loved . . .*; Williams', *what, shut grief in from us? We who have perhaps nothing to lose?* And the, *myself forgetting violence, and long betrayal*—of Robert Graves, the poem which introduces the first edition of *The White Goddess.*

Should we roar with laughter—or what do we have to do, with the moon, these days? Stendhal writes: "I am full of admiration for the shrewdness and unerring judgment with which women seem to me to grasp certain details; and yet the next moment I find them praising some dullard to the skies, allowing themselves to be moved to tears by a platitude, or gravely treating some hollow affectation as a sign of character. I cannot understand such folly. There must be some general law beyond my ken governing these matters . . ."

Robert Duncan, in a letter: "And I want them all as best I can, and so do you, any man: want to be free to give myself over to the sexual lure, to fall in love—and to learn the art of place and person, of tone and definition that might render the experience to itself. But it's a cheat to bring the accusation against ourselves or our lovers of selfishness in a situation that is of the essence 'thotless.'

"And a mixd hell on wheels to try to come to *love* that which has possessd us. Well, but then there is the figure of an hysterical female figure on a rollercoaster crying 'I simply love this.'"

## 2

Conversely, Wyndham Lewis' *Self Condemned* is a terrifying relation of more than 'one man's life'; it is a statement of the impossible distance of an intimacy, too often, these days. At the beginning:

> As soon as she saw that he was occupied with his correspondence (and she was not detained by her own, which had been nothing but a few bills), she shook off the contretemps of the *Princess Casamassima* discussion—such a highbrow feature for their breakfast-table talk was almost without precedent—and returned to the setting of her own little traps. The terrific success of the night before, and René had been in perfect honeymoon form, must really be put to some good use. The moment had come, it seemed to her, to seize time by the forelock while his eyes were still gooey and his brain still drugged with the fumes of the Venusberg. Her eyes shining, her waist arched in

and hips thrust out, she held up a page of her newspaper on which
were displayed a bunch of late-spring coats, a bait for those who were
so silly as to imagine that in warm weather fur coats grew cheaper.

"Now *that*," she exclaimed, arching her eyebrows, "is what, if you
ever had a really *lavish* fit—*that* is the sort of thing I should get you to
buy."

René looked up from his correspondence, momentarily stung almost to fury by the brazen naively mercenary calculations of the good
Hester, with her garishly stock notion of what was a propitious
moment . . .

This image is not a 'criticism' of anyone, or rather, I use it in no
such context. Nor am I concerned with the 'reality' of either character or situation, except that they are here—some pages (weeks,
months, countries) later:

> . . . "Will you kindly tell me at once what my wife has done," de-
> manded René.
>
> "What did she do?" echoed the policeman. And René noticed the
> change of tense.
>
> "She did nothing?" he asked; his lips trembled. "And if she has
> done nothing, why did you demand my presence here?" The ag-
> gressive tone provoked the reappearance of the unmodified jowl of
> the dogs of the Law.
>
> "She did do *something*, Professor. She threw herself under a truck."

It continues: ". . . The poor hair was full of mud, which flattened it
upon the skull. Her eye protruded: it was strange it should still
have the strength to go peering on in the darkness."

> René took a step forward towards the exhibit, but he fell head-
> long, striking his forehead upon the edge of the marble slab—the re-
> mains being arranged upon something like a fishmonger's display
> slab. As he fell it had been his object to seize the head and carry it
> away with him. To examine his legal right had been his last clear act of
> consciousness . . .

D. H. Lawrence writes: ". . . But if your wife should accomplish
for herself the sweetness of her own soul's possession, then gently, delicately let the new mode assert itself, the new mode of relation between you, with something of spontaneous paradise in it,
the apple of knowledge at last digested. But, my word, what belly-
aches meanwhile. The apple is harder to digest than a lead gun-
cartridge . . ."

# The Journals of Jean Cocteau

*The Journals of Jean Cocteau,* edited and translated, with
an introduction by Wallace Fowlie. New York: Crite-
rion Books, 1956.

The occasion of Jean Cocteau's election to the French Academy
(1955) has meant an increase of interest in his work in this country.
Actually, this kind of interest most concerns publishers and their
use of such events to provide "times" for concern with the writing
of this or that man. This is a perfectly reasonable exploitation of a
circumstance perhaps, but it can often lead to hasty thinking, editing, translating—and so on. The occasion forgotten, the book shows
its gaps and awkwardnesses, and ends by disobliging the very man
it assertedly hoped to honor.

The present book is an "occasion" book. Mr. Fowlie's introduction is twenty-nine pages long almost in defense of his uneasiness.
He was given a sizable task, clearly. I am by no means as familiar
with the material as he must be; but I am aware that it must have
been very difficult to select things out of it—it does not break open
into pieces, but is a texture of attention, endlessly reforming. At
times Mr. Fowlie can only shout his goodwill ("Membership in the
Académie Française will hardly slow him [Cocteau] down!"). But
his translation is readable, and given his word—"A fairly literal
translation seemed often to serve Cocteau better than an effort to
recast the original in order to find a style and phrasing more native

*New Mexico Quarterly,* Winter 1956–57.

to English . . ."—we will have to trust him, and also thank him, because no one has as yet done more, or as much.

This brings us, then, to Cocteau—not fatuously, please, because
I have taken pains, or have tried to, to separate him from his translator, and particularly, from the "occasion" behind the translator—
forever to be suspected. As Mr. Fowlie suggests (p. 3), Jean Cocteau
is not a widely read writer, although many people know his name,
and sense a half-glamour in it, for reasons they themselves continue to produce. He has, however, been recognized by his contemporaries for many years. The first sections of the book describe his
relationships with Satie, Max Jacob, Stravinsky, Raymond Radi-
guet, Pablo Picasso, Maritain, Proust, Diaghilev, Apollinaire. In the
American context, Ezra Pound mentions him several times in *Guide
to Kulchur,* once as follows: "To establish some table of values as
among men I have seen and talked with . . . Gaudier had and Cocteau has genius . . . By genius I mean an inevitable swiftness and
rightness in a given field. The trouvaille. The direct simplicity in
seizing the effective means."

What is his writing like, then? I would like to know too. I have
seen three of his movies, including *Beauty and the Beast;* know nothing of his poetry; read *Opium* when younger with great care (and
wonder—it was not at all what I expected, and was very strictly
written); and began *Thomas the Imposter* (remembering the kalei-
doscoping of short scene-images, with which it begins); and read
with what French I had, *Journal d'un Inconnu,* what I could of it—
excited to find the mind so capable of balance and continuance.
Cocteau writes:

*On Words*

I attach no importance to what people call style and that by which
they think they recognize a writer. I want to be recognized by my
ideas, or better, by my bearing. I make every effort to be heard as
briefly as possible. I have noticed, when a story does captivate the
reader's mind, that he was reading too fast, and gliding down the
slope. That is why, in the book, I skirt around the writing which
forces me not to glide in a straight line, but to start over again, to re-
read the sentences in order not to lose the thread.

When I read a book, I marvel at the number of words I find in it
and I dream of using them. I note them down. But in my work it is
impossible. I limit myself to my own vocabulary. I cannot go beyond
it, and it is so restricted that the work becomes a puzzle.

I wonder, at each line, whether I shall go on, whether the combination of the few words I use, always the same ones, will not end up by

blocking the way and forcing me to silence. It would be beneficial for everyone, but words are like figures or letters in the alphabet. They are able to reorganize differently and perpetually at the bottom of the kaleidoscope.

I said I was jealous of the words of other writers. It is because they are not mine. Each writer has a bag of them, as in a lotto set, with which he has to win. Except for the style I dislike—Flaubert is the leading example—too rich in words—the style I like, Montaigne, Racine, Chateaubriand, Stendhal, does not spend too many words. It would take no time to count them . . .

The sections into which the book is divided show a preoccupation with personalities, not Cocteau's nor perhaps even Mr. Fowlie's, obliged as he was by the concerns evident. Sections I (Childhood and Early Influences) and III (Testimonials) contain the bulk of it; and Sections II (The Writer's Character) and VI (Aesthetics) seem the most purposefully free, and useful. But what use we are intent upon, is what we must of course decide.

A use of words is a definition of words. This is not new, but worth, like they say, the repeating, always. The structure of language is at stake, so to speak.

There is also the question of "authorities," concerning which Robert Duncan, an American poet who has read Cocteau's work with care, writes:

What Joyce sees as "conscience" because he is guilt and sin centered, Pound sees as sensibility or Ibsen sees as awareness or Dante sees as Grace. Cocteau in *Journal d'un Inconnu* voices an aspect of the problem. It is here in the terms of the economy of fame. The work, as it is realized, is a flowering; and like all flowerings—the author here no more intending than a plant intends—an attraction; its emanations draw and repel, its colors exhibit or conceal. No matter! a host arrives, or hosts depart, of all sorts. This clustering about an emanation is its fame in which sometimes the plant can survive; thru which at times the plant comes even to flourish or, as in the relation of certain plants thru their flowerings with bees, to depend; or it may perish. All artists draw a sap out of solitude. The work of art flowers forth, ripens, and falls away from a vitality drawn out of a privacy, a secret source of the artist in the fields of time and space . . .

The relation of a poem to what the world calls events is similar. The "world" cannot view a poem as an event in itself, and seeks to translate as if the poem were referring to "real life." Yet for the poet, the reality of time and space which is realized in making, in a poem, is the real life.

[From an unpublished Notebook.]

The attempt to wrench segments from any completed work (happily called a *book*), to reassort, re-*time*, reaffix, etc.,—is not easily defensible. Most reasonably, it would be the act of the man who wrote the book or books. In this case, it is not. In twenty years there have been five books by Cocteau published in English; two were translated by the British poet and playwright, Ronald Duncan, one by the British novelist, Rosamond Lehmann. The fourth is a retranslation of the same novel translated by Miss Lehmann (no translator given), published in this country. And the fifth is the present book. I think we had better go back, and start over.

# Kenneth Rexroth:
## *In Defense of the Earth*

*In Defense of the Earth,* by Kenneth Rexroth. New York: New Directions, 1956.

*In Defense of the Earth* is the first more or less substantial collection of Kenneth Rexroth's poems since the publication of *The Dragon and the Unicorn.* The latter was a long philosophical travel-poem, so that the book I am reviewing more literally goes back to *The Signature of All Things* (1949), and is (as that book was) an accumulation of poems and translations of varying length and determination.

> Many of these deal with similar locations and events, seeking over and over again for the changing forms of an unchanging significance in stars, insects, mountains and daughters. They do not of course try to answer, "Why am I here?" "Why is it out there?"—but to snare the fact that is the only answer, the only meaning of present or presence . . .
>
> [Foreword to *In Defense of the Earth,* by Kenneth Rexroth]

Reading a book, or reviewing it—one comes to ask, what does the book have, for its ideas; and, how clearly are those ideas made evident? Rexroth's title demonstrates the area of his concern, large though it surely is, and open as well to the pitfalls of an overzealous generality. But one can, as he does, begin there.

The opening poems are for his wife, Marthe, and his daughter Mary. Those for his wife have, among them, some of the book's best writing.

*New Mexico Quarterly,* Winter 1956–57.

> . . . What do I know now,
> Of myself, of the others?
> Blood flows out to the fleeing
> Nebulae, and flows back, red
> With all the worn space of space,
> Old with all the time of time.
> It is my blood. I cannot
> Taste in it as it leaves me
> More of myself than on its
> Return . . .

This is the first idea. It is as well a broadening, in effect a deepening of something, such as:

> . . . Just born to die
> Nobody will ever know anything about it
> And I have nothing more at all to say.

Which is taken from *The Art of Worldly Wisdom* (1949), a book which marked the last large instance of Rexroth's experimentation in poems akin (as he notes) to those of Stein, Lowenfels, Arensberg, and Louis Zukofsky. After that time he made clear his intention to write in more "common" forms, and to give up at least the intensity of his concern to that point with syntactical formation, personally based. Perhaps my own statement here is unclear, but what was meant seems simply this: he became concerned with a poetry which people, in a half-hoped for generality, might be able to read, as put against that which apparently they could not—or at least this was not to be the concern of the writer.

This is the second idea, clear in this book—that people, who are being loved, attacked, or subjected to the varying attitudes of the writer, be obliged to hear that concern. The poem "Thou Shalt Not Kill" (for the memory of Dylan Thomas, who was himself proposed as a common voice) speaks like this:

> I want to run into the street
> Shouting, "Remember Vanzetti!"
> I want to pour gasoline down your chimneys.
> I want to blow up your galleries.
> I want to burn down your editorial offices.
> I want to slit the bellies of your frigid women.
> I want to sink your sailboats and launches.
> I want to strangle your children at their finger paintings.
> I want to poison your Afghans and poodles.
> He is dead, the drunken little cherub.

> He is dead,
> The effulgent tub thumper.
> He is Dead . . .

But—one knows what one 'speaks,' or else not. Put too blandly, such address is perhaps only equalled by the equal exhortations, to buy this bread, that butter, and to eat it all. More reasonably—the addition of "launches" to "sailboats" belies the echoing tiredness of the man writing, it may be, with the whole 'idea.'

More quietly (less 'common'):

> What can you say in a poem?
> Past forty, you've said it all.
> The dwarf black oak grows out of
> The cliff below my feet. It
> May be two hundred years old,
> Yet its trunk is no bigger
> Than my wrist, its crown does not
> Come to my shoulder . . .

I read the book making notes, so that I should not be overly embarrassed, coming to write of it. Which was my dilemma, but these poems are marked as follows: "Seven Poems for Marthe, My Wife" ("Positions of love—physical—loneliness. Images of possible loss—flat line. Praise.") "The Mirror in the Woods" ("Good—fairy story quality. Mirror."); "For Eli Jacobsen" ("Good—old-timers, liberals, workers—the good old days—won't come again. Courage—makes taste & feelings better. Ok."); "Time Is the Mercy of Eternity" ("Philosophical—'on poetry.' Up in the mts. Images of *moments:* description. Clear. *Alone.* All strips *away to 'knowledge'*"), etc., etc.

Perception, inside or out, is 'earth,' equally to be defended. In the "Japanese Translations" at the book's end, there is this one (by Ishikawa Takuboku):

> I do not know why
> But it is as though
> There were a cliff
> Inside my head
> From which, every day,
> Clods of earth fall.

# Edward Dahlberg:
## *The Sorrows of Priapus*

*The Sorrows of Priapus,* by Edward Dahlberg. New York: New Directions, 1957.

Manners are custom insofar as they represent continually and generally reaffirmed notions of value. We shoot to kill. We think to act effectively. The world is nine-tenths to be found in the way one moves through it, be that with resistance, longing, good nature, or whatever other possibilities of attitude exist.

For a writer this problem of "manners" converts, partly, to that of "style"—of which Stendhal said, it is the man. In America there are no very actually customary writers such as the English have. From Melville on, those men who have managed a formal distinction have done so with great labor, and *Moby-Dick* sweats a composite language of completely singular kind. It would seem that the American writer has constantly to refind, and, equally, to redefine wherein lies the value of the words he uses. Awkwardly, and persistently, this is what they seem to me to have done: Whitman, James—utterly unlike otherwise—and in our own time, Pound, Williams, Crane, Faulkner et al. To the European our "stylists" at times seem outrageously self-conscious; they do not at all write in a way that anyone might have. But I think that is, again, a reaffirming of this question of "manners" which has nagged at our dress, our food, our attitudes, ever since we first came to this country.

*New Mexico Quarterly,* Spring 1958.

The only way is the one way, and that way must be found by each of us, one by one. Perhaps we arrive at custom without any manners at all.

From the character of writing in his first book, *Bottom Dogs*, a novel published in the late twenties, to that now shown in *The Sorrows of Priapus*, Edward Dahlberg has come by no means unwittingly. *Bottom Dogs* is a flat, harsh work of realism; and for the last word, read the attitudes subsequent to Dreiser, the affective photographing of life sans relieving characteristics of sympathy. Why then this manner?

> Our annals are weak, and we know not our rivers; we cannot understand today which is Father Ra, the Egyptian sun, until we gather up yesterday, who is Osiris. These rivers are immense legends and would cure us of many ills, did we know them, for all nature is our corpus, and once we relinquish a part of the earth, we lose, in some way, the use of our hands, feet, loins, and spirit.

This is not a realism of any kind familiar to critics, though I would argue its concerns are ultimately just so oriented. For those familiar with *Bottom Dogs*, the language has certainly a new character of reference and tone. Yet the strong monosyllabic structure holds. Sentences stay closely based, running to compounds in passages of argument and explanation; but even there they end with even, flat statement, unmistakable contentual emphases.

*The Sorrows of Priapus* argues two main images: (1) a natural world, dominant in animal and plant, as corrective to that "understood," intellectually "purposed," defiant of natural authorities; and (2) a source-world, of New World histories, and custom, origin, whereby to secure continuance and understanding of a more primal sort. The last sentence in the book is: "Be primordial or decay." Which injunction—both to continually begin, and to begin with what you began with—can give some sense of the manner in point of content. The beginning note reads:

> This is fable and not natural history. The polestar of the writer is a legendary book, using geography, the beasts in the earth and in the sea, and voyages, as the source of maxims, mirth and an American myth . . .

The natural world is the "plural" world of the Greeks, and those around and before them. It is devoid of humanistic hierarchies; the trees are there as much as the man is, no matter he can chop them down. The second, the source-world, is that of the Maya, Aztec, ge-

ographers, the forms of land, and the rivers which mark them. In
Dahlberg's use it breeds overtones, insistencies, of great strength:

> Memory is our day of water tutored by want. La Salle sought virgin
> Tartars, descendants of Prometheus. He returned to Frontenac, but
> he had not found the Alpha of the river . . .

But what does that first sentence mean? It means that we remember what we have, because we do not have it. It means that fate does
not necessarily argue accomplishments.

> Water is death, but man must seek it. All our seeming wakings are the
> debris of evening waters; most dreams come from mean shallows, and
> are the digestive rot of secure bottoms; prophecies rise up from the
> marine depths ancient as the Flood. We are cartographers, unheed-
> ing the singing maggots, or bereft of the Angel.

Is it to gain an authority, the manners of authority, that Dahlberg
has developed such a "style"? I argue that its purpose is as follows:
to demand attention, for the content, the things with which it is
concerned. The book is a compounded book, formed of many
things; "many narratives have been employed . . ." The book is a
legendary *imagining*—from *imitārī* to imitate, or some form lost
"back there," in the same world; and derives its form from tales,
and writings, of men who were there, and provides for us the image of a "new world" which has filtered down to us.

Finally, pedantically, manners comes from *manus*, hand; and cus-
tom, at least possibly, in part, from *suescere:* to have it for one's own.
At least that can stand as an American reading of the work Edward
Dahlberg has done.

# *Evergreen Review,* Nos. 1 and 2

*Evergreen Review,* Nos. 1–2 (1957). New York: Grove Press, 1957.

The use of the "little magazine" format in contemporary publishing is a result of the wide increase in paperback publications generally; and must, I think, be first recognized as a commercial device rather than a use relating directly to contemporary writing. In fact, the little magazine per se finds itself in difficult straits these days. Increased publishing costs, more highly developed means of distribution, lack of independent subsidies, and like factors have all tended to push out any actual parallels to the old *Dial, Transition,* or *The Little Review,* which might otherwise have appeared. The increased use of little magazines by universities has also resulted in a generally academic tone which reaches over into reviews without such connection, e.g., *The Hudson Review.* Writers for these periodicals have usually a well determined axe to grind—not certainly their fault, but again the result of anterior preoccupations: in this case, that universities have come to expect their employees to be active in such publication, particularly the members of their English departments. The subsequent search for occasions has led to any number of specious revivals, and the independently creative writer—to use a well-worn phrase—finds himself more beside the point than ever.

What is a little magazine? It used to be, most usually, the publication of a group of *writers,* however restrictive that might seem. It

*New Mexico Quarterly,* Spring—Summer 1957.

was not, in any case, the publication of a group of publishers or teachers. At times a sympathetic editor, such as Ford Madox Ford, could, with an *English Review*, publish both Lawrence and Pound, no matter what each thought of the other. *Transition* practiced an almost voracious eclecticism, but one clearly committed to writers, not pocketbooks. And there were as well magazines such as *Broom* with a more narrowly cohesive editorial commitment. The late *View*, for example, was dedicated to American surrealism, with Charles Henri Ford and Parker Tyler as mainstays. In contemporary writing only *Origin* (which has now stopped publication) seems to have been committed to a group—its nemesis perhaps, but also its use. The writers it published were given means to develop their own idiom, with the very significant security of knowing there was a place where they might appear free of obligating "limits"—which is a very important security indeed.

The *Evergreen Review* has, as yet, no "group" and it is perhaps not to be expected of an essentially commercial publication. Publishers, reasonably, use such magazines as this as a form of advance publicity; Gallimard in Paris has maintained a review of this kind for some years. But this use will explain in part the hodgepodge character of *Evergreen Review* No. 1, despite single excellences such as James Purdy's "Cutting Edge." The contents include Sartre, Michaux, Baby Dodds, and Samuel Beckett—and these do not relate, nor is the eclecticism of such inclusion very interesting. Sartre's essay, "After Budapest," is not demonstrably an attitude with which the editors "agree"—or on which they stake their own political commitment—or by which they define a position they intend to maintain. It is, rather, an "example"—useful, but limiting, because it is an example of Sartre, not of an editorial program or policy.

This randomness is in some sense corrected in *Evergreen Review*, No. 2. Here a cohesiveness is obtained by giving over the issue to San Francisco writers; and Kenneth Rexroth leads off with a confused, but certainly explicit, "letter," maintaining the importance of *disaffiliation* to the writers involved. This of course implies liveliness and the like, but it also involves some error of generalization as does, equally, calling Jack Kerouac and Allen Ginsberg writers of this geographical "school," despite the impact they have had there. Michael Rumaker seems to me equally detachable. The more true members are, perhaps, Rexroth, Brother Antoninus, Duncan, Spicer, Broughton, and Josephine Miles—though these as well share many differences. There is, in any case, some danger in promoting geographical relationships; they are rarely significant, and add somewhat specious labels to writers who have troubles enough.

In both issues the problem seems coherence. The first relies primarily on an unabashed eclecticism, with the use of "names" to provide interest. This is a familiar practice. The second in turn makes use of a geographical "scene" (the publisher has printed on the cover SAN FRANCISCO SCENE in fact), and again the coherence is tentative, although somewhat more clear than in No. 1. But neither seems to me a very able substitute for a literal editorial policy or program, no matter the apparent limits of that commitment. It means of course that someone will be left out. It means, too, that several writers, or, in short, a group of writers will have precedence. But it means equally that something will be aimed at, and the editors will have arrived at the liberty of inviting writers to contribute to something more than a miscellany. There exist very clear "sides" in writing today, and they are not described by calling something "good writing." I should myself hate to see the *Evergreen Review* become, simply, another *New World Writing*—which can boast it prints writers of completely divergent opinion only because it has none itself.

I make use, however, of a writer's attitude in this review; and forget that it is not here the point. Readers will find much of interest in both issues despite my qualifications. "Baby Dodds' Story" in No. 1, for example, is a fine exhibition of a very free-wheeling prose; Michaux's tour "through the hallucinated hell of Mescalin" in the same issue is also a timely subject. And *Evergreen Review*, No. 2, is I think the most interestingly diverse and generally excellent instance of the "little magazine" in big publishing yet to be done. So, if I hope, it is mainly that it will become the occasion for writers it can now be claimed to be for readers. That will be the day.

# "To Build Castles in Spain"

*Ten Centuries of Spanish Verse,* edited by Eleanor L. Turnbull. New York: Grove Press, 1955.

*The Penguin Book of Spanish Verse,* edited by J. M. Cohen.
Baltimore, Md.: Penguin Books, 1960.

To anthologize ten centuries of any country's poetry would seem a
very ambitious job—and the more so, when the country is one so
vague in our minds as is Spain. I don't know that either Miss Turnbull's selection, or that of Cohen, succeeds altogether in giving the
necessary orientation. But such success would be in any case extremely relative. Briefly, I would prefer Cohen's book for these reasons: (1) his system of identifying authors in the table of contents
is uncomplicated and allows quick reference; (2) his prose translations, running beneath the Spanish text on each page in the character of unpretentious footnotes, make a very usable "trot"; and
(3) his material, although paralleling Miss Turnbull's in great part,
seems to me a more solid continuity. To these things, I should add
the fact that his anthology costs $1.50 less than Miss Turnbull's;
and consider the matter settled.

There is, however, a tendency evident in Miss Turnbull's book
that might be mentioned—because it seems without justification.
The translations which she has provided are often very curious.
They include, for example, Henry Wadsworth Longfellow's trans-
lation of the formalist Jorge Manrique's "*Coplas por la Muerte de su
Padre*"—and also Lord Byron's translation of "*La Pérdida de Al-*

*hama,*" which he calls "A Very Mournful Ballad on the Siege and Conquest of Alhama" reasonably enough. And there are a number of other translators present, who have that strangely insistent tone of great enthusiasm and limited perception. Again, that is why I favor the workmanlike continuity of Cohen's prose notes. But an instance may make the point more clearly:

> . . . *Como al partir del sol la sombra crece,*
> *y en cayendo su rayo levanta*
> *la negra escuridad que el mundo cubre,*
> *de do viene el temor que nos espanta . . .*
>
> (Garcilaso de la Vega, from "*Egloga Primera*")

. . . As when the sun departs the shadows grow and, as its rays sink, the black darkness rises to cover the world, whence comes the fear that strikes us . . .

(Cohen)

> . . . As at the set of sun the shades extend,
> And when its circle sinks, that dark obscure
> Rises to shroud the world, on which attend
> The images that set our hair on end . . .
>
> (Turnbull: Jeremiah H. Wiffen, translator)

Miss Turnbull would, I think, have been better advised to follow her own abilities; *Contemporary Spanish Poetry* (another of her anthologies, wherein she used translations of her own) seems to me a much happier example of her care and intelligence.

That done, there remains Spanish literature to be spoken of; and I feel as tentative here, as the usual American must. Both books are, in effect, a substantial offering of that literature, but I wonder how simply a reader will find their materials available, lacking much acquaintance with either literature or the peculiar characteristics of the national temper of which it is the form. It is true enough, as Cohen notes, that "For the majority, Spain is the country of a single prose masterpiece, *Don Quixote* . . ." For the American, we may add background instances of Spanish temper, such as Cortes, Coronado, et al., and of course Columbus (by Robert Graves' conjecture quite probably Spanish also, i.e., a Mallorquin from Soller, etc.). But then our orientation moves north. And although one may see bullfights in Nîmes, Arles, and other French cities close to the Spanish border, there is no such acquaintance with Spanish form allowed in Texas.

So then the background for this literature is also a problem, and we are left here with what references we can manage, wherewith to take hold of this work. Granted writing comes from a *place*, and the complex of attitudes there to be found effectual, I would recommend as a primer William H. Prescott's *History of the Reign of Philip the Second* (1855), simply because it conveys with all the singularities of 19th-century American intelligence, a world unequivocally *Spanish*, in a variety of relationships, both European (because this period was one in which Spain, contrary to usual position, was much involved in European politics) and Moorish (the opening chapters of Book V will place that relationship clearly in the reader's mind). What we have, in short, to manage is even the most minimal sense of what that "world" was—for ten centuries. Prescott will usefully let one look both backwards and forwards, and that is more to the point here than would be a work perhaps more modern or more accurate.

Continuing this sense of background, I would also cite a few *ideas,* more than actual references, which may have bearing. I don't know that we see, or can see, such areas "all of a sudden"; yet an idea, a perception of some aspect of that reality, can do much to help, no matter what questions of bias or opinion. For example, Stendhal comments on the Spanish character in his *A Life of Napoleon* as follows:

> Ferocious yet generous at one and the same time; hospitable yet unrelenting; lazy yet tireless when on the move, burned by his sun and his superstitious beliefs, the Spaniard offers all the freakish characteristics of an irascible temperament carried to extreme.

Continuing:

> The specific character of the priests is perhaps the main characteristic which divides Spain from the rest of Europe. The clergy in Spain is *resident.*

In her *Autobiography* Gertrude Stein writes:

> She always says that americans can understand spaniards. That they are the only two western nations that can realise abstraction. That in americans it expresses itself by disembodiedness, in literature and machinery, in Spain by ritual so abstract that it does not connect itself with anything but ritual. . . . They have no close contact with the earth such as most europeans have. Their materialism is not the materialism of existence, of possession, it is the materialism of action and abstraction.

Ramón Sender calls the Spanish poet ("if he survives") the most civilized man in the world today. I note that Elie Faure in an introduction to a collection of Goya's etchings speaks of "a kind of equivocal atmosphere wavering between Catholic cruelty and life on the one hand, and Protestant hypocrisy and morals on the other . . ." It will be, then, by such apparently disrelated comment, often incisively personal, that our own reaction may be stimulated, to supply that contact on which these, or any poems, will be dependent.

There are many poets in the two collections, otherwise, who will enlarge anyone's concept of Spanish or, equally, of world literature. Juan Ruiz, Jorge Manrique, Garcilaso de la Vega, Fray Luis de León, Baltasar de Alcázar—to note only those to the time of Shakespeare—are such men. Yet to say it that way quickly falls into speciousness. It is better to think of one poem. "Antonio Machado (1875–1939), a poet of great and individual simplicity, sober and reflective, and a great interpreter of the Castilian landscape. He defended the Republic, and died on the French side of the Pyrenees when its armies were defeated" (Cohen). This is one of his poems:

*Siesta*

    *En memoria de Abel Martín*

*Mientras traza su curva el pez de fuego,*
*junto al ciprés, bajo el supremo añil,*
*y vuela en blanca piedra el niño ciego,*
*y en el olmo la copla de marfil*
*de la verde cigarra late y suena,*
*honremos al Señor*
*—la negra estampa de su mano buena—*
*que ha dictado el silencio en el clamor.*

*Al Dios de la distancia y de la ausencia,*
*del áncora en la mar, la plena mar . . .*
*El nos libra del mundo—omnipresencia—,*
*nos abre senda para caminar.*

*Con la copa de sombra bien colmada,*
*con este nunca lleno corazón,*
*honremos al Señor que hizo la Nada*
*y ha esculpido en la fe nuestra razón.**

* Whilst the fiery fish traces his arc beside the cypress, beneath the tallest indigo-plant, and the blind boy disappears into white stone, and in the elm the ivory verse of the green cicada beats and booms, let us honour the Lord—the black trace of his kindly hand—who has compelled silence among the clamour.

To the God of distances and absence, of the anchor in the sea, the sea at high tide . . . He frees us from the world,—he is omnipresent—and opens us up a path to travel.

With cups overflowing with shadow and with this never filled heart, let us honour the Lord who made Non-existence and sculpted our reason out of faith. (Cohen)

# "Her Service Is Perfect Freedom"

*The White Goddess*, 3rd ed., by Robert Graves. London: Faber & Faber, 1952.

*The Poems of Robert Graves (Chosen by Himself)*. Garden City, N.Y.: Doubleday, 1958.

*The Golden Ass*, by Lucius Apuleius. Translated by Robert Graves. Harmondsworth, England: Penguin Books, 1950.

*The Twelve Caesars*, by Gaius Suetonius Tranquillus. Translated by Robert Graves. Harmondsworth, England: Penguin Books, 1957.

Robert Graves presents an attractive figure; he is diverse, he is multifaceted as some might say, he writes clearly and with engaging emphases. Many of his books—like the occasions which prompted them—may well fall away; but some, equally, seem squarely fated to stick.

So, what to think of *The White Goddess*? Is she really for real—because that has, it seems, been the question. Perhaps it is our ingrained monogamy that has made most readings of this book, ironically enough, a frustrated rejection of its proposals. The subtitle gives an orientation, however; the book is "A historical grammar of poetic myth." By its "historical," the text will depend on what is known in and of time; by its "grammar," will offer a wherewithal to "know one's letters"; and, by "poetic myth," will depend on those evidences, tales of the tribe, which poets, the makers in language, have used as a basis for their work. This in hand, one may read as literally as he cares to; but he would do well to see that the book is an "argument" as much in its own form and methods, as it is in the literal details to which it refers.

In short, this book is much concerned with an image of how poets have worked in this world, and of the "magic" source by which they have survived. Poetic faith, Coleridge's plea for a "willing suspension of disbelief," the timeless acknowledgment of the *other,* such things may, or may not, depend upon the matrilineal institutions which Graves exhaustively discovers. But his working premises of conjecture, of a formulative (basically) rather than an analytic ordering of the "what happened," are, I would argue, the only ones which will work in this area. He is right that the poet is a man peculiarly fated to move by such alphabets as he restores, and by such sidewise containment of knowledge as "The Battle of the Trees" demonstrates. Philosophically enough, the poet is here to prove nothing but the continuance of that which was given him on his arrival. The Muse, "the White Goddess . . . the Mother of All Living, the ancient power of fright and lust," etc., is both source and denial; seen as "generation" there is no other relevance possible. Because if you are a poet, you will know that presence of fate, against which you might, even effectually, interpose your own will—if you covet a quick death, and the loss of all you thought to honor. The principle of the animate, in language, is that "things" can become absorbed by their presence there, until their life, in that character, equally represents their force in other, more "literally" given, characters. This, in turn, can generate a power of reverence and recognition capable of continuance. The Goddess, whether characterized as the ultimately personal, or impersonal, wife, mother, queen, or simply the generically "unknown," is the most persistent *other* of our existence, eschewing male order, allowing us to live at last. The obedience of a poet's gratitude, for this, is the authority which you hear in his poems, and it is obedience to a presence which is, if you will, that which is not understood, ever; but which he characterizes as all that can happen in living, and seeks to form an emblem for, with words.

Otherwise poets, like other men, face the necessities of this life, in terms of the money needed to support themselves and their families. Graves has found his solution in making prose support his verse; and thinking of the diverse occupations which poets in this

country have used to accomplish the same end, it appears happy
for him that he has so managed. But the evidence indicates that this
way has had its problems. *Five Pens in Hand,* a miscellany of his
criticism, stories, etc., is reminiscent of the schoolman's "Publish
or perish . . ." With few exceptions (e.g., "The White Goddess,"
"Prologue to a Poetry Reading") nothing offers much purchase for
the problem with which Graves has been elsewhere concerned. If
nothing in the collection represents "any task or . . . any relationship . . . inconsistent with poetic principles . . . ," again "nothing" is
the explanation, by being what is said. The book documents, painfully, what is necessary to manage self-support by writing; how persistently one must be entertaining (cf. "The Whitaker Negroes");
how able to rise to any occasion (cf. "Legitimate Criticism of Poetry"). The process is the more uncomfortable, since the ingenuous
good nature back of it all will expose whatever the dictates of the
situation ask for—a situation as endlessly of no use as the minds of
the editors who create it.

Fairer purpose, better game, for this process is one which allows
a firmer grip on such "occasions," as Graves' historical novels have
previously shown. Two books, each in its own way, give quick example, i.e., his translations of Suetonius' *The Twelve Caesars,* and of
Apuleius' *The Golden Ass.* In America we read Latin poorly, if at all;
and translation is a thing on which we are more and more dependent. Graves' translation of Suetonius demonstrates a very certain "poetic" facility, an intuitive response to another man's mode
of speaking; and the text is thereby restored to wit and precision,
which are things often lost in the translation of Latin. Equally, his
transformation of *The Golden Ass* from a somewhat bawdy "classic"
to a whimsically moving, full-fledged "religious experience" is token
of "poetic" insight, notable here since the vision of the Goddess
(pp. 268–71) in other hands might have proved full of doubt or
awkward acknowledgment.

But it would be better to forget all of these books, to keep hold
only of *The White Goddess,* an act of poetic faith if ever there was
one—when you read Graves' poems. Coming from such a Hydra-
headed intelligence, they are nonetheless small, lyric, and often
commonplace in their concerns. When one thinks of the sheer bulk
of prose written in order to support their creation, one is staggered;
but that too is like the day, which passeth away. The point is, it does
not really matter how you write a poem, so long as you write it.

A poet's "handwriting," whereby he may be known, Graves has

termed the rhythms peculiar to his work; to which I would add, it is also the rhythm of his thought, of the ways in which he sees the "out there," and the "in." Graves' forms are primarily traditional, which fact may blur them for a careless reader; but he both uses and informs them in a manner unlike our own current "traditionalists." By which I mean that he is at home in them, thinks with them, and shapes the content of his obligation to their pattern with a good grace:

> *The Door*
>
> When she came suddenly in
> It seemed the door could never close again,
> Nor even did she close it—she, she—
> The room lay open to a visiting sea
> Which no door could restrain.
>
> Yet when at last she smiled, tilting her head
> To take leave of me,
> Where she had smiled, instead
> There was a dark door closing endlessly,
> The waves receded.

A constant acquaintance with any woman will take humor; it is the only footnote possible. No poet ever quite dares to make such reference to the Goddess, but a deep humor grows also from that association. This element is a constant in Graves' poems; "Questions in a Wood," "Woman and Tree," and many more, some funny outright, and some much more quietly, give evidence of that one male prerogative he has used for sustenance. Others, at last with bitterness, strike flatly on despair:

> Counting the beats,
> Counting the slow heart beats,
> The bleeding to death of time in slow heart beats,
> Wakeful they lie . . .
>
> ("Counting the Beats")

Despair or not, like it or not, the faith which Graves defends comes of belief, and is a renewal. You die many times to acknowledge one birth.

# A New Testament

Some years ago I had the opportunity to publish a section of this novel* in the *Black Mountain Review* (No. 7). I felt then (and continue to feel), that it was an extraordinary piece of work. At that time I also saw the book in manuscript in a form substantially different from the one which Olympia Press published in 1959. It had a more discursive manner, being in fact three books, one of which had been published in the United States as *Junky* (under the pseudonym, William Lee) and the other two having the titles *Queer* and *In Search of Yage.*

These books, then, made a trilogy progressing into the observation of a despair, with all possible terms of degradation, of commitment to sensation as an alternative logic to organizational 'goodness' or 'purpose.' The present book does that too, but in a form so much more telling in itself that it is immediately remarkable in that way also. For example, this book has no 'historical' logic of any significance. It follows a more real apprehension of life, as significant (or insignificant, the same) memory of detail, of frustrate invention upon the mock taboos of society, of humor used to weigh possibility, of echoing loneliness and repetition. This novel pictures society by coming from it—just as the image of The Rube comes from the cover of a *Saturday Evening Post*, with the catfish in hand, and recurs as innocence converted to use out of the pressure of needs the society itself has taught. The dirty words, so to speak, which the book contains are not the simple "shit," "fuck," "cock,"

*Outburst*, no. 1, 1961.
*William Burroughs: *Naked Lunch.*

and so on, that society has made use of from time immemorial—or rather they are here played upon for what they are, for any of us, the power of fantasy, of an ultimately successful touching, carrying with it all the fearful load of suggestion that any ad for a brassiere can demonstrate. It is that "fuck" here *is* fuck, not the guffawing punch-line to a giggling joke, but horror, ultimate in its *free* term. If we had the money (say it), what wouldn't we do . . . The inventions Burroughs plays upon the organizational man, the *square* gone rigid with logically coherent *method,* the sunken man or woman with the "condition" ("You think I am innarested to hear about your horrible old condition? I am not innarested at all."), the forms of authority or societal control taken to satiric limits of fantasy so naked it cannot remember the way any longer to another term or situation:

> Old violet brown photos that curl and crack like mud in the sun: Panama City . . . Bill Gains putting down the paregoric con on a chinese druggist.
> "I've got these racing dogs . . . pedigree greyhounds . . . All sick with the dysentery . . . tropical climate . . . the shits . . . you sabe shit? . . . *my Whippets are Dying* . . ." He screamed. . . . His eyes lit up with blue fire. . . . The flame went out . . . smell of burning metal . . . "Administer with an eye dropper. . . . Wouldn't you? . . . Menstrual cramps . . . my wife . . . Kotex . . . Aged mother . . . Piles . . . raw . . . bleeding. . . ." He nodded out against the counter. . . . The druggist took a tooth-pick out of his mouth and looked at the end of it and shook his head. . . .

"Wouldn't you?" Which, and why? The vacuum that is the condition, the nightmare without sound except that it *is*—and waits, patiently enough. Which control do you choose?

Burroughs says: "There is only one thing a writer can write about: *what is in front of his senses at the moment of writing* . . . I am a recording instrument . . . I do not presume to impose 'story' 'plot' 'continuity' . . . Insofar as I succeed in *Direct* recording of certain areas of psychic process I may have limited function . . . I am not an entertainer."

The terms of this book are responsible in that they make the *responsive* areas of intelligence and sensation their logic—beyond any hierarchy of social purpose, good men and bad, evil seen as a side issue (beside the side issue of the nominal 'good'). Its form is an increasingly narrow range of recall, of stories told and retold, in shortening phase, so that they end as an echo of a page, paragraph, sentence, phrase, word: *Wouldn't you?*

There is no way to explain need except to state it. You can solve what you will as you will. We assume that to prevent such issues as Burroughs derives content from, we need only cut them out, away from ourselves. So much of the world has been tidied up in this manner that it is probable that very few people either want to, or can, recognize the anguish their own faces make clear. But Burroughs has written from all the evidence of his own body and mind their testament as well as his own.

(Note written for Grove Press, which plans to publish *Naked Lunch* this year.)

# Ways of Looking

*Parvenus and Ancestors*, by Barriss Mills. Flushing, N.Y.: Sparrow Magazine, 1959.

*Experiment Theatre Anthology No. 1*, edited by Carol Ely Harper. Seattle: Experimental Press, 1959.

*Kô, or A Season on Earth*, by Kenneth Koch. New York: Grove, 1959.

*Mexico City Blues*, by Jack Kerouac. New York: Grove, 1959.

*A Red Carpet for the Sun*, by Irving Layton. Highlands, N.C.: Jonathan Williams, 1959.

*The Heart in Naked Hunger*, by Judson Crews. Ranches of Taos, N.M.: Motive Book Shop, [1958].

*The Feel of Sun & Air upon Her Body*, by Judson Crews. Eureka, Calif.: Hearse Press, [1962].

There are many things to tell us the nature of the world in which we live. A pragmatic response to such nature, for example, would place the house where water is to be found, and would avoid, equally, the desert or whatever other situation might be supposed impossible. Our reference is this nature, and in our use of it we cite the nature of ourselves, the needs and suppositions which describe us as actual. Perhaps at last it is all a dream—as they say—some ultimate mistaking of purpose. That aside, in poems as elsewhere

*Poetry*, June 1961.

a description is, like it or not, made use of, to speak of worlds and
to live in them. Adaptations of form and of purpose follow as an
outline, an acknowledgment of exterior presence.

Barriss Mills works between a part-time wish and (also hopeful)
a rejection of an easy taking, of anything, so that his poems are,
often, wryly wanting something he feels may not be had. An image
of his father becomes:

> . . . Remembering
> now my father and the begonias
> he could love and they, thirsty, silent
> accept unknowing his silent care.
>
> ("Remembering My Father and the Begonias")

Is that given as the despair, or the triumph, of care; or is it habit,
maintained to secure a continuity? The problem, as ever, is meaning—and relationship, as Iago elsewhere says:

> . . . I'll prick them
> till they've lived (and felt
> the world rush in upon them)
> a moment, before they die.
>
> ("Interlude: Iago Addresses the Audience")

Mills feels, I think, the nature of women as both a relief and a
curious threat, or problem, of adaptation, in the ease of relationship suggested, not with men but with all that men fumble in, the
world of things and intention:

> No man can feel it—
> the aplomb women are born to.
>
> ("Helen")

The poems in his book are often a happy balance of good humor
and a wistful attention to discrepancies. They are small in the range
of their attention, and seem even meant to be so, e.g., notes on the
"classical" moon, Venus, "Everybody Cried at Our Wedding," Pyg-
malion's "icy art," and money: "The money? nobody knew / by now
where it had gone." In that sense they are occasional—or better,
purpose described as provoked attention not so much lacking as
falling beside a more deliberate sense of purpose.

Purpose itself, of course, may well be ridiculous, implying relationships where none may exist—so that no tunnels to China succeed. The *Experiment Theatre Anthology* fails partly in this sense. It is
not so much that one rejects, just like that, "the *petit drame* or One-

Minute Play" which the preface to this book describes, nor even the "arena theatre in every living-room." But to say that "We can develop a Shakespeare so in a hundred years . . ." strikes me as pretentiously overhopeful.

The plays themselves, insofar as they depend on poetry for a means, seem garbled and cribbed, echoes of a high-school "Shakespeare," who is all too present as it is. Bad writing stays bad writing no matter what the occasion, and it is a poor trick to attempt to blur that fact by removing it all to a play:

> LEAH:   Jacob, hear me now,
> For I am yours, as night has been our vow:
> You cannot love, I see, but give me room
> To lay my heart, and God will bless my womb.
>
> > ("Jacob Hofstädter")

Which is unfair, out of context, and there are many other "tones" at work in the collection. For myself, however, there is little of interest and/or it is a world so cutely begged that it becomes offensive, the Living Room *qua* Ultimate Refuge for pains quite real enough but never, I believe, to be exorcised in this manner. Our world seems desperate enough to make us want to turn all possible occasions to use. But to say with the complacency of Carol Ely Harper, "We have taught young poets, unfamiliar with playwriting, to make the One-Minute Play from one's own poem, preferably an unsuccessful one . . ." makes cosy what is not cosy, and turns such art as her Shakespeare's into a harmless pastime.

It is this sort of easy reference (which the *Experiment Theatre Anthology* implies) that Kenneth Koch lampoons with a very gracious viciousness. It is a character of the *urbane* to play upon discrepancies, and to leave the unifying and observing intelligence—with final limits of sky and ground and people thereon—as the only real term. Koch's "epic," mocking and clever, marches upon all sorts of things, the cliché of Great Baseball Teams (the Dodgers) and of Great Events (the Coronation) among them. The hero, or one of the heroes at least, is, rightly enough, Japanese, and the progress of the story, so to speak, leaps about like a kid flipping stations on a television set. The villain of it all is Dog Boss, whose farcical origins are much attached to a German shepherd, who had bitten his mother's seducer, etc., while all were living on a houseboat, etc.:

> Dog Boss was there, a child of five; tears welling
> In both his eyes, he ran to shore to farms

And cried for help, but none could understand him.
'Twas summer, blazing. Then a cool breeze fanned him,
And he saw at his side a German shepherd
With wagging tail, who understood! They hurried
To where the lust-crowned living-boat was tethered
And found the pair. The shepherd roared and buried
His teeth in Blickly's thigh, whose muscles severed.
From that day onward, sailing down the Surrey'd
Be nothing to the boy, without a dog;
Sheep could not substitute, nor could a hog.

Finally the whole thing comes to a fading end, because the problem with such work must be that it can, patently, go on forever. As can likewise the world which it reports, with such inventive humor. But laughter, like love, among the ruins seems a reasonable act. It doesn't change things, so to speak. It simply makes them entertaining.

If Koch's world depends upon a satiric response to a chaos of value, then Jack Kerouac's becomes a simplification of that chaos, familiar to us now in Zen teaching. For example:

You start with the Teaching
    Inscrutable of the Diamond
And end with it, your goal
    is your startingplace,
No race was run, no walk
    of prophetic toenails
Across Arabies of hot
    meaning—you just
    numbly don't get there.

                                    (113th Chorus)

Kerouac's book is a series of improvisations, notes, a shorthand of perceptions and memories, having in large part the same kind of word-play and rhythmic invention to be found in his prose. It seems likely that much will exasperate because we are wary of that which does not make use of familiar continuities. We like the "story" of usual thought, and we are apt to distrust what so unembarrassedly wants to throw that all away. But Kerouac says:

Like running a stick thru water
The use and effect
Of tellin people that
            their house
            is burning . . .

                                    (126th Chorus)

So I write about heaven
Smoke for the scene,
Wanta bring everyone
Straight to the dream.

If you could only hold
    What you know
As you know it forever,
    instead-a
Moving from griefy to griefy,
    lament to lament,
Groan, and have to come out
    and smile once again . . .

(196th Chorus)

Perhaps the "big words" will be missed, or more, the manner which contains them—and the forms of wiseness and security which that manner of investment secures. It is not that simple to find a language whose emphases will be common perhaps. I mean that Kerouac may well distract and irritate more than he will teach. But the attempt is useful, with its clutch of old songs and childwise wordplay, jogging the mind to a simplicity, making the old wiseness foolish, the old foolishness wise.

Irving Layton also distrusts the deceptive distances in manner which the more academic poet is apt to fall heir to, that remove from the terms (if not the situations) of a common existence with other men and women, in a common place. For example, in his preface to *A Red Carpet for the Sun* he makes very clear the position he has chosen for himself:

> . . . What I've written—besides my joy in being alive to write about them—has been about this singular business of human evil; the tension between Hebrew and pagan, between the ideal and the real. The disorder and glory of passion. The modern tragedy of the depersonalization of men and women. About a hideously commercial civilization spawning hideously deformed monstrosities.

With that intent there can be little misunderstanding of his commitment, and the poems themselves (here happily collected into one substantial volume from twelve others which came before it) make clear the range possible to this kind of sincerity. Layton is, all at once, the most tender of men, and the most purposefully satiric. He uses the provincialism of his situation (Canada) to keep himself awake to the alternatives, and, being a Jew, he holds to a tradition of intelligence and compassion. Most simply, he writes in this way:

*The Madonna of the Magnificat*

I shall wander all night and not see
    as much happiness as this infant gives
to his plain sisters who are adoring him
and his mother cradling and covering
    him with her love.

She has borrowed the white moon from the sky
    to pillow his golden curls
and at her magical cry the dark roofs
the length of the street lie down
    like quiet animals.

The night will wear out and disappear
    like soiled water through the city's drains
but now it is full of noise and blessed neighbours
and all the tenement windows fly open
    like birds.

A world so made possible (in the mind of a man who will not give in to its pain) must be true beyond all contradiction.

What to say, then, of all those other worlds, equally the intelligences (or lack thereof) which have created them? It becomes less and less a "world" one may witness as an "objective" phenomenon. Nor does this seem a recent problem if Wyndham Lewis can write in 1927, "The material world that the human intellect has created is still there, of course; but as it is a creation of our minds, it will no doubt be found that we can even physically disintegrate it." That we can now do without question. Yet that hardly proves a relief.

Judson Crews has, for some time now, lived outside of the common areas of recognition, surviving by his persistence and by, as well, the respect those who have read his work with care have come to give. He asks for nothing and lives sparely in his work, a place for survival, where the test of a life is that which is possible in it, terrors of image, dream sensualities, hard thought, all given place. The twists of language (which his titles most quickly describe, e.g., "Sated in Lucid Devine," "Bale Thaw") define this same character of test, of meaning, curiously, of statement against statement, word against word. The problem of meaning itself is defined by him in this way:

*Of the Self Exceeded*

The page itself was part of the meaning
and the man reading was part

The sky above is part of the meaning
and the bird drifting like a feather

Because the page is as perfect as meaning
and the sky is as perfect as air

The mind is startled in face of perfection
it hides from the limitless air

The bird is perfection of air, of air
but the mind is lost short of meaning

Both books (*The Heart in Naked Hunger* and *The Feel of Sun & Air upon Her Body*) have this hardihood of thought; and both as well use the device of occasional photographs, of nudes, of flat building fronts, of many untoward things, let us say, to shock the mind awake with a somewhat wry invitation.

I find my own relief in such "worlds" as Crews and Layton have worked to make actual, admitting that such a feeling is a feeling— yet either man is openly concerned to make a way common to all, despite the seeming difficulty of Crews' images at times or Layton's insistence on values which must (fairly enough) discriminate. It is the size of the area involved by them which proves distinctive, and it is not that they make a world apart from that given me—which could only prove a competition. In one sense, we are all "nature" poets these days, and whoever can show a nature of world still possible, to others as well as "me," ought to be commended.

# The Fascinating Bore

*Poems,* by Algernon Charles Swinburne, selected, with an Introduction, by Bonamy Dobrée. The Penguin Poets. Baltimore, Md.: Penguin Books, 1961.

*Swinburne: A Selection,* edited, with an Introduction, by Edith Sitwell. New York: Harcourt, Brace, and Co., 1960.

Early in his book *The White Goddess,* Robert Graves provides this description:

> The Goddess is a lovely, slender woman with a hooked nose, deathly pale face, lips as red as rowan-berries, startlingly blue eyes and long fair hair; she will suddenly transform herself into sow, mare, bitch, vixen, she-ass, weasel, serpent, owl, she-wolf, tigress, mermaid or loathsome hag . . .

He continues, "The test of a poet's vision, one might say, is the accuracy of his portrayal of the White Goddess and of the island over which she rules. . . ."

This same figure is made use of in Mario Praz's study, *The Romantic Agony,* as a characteristic presence in Romantic literature, and it is in the work of Swinburne he believes "this type of Fatal Woman found its most complete form." Unlike Graves, however, who is himself involved in this same tradition, Praz depends much upon the sexual terms of such reference in Swinburne and the other writers with whom he deals. The question of Swinburne's al-

*Poetry,* August 1962.

golagnia—the association of sexual fulfillment with pain—is the key to Praz's own use of the work itself. For example, he summarizes Swinburne's "formula" as follows:

> . . . man, in his work, aspires to be 'the powerless victim of the furious rage of a beautiful woman [here quoting from Swinburne's *The Whippingham Papers*]'; his attitude is passive, his love a martyrdom, his pleasure pain. As for the woman . . . , she is always the same type of unrestrained, imperious, cruel beauty.

Whether or not such emphasis proves fair at last, it makes unequivocally clear the source of energy in Swinburne's early, and I think greatest, work. He himself, in the curious innocence of his nature, found it impossible to accept finally—or he could not use it as could Baudelaire, for whom he felt great admiration. In her introduction to *Swinburne: A Selection,* Edith Sitwell quotes from a letter of Swinburne's to his friend and mentor, Lady Trevelyan, who had warned him he was being attacked "on the score of his personal morality":

> I cannot express the horror and astonishment, the unutterable indignation and loathing, with which I have been struck on hearing that anyone could be vile enough to tax me, I do not say with doing, but with saying anything of the kind to which you refer.

It does not seem to me possible to answer as simply as does Edith Sitwell, "I cannot believe this extremely brave man was a hypocrite." Nor does it seem otherwise possible to settle the question as does Bonamy Dobrée, the other editor here involved:

> One need not close one's eyes to these things in Swinburne; indeed to do so would be foolish. Most men and women have in them vestiges of such destructive impulses, which normal beings turn into more beneficent channels, or suppress, but which Swinburne had no wish to hide. Such things need not concern the reader who seeks in poetry for imaginative release, for support of the more directive energies, for relations he can contemplate and ramify; they belong, rather, to the realm of psychiatry, and, so far as this Introduction is concerned, will be left there.

It is a little ironic that Swinburne found just that "imaginative release" and the "support of the more directive energies" which Dobrée notes in the writing of the very poems which raise these questions. And there the reader must follow him, or else lose contact with all that ambivalence of experience for which the poems serve as means. Had it not been for the complexity of Swinburne's sexual nature, his work would be only a thin exercise of technical virtuosity few in fact have so acquired, yet which, by itself, serves little. It was his genius that in these poems he could so resolve, with such art as he had, "such destructive impulses."

Even in Swinburne's sense of liberty, "what his poetry sings out loudly," as Dobrée puts it, there is much equally equivocal. Those familiar with the writings of de Sade—"that illustrious and ill-requited benefactor of humanity," Swinburne calls him in a letter to Monckton Milnes—will recognize the basis for Swinburne's own antitheism. For example, here is a brief instance of de Sade's argument in *Dialogue entre un Prêtre et un Moribond.*

> PRIEST: Who can comprehend the vast and infinite designs of God upon man, and who can understand all we see?
>
> DYING MAN: The man who simplifies things, my friend, and especially the man who does not increase the causes the better to muddle the effects. What do you want with a second difficulty when you cannot explain the first? And since it is possible that Nature quite unaided has done all that you attribute to your God, why do you want to look for a master for her?

Swinburne makes use of a like argument in "Hymn to Proserpine":

> Wilt thou take all, Galilean? but these thou shalt not take,
> The laurel, the palms and the paean, the breasts of the
>     nymphs in the brake;
> Breasts more soft than a dove's, that tremble with tenderer
>     breath;
> And all the wings of the Loves, and all the joy before
>     death . . .
> More than these wilt thou give, things fairer than all these
>     things?
> O daughter of earth, of my mother, her crown and blossom
>     of birth . . .
>
> I am also, I also, thy brother; I go as I came unto earth.

*Atalanta in Calydon,* described by Edith Sitwell as "indisputably Swinburne's greatest work," was also his first published book. Our knowledge of it is now usually confined to the choruses, "When the hounds of spring are on winter's traces . . . ," and "Before the beginning of years . . . ," and perhaps others like these. We cannot read it as the great release from Victorian limits it then seemed.

Although Browning, with some accuracy, felt it a "fuzz of words," Ruskin thought it, symptomatically enough, "The grandest thing ever done by a youth, though he is a demonic youth . . ." The play is, whatever else, a beautifully maintained control of means upon a classical theme, of no great depth of thinking—on Swinburne's part at least, since de Sade is again the clue to its logic of argument. But if sounds alone can engage us—and Edith Sitwell provides much provocative comment on this score—then we should be satisfied with this:

> And I too as thou sayest have seen great things;
> Seen otherwise, but chiefly when the sail
> First caught between stretched ropes the roaring west,
> And all our oars smote eastward, and the wind
> First flung round faces of seafaring men
> White splendid snow-flakes of the sundering foam,
> And the first furrow in virginal green sea
> Followed the plunging ploughshare of hewn pine . . .

Yet the most incisive of Swinburne's poems remain those in which he underwent the "test of a poet's vision," in Graves' sense—or when his concern with the terms of his algolagnia is unmistakable, as here:

> As one who hidden in deep sedge and reeds
> Smells the rare scent made where a panther feeds,
>     And tracking ever slotwise the warm smell
> Is snapped upon by the sweet mouth and bleeds,
>
> His head far down the hot sweet throat of her—
> So one tracks love, whose breath is deadlier . . .
>
> ("Laus Veneris")

The major part of Edith Sitwell's selection comes from *Poems and Ballads* (1866), and includes the whole of *Atalanta in Calydon* (1865). Dobrée ranges more out of necessity, since the Penguin selection intends to represent the whole body of Swinburne's writing. After Swinburne's "rescue" by Watts-Dunton (with whom he shared a household for the thirty years until his death in 1909), there is little of interest in his poems. Perhaps it was the confinement from his excesses that quieted his earlier energy. It was Watts-Dunton's assertion that, "From this moment (1879) Swinburne's connection with Bohemian London ceased entirely." But much had in fairness stopped before that, it would seem. *Songs Before Sunrise* (1871), written in hero-worship of the Italian political exile Mazzini, shows increased diffuseness and verbosity despite the occasional interest of a poem like "Hertha" or "Hymn of Man." Still both these last become a tedium of accumulation and patterned manner. The intensity is gone.

It is doubtful to me that Swinburne can now be of much use to us. We have come, or have tried to, so far from the manners of that period, moving toward (as Grierson notes in his monograph on Swinburne) an increased use of spoken rhythms. This is why, perhaps, Swinburne's poems must seem so interminably artificial a contrivance so very often. Or perhaps it is, as Robert Duncan suggests, that Swinburne's "pleasurable pain/painful pleasure specialty may have something to do with his aesthetic in the actual poem—going on almost unbearably as he does. The fascinating bore in discourse is a sadist in that way."

# Preface to *Sticks and Stones,*
## by George Bowering

The words will become a world, sustaining the occasion of thought —which is to think of things, in that complex of all that had been thought, might be, and felt equally. This is not, after all, to find an escape from what problems may exist in all senses. Feeling alone prevents it, and the impact of distortions, which make of common reality an immense tension of impossibility, must be first felt to then be dealt with.

But in the care with words, a world occurs, made possible by that care. For example, Williams writes, "If the language is distorted crime flourishes. It is well that in the unobstructed arts (because they can at favorable times escape the perversions which flourish elsewhere) a means is at least presented to the mind where a man can go on living."

Bowering begins to live at this point, finding a world opening to his sense of it. How can it be otherwise? And he has it:

> so that it is the walking of the voice
>
> the
>
> opening of doors and the walking
> on floors
> and the closing of doors
>
> the swinging of arms
>
> and the talking of the voice . . .

George Bowering, *Sticks and Stones* (Vancouver: Tishbooks, 1963).

All senses come to their occasion in this use of them. And things are not hostile, let us believe it. If the means stay true to such occasion, all sense may then focus:

> Thinking what?
> happens in the
> swing from one
> step to the touch
> of the next—

or otherwise, says "The older we got / the shorter the climb . . ." If one is to live, and what else would we have him do, then it must perhaps be that he take in hand all that first comes to hand, the sight, for example:

> In the white moving
> over the sky
> there is no future shape
> or any moment before . . .

Wise enough to know better, and to want to, beginning at the beginning, where taste, sight, air, a night's walk, or a morning, love found in another, all the perpetual occasions begin to take root— this seems wise enough.

# "Think what's got away . . ."

*The Hazards of Holiness,* by Brother Antoninus. Garden City, N.Y.: Doubleday, 1962.

*Traveling through the Dark,* by William Stafford. New York: Harper & Row, 1962.

*Imperatives,* by Anthony Ostroff. New York: Harcourt Brace & World, 1962.

*Uncle Dog,* by Robert Sward. London: Putnam, 1962.

*Children Passing,* by Richard Emil Braun. Austin: University of Texas Press, 1962.

*A Wedge of Words,* by Frederic Will. Austin: University of Texas Press, 1962.

*A Local Pride,* by Raymond Souster. Toronto: Contact Press, 1962.

*Run with the Hunted,* by Charles Bukowski. Chicago: Midwest Poetry Chapbooks, 1962.

*Letter to an Imaginary Friend,* by Thomas McGrath. Denver: Swallow Press, 1962.

*My Friend Tree,* by Lorine Niedecker. Edinburgh: Wild Hawthorne Press, 1961.

One tends to value any kind of statement for what one can take from it as a content, or a state of feeling some way about something, a viable association between what the statement has "said"

*Poetry,* April 1963.

and what terms of response it can gain in who hears it. We learn young that the way in which some thing is said, the tone of voice, the literal words used, and all the relations implied in the context of their use—all these say "things" too. It is equally a commonplace that in a poem such content may have, finally, a greater value for the reader than the literal facts the poem is otherwise making clear.

The work of Brother Antoninus begins, first of all, with a very emphatic content, characterized by him as follows: "A poem, like a dream, is a 'whole' to the extent that it registers the mystery of the psychic complex which produced it." *The Hazards of Holiness* is a collection of specific tests, of "scalps torn dripping from the skulls of interior adversaries," which last way of speaking will not outrage those who are willing to admit that a "Dark Night of the Soul" may exist for a man who attempts to find himself in relation to God. Again as Brother Antoninus says, "These are the terrible wrestlings his verse begins to register; and this is the harrowing ambiguity, so fraught with terror and mystery and meaning, that cross-riddles this demon-haunted realm."

Such a way of speaking will have, of course, an immediate impact, and it will either be one of respect and sympathy for the man who has so endured, to speak, or it will be perhaps a questioning of such an invention of agony in a world so substantially tormented. Either response will here depend on the reader's own relation to the literal facts dealt with, the faith in God which is the issue. But, in either case, there can be without such question a simple response to the ways the words are working, as here:

> Christ-cut: the cedar
> Bleeds where I gashed it.
>
> Lance-wound under the narrow rib.
>
> Eve's orifice: the agony of Abel
> Enacted out on the Tree.
>
> Blood gushed
> From the gash . . .

The heavy, harshly stressed alliteration is sign of the intent, and it is, at times, a rhetoric that is present apart from demands of specific content; I find this most the case, for example, in the more dramatic poems, as "Saints" and the two parts of the title poem. I do not like—and it is my taste which qualifies: "Herodias, that corrosive female wrath, / Black grasp of the invidious breed, / Blanched, swore blooded reprisal . . ." But I cannot avoid or deny the force of

this language, despite my own characterization of it as often melo-
dramatic, that is, an enlargement of occasion purely willed. What
the poems effect is a language, itself a formality, a distinct way of
engaging feeling, a testing of tones of response and recognition.
They speak in one voice because their occasion—despite the variation of subject—is always the same, the search for substantial faith.

The poems of William Stafford are, in some contrast, much quieter in tone. But, despite the frequent colloquialisms, an equally
conscious rhetoric seems to me at work. For example, it is present
I think in this kind of balance of manners: "no acrobat of salvation, / I couldn't help seeing. . . ." Stafford familiarizes his reality,
makes it often subject to a "we," generalizing in that way the personal insight. The primary tones of his work are those of nostalgia,
of a wry wit, often, which can make peace with the complexities of
times and places. He says "that some kind of organization / is the
right way to live." The danger is simply that things will become cozy
("The earth says have a place . . ."), and that each thing will be hu-
manized to an impression of it merely. When the irony can outwit
this tendency, then an active intelligence comes clear. In the following poem I am put off by the personifications of the first verse, but,
in fairness, they do underline what becomes the point of the second:

> *Found in a Storm*
>
> A storm that needed a mountain
> met it where we were:
> we woke up in a gale
> that was reasoning with our tent,
> and all the persuaded snow
> streaked along, guessing the ground.
>
> We turned from that curtain, down.
> But sometime we will turn
> back to the curtain and go
> by plan through an unplanned storm,
> disappearing into the cold,
> meanings in search of a world.

Formalization of intelligence, or whatever to call it—that is,
the manner which wants to invest subject with its own wit before
there is any subject—can become a great problem. At present there
seems still a "style of the period" which got its authority from the
work of the New Critics, and which still lingers, heavily, despite the
fact that it grows increasingly out of fashion. All fashion is a distraction, and perhaps old modes, in this respect, are really more pleas-

ant than new ones. But I must object, just that I lived through it, to the manner in which Anthony Ostroff writes. Here is the first poem in his book:

*Matinal: The Stockyards*
Wooly wooly
The bright brick shines
The sheep's feet peck there
All in a line

And lines in lines
Moves out on the wet
Brick in the light

The sheep forget

This is not the primary tone of the book, or, rather, the way in which the poems are usually organized or directed. The book is really a collection of literary manners, exercises, in conventional styles of our day. There is a "Dirge" ("Where are the lips, the breast, the thigh / That were such poetry . . ."), a "Folk Song" ("Sing death-ily, deathily, deathily sing. / The crops are to seed and the seeds are rotting . . ."), and other usual visits to the country, elegies, "littlest sister," and so on. The technical means seem competent, although stiffly present—again, the will "to write" "a poem" is dominant. And the intelligence is so battered in the process of getting it all, just so, together, that very little otherwise gets said. It is taste, as ever, balking, but I cannot react any longer to tricks like this one: "The library thinks of itself I think . . ." I question that anyone is thinking at all.

Problems coming in pairs, Robert Sward joins Anthony Ostroff to drive the point home. What are literary "manners" and how can we be rid of them, so that poetry can become again an active invest-ment of all the range of language and all the reality which can be found there? Sward's humor is a good sign, but why destroy the poem with banality:

Hello wife, hello world, hello God,
I love you; hello certain monsters . . .

And why insist, so often, that the range of experience dealt with has to be an itsy-bitsy business of tiny tots and their ironic elders? The assumption that all childhood memories—or these curious rec-ollections that now pass as such—are intrinsically valuable baffles

me. In Sward's book there are also letters to a psychiatrist, take-offs
on advertisements, odd animals (and again I wish these could be let
rest), and other arch inventions. I like best those poems in which he
does invent, wildly and wittily ("Beach Scenes—and Other Scenes"
for one), but here also the wiseguy manner grows tiresome.

It is curious, if terrifying, to see how deeply a literary manner
can cut into resources that must, at some level, be holding the whole
unwieldy coherence together. Richard Emil Braun has a complicated and interesting mind, but he wants to say everything in one
breath, not so much grandly as conclusively:

>         The bodies of the children
> whose characters I am hired to strengthen are grotesque:
>         faces eruptive, extremities
>     disproportionate, voices stridulous.
> The ensemble, ugly with cruel, abrupt
>     asynchronous growth cripples their minds
> which I am paid to fortify by means of Caesar . . .

And I can sympathize with what's going on in his head, so to speak,
having taught Latin to such children in the Southwest. But what
happens, then, to the poem—is what I question. I am not, I hope,
being sentimental. In any case, he tends to "subjectivize" the poem's
content to that point where no possibility of what's outside him remains volatile, free in its own term, even when he "speaks" in the
guise of the several voices he chooses, as in "Late Promenades."

When the literal thought of the poem has energy, then a sharper
gauge of means seems to occur. There is not that working up of
a subject so dulling in Ostroff, or so glib in Sward. Frederic Will
writes in a traditionally developed manner, but he feels perceptions
in a poem specifically:

> *Across the Street*
>
> Those berries on fire from fire:
> I shall repair
> Losses of passion here.
>
> Memling would have held the instant
> Sure in a cardinal's hat
> Taking it down in sight.
>
> I am less sure.
> What will not cool from the word,
> Ashed in the very instant?
> Lost, when heard?

The last line gives pause, certainly, for reflection. I wish something freer, quicker, might have been found for the statement of the second two lines; Memling is also a distraction, though that is clearly my opinion. I don't like the "Ashed . . ." in the next to the last line. But the poem is interesting, it says something beyond a manner; and no matter what I may cavil at, I hear it.

In a like sense one hears this poem by Raymond Souster:

> *Morning Certainly*
>
> Coming back from away out, a darkness,
> there is light at the window
> my clothes are on the chair, as if waiting,
> there is even
> someone in bed with me.

After so much self-consciousness and preening, I like the flatness, the very openness of this language. It is simply said, but I had never thought of it that way, and I am left, quietly, with the perception.

But it isn't all that quickly an issue of a vocabulary because Charles Bukowski uses very open speech, and common sentiments and references. But not the same thing comes of it; ". . . hooray say the roses, today is blamesday / and we are red as blood . . ." does not think in the way that Souster's poem thinks. Souster also at times drops to a level of response that he knows too well, feels even too comfortably, despite the pain of the reference. The starved, the poor, the bewildered, the dragged, sullen reality of usual life does not want, or not want, to be a poem. The work is still to be done.

Even a life is no continuity, it happens here and there, *now*— then it was or will be. *Letter to an Imaginary Friend,* by Thomas McGrath, is very moving in the world it makes tangible in its opening sections, the harsh farm world of a young boy:

> . . . I couldn't quit. I came out of sleep at four
> Dazed and dreaming and ate my food on the run,
> And ran to the barn . . .

Then it tends to become programmatic, crossed by defined purposes, as are even the terms of love it meets with early. Approximations of reality take the place of literal orders, or, more fairly, the reader is given attitudes rather than precise contexts: "Now in the chill streets / I hear the hunting, and the long thunder of money. . . ."

How can such life be told? In his introduction to Lorine Niedecker's *My Friend Tree,* Edward Dorn makes a useful comment: "What

is in will come out, it does not always work the other way. . . ." And
he ends by saying: "I like these poems because first they attach an
undistractable clarity to the word, and then because they are unabashed enough to weld that word to a freely sought, beautifully
random instance—that instance being the only thing place and its
content can be. . . ." I cannot believe that there is anything, finally,
to be proven. All we see, we see. By nature, then, and of course
unfairly, I will stick with Miss Niedecker, who writes:

> Remember my little granite pail?
> The handle of it was blue.
> Think what's got away in my life!
> Was enough to carry me thru.

# The Beat Voznesensky

*Selected Poems of Andrei Voznesensky.* Translated by Anselm
Hollo. New York: Grove Press, 1964.

It is difficult to read Voznesensky's work apart from the various
uses to which it has been put, and is to some extent still serving in
this present collection. Immediately there is the fact of his being
Russian, and young, and—most insistently—an evidence of the political *thaw* which reached a peak in the winter of 1962. There is,
further, his relation with Pasternak (emphasized in Anselm Hollo's
introduction) and the implications of that fact. And, finally, his
public association with Evgeny Evtushenko has emphasized the social aspects of his activity. The jacket notes say that his latest collection, *The Three-Cornered Pear* (all of which is included in this volume), had advance orders of more than 100,000 copies prior to
publication. Response of that order in itself defines a use of poetry
rarely experienced in this country.

It is necessary, then, to make some qualification of the situation
which he has shared with Evtushenko. Edward Dorn, writing of the
latter in *Kulchur 8*, makes a useful (if wry) definition:

> . . . For instance there is Yevtushenko. He is feeble-minded . . . in the
> way reserved for a modern intellectual, i.e., he doesn't say anything.
> He is precious about borders! He would campaign for a cheap inter-
> national right-of-way. He likes it in the country. My My. He likes
> Ernest. A most exact indicator of a facetious taste. He desires the
> reign of the simple-minded middle class worker in enthusiasm and

*The Nation,* November 9, 1964.

sensitivity and his excuse is assured him because he is Russian without
the wild Russian mind, in other words he is a member of the first of
the world fraternities (used in the college sense): U.S.-Russia. . . .

If Dorn quickly summarizes what may well be a more complex
instance of literary *populism*, I believe him accurate nonetheless.
Evtushenko's poems—such as have been translated in the Penguin
collection, for one—are very bland generalities.

Elements of this generality are also evident in Voznesensky's
work. Here, for example, one finds an idiom derived from a loose
reading of "beat" poetry, masked as "public" value:

> . . . Up into the mountains and into the beards
> into the sea the rivers run dry the fish are dying. . . .
> Rolls-Royces are fucking our women,
> radiatoractivity. . . .
>
> ("Beatnik's Monologue")

But it proves a content equally vague in any idiom, and it appears in the earlier poems as "The artists take leave, / Bareheaded,
enter / The humming fields and forests / Of birch and oak, like a
church . . ."

Such writing seems a most tired sense of what we are literally involved with, as a political entity (the "people" notwithstanding), or
as an individual entity—quite distinct from such apostrophe as "O
you who had plenty soul"—which is the line directly following on
what I have quoted from "Beatnik's Monologue."

There is no need that I can value to read a poetry imitative
merely of terms the American has so much more sharply *known*,
and insofar as Voznesensky writes "like" a *beatnik* (in Hollo's translations, at all events), he is dull indeed. He is not in any sense an
Allen Ginsberg (who is not, be it emphasized, a *beatnik*) nor is he
possessed of like force. But there is a third point from which to
measure, in the work of Lorca.

Lorca is a poet close to Voznesensky's attention—one, in fact, he
particularly honors:

> . . . I love Lorca. I love his name, hovering lightly like a boat, hum-
> ming like a gallery in a theater, vibrating with the sensitivity of the
> moon-disk of a radio relay station; smelling as bitter and intense as
> orange rind. . . .
>
> ("Lover of Lorca")

In this prose poem he speaks most clearly of his own sense of poetry, and the intensity with which he wants to invest his metaphors

takes as its example Lorca's—"Those wildly sprouting metaphors of Lorca!"

Comparisons are deceptive, but Lorca's use of America does make clear what Voznesensky's tends to make bland. In "Ode to Walt Whitman," for example, a language specific to the literal feeling occurs, and the revulsion felt by Lorca, in the pain of his experience, is explicit: "Agony, agony, dream, ferment and dream. / Such is the world, my friend, agony, agony. / Corpses are decomposing under the clocks of cities; / war passes with a million grey rats weeping, / the rich give to their mistresses / small illuminated moribunds, / and life is not noble, nor good, nor sacred. . . ." Against this, Voznesensky's response reads weakly:

> . . . Under the firehose spouting out endless driveways
> my ears were turning like windmills
> O godless gasoline poisonous America
> Coca-Cola and tolling bells . . .
>
> ("Another Beginning")

When metaphor becomes a recognition of something more than echoed banality, when feeling gains the active transformation of literal things in relation, another Voznesensky comes into focus, and he is not the generalized intelligence of good intentions:

> . . . My cries have been torn onto miles of magnetic tape
> an endless red tongue, snaked round a big spool
> I have been taken apart dismantled and dragged to
>     interrogations. . . .
> There I am, crucified and transparent, riddled with photo
>     bullets
> their fingernails, rusty, are trying to scratch at my heart
> "Does it hurt Mr. Voznesensky?" . . .
>
> ("An Extorted Divagation")

It becomes a protest against all distortion, but most of all his own. Here as well it is possible to feel him one who, without sentimentality, fights for the preservation of an individual sensibility. It is from this paradoxically quieter sense of himself—the *place* I feel him finally to be—that he writes:

> . . . I have tried
>               in the shooting-galleries
>      for 100 points with 10 bullets
>      but thank you for not letting me make it,

for lighting up my small transparent guns
illuminating them like a red fist
appearing in a rubber glove;

"Andrei Voznesensky"—enough,
no word, no little doggie to be left behind . . .

("Autumn in Sigulda")

# Judson Crews

It is a little hard for me to separate my own affection for Judson Crews—as a man who has so often helped me with such a quiet sympathy—from my sense of his work as a poet. I feel, in this case, no very actual reason to. He is an isolated man, despite the continuity of his various activities, as bookseller, printer, editor, in all of which one marks the persistence of his energy. But he is not a part of a 'group,' nor does he invite this kind of identification. His poems are singular effects of the constancy of one man's attention to the oftentimes 'faceless' reality of a world, which can baffle, hurt, yet call for an endless attention and response.

I am most struck by the character of his language, evident in the selection of poems which follows. He feels the words with a marked sensuousness; they are 'real' to him, which is to say, each one offers itself to his imagination as might the texture of wet sand, or silk's softness, or smoke in air. His words are volatile. They open into guises of feeling, of senses of things, beyond the literal nature of their meaning. Often they create a feeling of deep nostalgia, and of that blocked dilemma of feeling which will not be recognized by those to whom it is offered. The women of his poems are so lovely in their being, in that they contain forever the reality of touch. But access to them is neither simple nor to be taken for granted. They will never be 'there' so simply for the mind's intention.

This world, then, is real—as one comes to know it. In it men falter, grow confused; women grow tired of their prize. Yet the words hold them, in this man's care.

*The Desert Review*, Spring 1964.

# A Note for *Thread* and Fielding Dawson

I have long been impressed by Fielding Dawson's abilities as a writer. His consciousness is *in* his writing and that is, for me, a rare and useful fact. Speaking of stories, he said once that unless they *take a turn on their own,* they can come to nothing. He meant, simply, if one write only what one intends, as some presumption always to be respected, then intentions are really all one ever comes to— good or bad. There must be a further place where all the assumptions of significance are lost, and some much more *present* instant of integrity can occur. Such location has its obvious dangers, and yet I do not see, personally, how they are not to be risked. It is foolish to define as 'control' an ultimately rigid formula of effects— 'gimmicks' as they are called in the States, the cheap clichés of a tired so-called 'industry.' Control here means the recognition of a moment to moment term of possibility, which is *not* static, but rather so volatile in its nature it demands all possible articulation of attention—to give shape to smoke in air.

Fielding Dawson, *Thread* (London: Andrew Crozier, 1964).

# A Note for Kenneth Irby

The sense of *place* in American poetry grows increasingly insistent, but it is not one simply of what sort of house you happen to have, or anything akin to mere description. It is, more deeply, that experience of location which is out of time, and the history of traditional order—a location which is, instead, one of the literal fact of space, and the ground which occupies it, literally under foot.

That fact is all the more evident in the writing of those who had the middle west as the first place they knew. For Kenneth Irby it becomes:

> . . . because it's me, and only there
>
> can I go in—
> the circle to focus
>
> comes narrower,
> the land
>
> presses up
> like flesh
>
> toward the hand . . .

More, he carries this response, and measure, of his experience into all the terms of that experience, as he moves away from this place— yet always, to my mind, looks for the reality of the first known way of feeling.

Men as he, it would seem, had no easy way of being even where they first were. Historically, we know the loneliness and what it led to, in the first people to take root there. The woods shrank back,

*Duende* 8 (September 1965).

and the grasslands opened before them, seemingly an endlessly vacant possibility. Touch is not simple. Feelings tend to draw back
from what they know as such emptiness. An endurance not at all
romantic seems to take hold.

But the inner terms of feeling nonetheless survive, looking always for their possibility—calling to friend, to brother, to whatever
can and will acknowledge them. I read that fact in these poems too,
finding such an intensity of longing it is at moments hard to acknowledge—just that a man is facing so unequivocally what he has
been given to accept.

The terms are common, however—ours as his. We will find a
world only as he does, by loving it.

# Frederick Eckman:
## *The Epistemology of Loss*

*The Epistemology of Loss*, by Frederick Eckman. West La-
fayette, Ind.: The Sparrow Magazine, 1963.

The title of this book gives an accurate sense of its content, and, as
well, the manner of its feeling. It is an "epistemology" wryly considered, for the most part, and also one which moves from the feeling
of knowing something to the ironic situation here of what is known,
and how it is known—and finally, to that sense of 'what for,' which
provokes the rhetoric of:

> . . . Mother of silences,
> Invoke the blind rosebush below, whose round
> And scarlet sounds ring fence-notes heaven-high,
> That is the singing echo of swift wings
> We choke not, chance not, fling not away
> Our leaf and passport through this atmosphere;
> But glide in cloudy echelon of rose,
> Beyond the heat-streaked doppelgänger Now . . .
>
> ("July: A Devotional")

It is an actual nightmare which is felt, unrelieved, or if at all so,
then simply as that 'relief' the intelligence may suppose when it
has reduced the person it inhabits to something "Cold with terror,
rigid as a beast/held in some pit or trap . . ." There is a persistent
sense of an animal rage, and bafflement—a frustrated physical
anger that wants to strike out against that which has hurt it. But

*Elizabeth*, March 1965.

there is also the continuingly ironic emphasis on the uselessness of such acts—as here, in a poem called "Hurry, Hurry":

Say: "Heart is a black stallion,
evil as midnight. His eyes
glint fire, his hooves can murder.
He thunders across the world."
Say & say. Meanwhile the heart
spurts out its fury, embers
to cold ash, calmly nibbles
gray grass in a gray meadow.

The book has, however, another way of speaking to my own mind even more moving—in which a quiet is left to "say" more than does the violence of what I have quoted. It is not simply that this tone is more malleable, or that it lets the reader develop his own assumptions—but that it comes so directly from what it involves, a literal pain which can only say what it literally feels. "Omega":

What is there
to be said
when everything
has been said?
*Words? Words*
*are nothing!*
This from you
in another spring,
& once more the
flowering Judas
betrays us, o the
sprawling wisteria
purples across our
crumbling wall.
The flowers, they
too will decay.
No, you are not
right, but neither
(o my lost love!)
are you wrong.

If—as Pound once wrote—"Nothing counts but the quality of the emotion. . . ," one has in this poem a measure of that possibility.

# A Note for These Poems . . .

There is no simple way to say anything—unless by that accident which is feeling, one is given, literally, the words in their own terms. It is here it all begins, an endlessly possible world. No one earns anything by it, nor can it be come to as an intention. What it all means is insistently more than any one sense of it will offer. Again and again it will happen, and in that demand its own occasion.

I can no longer remember what it was led me to try to write poems. I had no articulateness, and no sense of a place where such activity might be possible. But I don't think one knows more than that one has to and/or does write as he can.

David Franks has equally no alternative. There is no other way to say it.

> In a dream one sees it,
> a tongue, his own, floating
> in a small bowl . . .

A long time ago Yeats said, *In dreams begin responsibilities* . . . This one is adamant.

David Franks, *Touch* ([Baltimore]: Red Wheel Barrow Press, 1965).

# Rainer Gerhardt: A Note

I felt very close to this man—selfishly, because he gave me knowledge of a world I had otherwise no means of knowing. We were of
the same age, but the life he had been given was far from that I
knew. When he spoke of growing up in the Hitler *Jugend,* of the
final chaos of his feelings and senses of possibility after he had been
drafted into the army—of his desertion, then, to Tito's forces in
Yugoslavia—finally, of all the world of chaos after the war, of his
marriage and his two young sons who had to go daily through
streets of collapsed buildings often with bushes pushing through
the rubble—of the hope of a magazine, then small books, of what
Ernst Robert Curtius characterized as *the most hopeful sign to come
out of postwar Germany,* the first issue of *Fragmente*—when one witnessed the complexity of his life and all that it had been forced to
acknowledge, there was no easy way to resolve all that he did, in his
own person, force one to see.

I most clearly remember him, not tall, somewhat stocky, dark
haired, his skin a little heavy with all the starches that made up the
common diet—or more clearly, the curious concentration, persistent, often enthusiastic, but never a whim only or a momentary
excitement. He took such care with things—of myself, when I came
to see him with a friend, Ashley Bryan. We found them living in
Freiburg in one room, Rainer, his wife, and the two children. They
gave us their beds and slept on the floor. I had a pair of old, scuffed
combat boots I was wearing, and found them the next morning

*Work,* Winter 1965–66.

polished to a high shine, by Rainer's wife. Then Rainer came back with myself and Ashley, by way of Paris, to Aix-en-Provence, close to which we lived in a small town called Fontrousse. He stayed with us there a week, and it was his hope that he and his family might immigrate to France. They never managed it. I remember the day before he was to leave, I had come down, it was morning, and he was standing looking out through a window in the door, at the long side of Mt. Sainte Victoire, that faced our house across the fields. He was crying without sound, one could see the tears on his face.

He spoke to me of what he felt to be the community, the complex of people any city or town describes. He felt that a writer was not distinct from such a unity, but rather helped very literally in its definition. In contrast, he felt an isolation in Americans which bewildered him.

What he hoped to do was so much, and is most simply illustrated by a partial list of the contents of the first two issues of *Fragmente*— all that he was able to publish before his death: Pound, Bunting, Michaux, Césaire, Olson, W. C. Williams, Montanari, Perse, Artaud, Alberti, Lu Chi. He wanted to bring back into the German context all that writing he felt the war had blocked, and at the same time he could not accept such makeshift 'official' translations as would leave out eleven lines of *The Waste Land* on the grounds 'they were too difficult.' He wanted it right with such an unremitting intensity.

The last year of his life I had too little sense of, involved as we then were with our immediate living. I realized that money continued a large problem, and his ability to get some income from radio scripts and like work had been affected by his increasing depression. They had lost the room they had been living in, and for a time depended on a tent. Another passing friend told me of having been in Germany, and of meeting Renate, Rainer's wife, standing out on the road hitchhiking in a heavy rain to the city where she hoped to sell some of Rainer's scripts. She told him that Rainer now went for long periods all but incapable of speaking, and that he would sit by himself in the park, where she would then go to sit by him, for what moments he could speak, or work, trying to continue with all that he had undertaken.

To speak of his poems is for me most difficult, because I could not read them simply in German, and, beyond that, had only a partial sense (very much so then) of what specific difficulties and possibilities German poetry had as context. He said once, *the idyll is our weakness*. Trakl was close to his own terms of imagination. Benn's technical facility he respected, and he found, also, accuracy in the deep irony with which Benn characterized the world. But I was certainly aware that in his last book, *Umkreisung* (1952), all the care he had given to his translations of men as Pound, and Olson, and Williams, was beginning to find root in his own work. He seems to have read the necessity very deeply.

I felt such a bitter waste, at the news of his death. I feel it still, simply that he was so much the cost of his own time and place—and so incredibly brave in his confrontation of that fact in himself. There was no way to move in any easy sense beyond the past, and there never will be.

*January 20, 1964*

# Introduction to *Thongs,*
# by Alex Trocchi

At times world (consciousness) seems containment absolute in all systems. As—"All Systems GO . . ." Expanding consciousness is burst out—as pressures "grow" in paradoxic isometric tensions. Patterns are, so to speak, points of the sphere—"points define a periphery." *Blow your mind* . . . The truth is that all *is*—a living center.

For the Puritans—William Carlos Williams called them tight, *small* seeds of distrust and endurance—the experience of the *outside* is primary, and the edges of their world, in either "direction," are the terminals, the terms. Charge them, as you might a battery, and the organization, or organism, tenses and extends—the phenomenon of increase. It was the peculiar stroking of this life by the experience of space in the 17th century that affects the world in continuing forms—which the Puritans distrust and attempt to contain. Morphology—the *logos* of forms—in McLuhan becomes a "How-to" manual, and *sells* information in the modes it would qualify. It "shows" you so that you'll "know where you are."

Complex, then, of sexual possibilities: input, output—modulations in the terminal experiences. This way and that—leading to William Burroughs' Cut City—mind tapes, genetic taping—the great mart, distributes the world in *substance.*

"Puritan"—sexual possibility an inverse ratio to the degree of self-responsibility. "Is this trip necessary?" *Must* (a familiar expression to this "way of life") I do this, is it *really* necessary? Modes of people having this life-order seem to range from self-shrinking,

Alex Trocchi, *Thongs* (North Hollywood, Calif.: Brandon House, 1967).

convenient-to-others commitment, *self*-imprisoned paranoids to harsh direct noninvolved absolutists, whose actions *never* respond to what they experience.

*Hurt me*—so that I may feel *pleasure*. Each agency of thought in this situation effects the same condition—from the Old Testament to Samuel Beckett's *How It Is*. Pain is the measure of possible value, the primary in all cases.

Stendhal questioned, is pleasure the absence of pain? But the Marquis de Sade proposed, with a logic not unlike Freud's, that pain was perhaps the most *formal* means society had evolved for the experience of itself. In *Thongs,* as in the other novels he has written in this genre, Trocchi defines the *isolation* of persons in sexual rapport, and the *facts* of life as unrelieved in all possible senses. The two human conditions most evident seem the intellectual and the animal. There is no "love" felt as a convenience of possibilities for "other" relationships. Gertrude insists upon a Platonic experience of identity: "The triumph is in the rising beyond the painful into Pain. Once that leap out of the self has been made, it is an anticlimax to go back . . ." Insofar as other persons of the novel betray a sympathizing attraction to each other, or want, as Gertrude says, "to go back," they fall away, as Harry or the Prince in the closing section. Only Miguel is possessed of a like intensity:

> I am alone. The Prince is alone. Miguel is alone. The Prince lies. He tries to tell me that I am not alone. Miguel tells the truth. He tells me that I am.
>
> Miguel my love, be my executioner!

So ends the book. I leave these notes as they are in hope that the reader will find his own occasion to think of what "Puritanism" is, and to consider—with a little of that lovely wit Trocchi is so possessed of—just what it is, and has been, *to love*.

*July 28, 1967*

# AM

There is a sense to him that intrigues me—of an Ancient Person, a curiously insistent Messenger. We were sitting on the beach, talking, and it was a gray day, the tide well out, so that all seemed distant and level. The children were close to the water making forms with the sand. He has lovely clear eyes, a gray, and he comes from the water in that way, sea water, from some far off place as one says in the stories.

Momently we were in New York. He had knocked on the door and now entered, wearing a lovely Edwardian suit, a lovely cloth it was, wool. He handed my wife and myself the pipe, and again moments later, we were walking on the street, and into a charming old building where he helped me ascend the pulpit, and I read from the text though the winds about me roared and the waves did lash. It may be that he is the Caretaker—or taker of cares—and shows one the way.

I don't really know, nor perhaps does he. Again moments later he wrote us from India, was making divers pilgrimages, was climbing a mountain with the people, of all ages, wrote from the moment's calm as they sat, resting, drinking tea, the old and the young. The room filled with an icy air, possibly dust too, the mind was struck by what he said.

I will not argue his presence. I will respect what he has written here—a text in no need of qualification. What his words say, they say.

*October 31, 1968*

Preface to Alan Marlowe, *John's Book* ([New York]: Poets Press, 1969).

# Introduction to *Krazy Kat/ The Unveiling & Other Stories,* by Fielding Dawson

An *instant* motion—as when the road twists, suddenly, or else, dropped in the river, you see the ball float out, then, caught in the current, go on, round the bend. Perhaps Fielding Dawson is in fact incarnation of some wild Steamboat Captain, and certainly Mark Twain—in that both make words a literal condition of experience—is part of him too.

A few days ago, in Leavenworth, Kansas (which has four prisons and old-time spade bar with blackjack dealer practicing, at the table back of us white boys)—a man comes up, to talk, who is using a crazy vocabulary of midwest forties cliché, *he's a good joe, I know the ropes*—all like that, with sort of a sad smile too, just that his friends had faded off and the incredibly bulging blonde he'd picked up had gone too, while we were talking.

It's like that language, like an old album of pictures, one could make a collage of, but *not* a 'description'—rather, an enactment, of what that language continued to carry as its own condition. *Movietone,* in this sense, is a fantastic Cultural History—like they say—of a whole era.

But again, *movement*—I have never seen a writer capable of such fast shifts, so instantly, nervously, exact. Think of what's got to, with such unobtrusive statement, in *Early in the Morning,* i.e., how it's always there, in your eyes, and yet the hand *is* quicker than the eye, as usual.

*Worte sind auch Taten* . . . It's funny it should be a German, Witt-

Fielding Dawson, *Krazy Kat/The Unveiling & Other Stories* (Los Angeles: Black Sparrow Press, 1969).

genstein, who tells us that—Americans, who always used language
like an axe. From the twenties, people like Ring Lardner, from the
thirties, Hammett and especially Chandler—who make of words a
literal texture of place and person. I value Fielding Dawson as the
present Champ of said possibility.

He also likes baseball. I'm sure it's as much the language as the
game. He loves anything, where it really is. He's a deeply gifted
writer. He's a very lovely man. Open the goddamn door and say
hello.

*May 9, 1969*

# For Diane

I've loved women all my life, this one especially—and for once I think I really know why. Williams, in a late poem, ends by saying, "The female principle of the world / is my appeal / in the extremity / to which I have come." We stretch out long on the earth, as men, thinking to take care of it, to give it specific form, to make manifest our experience in how we take hold. Yet there is no one there unless this *other* person of our reality take place too, with a generosity only possible in that act. Diane di Prima is fact of that "female principle" whereof Williams speaks—not simply, certainly not passively, but clearly, specifically, a woman as one might hope equally to be a man.

I am not speaking of roles, nor even of that political situation of persons she has so decisively herself entered at times. Nor of children and homes, though she has made both a deep and abiding pleasure in her own life and those related. It is some act of essential clarity I value—which in these initial occasions of her writing is already moving to declare itself: food, places, friends, nights, streets, dreams, the way. She is an adept and flexible provider of the real, which we eat daily or else we starve. She is kind but will not accept confusion. She is beautifully warm, but her nature balks at false responses. She is true.

Growing up in the fifties, you had to figure it out for yourself—which she did, and stayed open—as a woman, uninterested in any

Preface to Diane di Prima, *Dinners & Nightmares* (New York: Corinth Books, 1974).

possibility of static investment or solution. Her search for human center is among the most moving I have witnessed—and she took her friends with her, though often it would have been simpler indeed to have gone alone. God bless her toughness and the deep gentleness of her hand!

*Buffalo, N.Y.*
*March 8, 1973*

# Foreword to *The Sterile Honeycomb,* by Arthur Axelrod

It's very hard to think of Arthur gone. His cranky, dependable humor had become a real part of my own life, and I think I depended on him as much as he did on me. When one's older, so to speak, the young tend to rush past, and if they stop, it's to check out what one's got that might be of use, and then to be off again. That fact is certainly human, but I'm moved also by those with whom one can share some certain recognition of the human place—and realize it is both particular and common to all.

In that sense, I'll talk to Arthur as long as I live, which has an obvious human limit also. It isn't that I, or other friends relating, didn't know the pain and confusion and intensity of Arthur's feeling of isolation, or that we wanted to leave him in it god knows. He took me off that hook many times by that same humor which relieved me in other dilemmas of my own. Despite what seemed at times his insistent demands on his friends to respond, he had a very specific perception and generosity, which let them go about their own lives. He was extraordinarily tough, humanly brilliant by any measure I'm aware of, and if he exhausted people, no doubt they were there to be exhausted.

My first meeting with Arthur must have been in Ed Budowski's Student Bookstore on Main Street across from the university. In 1966 that bookstore was a center for a lot of people, particularly for the poets local or visiting. Ed told me that Arthur was even at that time an habitué, first brought by his parents, but subsequently arriving on his own to check out the new books and to meet the divers

Arthur Axelrod, *The Sterile Honeycomb* (Buffalo, N.Y.: privately printed, 1975).

visitors. I was impressed and intimidated often by his encyclo-
paedic knowledge of contemporary poetry—or call it simply *poetry,*
because his range of information even at that early age wasn't limited simply to what was topical or in style. No doubt at first I must
have felt him some quirky, diminutive kid, reveling in poets the
same way one might in football stars or opera singers. But the more
we talked, the more I learned that his commitment and clarity were
facts of his life, not tokens of a time in it. The first poems of his own
that he showed me (some of which will be found here necessarily,
whether or no he himself would have included them) were characteristically *young man* poems, concerned with all the old *young* problems in an expectedly usual way. Underlying, however, was a kind
of texture, a movement, of the words which no one 'learns' arbitrarily—a gift, in short, as actual in Arthur's experience of words
and his use of them as it is in any other poet one might name. So
the *thing said,* in those early poems, was one thing, common as the
age sixteen, but the apprehension of an almost tactile sinuosity,
a substantive feel for the conjunction of this word and that—this
*grace* was unequivocally particular.

I might have said then, he didn't write like me—which was paradoxically a pleasure. I didn't want disciples, and he was poorly
equipped to be one, thankfully. Our meeting ground in this respect
could be Denise Levertov—we both thought she was terrific—but
we'd then disagree as to Allen Ginsberg's *The Fall of America,* which
I wanted to praise sans exception and which Arthur wanted to toss
out as too blowsy and rambling. Thus we'd argue, usefully, and
Arthur never gave nor expected quarter. I in turn learned a lot
about my own assumptions.

A few weeks before his death he asked me if I'd do a prefatory
note for a collection of poems he had in mind to put together.
My answer was certainly yes, in no way equivocal—I thought he
counted, and as a friend, I was pleased to be of that use. One sad
fear he had was that what he did didn't matter, that it would be not
only forgotten, but never really considered—and, humanly, we
must many of us have known that lonely feeling. The poems here
collected will many times return to it. Finally, it isn't to the point
that we may fail one another—but that we never even know we've
lived in the same world together can't be accepted. Arthur's life was
short, often bleak, often isolated—but also with guts, with heart,
with intelligence and response, with places of inexplicable grace
and clear beauty. He loved it, he hated it, he lived it. These poems
were his resource.

# Gee Gerry G . . .

Keep it personal, I tend to think—so, lovely flashes of memories, of this dear person. Like time he was doing TV children's program, the loping monster spider they could hardly freak out at it was so benign. Viz., himself. I love the shy excitement of his voice, the particularity with which he catches to consonants. Likewise his eyes, of a faded flashing blue. He's got a great beard now, reddish, a kind of Anglo-Scots Santa Claus.

He's always been good to me, god knows. Times he was restless and couldn't sleep nights in early days Vancouver, he'd drop in and we'd drink and talk, round and around. He told me once that something like two generations of his family had had the same English teacher in grammar school—grounds for life in one place, surely. He's often a bird who seems to be sitting on the roof for awhile, just looking down with bemused regard for those below.

When he moves, language, body, mind and eye, I get a sense, even a whiff, of some post-gun-powdery smell. Which is so good, quick, to the nose. He's a very fast, sweet perceiver, the sweet Jesus of local streets. No cross ever finally necessary. Or, as he would say, "save the postage & come yourself!"

Well, standing here in the wings, so to speak, could put it, "Ladies and Gentlemen, welcome to the greatest show on earth," which *is*, after all the distractions, *human,* and right here and now. You're

Introduction to Gerry Gilbert, *Grounds* ([Vancouver]: talonbooks, [1976]).

going to love it, because it loves you. So—ticket's in your hand, eye's in your head, ear's in your body. Let's go.

*Placitas, New Mexico*
*August 22, 1976*

# Lew

First flash memory of Lew Welch is at party after some event at Berkeley Poetry Conference '65, and we're on interior, upper balcony, swirl of dancing people below, and he's pointing to one thus extraordinary, a pounding, muscular woman wet with sweat and visible ecstasy as she keeps the beat, like they say. That was Magda, last companion of Lew's life, who could speak here far more usefully of what he was, and continues in heart to be, as complex human being. What I knew, and that all too briefly, was fellow poet and *man*—literally one from whom I could learn in that respect.

I'd met him much earlier, at celebration for Gary Snyder's first going to Japan—a mussel feast on McClure's Beach mid-fifties—spare, quick seeming man, recall running into surf with him, wow, cold! But not much subsequent till conversation mid-sixties, when at one point he was telling me how he & friend at Reed had made intensive study in order to locate the theoretically ideal place to live in this world, climatologically and elsewise speaking, and settled on Santiago, Chile—where, as Lew said, river runs fresh from mountains to east, direct through city, then to western sea. Terrific—all in the delighted mind. He was an intensive perfectionist, hard on himself in this respect since he felt that many of his own poems were lacking and so refused their publication often. "Alice Herlihy had hard hands . . ." He's saying that now (on tape playing next

"*. . . where ring is what a bell does*": *an appreciation of Lew Welch,* collected by S. Fox. Boston: The Stone Soup Chapbook Series no. 10. Boston: Stone Soup Poetry, 1976.

room, generous talking to students, California, April 22, 1967). Can you hear that ear? As he emphasizes, taking it from Williams, "melody in American speech is percussive . . ." You have the information apart from the literal poems, where it's all come true, in *How I Work as a Poet*—great, clear compilation of his own insights and commitments.

Lew's loves, Stein, Williams, docks and people yakking it up, language in the physical mouth and ear—all prove the actual, energizing *world* (a man's lifetime), and words, the substantive *things* of speech you must listen to as much as understand, viz., "Let's take out the car and park it/ at the big new supermarket . . ." He's *singing* it.

In fact, seeming simplicity of Lew's statement masks delight of *melody*, if you only read it with eyes. Like abstract items make lasagna on page of cook book tasteless, if no actualizing goodies meld with simmering heat, etc., etc. Like—don't just sit there, *do* something.

He did, risks of mind, risks of body—heavy drinking till depressions got impossible weight. Still—there he specifically was, in his own hands.

*Buffalo, N.Y.*
*September 19, 1976*

# A Note for Hilda Morley:
## *A Blessing Outside Us*

Hilda Morley I've happily known for years now, one of those insistent *sisters* who invite the world with seemingly innocent provocation of its own dumb vulnerabilities. Put more clearly—I recall so freshly the fact of her then, like some extraordinary English milkmaid, walking along through 'Black Mountain' as on some summer day. One time she and her dear husband, Stefan Wolpe, invited Olson and myself to dinner, *paella*, as I remember—which was excellent, and we ate with great satisfaction until a small bit of Brillo surfaced in Olson's plate, occasioning disgruntlement on his part, but I like to think I would myself have eaten it, had the honor been mine.

It is now, of course, years later, and I read these extraordinary poems with another sense of honor, and wonder for their *physical* clarity, their reliance on *sensual* dimension, whether or no the terms of human life elsewise the case be simple. Possibly the despair at some times confronted, the painful sense of anguish, even the frailty or weakness a human reality has finally to admit, are survived, literally, by virtue of the body's appetite, to move, to see, to feel, to know, to eat.

Her grace is truly of that order. As she says, "so the heart's fire was shaken/ into its powers . . ." Robert Duncan remarked that American poetry is not characteristically *sensuous*—as if the Puritan tradition we have had, each one, to survive had left this specific mark. In contrast—and despite what they have otherwise at times to 'say'—these poems dance with such a *human* body, and that *health* survives all.

Hilda Morley, *A Blessing Outside Us* (Woods Hole, Mass.: Pourboire Press, 1976).

# Foreword to *Sojourner Microcosms,* by Anselm Hollo

There is a quality in Anselm Hollo's person and poems which I value absolutely, and would call, for lack of a better term, a persistently integral *manhood.* For myself, the world is often a flux of shifting centers, a diverse and irresolute complex of 'points of view'—as if, each time, what might stay as measure of acts, either those of others or of my own, had insistently to be discovered in the moment. Which may well be the fact of one's Americanism, that this world has no incremental experience or habit with which to take hold and make judgment.

But, truly, the point is that Anselm Hollo is not only 'European' but a Finn, which is to say he has both the solid human realness of the Nordic and also the intensive visionary mind of those specific people. There is always a laughter in him, an extraordinary chuckling roar that is not mocking or contemptuous. It is literally the laughter of a man who lives daily, humanly, in the physical event of so-called existence—and, despite its trials and troubles, finds it good.

Here, then, the wit, the deftness, the active life of a primary man come again and again to form, to a thing said in the abiding pleasures of that possibility. No one will ever know more or less.

Anselm Hollo, *Sojourner Microcosms* (Berkeley: Blue Wind Press, 1977).

# Introduction to *The Manner* Music, by Charles Reznikoff

A story is an extraordinary human possibility, and people have been making use of its resources no doubt since time, like they say, began. There are, of course, many stories, and many ways of telling each story—many, many variations and points of view and opinions as to what, after all, was the point. *What happened? Well, it was like this* . . . So the story begins, or might, to tell *what happened,* or might have happened, or didn't.

One had not known, sadly, that Charles Reznikoff wrote novels. That a man should have such quiet and singular genius so modestly put aside (by himself) is regrettable. So much does shout at us, belligerently claiming attention for its style or its intelligence or its newness, that a story such as this one, so shyly assertive of what it so truly knows, is, humanly, such deep relief and reassurance—that one of us *can* care. The circumstances involved with its writing are briefly summarized by its present publisher, John Martin, as follows:

> I have recently gone through Charles Reznikoff's lifetime accumulation of manuscript, and was thunderstruck to find a carefully typed, completed novel, which he apparently never mentioned to anyone, or submitted for publication. It was, I think, composed in the early 1950's and is called "The Manner *Music.*" It is autobiographical, with one character, the narrator of the story, representing an aspect of Charles himself—the Charles who worked as a drummer, selling

Charles Reznikoff, *The Manner* Music (Santa Barbara, Calif.: Black Sparrow Press, 1977).

ladies' hats, who was disillusioned at trying to find the leisure to write, at getting his poetry accepted, etc. The protagonist of the novel, called Jude Dalsimer, is the Charles who never doubted his worth as a poet and who was determined to live out this destiny regardless of circumstance. A third character in the story, called Paul Pasha, is a portrait of Charles' most faithful friend for many years, who was a successful motion picture producer.

I believe this novel was written in response to a letter William Carlos Williams wrote Charles in the late 1940's, at a time when Charles' career was at low ebb, urging him to continue writing at any cost, and if possible to write a novel . . .

Stories are changed in telling, of course, so this one is not a simple rehearsal of a part of a man's life. There are, in fact, many stories here, "the manner, *music*," an interweaving of a complex of "things" happening, being recalled and told. The plot is an ageless one, the story of two men who have known each other since they were boys. One tells us what he knows of the other's life, as he is witness to it but also as the other tells him of it. Times are reasonably good, then are not, then come to the anticipated disaster. Jude Dalsimer, whose life is the novel's center, will not give up his *music*, which is not a secure means of livelihood as his friend well knows, having himself yielded similar hopes for a more dependable job. But, for Jude, it is the means of transforming all the welter of emotion and event into an articulate form. Neither his wife nor friend, nor anyone else, for that matter, can understand it. But, as his friend finally says:

> If Jude had wanted to write music and had not done his best to do so, he might have lived longer and more pleasantly but, as he might have explained, it is as if one enlists in an army or perhaps is drafted: he must fight and may fall but may not desert. Most do, of course. I did, I suppose . . .

However, the bare bones of the plot tell little. As the two meet recurrently, over the years, each time Jude rehearses for his friend the circumstances provoking the music, which he then plays for his patient listener. This "background" can be the hauntingly provocative fact of a dog's having followed him, or a party at the house of his boss, the movie director, Paul Pasha, where the conversation leaps from "subject" to "subject":

> *All this learning was pleasant to the guests who were covering much time and space with little trouble.*

Or it can be, instantly and harshly, full fact of the times:

> *Then the chairman called on a young German who had escaped from a con-*
> *centration camp. "I was to speak on the literature now written in exile by the*
> *refugees from Germany," he said, and the diners leaned forward to listen, al-*
> *though he spoke English well enough and clearly. "But I cannot talk about any*
> *such subject now, for I had an experience today I must tell you about . . ."*

Then that story follows, as do others, layer on layer, arriving at no simple point or conclusion, but, instead, gathering into a multiple density of impressions, and impacts, events, of literally common people. The two friends frequently eat together, and there is always an overt calculation of the provision, of the people employed in it, a comparison of its resources as against another's. There is the Jew in the Gentile's world, the explicit or tacit confrontation. There are the successful men and women, and, as the story goes on, the unsuccessful and destitute. There are insistently places, so plainly yet vividly remarked one will never forget them:

> Further on, the lonely street passed the foot of a cliff and suddenly
> among the boulders, right above a drop of twenty feet or so, a man
> stood up, face as grey as stone, clothes dark with dirt: he might have
> been a wild animal that had made its home there, almost indistin-
> guishable among the rocks, and he, too, looked at me. I saw a path,
> at least a slope, down which he could come if he wanted to and his
> nerves were good enough. I suppose they were, to stand where he
> did. But he did not move. The cliff rose above him for a hundred feet
> or more to the cement foundations that outmeasured the houses
> themselves. Then he turned and began to pick his way slowly among
> the rocks along the cliff.

The friend, who is listener and witness, has no exceptional judgment to make. He tells the story as it is told to him, and otherwise recounts his own observations and impressions. One feels that his interest in Jude is fact of old loyalty, and some curiosity to find out, each time there is the possibility, what has become of his old chum. His own life is not primarily involved, nor told, except for the brief information of his selling trips. He has feelings, criticisms at times, but he has nothing to say that will change a thing. His life will go on, certainly, with or without Jude Dalsimer.

How common a situation—someone one used to know. Nothing finally so remarkable about that fact, or any other like it. Certainly nothing heroic in this case. And yet it seems to change everything, with its futility, its despair. Why is he telling me this, one wants to say—as no doubt Jude's patient friend must often have said to himself, or *playing* me this, this *music* I neither like nor understand.

I am afraid, however, that I listened to other of Jude's enthusiasms as I listened to his playing—politely but at heart indifferent.

Why can't *that* be understood. And yet—it seems to change everything. Charles Reznikoff's power as a poet, always, and now in this novel, without exception, is his singular ability to state the case—not the right answer, or the wrong one—but the *case*. Put most simply, as he himself does in a manuscript found among his papers at his death in 1976, "First, there is the Need":

With respect to the treatment of subject matter in verse [or in this novel] and the use of the term "objectivist" and "objectivism," let me again refer to the rules with respect to testimony in a court of law. Evidence to be admissible in a trial cannot state conclusions of fact: it must state the facts themselves. For example, a witness in an action for negligence cannot say: the man injured was negligent in crossing the street. He must limit himself to a description of how the man crossed: did he stop before crossing? Did he look? Did he listen? The conclusions of fact are for the jury and let us add, in our case, for the reader.

*San Feliu de Guixols,*
*Spain, 1977*

# Preface to *Nolo Contendere,*
# by Judson Crews

It's presumption indeed to interrupt another man's altogether competent conversation, especially before he's even had chance to begin. But—Judson Crews is a modest man and a most honest one, and he won't tell you himself what I think you have right and reason to know. For one thing, he is a man of absolute principle, by which I mean that he has taken explicit care to consider the world and he has come to some conclusions—not to lie, not to cheat, not to murder, not to kick one's fellows when they're down. You'd be surprised how few people ever get around to thinking about such things, much less to taking a stand.

For years Mr. Crews lived in Ranchos de Taos, New Mexico, with his wife and two daughters, working as a pressman for the local newspaper at one dollar an hour. At the same time he published a number of little magazines, *Suck Egg Mule, Poetry Taos, The Naked Ear,* among them, and a series of his own books—and usually he put a photo reproduction of a naked lady in each one, as much as to say, if you can't 'understand' these poems, you might test your powers on this person; i.e., I'm sure that God loves us all.

Coming from the East, I had a larger than lifesize sense of Texans. When we were still kids, a friend of my father's just back from Texas brought us a donkey in a taxicab from Boston, after having got it that far by train. So it was clearly a real place, and when I later read of the Alamo and who was there, and how they literally held

Judson Crews, *Nolo Contendere* (Houston, Tex.: Wings Press, 1978).

out till the last man went down, I hoped one day to know the people of that state because it seemed they might well be a little bigger, a bit more ample, more generous, and factually finer than their somewhat bedraggled countrymen. Sadly the events of the past twenty years have cut that dream down to very meager size—and I'm sure we've all met a lot of Texans, like they say. But I'd still like to remember, as a company, Sam Houston, Robert Rauschenberg, Janis Joplin, Judson Crews, and Freebelly Norton, just that he *was* the first Texan I ever met (it was the Second World War) and certainly he was no disappointment.

So what does this have to do with Mr. Crews' poems? A great deal, in fact. You can't make an omelet without breaking eggs. You can't get an egg to break without a chicken to lay it. Mr. Crews is not so simply an autobiographical writer, and I don't know whether or not he's done all the things he talks of in these poems. I'm damn sure someone has—and that their wry, laconic, sensitive perception is fact of very human experience. *Integrity* is a very apt word for Judson Crews' way of being human. He won't do what he doesn't believe in doing, nor will he say something for simple convenience. That's cost him a lot at times, jobs included, but you can no more be a little bit committed to telling the veritable truth than you can be a little bit pregnant. So you might as well go for broke.

One day, when we're all, as Jack Kerouac put it, "safe in Heaven, dead," I'm sure that Judson Crews will be both remembered and honored for the loner wisdom of what he had to tell us and that wild down-home elegance of what one might call his delivery. Like in that knife fight when the one guy says, you never touched me!— and the other says, just try to move your head—maybe it will take time to catch up with this dear man's delights. But if you're reading this, you're surely getting close. Onward!

*Placitas, New Mexico*
*June 30, 1978*

# Preface to *The Blind Receptionist and Other Poems,* by Robert J. Richkin

The reality of world, as it were, has become increasingly a pre-occupation with secular, social, and political aspects of person. If a previous and insistent rationalism had argued our virtues only as habituated roles—fathers, mothers, husbands, wives—the present would define us equally as an ideology, a *this* or *that* seen primarily as social and economic within the pattern of a community no less remote than heaven's itself. But it would seem that the farther we come out, into a daylight world of explicitly tangible states of things and feelings, the more an equally decisive part of us lives with compensatory intensity *inside,* forcing us to survive the nightmare split of identity. Because we are not one, but two, or three—and we cannot exorcize the old stories by telling, simply, new ones.

These poems tell a story of a literally archetypal *pain*—which must have begun with consciousness itself, recognizing desire as that which would take it beyond itself, into a world where its own presumption of integrity would be shattered like a mirror. There is a simple ritual of numbers, for example: one/I; two/you; three, the world. That crisis, of the step from one to two, is unremitting, and there is no return.

The thread of story here, then, is a primal *mythos:* "You can be known by anyone/ who is willing to watch you die . . ." All things given, valued, yielded make not only no difference but fail with the silence of snowflakes. An absolute silence is the only answer—to all entreaty, cajoling, endearment, contempt, and, at last, despair:

Robert J. Richkin, *The Blind Receptionist and Other Poems* (New York: Blue Mornings Press, 1978).

my childhood forever descending
into the tunnel of dreams
colorless and crying for sleep
little bedrooms
neatly arranged in my head
and mine, maybe
in some other tender memory
in some other tender heart
for the love
of some other life

In the old stories it was the hero's own life which was given in pledge, beyond any hope of redemption—and so the fact of being *human* was entered deliberately, painfully, step by bloody step. Who could say where it would lead, or end—and can one now say, we know? I do not think so. Yet there is *no* other way, for any of us, and if there is some one of us *willing* to offer his life as forfeit, even we may find means to live.

# Foreword to *Running Grass: Poems 1970–1977*, by Peter Levitt

Peter Levitt tells a charmingly useful story of himself, to wit: He was one day walking the streets of Los Angeles, and a classic black heavy comes up to him and asks his help apropos the following. It seems a local bartender owed him some money but wouldn't pay off, so he figured that if Peter were to come with him, not get involved you understand, but just stand in the doorway where the man could see him, then he'd come across. So Peter, being of sympathetic disposition, accompanied his new friend to the bar, took his position at the door while the other went in to accost the bartender—and then, to his wonder, he sees him pull out a gun, point it at said person, and ask for all the money in the till. At which point Peter splits.

The point is, it truly takes a "willing suspension of disbelief," as Coleridge put it, to get into this world at all. It isn't just taking a chance, to see whether this or that will pay off, but climbing out on the proverbial limbs forever, no matter the cynical laughter of the very probable observers. Jesus, a *poet,* man? You got to be kidding. What do you do for real?

I was young once, like they say, and I've hardly forgotten what that all was like. Certainly *love*—of all that would stand still for it, and of the words you could give them instead of the rent. There's a very close company between so-called con men and people of Mr. Levitt's and my disposition. I suppose the only difference is that

Peter Levitt, *Running Grass: Poems 1970–1977* (Point Reyes, Calif.: Eidolon Editions, 1979).

they're trying to get out, while we are trying to get in. Again it's our wistful naivete that saves us.

It's a particular pleasure to be even this small part of this active demonstration of what poems can do. For example, consider the shopping list here turned to mantric power: *tomato sauce/ mushrooms/ and dog biscuits* . . . Or the melos of *let seeing, let/ sighing, empty/ persons filled/ with love,/ be enough, ever.* Or the whole damn world: *Landscape for Han-shan.*

Finally—because there's a definite Chinese edge here—consider Pound's translation of this Confucian analect (XVIII, 1.): "He said: Those who know aren't up to those who love; nor those who love, to those who delight in." Fair enough.

# Xmas as in Merry

Robert Duncan tells the story of a professor at Berkeley who began his lecture on Melville's *Moby-Dick* with the rather provocative announcement, "You've heard a lot about this novel's being symbolic of this and that, but to me it's nothing but a whopping *good* sea story . . ." Shyly, in part, I'd like to make the same pronouncement about Gilbert Sorrentino's novels, which begin, years ago, with *The Sky Changes*, the classic first novel of young love, its occasions, persons, and ultimate despairs. Knowing its author, I knew how specific in fact this book was to his life, and that moved me, rightly or wrongly. There is, for example, a Christmas Eve scene which I've never forgotten. It's a bleak night in a barren apartment. The kid's mother has gone out with one of a multiplicity of "uncles." Under the terrifying tree, if you can call such a meager collection of shedding sticks that, is the single small present, which, after some bemused consideration, the kid opens. It is a tin, mechanical, wind-up pig. And the kid's question, which echoes through all time and space for me, is, who would want it?

That pig comes back in the latest of Mr. Sorrentino's novels, *Aberration of Starlight*, although he's mentioned only in passing, simply an instance among many of the ex-father's sleazy presents as noted by the boy's mother—recalling that the pig had a little drum it beat when wound. So the question had been, who would want a little tin pig that beat a drum . . .

What briefly I'd like to emphasize is the moral disposition of

*The Review of Contemporary Fiction* 1, no. 1 (Spring 1981).

Gilbert Sorrentino's writing, both prose and poetry—and the fact
that an initial detailing of the world, as his first two novels, *The Sky
Changes* and *Steelwork* introduce the persons and place significantly
his own, emphasizes his explicit concern as to *why* the human world
suffers so remarkably and so stupidly its persistent inabilities of
judgment and perception. There are moments of intense anger,
contempt, compassionately ironic sympathy, even a yearning disposition to s ve something, in Mr. Sorrentino's narratives. One can
hardly *not* recognize how much this writer cares about the qualities
of feeling and act in the human world he shares with others. *Imaginative Qualities of Actual Things* (the title itself a quotation from an
equally moral writer, and a significant model for Mr. Sorrentino,
William Carlos Williams) is an intensive judgment of the specific
world of artists and writers of the New York sixties, say, Max's Kansas City Before the Fall. It engages its various subjects most intentionally—real details from real lives—so that two thus, feeling
themselves maliciously parodied, will not speak to him ever again,
etc. But this is a risk the writer presumes to take, in this case with
full responsibility. The necessity to make judgment, to define value,
is *always* primary in this writer, no matter the formal means employed or the technical pattern.

In short, I feel Gilbert Sorrentino's continuing preoccupations as
a writer have insistently to do with factors of relationship, really of
the most usefully obvious kind (mother to son, husband to wife,
friend to friend), and with the senses of place qualified as *a time*,
that is, lived in and remembered. He will run a great many changes
upon these possibilities—often wryly, nostalgically, with wit and a
secure invention. *Splendide-Hôtel* is, in this way, not only a tour de
force upon the possible categories of alphabetic 'order' and language but also a whimsical self-invention and recall including heroic "models." (Myself there, for example, in the reference to *Mr
Blue,* I came upon much as an old photograph, and deeply enjoyed
the permission.) We all make ourselves up, if that's the point. Mr.
Sorrentino's competence in respect of his technical resources is part
and parcel with his long time admiration of Louis Zukofsky's abilities as a poet—which, characteristically, he made most emphatically
public in the *NY Times Book Review.* (Here one should check out *all*
the critical writing he has done—for *Kulchur,* for example. Note
that he *always* writes in the imagination of an *active* responsibility of
anyone apropos the kind of world humans do make in which to
live. He puts his values very unequivocally *out front.*)

Therefore one distraction for me, as reader and fellow writer, was to come upon this in the jacket blurb for *Aberration of Starlight:* " . . . stories that Mr. Sorrentino further enriches by using a variety of literary methods . . ."—which fact, somehow, is none of the publisher's *or* reader's business, dumb as that sounds. Or it was disappointing to find this same novel reviewed in the *NY Review of Books* from the same 'point of view'—Sorrentino's resources as stylist (as we used to say). But I've not read *Mulligan Stew,* the novel which brings his work this location—but I will, and have the gall to presume I can accurately anticipate the nature of its pleasures—which will be terrific. And so . . .

It's most interesting that some of the most impressive moral writing ever was done by prose writers capable of exceptional 'stylistic' invention. E.g., Melville, Sterne, Joyce, Céline, Lewis, et al. Feeling, even more than necessity, may well prove the crucial 'mother.' Gilbert Sorrentino may not approve his general life's company very simply, but he markedly and persistently cares, and in that feeling makes language the instrument of response and judgment it must, of necessity, be. If he has demonstrated a master's skill in *how* a novel may be put together these days, you can be certain that what has to get said is still his point. It's still a possible Christmas somewhere, and there are still kids—and tin pigs.

# Poetry of Commitment

*Endless Life: Selected Poems,* by Lawrence Ferlinghetti. New York: New Directions, 1981.

*Selected Poems,* by Daryl Hine. New York: Atheneum, 1981.

*Only the Dreamer Can Change the Dream,* by John Logan. New York: Ecco Press, 1981.

*Selected Poems, 1958–1980,* by Gilbert Sorrentino. Santa Barbara, Calif.: Black Sparrow Press, 1981.

It wasn't so long ago that many of the poets of this country had intentionally and intensively to do with political and social terms common to us all. Whatever their disagreements otherwise, they came together in the integrity of their public commitment. Even now one may regain some sense of those days in Norman Mailer's *The Armies of the Night* with its vignettes of political protest in which the unlikely company of Denise Levertov, Robert Lowell, Ed Sanders, and many, *many* more all stood up and were counted, and took the consequences. Our lives these days have certainly grown quieter, more muted, and the oblique blandness of much of the poetry now written must be an effect of the national temper. Even the proposed emotions seem largely symbolic.

These four books of selected poems—by Lawrence Ferlinghetti, Daryl Hine, John Logan and Gilbert Sorrentino—are therefore a

*Washington Post Book World,* August 2, 1981.

curious recollection of a time some of us only remember faintly, and some not at all.

*Endless Life: Selected Poems* (New Directions) is Lawrence Ferlinghetti's own selection from some 40 years of his work, and I think the result proves a sturdy rehearsal of his virtues: tough, public humor and accessibility. If J. Edgar Hoover (remember him?) once said of this poet, "it appears Ferlinghetti may possibly be a mental case . . . ," he is surely that person we dearly want the wit of, faced with such "institutions" as Hoover suggests, inside or out:

> The world is a beautiful place
> > to be born into
> if you don't mind happiness
> > not always being
> > > so very much fun
> ("The World Is a Beautiful Place")

From the early poems, with their wry, backhanded literacy and good-natured hope, to the final poem, a "work-in-progress" in which the insistent repetition of "Endless" is both an ingenuously proposed belief ("Endless the splendid life of the world/ Endless its lovely living and breathing") and a bitterly ironic emphasis ("Endless the waiting for God and Godot/ the absurd actions absurd plans and the plays/ dilemmas and the delays . . ."), one is made to recognize the public consequence of any personal existence. We don't, we cannot, live alone:

> Home to the bed we made
> and must lie in
> with 'whoever'
> Or home to the bed still to be made
> of rags & visions
> the bed whose form is pure light
> (and unheard melodies
> dark despairs & inchoate ecstasies
> longings out of reach)
> Who to decipher them who answer them
> singing each to each?
> > ("Home Home Home")

No doubt this will read nostalgically to some, appropriately enough. There is, however, another kind of nostalgia present in Daryl Hine's *Selected Poems* (Atheneum). That part of Canada from which he comes, British Columbia, has still a significant incidence of literal "colonials" and, in yet another sense, the place of his "home," Vancouver Island, is self-consciously more "British" than the mother country. So one feels an unexpected kinship in his tone with writers as various as Edward Braithwaite and Alan Curnow, who are also far from the initiating places of their imagination. Therefore Hine's poems often read as tests of some imagined order, demonstrations of a questioned ability, although who has so questioned him or thus set the test is never clear. There seems some haunting specter of taste as well, a demand for a practiced urbanity, cosmopolitan and cool in bearing, yet often forced to a shrillness tacitly hysterical:

> Ithyphallic, dactyl,
> Iambelegiac,
> Such cosmetic measures
> Seem preservatives or
> Spices to embalm the
> Evanescent sentence.
> Metrical devices
> With corrective lenses
> Bring the phrase in focus.
> Form is recognition
> Of an underlying
> Symmetry in something

("My Optics")

Of course this is a put-on, and becomes rather brutally more so. But it is an isolating use of humor, and it may be noted that much of the writing has the tone of a private joke, if not the fact. I am most moved by the poem no doubt the most ineptly vulnerable, "A.B.C. Diary," concerning the return of its author to his home. It is a grimly unfunny text despite the omnipresent "wit":

> My family present me with a bill
> Overdue and unreceipted still?
> I'll pay it if it kills me, and it will.
> Funny, under so much natural beauty
> To discern the dull death's head of duty
> Fixed in an uncompromising grin!
> We resident aliens end where we begin.

That particularly common wish to be one of the elect, to have the final authority of a generalized and generalizing "we," seems to me antithetically distant from the person of John Logan's selected poems. As he says, *Only the Dreamer Can Change the Dream* (The Ecco Press), and it proves of necessity a lonely and harshly difficult undertaking. If there is to be, finally, no appeal to a securing system, of whatever order or need, then measure and judgment have only the fact of one's life as context, and that situation would define the specifically human. This, I feel, is John Logan's undertaking, and the poems record, densely, compactly, the progress of both art and life in a remarkably explicit communion. From the very first poem his "we" is the factual company of friends, and the "I" of his writing is unabashedly—*Americanly,* one wants to say—the real John Logan of his own perception and experience. He shambles, dances, feels and falls as he is able, and if one occasionally grows impatient with his sometimes sentimentalizing affections, one would hardly chide him for their being here—because *he* is here, and that is the *humanly* endearing point.

In fact, no one of these poets can be more eloquently present than he, and that is a very large value in these times of proliferating masquerade. There is a lovely poem included here which, when I first heard him read it, brought the proverbial tears to my eyes—it was so nakedly present in its feeling. It's a poem found late in the book, a poem of a little over seven pages so it cannot be fairly represented. However, here is some suggestion of its power:

> And you—you danced with me,
> sometimes led
>                 sometimes followed.
> I knew what loving meant
> and for the first
> time pointed myself toward your woman's heart—
> tried to touch it with my groping, masculine hand
> as I felt you grip
>                 me
>                         and ungrip me
> with your closing and opening body.
>                         * * *
> The great, bright, moon shaped crab creature
> rests, having just crawled up on the shore.
> Land leans away from the sea.
> A giant cloud, changing shape, leaves the sky
> black or blue or gray.
> The crimson crowned, great eyed king is dead,
> but long live his shriveled child!
> Every troubled, dreaming young man

lets go the girl in his hand.
And the tired parents of each of us
turn over to sleep at last.

("New Poem")

If Logan echoes the great, tender hopes of the old-time High
Modern and can recall such weirdly provocative puns as "Germs
Choice" while, incidentally, admonishing Hart Crane for commit-
ting suicide, then Gilbert Sorrentino's *Selected Poems, 1958–1980*
(Black Sparrow) reads as a remarkable survival of that appetite all
those masters had for language, for what one could make, literally,
out of words. Sorrentino is the only writer of the present company
whose authority extends equally to the novel (*Mulligan Stew* brought
him international acclaim in 1978) and whose work as a critic (specifically, his unyielding support of the late Louis Zukofsky) was
often a daily affair as well as a lifelong commitment.

The physical solidity of this book, the literal bulk, is a great complement to what Sorrentino has put into it—said simply, *a lot.*
Though I have known his work for years, I am fascinated to have
so much of it in one ample collection, so that one may see the continuity of his invention, his delight in the toughness, the *humor,* of
formal design, the playful echo of those he has loved and used,
such as William Carlos Williams. He is here as he imagined all those
years ago one might learn to be, and he is very good. Best therefore
to let him have the last word with what is the last poem in his
book—"the latest," as Charles Olson would say:

To wear those old moccasins with the backs
Broken down and sockless as well was a fashion
Germane to certain modes of departing. All now
Dark as the grave and silent and the streets
Though trafficked as always are not trafficked
By them. The awesome nonchalance with which things
Disappear. Not to be thought of as complaint
But as a kind of knowledge that is incommunicable
Because who cares? Who relentlessly peers
At his own materials his impedimenta Blotters
Paper flowers yearbooks photographs faces
That were young a minute or two ago and
Experience sits as it sits ten letters
Useless but to get "the story" told to prove
Again oh again and again that love although
Insanely difficult is as they say It.

A certain turn of the head the registration
Of laughter and all of it always going away
Going away as Who sits words skirling out
Of him too seeled in a mode of departure
Stepping out smartly toward the silence death.

("Bright Nightgown," by permission of Black Sparrow Press.
© 1981 by Gilbert Sorrentino.)

# First Prize

Although I didn't know it at the time, the title of Douglas Woolf's first novel, *The Hypocritic Days,* comes from a poem of Emerson's, "Days":

> Daughters of Time, the hypocritic Days,
> Muffled and dumb like barefoot dervishes,
> And marching single in an endless file,
> Bring diadems and fagots in their hands . . .

It's a curious beginning, this echo of a determinedly New England root, for a story that has to do with the LA aches and pains of becoming a so-called person. But that's not really its point either. Better (again Emerson)—"Things are in the saddle / And ride mankind . . ." Or—"Give me truths; / For I am weary of the surfaces, / And die of inanition . . ." There has been persistently in Douglas Woolf's writing an unremitting judgment of the grotesque banality of such "surfaces" and a remarkably tender allowance of those trapped 'between,' as it were, a nonexistent 'top' and 'bottom.'

Anyhow! My own relation to this all begins with getting in the mail in Mallorca, sometime in mid '54, the manuscript of the novel. I had (and still have, in obvious ways) a disposition that wanted *one of each,* and the fact we had published, as The Divers Press, (my) short stories, several collections of poetry (Paul Blackburn, Irving Layton, Martin Seymour-Smith, who was my initial collaborator on the press, and Katue Kitasono, in his own translation), and a kind

*The Review of Contemporary Fiction* 2, no. 1 (Spring 1982).

of belles-lettres, Olson's *Mayan Letters,* meant we now needed a novel to prove the range of our competence and serious intent. So at least I thought, and reading Douglas Woolf's novel, I recognized the very lucky coincidence of what we both wanted.

But so much more—corny as that will sound. I don't know about you, like they say, but remember this was the first novel I'd published. (Apropos, there's a story of Thomas Seltzer, the publisher, which Henry Wenning told me years ago—he was trying to compliment Mr. Seltzer on his exceptional list of authors, e.g., D. H. Lawrence, but Seltzer kept demurring, saying that they were simply the only ones he could get.) I don't recall that The Divers Press paid anybody anything—it was my first wife's modest income that kept any of it going—and so our choices had to be limited to writers as existentially defined as ourselves. Later I came to know that Douglas Woolf had literally rejected a patrimony that would have made things much easier, although the presumption is large (and offensive). I think he forever rejects any situation that 'signs him up,' 'provides for him,' makes his own qualifications and responses necessarily secondary to the 'big one'—whatever. His book was *very* good. Somehow one had not anticipated that, something out of the air, nowhere, so extraordinary, so specifically *written*:

> . . . But then it invariably happened, as it now did, that his father smiled at him with the appearance of such genuine fondness that he was compelled to admit if any love at all were in this room it was he himself who at the moment aped it.

It's twenty-five years later and the people of this painful rite of passage stay vividly in mind: the dwarf father, Chick; the senile Uncle Sam with his upside-down flag; the sort of Beach Boys gang, who make a usefully puerile company for their crippled fellow, Lloyd; Mr. Lippincott, Lloyd's father—who's responsible for the ending; his mother, faint and inept; Charles' girl friend, Jan. His friends Rollo and Billy Hart. Even the way the pornography Mr. Lippincott apparently switched into a usual film has a gritty, unexpected tenacity: "At first his stunned mind wanted to believe the girl had merely ducked her head to nibble a banana, a large, ripe banana the man held in his fist."

Possibly it's the fact that Douglas Woolf has a tone, always, of wry, persistently awake question, of a superficially bland but harshly abrasive content. Ed Dorn writes very usefully of his work: " . . . satire is only one of the pointed elements. And even then, taking the dictionary as a guide, irony is more the important rule for him.

A dissembler of speech . . ." ("The New Frontier," *Views*, p. 57). There is no way off its hook, no shared laugh that lets it all fade out, which, significantly, is the title of his second novel—which has the one happy ending I recall, of sorts at least. Again—certainly as age approaches—one will not forget simply the hero's trying to sell Xmas cards with his crony, or the awful, graceless, unremitting and unfair battle he has with his granddaughter, Gloria. There is a way in which Douglas Woolf vindicates the mawkish American pitch of "Give me your etc etc"—he gives them deathless representation at least, the old, the mad, the hopeful, the fucked up. There's nothing funny about it, no matter one laughs.

Given there's more and more, and will be, and that the times now move to some convenient epiphany of Woolf's World, I'd like to think of the honors he might be afforded, i.e., I think we can afford them, at last. Of all the others of his various company, from Wyndham Lewis to Nathaniel West, from Socrates to Sorrentino, there is no one quite like him, so quiet, so quick, so gentle on your mind, so truly at your throat. Let's give him *everything*.

# Cowboys and Indians

It's always impressed me that Bill Eastlake was born in Brooklyn, just that he's so particularly and adamantly Western, however vague now that term becomes. Much like Edward Abbey, with whom I first went down from Taos to meet him in the mid '50s, that wonder of an imagined place had somehow met with its actuation in fact, and the intensive demand both men bring to anywhere they are, being Easterners I'd like to say, got response in this otherwise gritty, barren, wind-blasted, inhuman, godforsaken and altogether dear desert, the so-called Southwest. As it happened, I had written Bill his first fan letter, from Mallorca, having read a story of his, "Little Joe," in *Accent* (Autumn 1954). I was trying to get active prose for the *Black Mountain Review*, and his writing, with its asperity and singular (almost 'existential') point of view, call it, caught me instantly. This story, be it said, was far from the setting of his subsequent writing, involved as it was with children and their teasing of a bigger one, "Little Joe," who is retarded—and a tree they variously climb, which still sticks in memory as a wondrous, literal center. Bill took my letter as some signal of international recognition, which thankfully and deservedly he did finally get but not that year. I, in turn, never did have a chance to publish him in the magazine because it collapsed very shortly after. It wasn't till Donald Allen invited me to collaborate with him on the editing of *New American Story* (1965) that that could happen in any respect.

*The Review of Contemporary Fiction* 3, no. 1 (Spring 1983).

At the back of that book are printed brief statements by the writers included (Ed Dorn, William Burroughs, Amiri Baraka, Michael Rumaker, and Jack Kerouac among them). What Bill says is writ large but its legitimate emphasis becomes, if anything, more clear in the years since:

> Someone has got to believe in a future. Someone has got to give us a religion we can go by, and the truth is defeatist. Only the artist can give us the emotional ecstasy, the defiance in face of facts, the joy of life that will make us conquer ourselves and go into the future, a future as bright as a mirror and colored with all the imagination of the young. If there is no future then the artist will make one. It is the unique ability of man and the supreme triumph of the artist. The artist is the best in us all. He is the true creator and art is the only religion worthy of man.

These are not the sentiments of a postmodernist; that is, such regal hopes or measures for human potential would find no place in that disposition. But as he says, in this same note, " . . . writers never grow up. The artist is forever a child, a child in that he has that first wonder for the world." In other words, this is not a situation of world intellectually disposed, however intelligent participation in it may be or recognition of its nature may prove. It is a vision, a dream, we variously recognize, so that Bill is, if anything, a very old-style writer indeed, a storyteller who knows that the wonder is the telling, always was, always will be, and that it is only by such apparently discursive address to it all that anything, of anyone, anywhere, anytime, will ever get said. I.e., you don't know it. You are it. So tell it like it is . . .

I think I can say fairly his heroes were Faulkner and Hemingway. I know he greatly respects them and put himself to their texts as measure of his own. He strikes me as a Hemingway with a sense of humor, a Faulkner with wider, more complexly simple space to move in. Or something to that effect. Comparisons are truly odious, if there's to be no factual engagement of terms—and that one can most simply manage for oneself, i.e., read all three. The cowboys and Indians of *Go in Beauty* (1956), *The Bronc People* (1958), and *Portrait of an Artist with 26 Horses* seem a perfect métier for his information of that world he both proposes in imagination and also daily lives in, as objectively determined fact. That dryness, that fact of the specific thing to be dealt with, that vast roominess the displacement of an inch might well crowd, a time without seam or accessibility, and person, often, a furious small Stephen Crane-like dot in the sand—this is neither human place nor time to be thought through and therefore settled, once and for all. Insofar as humans propose to deal with this world, consciously, they will forever be perversely separated from it, balanced on its edge, at best, looking in. So it is one of his charming Indians can truly say, *well, at least I didn't go to Yale.* . . . And anyone with any wit at all must forever hanker to be in *The Bronc People*'s incredible white convertible as it leaves the so-called road and plunges straight out into the river—and on, by god, still going!

There's a part of Bill that will always be hooked on teasing, on poking his finger through the obvious hole. I recall an evening he spent largely questioning Joseph Wood Krutch as to how he could have spent a life devoted to an author as inhumanly dull as the one who wrote *Rasselas*. I think he even expected an answer, though I don't think he got one. Likewise he put much the same effort into catechizing kids of an intensely Catholic family as to what might be *their* sense of it all. He is merciless in these preoccupations. Another time, when we were visiting again, he sent Ed Abbey out into a veritable blizzard (so it proved) to check the horses in a pasture some distance from the house. After some time Ed did finally make it back, but as he would tell you, it hadn't been easy in the blowing snow. He told Bill he'd come very close to x-ing one of the horses, slitting its belly and crawling inside—an old survival tactic that Bill didn't take to at all, at least not that night with, proposedly, one of his dear horses the sacrificial victim.

Both Bill and his wife have been so specifically good to me and mine over the years I can't end any such note as this without particular instance. For example, when we'd come back from Guatemala the early summer of 1960, they contrived to get us use of her brother-in-law's place, an old institutional conference house up in the mountains above Cuba, and so we could relax and regroup sans the awful dilemmas of no place to live with four kids and no money. I had an oddly persistent wheeze that summer, accompanied by a low but tenacious fever. The prognosis was bleak, i.e., either lung cancer or tuberculosis (which last meant I'd lose the prospective employment at U.N.M., if I did in fact have it). I was supposed to take it as easy as possible, but Bill, thank god, had other plans. He showed up one day to roust me out for a ride up to the high mesa of those mountains which go all the way east to Santa Fe. Once up and out, I found the world becoming a wondrous place as we rode higher and higher, threading through the oak brush, meeting with Indians trailing horses, spotting the occasional old-time home-

steader who might well have got there before the territory had
become the present New Mexico (1912?). Then we came into the
meadows, with creeks and knee-high grass, and miles and miles of
open sky and mesa. No wonder he has spent so long in its spell, and
has so adamantly insisted upon its measure as against the tediously
convenient and small fact of this or that passing appetite. This
world, at least in mind, will forever be before and after all others. It
is the one, so to speak.

Finally we were coming back down and Bill's horse, a wildly good-
natured but dead-mouthed quarterhorse, Poco Mas, managed to
lodge Bill and himself smack up against a barbed wire fence, so
that Bill's left wrist was caught between the pommel of the saddle
and the wire. I managed to back the horse off without problem and
then wound a bandana I characteristically had with me in those
days tightly around his wrist. Then we headed down to his car and
drove in to see Dr. Johnson, the bright woman who had the clinic in
town and was the only medical resource for many miles indeed.
After asking me what I was doing out of bed, she checked Bill's
wrist and gave him a tetanus shot. I remember her showing him
photos of classic broken wrists—they look like a fork, she said, the
way they go—so as to reassure him his was ok. So that was that,
except for a lovely echo sometime later when my wife was talking
with his, during a visit. You know, she said, Bill thinks Bob is a great
*writer.* Somewhat surprised, my wife answered, I didn't know Bill
particularly cared for poetry. No, no, was the answer, *not* writer,
*rider.* . . . You be "the great writer," Bill, because you damn well are.

# Ted Berrigan's Death

Ted Berrigan's death leaves a hole of adamant loss. There won't be another like him, ever, and what's left as always to do is to remember that, and what his writing was all about, and how, with such disarming simpleness, it could hold the largest imagination of human relationships and the world in which they are given to be.

Robert Duncan spoke of him as a genius of *pathos,* a power that could move the heart so commonly, simply, as in one of his great poems, "Things to Do in Providence." His insistent ritualizing of his friends' names, his lovely rehearsal of them, often as a poem would begin, to make the company of his life become the place where all authority of speech might then occur—what a generous *and* American act! I recall a British friend's irritation on hearing him do this, at a reading he gave with Jim Dine in London years ago ("Ted / is ready. / The bell / rings . . ."), and saying something like, "*I* don't know those people . . ." She missed the point altogether because Ted would dearly have liked her to know them— they were the greatest friends in the world.

He *was* an Irishman from Providence, which always moved me. Together with Charles Olson and John Wieners, he was my particular New England—certainly all I ever knew or believed in. I loved the way he took on New York and not only made it but so permeated its New York style, like they say, that I do think he's finally as evident in that manner of poetry as is Frank O'Hara, whose work he so loved. But the pace and rhythm of his poems, the

*Exquisite Corpse* 1, nos. 8–9 (August–September 1983).

seemingly open way of the words, the commonness of them, the literal action of what happens, the content at once so obvious and so resonant, all that is inimitable, however large the appetite now to possess it.

Then, as with Mr. Wieners, he remains forever in mind as a great gentleman, an exceptional one. He taught manners, and common caring, by his own example. Despite he was a hard man to interrupt (!), he certainly heard you. I remember my own applications to his attention got always a courteous reception and response. He had great honor—put most simply as he did, "Give it your best shot . . ." "I'd like to take the whole trip . . ." He made an extensive, particular, possible world of his life and lived there difficultly sans complaint.

The raw shock of his death, no matter he or anyone else expected it, makes no room now for spelling it out further. You will hear his wild tremulous wistful reflective engaging way of saying it in any work of his that you read or hear him reading. Thankfully there is the substantial collection of his poems, *So Going Around Cities,* and the reissued *Sonnets,* and much else. It won't bring him back but it's what he left, solid as a rock.

# William Corbett: Two Books

*Columbus Square Journal*, by William Corbett. Angel Hair
Books, 1976. Reissued by United Artists, 172 E. Fourth
Street, #9B, New York, NY 10009.

*Runaway Pond*, by William Corbett. Apple-Wood Books,
1981. Box 2870, Cambridge, MA 02139.

The sturdiest preoccupation in poetry at the moment seems to be
that with language-centered writing. It's given a singular genius
like Larry Eigner a whole and very useful new ballgame, and on
both coasts its principals have the character of self-determined and
remarkably coherent activity in publishing as well as in composition. It's to the point that William Corbett shows up occasionally in
this company—as critic as well as contributor. If one thinks of specific friends of his life, Clark Coolidge, for example, or Bernadette
Mayer (one of the three dedicatees of *Runaway Pond*), or Michael
Palmer, Lewis Warsh, Lee Harwood, et al., then one may recognize a continuity from elders such as Ashbery or Schuyler to the
younger Charles Bernstein or Michael Davidson. But, like so many
attempts at such doctrinal neatness, putting Corbett in boxes fails
entirely.

I would sooner say—like they say—that Corbett shares very remarkably with Robert Lowell a *tonal* quality, a specific surface of
words and how they sound literally, I find almost not at all in other
poets. It's a texture made vivid by an ear I'd think as good as ears

*American Book Review* 5, no. 6 (Sept./Oct. 1983).

get, a playful, persuasive ear (unlike Lowell's droll and often violent ironies), a charmingly nostalgic ear (a Charles Ives of idioms!),
and a physically precise one, which its owner obviously values as a
means of getting around in the world. The densities of the writing
come from the particularizing of consonants:

> . . . Myself, I spent summers
> of my childhood in the northeast
> corner of Pennsylvania East Mauch Chunk
> later Jim Thorpe and miss driving out
> at dusk to look for deer the sweet
> langour of those long summer nights
> close TV nights safe watching
> wrestling after greeting those out
> for a stroll from the front porch.
>
> *(Runaway Pond*, page 32)

More, both texts are "developmental," accumulative and reflective, often, in their content. Both are proposed as "continuities,"
*Columbus Square Journal* a "day book" of writing from "12 October
1974–12 October 1975" with recurrent moods, things in mind,
echoes of others—and *Runaway Pond* is also well anchored in a *day's
place*, albeit several, with turns of season, city to country, past to
present, a dumb loss of pond to sad absence of father, equally
willful and resonant.

What gets said in any of these poems is complexly familiar:

> 7 January
> I gave up my husband
> then my wife. He moved away
> I walked out on her
> got a writ, a lawyer
> wrote out our lives' garbage
> not for love or money.
> The children looked after themselves.
> I lived alone together
> alone apart. He was a bully
> beat me until I let
> the world know. She was cold
> without heart two years
> out of eight we kept
> going away we kept coming back
> to piss and moan, to pick fights

getting close to cutting loose
from each other. White Red Black
Come then blood then ink.

(*Columbus Square Journal*)

Narrative is a dependable resource but a story forever beyond
solution or resolve. It is specifically a *life*, which again makes a parallel with Robert Lowell's work but equally with poetry as various as
Charles Olson's or John Wieners'. Possibly it is New England which
demands such witness, both of it and oneself. The tenacity of place
in all its emotional and physical presence is unique in Corbett's
writing, certainly in relation to his contemporaries with very few
exceptions.

Finally one wants to say so much more than one can, in brief, because this poetry (and these are but two of its collections, however
remarkable) has such capable and ranging articulation, so quietly
present. There is no one more gifted with respect to knowing how
*and* doing it. But were it a case even of such brilliance, simply, there
would be, finally, much to compete with it. One believes with
Pound, therefore, that *nothing counts save the quality of the affection*,
and *only emotion endures*. The ground, the world so recognized, is of
primary human value:

        . . . I want
    to roll out of bed and get it on paper
    before the water has boiled, the hours
    pass and my arthritic hands clench.

(*Runaway Pond*, page 40)

# No Matter What: A Note for *Collected Poems*, by William Corbett

A friend here had remarked recently that when he was in school, the proverbial one-room schoolhouse, in fact, they were taught to identify the local wild flowers and plants by means of large placards, the reproduction of the plant on one side, and the data relating on the other. So one could therefore walk out into a specific world of a shared and common information. Despite the fight now to save the environment, which word shares with 'world' a very wide application, there is little place indeed one is taught so to recognize and admit, to know by those ageless means of "habits and haunts," in Charles Olson's phrase, the particulars of where one physically is.

D. H. Lawrence had early nailed the wistful American aggrandizement of nature in his note on Crèvecoeur in *Studies in Classic American Literature:* "NATURE. I wish I could write it larger than that. N A T U R E. . . ." Such 'nature' is, of course, confined to the country and goes along with bears and bobcats and blueberries. But this is *City Nature,* what another artist of William Corbett's habits, Claes Oldenburg, had argued was just as actual as the rural kind and being intensively the fact of human nature, finally far more interesting.

The skills of this poet are so quietly and firmly established in his work that one is apt to forget about them in either reading or hearing—which is, of course, their mastery. If one takes as gauge the following proposal of Zukofsky, then the genius becomes apparent:

William Corbett, *Collected Poems* (Orono, Me.: National Poetry Foundation, 1984).

How much what is sounded by words has to do with what is seen by
them, and how much what is at once sounded and seen by them
crosscuts an interplay among themselves—will naturally sustain the
scientific definition of poetry we are looking for. . . .

[*"Poetry"*]

Corbett's factual love for words, his trust that they will say his mind
and feeling, that they literally matter, is profoundly engaging:

> Christmas
> A sleigh's wooshing hush
> running fresh
> jolly comice pear wobbles
> on the table    white bells
> let nothing you dismay

[*"Montpelier Biscuit"*]

Nor has any poet more fixed a place in language, called it to be
there as all that knowing it, and recalling, and having a life, lives,
there, with all that these mean and have to mean—all that that ever
can be. "February 29th," for one instance. Or the complex "Runaway Pond"—or "Vermont Apollinaire":

> I cannot carry a tune
> Not in a bucket one note. . . .

Whatever it is that poetry asks for, what it needs to survive and to
be listened to, I can hear or see none of it without a human pattern,
that stain or wear or humor or fear that it not last, that makes
things said a hopeful enterprise, a whistling in the seemingly endless dark. Much like the story of the boy walking through the grave-
yard, who sings because he is afraid, I need a company, even my
own voice if there is no one else's. But how dear to hear another's!
What relief to know that someone is truly there.

*Waldoboro, Me.*
*July 3, 1984*

# An Afterword to *Splendide-Hôtel,* by Gilbert Sorrentino

I've been trying to pay respects to this work since first reading it in someone else's home, in that curious disjunct that made it theirs and not mine despite I was a person of its text and was probably more there, "heading toward Indianapolis," than I was even in reading it. I too loved Rimbaud, that wildly youthful genius who had changed all of French poetry forever before he was even twenty years old. I pondered his "Voyelles" and tried, in careful manner, to deracinate all my senses. In the early 1940s, with the whole world blowing up around us, it seemed a sufficiently modest proposal. So I note with interest that *Splendide-Hôtel* was first published just about one hundred years after the first of the *Illuminations* were written.

Albeit there are many presences in this remarkably particular book, the two who make context for the imagination it "so much depends upon" are, of course, Arthur Rimbaud and William Carlos Williams, and Gilbert Sorrentino's homage to Williams' authority is always emphatic: "'Look at what passes for the new,' the poet says." Rimbaud is source for the title, both it and the motto being taken from the first of the texts in *Illuminations*, "Après le Déluge," in which "As soon as the idea of the Deluge had subsided," there begins a divers coincidence of actions, some sophisticated and reflective and some of primal innocence. "Caravans set out. And Hotel Splendid was built in the chaos of ice and of the polar night." Or as

Gilbert Sorrentino, *Splendide-Hôtel* (Elmwood Park, Ill.: The Dalkey Archive Press, 1984; reprint of New Directions edition, 1973).

Sorrentino writes in his second sentence: "Thus, any story." It is in just so simply *seeming* a manner that words become the reality we had only believed them to be issue of.

Rimbaud's heroic definition of the artist previously mentioned would be immensely attractive in itself, but even more to be valued—as one thinks of the hundred years—is the formal improvisation he was able to make hold against the canons of French literary style. Baudelaire's *Paris Spleen,* which one presumes him to have known, would be a useful precedent, but it does not anticipate the genius of his own invention or the impact it will have on *all* formal device in French poetry. "For Rimbaud," as John Porter Houston aptly says in *The Design of Rimbaud's Poetry* (1963), "a style is a system suited to a specific poetic conception and not to an author's characteristic mode of expression."

With that useful point in mind, one can then judge the parallel of Williams' situation in the composition of *Kora in Hell* (1920) or the *Improvisations,* as he also calls them: "I let the imagination have its own way to see if it could save itself. Something very definite came of it. I found myself alleviated but most important I began there and then to revalue experience, to understand what I was at—" (*Spring and All,* IX, 1923). Ezra Pound's response was wryly abrupt: "But what the French *real reader* would say to your *Improvisations* is Voui, g(h)a j(h)ai déjà (f)vu g(h)a g(h)a c'est de R(h)imb(h)aud!!" The quotation comes from Stephen Fredman's *Poet's Prose* (1983) and is used, paradoxically, to emphasize that Williams did *not* know Rimbaud's work specifically—or, to quote another of Fredman's sources, Mike Weaver: " . . . as Williams informed René Taupin, his knowledge of French culture was visual and not literary."

So it is, curiously enough, Gilbert Sorrentino who serves as their introduction in many ways indeed. As one might well expect, the factors and habits of his attention are solidly American, as are Williams'. Thus Rimbaud's *A* in "Voyelles" ("black hairy corset of the bursting flies which buzz around the cruel stench, gulfs of shadow") becomes ground for more thoughtful consideration in Sorrentino: "On the bookcase, a fly. In the mind, A."

So too the *d* of the word "glazed" in that most familiar of all Williams' poems:

> so much depends
> upon
>
> a red wheel
> barrow

glazed with rain
water

beside the white
chickens

"I take the d of that word as my excuse for this chapter" ("D")—
which has been at such pains to separate writing from the simple
excuse of an intention. "One wishes to say simply that the writer
cannot escape the words of his story, he cannot escape into an idea
at all."

Neither can he escape the compacted habit his life has been
given. "I walk through the world, aging with each step. It is the
only world I have, and I am compelled to accept its raw materials,
that is, those materials it is given me to deal with. One must find
some structure, even if it be this haphazard one of the alphabet."
There is no securing point, no compelling and relieving reason.
Yet, as with Williams, he knows the perfect: "K-K-K-KOUFAX!"

There is also the *moral* of the writing, any writing, that he shares
with Williams, "the government of words." "They want politics and
think it will save them. At best, it gives direction to their numbed
desires. But there is no politics but the manipulation of power
through language. Thus the latter's constant debasement." So it
is that the "President" is simply a figure precise to an imagination
and conduct, "who takes care to cross all his t's. Yet he cannot hear
this tolling bell." Or, "the true President of the Republic," Lester
Young. The Prez. "He holds a tenor saxophone. On the bed is his
clarinet." For *C*.

But all this seems to have been said, or about to be, in that such
work as this takes one far beyond the limits of a prescription. Always something, like they say. Always room for one more.

# The Gentle on the Mind Number

The caveat that death makes adamant is significantly ignored by all who keep on breathing. In this case, it is no different nor would Brautigan presumably have wanted it to be if he was at that point in any sense concerned. Despite the meager industrial interests already at work on the bleak legend, i.e., those who will tell us the true story, of what deadend circumstances, etc., the fact is still that Richard took responsibility as ever, and killed himself as factually as he'd do anything, like turn out a light or write a novel. He was not sentimental in that respect, albeit he could cry like a baby if drunk enough and with sufficient drama in the occasion. But he could stop it on a dime, and I can't believe, drunk or sober, that he ever finally looked on the world with other than a cold eye—not hostilely but specifically.

What's often forgotten is that he was a remarkably articulate writer, a determined one in its resources. His particular teacher was Jack Spicer and there is no one who more called for, literally demanded, that writing be intelligent, perceptive, conscious recognition and employment of words and the complex system of their event. Brautigan's writing seems so simple, " . . . the lobby is filled with the smell of Lysol."

> The Lysol sits like another guest on the stuffed furniture, reading a copy of the *Chronicle*, the Sports Section. It is the only furniture I have ever seen in my life that looks like baby food.

*Rolling Stock*, no. 9 (1985).

It's like an ultimate dominoes, ultimate attachments, endless directions and digressions, but all a surface or a skin of unvarying attention, a wild, patient humor, an absolute case in point.

*Trout Fishing in America* is dedicated to Jack Spicer and Ron Loewinsohn. There's a great picture of Loewinsohn and Richard they used for the cover of a magazine they edited together in the sixties, *Change*. Brautigan was in his middle thirties before the big time hit him. He said once his average annual income had been about $950 up till then. His childhood was classically awful, dirt poor, mother, step-father to whom he's given when the two separate and his mother takes his sister. He told a story once of cooling himself in his sister's hair, locked in fever, in some bleak motel they were living in. He hauled himself up from nothing to be the most influential writer of his specific generation, prose or poetry, you name it. You could hear him and you didn't forget it. It was like, think of this, this trout, like *this*. He was a great pro.

He was a loner and that didn't seem to be easy except for the situation of writing. He loved his daughter very much and tried to be and was a careful, resourceful father. He was very proud of her.

This attempt to say something is a weird and lonely exercise. I hate it that no one was there to say goodbye, or hello—that he could be dead that length of time, almost a month, with no one's coming by. They thought he'd gone to Montana. The people there must have thought he was in Bolinas. I know that he didn't make it easy to get next to him, like they say. Still that's a distance no one needs.

One time we were leaving some chaos of persons together, in the 60s it must have been, and just as we were at the door, Richard, looking back in at it all, smiles and says, let's leave them with the gentle on the mind number . . .

*Help Yourself*

Sir Richard Comma
three dots for a dime

drummed into my head
abstract pavement

as opposed to dirt
no move from the end

to the middle. Style's
a hug, a friend's

true pleasure.
To be home

is to have a friend.
Van Gogh in Amsterdam—

streets an easy size,
the canal in harvest moon

moonlight, walking with
David Gascoyne, with

Michael Hamburger.
Richard's friendship—

dear Richard met me,
you know what talk's like?

                                                    1/8/84


Now he's dead. You figure it out, i.e., you got something to do
you better do it now, friend. Onward.

# With Crusoe, on Familiar Shores

There was a moment, just a few years ago, when a human, simply one of us, suddenly saw the world from such a distance in space that all of its surface resolved as a single sphere, that familiar globe of our childhood. One wanted heroic acknowledgment, words so to dignify this remarkable and pristine sight of Henry Vaughan's "eternity" that no human eyes had hitherto witnessed. But the voice, as I recall, said only, *I can see all of Florida and part of the Mississippi basin* . . . Pragmatic though it was and even had to be, the statement said nothing either of the world left or the world come to.

Yet Defoe's story of an equal adventure, despite its determined fiction—it is the first novel to be written in our common English—became almost instantly the measure for all such tales ever after. Robinson Crusoe has had the respect of a bizarrely incongruous company, from Dr. Johnson to Franz Kafka, Virginia Woolf to Alexander Pope. Mocking the romantic disposition of its enthusiasts, Rimbaud made a verb of this persistent novel's hero in one of his early poems: "Le coeur fou Robinsonne à travers les romans . . ." But in two lectures given in March 1912 for much-needed money, James Joyce proposed that Robinson Crusoe was a far more representative Englishman than John Bull ever was. The qualities of this person—"the manly independence, the unconscious cruelty, the persistence, the slow but effective intelligence, the sexual apathy, the practical and well-balanced religiosity, the

*Harper's,* September 1985.

calculating silence"—are particular to a very substantial place and time, the early eighteenth century in an England of some 6 million people, 2 million of whom were by Defoe's calculation Dissenters, that is, Protestants who had been variously sympathetic to the Puritans and who, following the Restoration, were therefore held responsible for the excesses of the Commonwealth.

I take these facts from several sources (Richard Ellmann's biography of Joyce, for example, and James Sutherland's excellent study *Daniel Defoe*). However, my point is a simple one—that our relation to this forthright story of shipwreck involves the recognition of habits most familiar, for instance, our unquestioning respect for someone who, as Joyce put it, "shipwrecked on a lonely island with a knife and pipe in his pocket," "became architect, carpenter, knife-grinder, astronomer, baker, ship-builder, potter, saddler, farmer, tailor, umbrella-maker, and clergyman." He can *do* so many things, as we say. Surely that argues well on his behalf.

In fact, it is a perverse delight that our "first novel"—whatever that may finally mean—is a narrative told in the first person, and that for over half its length there is no other voice at all except that of a parrot that has been taught to say, among other things, "Poor Robinson Crusoe! Where are you? Where have you been? How came you here?" It is an exceptionally real story for contemporary lives, having no island, it is true, nor any hope that some passing ship will find them, their money still wadded, stored up, in boxes, banks, or what have you. But the isolation, the intense value of things (*any* things), the preoccupation with keeping busy so as to assuage loneliness, the foursquare application of brutally simplistic principles—these we know indeed. In a changing social and economic disposition of what we had presumed to know, we are also cast away, washed up, forced to learn rigorously altered manners and methods. We peer from suburban windows with much the same question as Crusoe, who, having come upon a human footprint in the sand after fifteen years of no one, "the very print of a foot, toes, heel, and every part of a foot," can find no relieving explanation. And what does that dilemma provoke as feeling?

> . . . after innumerable fluttering thoughts, like a man perfectly confused, and out of myself, I came home to my fortification, not feeling, as we say, the ground I went on, but terrified to the last degree, looking behind me at every two or three steps, mistaking every bush and tree, and fancying every stump at a distance to be a man; nor is it pos-

sible to describe how many various shapes affrighted imagination represented things to me in; how many wild ideas were formed every
moment in my fancy, and what strange unaccountable whimsies came
into my thoughts by the way.

It is, of course, a pervasive, displacing fear—that a balance, however ironic, a place, however confining, will be lost, violated. He has
become so *one* that no other can be recognized as simply another, a
peer, human company and solace. There must be a hierarchy in
which one is above or below, dominates or is subservient, wins or
loses. It is to the point that Crusoe now becomes successful, secures
Friday as tacit slave, outwits both natives and mutineers, and so on
to the requisite happy ending, whose moral has a peculiar authority
for us, whatever we may say to the contrary. It is that faith reveals
an advantageous "Providence," one willing to strike a bargain and
to pay its supporters a handsomely explicit reward. Nor need one
wait. The arrangement provides an immediate return.

Defoe had been long acquainted with these tenets, being a busi-
nessman of various successful ventures, if an eventual bankrupt. He
was also a committed Dissenter, who supported himself by producing pamphlets and tracts on topics of the day. One in particular,
*The Shortest Way with the Dissenters*, a harshly satiric hoax, proposes
that the government rid itself of the dissident group by executions
and exile. "If one severe law were made, and punctually executed,
that whoever was found a conventicle shou'd be banish'd the nation
and the preacher be hang'd, we shou'd soon see an end of the tale;
they wou'd all come to church, and one age wou'd make us all one
again." This remarkable confidence in irony caused him to be attacked by both sides.

One might think that his turning to fiction (or, more accurately,
inventing it, even at fifty-nine) was so inspired. But during the five
years of that activity—beginning with *Robinson Crusoe* (1719) and
including *Moll Flanders* (1722), *A Journal of the Plague Year* (1722),
and *Roxana* (1724)—he continued to produce essays and pamphlets, employment that had sustained him since his bankruptcy in
1692. What one suspects is that his brilliant powers of reflection,
surmise, and proposal wanted a less constrained occasion. He certainly knew the particulars of the world. The novels gave him the
chance to use that information most amply. For example, the frequent reports of shipwreck during the period, including that of
Alexander Selkirk, whose story is said to be the one Defoe used
in the writing of *Robinson Crusoe*, have characteristic recourse to

divine will. But the making of this specific person, this curious Puritan amalgam, proves something far more complex and enduring. Crusoe's presence—his cranky determinations, naively effective presumptions, insistently pragmatic values—much echoes in our own.

Not that we need reminding that the Puritan disposition of our culture is the bedrock for all else that may inform it. We are usually persuaded by appeals to our own advantage, find touch almost always difficult, suppose ourselves lonely yet are easily displaced by any presumption of another, have what we consider tender hearts while being capable of great social violence. Though we are patently secular, we have a sense of inherent righteousness, as if a god were truly on our side. So it is that in times of imminent national crisis—an election pending and foreign and domestic relationships in tatters—we can consider the issue of the legal status of prayer in the schools to be of paramount importance. Such ability to have overbearing purpose, no matter how fantastic, mistaken, or unpleasant, is both our apparent need and our insistent determination.

Various readers of this novel have proposed its narrative as an allegorical "quest," a searching after divine reconciliation and providence. Surely it is that, even explicitly. But again in a fascinating echo of our habits, it is difficult to say which comes first, the desire or the need, the hope or the advantage. Possibly these pairs are, in fact, one. Certainly they are for Robinson Crusoe. The poet Charles Olson used to say, when Wordsworth starts talking to his sister Dorothy in a poem, *Look out!* Because that's where he gets sententious, where he begins finger-wagging and generalizing. Just so "Poor Robin," whose apostrophes to the footprint as manifesting "Divine wisdom" are as tedious as might be expected and not at all convincing. He is, by his own statement, far more apprehensive of unidentified "savages" than he is of any "Devil." With a canny argument he proposes that the Devil would never put such a mark in such a remote place, "where 'twas ten thousand to one whether I should ever see it or not, and in the sand too. . . . Abundance of such things as these assisted to argue me out of all apprehensions of its being the Devil. And I presently concluded that it must be some more dangerous creature. . . ." Verily, a true pragmatist!

He is also a peculiar enthusiast, for having settled in Brazil as a planter after all the early vicissitudes of his foundering existence, he is easily persuaded to act as "supercargo" for the purpose of securing slaves from Guinea. He has been one himself, but of course his situation now defines him as otherwise, and he is inevitably open to the opportunity of the moment. This voyage provides the setting for his shipwreck, and for what readers over the years have always remembered as the story: his years as a castaway, the meeting with Friday, and their eventual rescue.

The book begins, however, with as impressive a panegyric to stay-at-home middle-class sentiment as one might hope to find. The "middle state," Crusoe's father tells him, is "the state of life which all other people envied," "the just standard of true felicity." But Robin doesn't listen, and by the book's end he has gained an affluence far more than a "middle fortune" might be thought to provide. This depends on our reading the edition that includes the final three chapters, which describe Crusoe's adventures following his return.

Otherwise, we leave him at that moment when he "arrived in England the 11th of June, in the year 1687, having been thirty-and-five years absent." A haunting, equivocal prospect, either in mind or in fact, not only because the present may be discovered as a place of utter unfamiliarity but because the past, all those claustrophobically vast particulars of physical, daily existence, is fading as surely as all memory, all elsewhere that ever was. I suspect that this aspect of the book's experience, which is common to any book once we have done with reading it, haunts us more than is often the case.

Whatever paradigm or moral it may prove, the wonder of *Robinson Crusoe* finally is in its writing, the word-by-word accumulation of feeling, of location, of a fibrous content of presence. Ostensibly the voice is Crusoe's. But of course a person is writing it all, pacing, inventing, appropriating, determining each detail, what shall be its company, whereto all shall be directed. There is a paragraph just after Crusoe has managed to reach the shore:

> After I had solaced my mind with the comfortable part of my condition I began to look around me to see what kind of place I was in, and what was next to be done, and I soon found my comforts abate, and that in a word I had a dreadful deliverance, for I was wet, had no clothes to shift me, nor anything to eat or drink to comfort me, neither did I see any prospect before me but that of perishing with hunger, or being devoured by wild beasts. And that which was particularly afflicting to me was, that I had no weapon either to hunt and kill any creature for my sustenance, or to defend myself against any other creature that might desire to kill me for theirs—in a word, I had nothing about me but a knife, a tobacco-pipe, and a little tobacco in a box. This was all my provision, and this threw me into terrible agonies of mind, that for awhile I ran about like a madman. Night coming

upon me, I began with heavy heart to consider what might be my lot if there were any ravenous beasts in that country, seeing at night they always come abroad for their prey.

As the last sentence emphasizes, it is what everyone knows—the stock-in-trade truths, the prejudices—that makes this work so solid, so reassuring, no matter what it tells us. The grace of its writing is so undemanding, so common. The genius, then, of Defoe's invention is this painstakingly accumulated person, who, as any one of us, believes he *can* know, and so lives.

# Kenneth Koch's *Selected Poems, 1950–1982*

---

*Selected Poems, 1950–1982*, by Kenneth Koch. New York:
Vintage, Random House, 1985.

Inevitably people seem bemused by humor, if not actively offended.
Kenneth Koch has paid the dues of that situation in a number of
ways. He's presumed to be confident in his laughter and to be certain of company concerning what amuses him. Neither is very true
at all. No one of my generation remembers more accurately or
more fully the seemingly incredible grounds for taste and right
thinking that our youth had to deal with. Reading the present collection—and I've read him persistently—I recognize once again
the heroism of his particularizing anger and the consummately
learned abilities that have enabled him "to play a game" of such
lonely condition and "to be serious" in a way so hidden from usual
habits of recognition.

John Ashbery knows it well, and goes his own brilliant way. Frank
O'Hara was its obvious genius also, but his characteristic casualness
was more sympathetically open to the randomly met. Kenneth
Koch was shier and therefore, paradoxically, seemed more secure.
But if one read "Fate," for example, or the truly extraordinary "To
Marina," some sense of the actuating experience and risk must
come through.

In any case, my delight in this poetry and respect for what he's
got done, as this partial selection demonstrates so substantially, are

*The Poetry Project News Letter* (New York: The Poetry Project at St. Mark's Church,
NYC, December 1985).

very great. For one thing, he never forgot where we all began, so
that in the poems there is often a wildly parodic judgment of the
cul-de-sacs of that time, the dead ends then so touted. He notes
that he could not take excerpts from *Ko* and *The Duplications*—
which is a shame in that their singular force as narrative—Kenneth
as master of any shaggy dog that ever lived—may therefore be
passed over. But he is a very conscious formalist and knows that
such pieces as might be taken out would forfeit the whole, like
they say.

His odes have always been terrific, especially in times of one's
own self-serious immolation. "On Beauty" answers a question that
Keats left as an insistent solipsism, however movingly. Reading, one
gets not only signs of the time but a time so accurate you could set
your watch by it. So the future is where it always will be, and the
past an active present at least that doesn't have to wait till Christmas
to be opened.

Years ago Kenneth read at a public gathering a poem he knows
I like especially, probably because it is less overtly, subversively,
funny: "Sleeping with Women." The sounds, rhythms, so gather in
that poem, so quietly, physically. I guess I felt entirely safe with it.
Now I'd like to say how much I've felt about *all* he's written—that
it's kept the faith immensely, and the *human* world its own significant fact, in mind, in heart, in common.

# Gone Fishing

A *Day at the Beach,* by Robert Grenier. New York: Roof
Books, 1984.

What locates in us as "information" has a diversity of patterns,
of grids, places of various impingement and authority. We know
without the least obligation of wanting to, that the language itself
"speaks" insistently in its own "system," of syntax, of community, of
all those bits and pieces that conjoin to say far more than any one of
us might either intend or be capable of stating conclusively. The
simplest seeming proposals—in fact, any of those which begin with
that singular pronoun "I"—fade in the immense condition of common place, that so-called "world" in which all of necessity has to
find itself. Robert Grenier is a poet, therefore, of great interest because his work takes place at the double edge of hearing and saying
things—"things" which are neither simply one nor many, nor material only, nor abstract, but the complex conjunction of all such, as
it leaves and enters simultaneously *A Day at the Beach.*

That, of course, says it with awkward, generalizing emphasis. But
I want the occasion of this writing explicit. There are no didactic
grids of imposed location more than the title itself makes evident—
that is, no formal poems more than the instant coherence of language itself or the complex of feelings, thoughts, that move to

*The Poetry Project News Letter* (New York: The Poetry Project at St. Mark's Church,
NYC, December 1985).

make use of it—with humor, reflection, sadness at times, and all the consummate ability to hear and make evident the sounding of words themselves:

> *Sunshine*
>
> I think almost without limit

Here the playfulness of the echo, of rhythm, of sound, makes actual what "limit" is.

*A Day at the Beach* offers, then, a remarkably specific place, and its ground is quite substantial. If one values the act of thought as it feels the world evident, *thinks of it,* like they say, *and* listens, then this book will be pleasure indeed. I mused for years on the reputed Chinese apothegm, "How is it far if you think it?" In this book also, the wonder is in what is.

# From the Language Poets

*In the American Tree,* edited by Ron Silliman. National Poetry Foundation, University of Maine at Orono, 1986.

Whatever poetry may prove to be at last, the very word (from the Greek *poiein,* "to make") determines a made thing, a construct, a literal system of words. We are, of course, far more likely to think of a poem as a pleasing sentiment, a lyric impulse, an expression of feeling that can engage the reader or listener in some intensive manner. But, whatever our disposition, it is well to remember that there is a diversity of "poetries" in our world.

As Ron Silliman, the articulate and resourceful editor of *In the American Tree,* puts it in his introduction to this significant anthology: "The more pertinent questions are what is the community being addressed in the writing, how does the writing participate in the constitution of this audience, and is it effective in doing so."

The Language Poets—a qualification with which all seem uneasy and which Jackson Mac Low, an elder poet of this company, discusses in this book with provocative clarity—have been a vivid presence on both coasts for some years. Particularly in San Francisco, they have served to engage active political dispositions as to what is the requisite "nature of poetry" and who or what significantly informs it.

They are certainly "experimental" if the *mental* of that word is to be taken seriously, and their mindedness is an especially attractive

*San Francisco Chronicle Review,* September 28, 1986.

feature of their various work. That is, they enjoy thinking, they like the *thingness* of language, they presume—I feel correctly—that "the government of the words" is a most critical factor in our lives "since it is," in William Carlos Williams' phrase, "of all governments the archetype."

Because of these preoccupations, they have at times been confused with the academic Structuralists and, without question, they share much information with this more institutionalized company. The people found here, while predominantly white, middle-class, etc., are not primarily teachers; and, when they are, they are not of the authorized kind, as the "Contributors" information concerning Robert Grenier's background makes most clear. That is, although he would seem to have appropriate credentials, he cannot find a job.

I find it fascinating that they are such a self-determined "voice" from an otherwise all too silent majority these days—one which, seemingly, makes few moves of its own initiation. The parallel for the company here may well be the wunderkind of computer technology, or anyone who has made a determined response to the extraordinarily rapid shifts in the epistemological base—our fund of and access to what we once called "knowledge" but would now think of more often as "information."

Therefore, a great deal of the writing has active rapport with the resources that the system of language itself provides and plays upon patterns of syntax and reference with remarkable effect. Yet, in his introduction, Silliman emphasizes that such effects are not the final concern here but rather "what, in the last part of the twentieth century, it means to be human."

Put as useful parallel, language poet Charles Bernstein's point in "Writing and Method," his essay included here, makes much sense: "For both poetry and philosophy, the order of the elements of a discourse is value constituting and indeed experience engendering, and therefore always at issue, never assumable." The whole essay is well worth reading for its unique clarity and the compact summary of usual models of reading/writing relationship that it includes.

Certainly one will have favorites and I have a lot of them here, as it happens: Robert Grenier and Charles Bernstein, and also Barrett Watten, David Bromige, Fanny Howe, Susan Howe, Stephen Rodefer, Bernadette Mayer, Bob Perelman, and others. Michael Palmer's "Echo" must be, surely, one of the great poems of the period, just as Clark Coolidge's work is now a contemporary classic.

But that all sounds too much like chitchat at some gallery opening, however heartfelt. Trying to say why I value this work so
much, I thought of Bob Dylan's "There must be some way out of
this. . . ," this terrifying impasse of imagined worlds and all the language that has created them. The brilliance of the writers collected
here is not simply literary. Their response to the world, however
demanding, is intently communal. They are asking—often with
great wit and heart—that we recognize that language itself is real
and we must learn to live in its complex places.

# A True Poet

*All true poets are gay, fantastically humorous*

PATRICK KAVANAGH

There is insistent particularity to the writing of Patrick Kavanagh, a wiseness of local reference, as one says, whereby to locate the time, place, and person of all that may occur. As young men, we were long warned by Pound to go in fear of generality: "Any tendency to abstract, general statement is a greased slide. . . ." Of course, such concern might be set aside if the subject were love or war or our own immaculate feelings, yet it was clearly a help to know in some respect that it was ourselves we were talking about. The lure of *meaning* forever invites us surely.

I came to Kavanagh's poetry late, rather dumbly considering one is finally responsible for one's own information. It was the year he died, 1967, after his having been at the International Poetry Festival in London in July. Charles Olson had been there also, as had Ungaretti and Auden and others one might expect. There is an "Addendum" which his brother, Peter Kavanagh, includes as a small blue sheet in the present edition of *The Complete Poems of Patrick Kavanagh* (1972), happily reminiscent:

> But since the arrival of the Beatles and the Stones
> Anything goes

Patrick Kavanagh, ed., *Patrick Kavanagh: Man and Poet* (Orono, Me.: National Poetry Foundation, 1986).

And I am glad
That freedom is mad
Dancing with pot
Hurray hurray
I say
For this beautiful day.

(Extempore at Poetry International '67,<br>London, 14th July 1967)

Some time after, I'd asked Olson what he had thought of the festival and who had impressed him. Just two, as it happens: Kavanagh and Ungaretti. In the usual welter of professional and/or political maneuvering these two, he said, could make of the weather, or any such fact of common, human experience, a profoundly simple, wondrous music. Those are my words, of course, but it was his point that they were so unambitious to be apart, singular, different, and that what they said, the so-called subjects of their poems, was so plainly evident, open to all. Best that one give an instance:

*The Ploughman*

In these small fields
I have known the delight
Of being reborn each morning
And dying each night.

And I can tell
That birth and death
Are nothing so fierce
As the Preacher saith.

But when life's but a day
The womb and the tomb
Press lips in fondness
Like bride and groom

And when a man's a ploughman
As I am now
And age is a furrow
And Time a plough,

And Infinity a field
That cannot stretch
Over the drain
Or through the ditch.

One's heard much of the attractiveness of Irish speech, of the gift of the gab, which is certainly to the point with respect to any poetry, i.e., it helps. Kavanagh, it would seem, never shifts an accent or a movement against the common pattern of saying it, and his rhythms keep sensible to this measure whether placed in an explicit form or permitted to range more at will (as in the "Extempore" quoted):

> Bicycles scoot by, old women
> Cling to the grass margin
> Their thoughts are earthy but their minds move
> In dreams of the Blessed Virgin
> For one in Bethlehem
> Has kept their dreams safe for them. . . .
>
> ("Christmas Eve Remembered")

Reading this, curious parallels come to mind, widely divergent in time perhaps, but of the same kind as best I understand it: Villon, in the relaxed seeming doggerel which has such power of canny wit; or, much later, Tristan Corbière, specifically, "The Ballad of the Good Saint Anne" (which I first read in Pound's quotation of it in *Make It New*); or my own contemporary, Irving Layton, "The Madonna of the Magnificat," for example. Burns, Heine, Skelton— that is, a *tone*, a prosody intimate with a voice speaking so that whatever is said with whatever result, that *way* of speaking is instantly clear. When it can engage a whole people's communal language, it becomes its collective power of expression, to put it mildly. If, as years go by and one gets older, there can be no transcendent resolution, or none more than a literal accommodation and the humor that permits it, then that is the truth of the power as well. It does not change things, so to speak, it reveals them. So Auden says rightly, that poetry makes nothing happen unless one consider such revelation a contradiction of his comment.

Apropos, I was impressed by Kavanagh's great care for Auden, putting him in company with Shakespeare, Dickens, Homer, and Swift. There would seem little in common between the Irishman's roots, as he puts it, in "the usual barbaric life of the Irish country poor" and the urbane Englishman's. Yet one hears the common voice in each case, and Auden has what Kavanagh most values, an insatiable appetite for all the possibilities that poetry offers: "A great poet is a monster who eats up everything. Shakespeare left nothing for those who came after him and it looks as if Auden is doing the same." More, "He is amoral" by which he means, beyond the limits of teaching or the hope to add "anything to life," and there is, finally, "no message but only energy," "detached from this

earth-bewitchment" as Blake or Pope, Swift, Cervantes, Homer.
"For comedy is detachment, the view from above" ("Auden and the
Creative Mind," *Collected Prose,* 1967).

It's proposed often that Kavanagh's most impressive work is
"The Great Hunger," and one can understand why—given the limits of such choice. The poem, in fourteen sections, is the relentless
narrative of a classic peasant small farmer, Patrick Maguire, whose
locked, bleak life is given us without the relief of broad humor
or generalizing satire. It is all too true, like they say, and what
irony one finds is of acid clarity, only making the point drive home
the more. As life increasingly passes him by, his last hope becomes
thus meager:

> The schoolgirls passed his house laughing every morning
> And sometimes they spoke to him familiarly—
> He had an idea. Schoolgirls of thirteen
> Would see no political intrigue in an old man's friendship.
> Love
> The heifer waiting to be nosed by the old bull.
> That notion passed too—there was danger of talk
> And jails are narrower than the five-sod ridge
> And colder than the black hills facing Armagh in February.
> He sinned over the warm ashes again and his crime
> The law's long arm could not serve with "time."

Later Kavanagh spoke of the work with a reservation, namely
that though there were "some queer and terrible things" in it, it
lacked "the nobility and repose of poetry." He says this in a piece
called *Self Portrait,* initially a television script. What he says also is of
much use:

> There are two kinds of simplicity, the simplicity of going away and the
> simplicity of return. The last is the ultimate in sophistication. In the
> final simplicity we don't care whether we appear foolish or not. We
> talk of things that earlier would embarrass. We are satisfied with
> being ourselves, however small. So it was that on the banks of the
> Grand Canal between Baggot Street and Leeson Street bridges in the
> warm summer of 1955, I lay and watched the green waters of the ca-
> nal. I had just come out of hospital. I wrote:
>
> > Leafy-with-love banks and the green waters of the canal
> > Pouring redemption for me, that I do
> > The will of God, wallow in the habitual, the banal
> > Grow with nature again as before I grew. . . .
>
> —and so in this moment of great daring I became a poet.

So too, at this point it would be tacitly useless to insist more than can one final quote from "The Wonders of Love," a late poem:

> Do not delay, for the moon
> Will be round at our back window soon
> And we will see the cool sheaves
> Of wheat with its golden believes
> And plenty of room for a prayer
> As gay and as wild as we are.
> It is not a joke that I make,
> I labour for happiness sake
> And I ask you to dance with your thought
> For all other pleasure is not.

# Preface to *The Leafless American,* by Edward Dahlberg

The immense loneliness of this country's people has been an insistent preoccupation of its most articulate and characteristic writers. One thinks of the various heroes of Edward Dahlberg's imagination, Melville, Dickinson, Poe, and Thoreau among them. Even Whitman's great "epic" is the self's cry *de profundis* for an annealing company.

In his introduction to Dahlberg's initial book, *Bottom Dogs* (1930), D. H. Lawrence emphasized the great price Americans had had to pay for the settling of "the New World": "America was not colonized and 'civilized' until the heart was broken in the American pioneers. It was the price that was paid. The heart was broken. But the will, the determination to conquer the land and make it submit to productivity, this was not broken. The will-to-success and the will-to-produce become clean and indomitable once the sympathetic heart was broken." The very title of this present book and the poem from which it is taken make the same emphasis: "Homeless, denatured ghost of many/ leafy races, where do you blow? who/will gather you up?"

It may be that there is truly no hope for any one of us until we remember, literally, this scarified and dislocated place we presume humanly to come from, whether the body of ground we claim as home or the physical body itself, which we have also all but lost. Dahlberg has made this determined gesture of renewal and recog-

Edward Dahlberg, *The Leafless American and Other Writings*, ed. and with an Introduction by Robert Billings (New Paltz, N.Y.: McPherson, 1986).

nition again and again in his work, and if he is, as some feel, the necessary Job of our collective American letters, he is also a resourceful friend to any who would attempt their own instruction and survival in the bedlam of contemporary life.

Because we have neither a history simply available to us nor the resource of a community underlying our acts, no matter their individual supposition or nature, we work in singular isolation as writers in this country. Unlike our European counterparts who work in modes and with words long established by a communal practice and habit, we have had to invent a syntax and address appropriate to the nature of our situation as "the last first people," in Charles Olson's phrase from his work on Melville, *Call Me Ishmael,* a text with which Dahlberg was much involved as it happens. Therefore the extraordinary rhetorical resources of Dahlberg's writing are intensively American in nature and uniquely willed by the needs of the writer himself to fashion a world of significant human value and practice.

In like sense his irritation with and attacks on this country's binding Puritanism are focussed upon the loss of a physical life, an ability to respond sexually without guilt or confusion, to admit the body itself as actual. When he proposes "Our history is the tragedy of separation," it is "separation" in all respects, from place, from person, but most of all from one's own self.

But I presume far too much upon the eloquence of this writer's genius, and it is far better that one read him directly, much as one might a friend's significant experience and advice, rather than as my point of view, however admiring. He has much to say to us.

*Waldoboro, Maine*
*July 16, 1986*

# Foreword to *The Collected Poems of Marsden Hartley*

Years ago, when I was importuning the ever generous Dr. Williams for some contribution to *The Black Mountain Review,* he sent me, among other things, "Two Pieces," the first of which was called "Beginnings: Marsden Hartley." "Beginnings" of what, I wanted to know—of Hartley's extraordinary genius as an artist? of a time in the world? of Williams' own insistent flowering? Characteristically there was no simple focus, but the details and the affection are very moving:

> In one way I am not at all the man to write of Marsden Hartley. I know nothing of his sea-going ancestors, his down-east background. For that very reason, perhaps, since he spent his life, while I knew him, in an escape from that, seeking as a painter of pictures, to follow a life not as far removed from his hereditary one as might on the surface be indicated, I knew this phase and sympathised with him in it. He was in addition a poet, a writer with a delightful prose style which fascinated me. Besides I had had a father of the same remotely English blood who looked like Hartley, at least to the length of his nose, a nose, Dad used to say like the Duke of Wellington, a Roman . . .

One finds the same tone of warm respect in the way Williams remembers him in the *Autobiography,* clearly a man he was much attracted to over the years.

It is Hartley who brought together Williams and Robert McAlmon, which meeting led to an intensive friendship and the crucial

*The Collected Poems of Marsden Hartley, 1904–1943,* ed. Gail R. Scott (Santa Rosa, Calif.: Black Sun Press, 1987).

magazine *Contact*. Hartley contributed to its first issue. Again and again Hartley shows up, so to speak, in the annals of the period as when one reads this passing reference to him *qua* explanation in Gertrude Stein's *The Autobiography of Alice B. Toklas:*

> We were fond of Rönnebeck [a German sculptor who was Hartley's particular friend at this time] and besides the first time he came to the house he quoted some of Gertrude Stein's recent work to her. She had loaned some manuscript to Marsden Hartley. It was the first time that anyone had quoted her work to her and she naturally liked it . . .

His rapport with active contemporaries is very impressive and they range from John Reed to Alfred Stieglitz, his primary dealer at 291 (1909). There is a lovely snapshot of him sitting with Pound and Léger at the Dôme in Paris, 1924. A year earlier his first book, *Twenty-Five Poems*, had been published in the same city by McAlmon as the Contact Publishing Company, whose other ventures included early work by Stein and Hemingway. He appears in the definitive journals of the time, *Others, Poetry, The Dial, The Little Review,* et al. Yet such a simple image of success is deceptive, and some sense that he shares in the intensive literary definitions of the period—as do Pound, Williams, Marianne Moore, Stein or yet another friend, Hart Crane—would be untrue.

Hartley's poetry is specifically personal, an expression of feeling, a various response to the world *out there* he feels he can afford. It is also, in Emily Dickinson's words, his "letter to the World/ That never wrote to Me— . . ." Recalling the painful situation of his childhood in Maine—born in Lewiston, his mother died when he was eight, and four years later, after marrying Martha Marsden (the source of Hartley's subsequent first name, to which he changed from Edmund in 1906), his father moves to join family in Cleveland, leaving Hartley with an older sister in Auburn, whose own family he not long after helps to support by leaving school early and getting a job in a nearby shoe factory at $3.00 a week—one must think that his art, no matter its sources otherwise or its exceptional gifts, has a great deal to do with what one can call, albeit loosely, compensation, an attempt to gain psychological respite or balance. For example, the family itself as a human term had almost fetishistic resonance for him as a letter of an old friend, Adelaide Kuntz, makes clear:

> The last time I saw Marsden was on a hot summer Sunday late afternoon, just before he set off on his last visit to Maine. He had lingered late in town as if loathe to depart and as if saying many wordless

goodbyes. We met by chance in the Museum of Modern Art and I had
with me my son, then sixteen, whom he had known from the time he
was born, but had not seen for almost a year because the boy had been
away at school. Marsden was overjoyed to see him again, and now almost a man, and very formally invited us to dinner "out of doors on a
terrace." He finally decided to take us to the roof of his hotel, where
we dined in the sunset overlooking "the towers of New York" which
he loved. He seemed completely happy and proudly introduced us
to some of the inhabitants of the hotel as we went to and from our
table. "Now they can see that I am not just that weird lonely man they
have thought, but that I have a family too—May I call you that?" It
was infinitely touching to me, especially as I sensed his pride in being
able at last, after all the years of fear of spending, to entertain his
friends with some lavishness. I shall always remember him like that,
with his extraordinary gaze steadfast under the glow of the late sun in
his face . . .

The prosody of Hartley's poems is also "personal," which is to
say, it is primarily his own invention, the heightening of a prose line
so that it can move with the flexibility of music (which he loved indeed). The way he turns in (*plows under,* I want to say!) rhyming is
fascinating in its effects, and his ear for cadence, especially in the
late poems, is very articulate:

> When the surf licks with its tongues
> these volcanic personal shapes, which we,
> defining for ourselves as rocks, accept
> them as such, at its feverish incoming—
> isn't it too, in its way, something like
> the plain image of life?
> Those restless entities disturbing solid
> substances with a curious, irrelevant,
> common fret— . . .

("Indian Point")

I recall first seeing this poem sandwiched in between those of Eliot
and Robinson Jeffers in Conrad Aiken's Modern Library anthology,
*Twentieth Century American Poetry* (1944), and finding it then, as now,
unique.

Hartley emphasized markedly the objective resources of art,
both in painting and in poetry. He was defensive concerning any
sense that art came of itself, without an intensely conscious delib-
eration. Yet in a 1941 letter to McAlmon he writes: "All my poems
are written first draft and left." That apparent ambivalence as to

whether one's art is deliberately or intuitively made is especially familiar to American artists, and the more so if, like Hartley, a large part of their background has been self-taught. His training as a painter was one thing, but as a poet he had only his own interests and instinct to guide him, and he clearly felt a vulnerability pertaining. However, his feelings are never absent in any instance of his art and like his hero, Walt Whitman, he so places himself in his poems that "Who touches this book touches a man . . ." As he says in "The Business of Poetry," a magnificently various discussion which he published in *Poetry* in 1919: "We present ourselves in spite of ourselves."

It is, then, this curious, reflecting voice that becomes so moving. Its authenticity, of course, is immense and it is both intensely local and universal at one and the same time. Its size is intently human, thinking the world into meaning, piece by piece. Again his friend, Mrs. Kuntz, says it most aptly:

> He was not really a talkative man—but he saw more with his blazing blue eyes than anyone I ever knew, and he thought constantly and he wrote a great deal. His mind functioned with little rest—he told me once that he always kept pencil and paper by his bedside and that when he woke in the night and couldn't sleep, he could write down what he was thinking. Marsden Hartley was an honorable man, a really loyal friend . . .

Here he can speak for himself.

*Waldoboro, Maine*
*July 30, 1986*

# Foreword to *Trumpets from the Islands of Their Eviction,* by Martín Espada

The common disposition toward poetry has been long schooled by determinations of privilege and similar academic investment. So taught, it colonizes in the strictest of senses, patronizing its hosts, exploiting the common ground of human feeling for isolating details of style or taste. So again in school we learned of its difficulties only, the oblique reference of its superior information, the presumptive authority of its diffident gestures. Thus qualified, poetry became a markedly foreign world, both alien and alienating, and we were rarely if ever its people. It would not speak to us and we were finally ignorant of its ironic language.

But the actual world, thankfully, is one in which a plurality of poetries exists—not simply this one, or any such *one,* but many. The poet William Carlos Williams puts it most compactly: "Therefore each speech having its own character the poetry it engenders will be peculiar to that speech also in its own intrinsic form. . . ." Whitman had said that to have great poets, one needed great audiences—those who might hear intimately, intensely, the common voice in the singular person. The point is that this art can never leave the common body of its own communal life. It is not an *I* but "the wind that blows through me," as D. H. Lawrence has written.

Martín Espada is a poet of great communal power and he is also, with equal resource, the voice of intensive isolation. He says, for example, that he began to write as an adolescent because "nothing

Martín Espada, *Trumpets from the Islands of Their Eviction* (Tempe, Ariz.: Bilingual Press, 1987).

matched me." Small wonder that he felt so when one recognizes that after his family leaves the projects in Brooklyn—he is then about thirteen—their various locations (Valley Stream, Long Island, several towns in Maryland) are far removed from the communal habits of their Brooklyn neighborhood, whatever its limits had been. Racism becomes an insistent qualification and response insofar as these new communities are instance of "White Flight," i.e., a social migration of the period formed by those wishing to maintain a racial privilege. In these malignant camps of entrenched prejudice, Espada feels "less and less in touch."

So, expectably, Espada says that it is the resulting sense of dislocation that moves him to write, but he also proposes that this experience of being an outcast is literally the determinant in all Puerto Rican immigrant life. It's an old saying that a Puerto Rican spends more time in the air than on the ground. Harshly, complexly, "The Spanish of Our Out-Loud Dreams" makes clear with consummate tenderness the irrevocable transitions, seemingly without end:

> . . . Last night you cried,
> your black eyes shimmering darker
> than the room
> where we tried to sleep,
> crying like your father cried
> when you pulled away
> from the hospital bed,
> and for all the nights
> we have wandered with stuffed bags,
> not staying long enough
> to learn the language . . .

As he said of this poem, it is the insistent theme of migration, "The Spanish, etc. The third verse is really what it's all about."

The book's title poem is, of course, the complement, the "islands," the places left, or that one is going to, or has come to, or is leaving. He says wryly, "We're always being evicted. The 'trumpets' are our resistance to that, through identity, or more actively."

He is by no means an old man—twenty-eight—and yet his life has been so many determining places. Like the University of Maryland, where courses in creative writing and modern poetry make clear that "whatever I'm writing, it's not this." He stops writing for three or four years, he says. He has no models at first. "I didn't know it had a name." Certainly not those offered—Yeats, Eliot, Crane, Stevens—if the active terms and reference of his experience are to be respected and used. Finally, when he's about twenty and living elsewhere, a friend, Luis Garden Acosta, gives him a copy of *Latin American Revolutionary Poetry* (edited by Roberto Márquez and printed bilingually) with Pedro Pietri's classic poem of Puerto Rican community, "Puerto Rican Obituary," facing Ernesto Cardenal's rehearsal of Somozan corruption, "Zero Hour." "And the spark was lit. . . ." The connection: "People can write about *substantial* subjects. . . ."

At this point the father, Frank Espada, is an intensive key, I think. One can see, in fact, the bridge his life makes as definition for his son's in the title poem but even more complexly in the poem on the grandfather's death, "El señor está muerto": "son's body huge with a father's life." In turn, it is the literal community and person of Frank Espada which so invests his own son's commitment. It is his father's family and relationships that preoccupy the son finally. His father is a gifted photographer with determined political address and some of his work appears as an active complement to the poems in Espada's first book, *The Immigrant Iceboy's Bolero* (1982). He makes the point that his poetry "is always about more than me" and that it insists on the *outside*, echoing emotionally, politically, and esthetically determinants in the father's own life. He speaks of the fact that his father's photographs were "always on the wall" despite there being long periods of inactivity, and that he sees himself as a "black and white" poet, for whom the principal agencies are foregrounding and shadow.

There is also the sense of *advocacy*—it is such a pervasive voice in this writing!—that Espada has in so many ways engaged. Thinking again of those "determining places": as a student at the University of Wisconsin in Madison, his interests are history (this is the major for the BA he holds, and it contributes curious data, as he says, such as the fact that Douglas MacArthur and Carl Sandburg both served in the US Army in Puerto Rico), radio journalism (a three-part documentary made in 1982 from material gathered in Nicaragua and broadcast on National Public Radio and elsewhere is an early national advice of circumstances there), and film—ultimately too expensive. *And* poetry. His first reading is at a bar in Madison where he also works as a bouncer.

But the job of most significance would seem the one he falls into by chance while working as a clerk in the state mental health system. The lawyer who had been responsible for representing the rights of patients leaves unexpectedly for a better job. So Martín Espada becomes the whole Advocacy Pool, simply because there is no one else so trained or at all interested. He had dropped out of college at this point, had just turned twenty—and must have been in some common crisis as to what his own life was finally to be. In any case, he "soon knew the statutes cold," as he put it, "Chapter 51.61: The Patient's Bill of Rights."

Again, *advocacy* is the crucial term—"speaking or writing in support (of something)" as the dictionary defines it. But the meaning is more active in Espada's own qualification: "persuasion, making the case, putting it in human terms, quoting directly from the people. . . ." He says of the poem "La tormenta" that it's a translation in part from the young boy ("A boy with wide ears / and one shirt, / he walked across Guatemala, / México and Arizona to get here . . . He wants to be called Tony / in the United States . . .") who was "quite mad. . . ." *La muerte es una tormenta.* "I couldn't say that, only he could say that. . . ."

As of this writing [April 1986] Martín Espada works as a lawyer for the META project in Cambridge, an organization involved with the legal context of civil rights for immigrants and with bilingual education laws in particular. He also teaches poetry to sixth, seventh, and eighth graders at the Agassiz School in Cambridge, a very different world indeed. No doubt it is poetry itself he speaks in defense of—or simply makes real for the beleaguered young. That he's a lawyer too must amaze them—with a three piece suit! Perhaps he can save us all.

Whatever their circumstances poets make a world, piece by piece, as best they can. Those most able are most ample—like Pablo Neruda, a particular hero of Espada's. When the distances become inexorable, the language disjunct, the place and person lost in meager time and circumstance, when all that's left is what one can finally say of it (or anything), then painfully, particularly, poets remember, put back together the broken fragments of the dismembered community. It is the power and the glory of their art. It is also why there is not one singularizing poetry but rather a host of annealing and restoring poets, who are as related to the people as ever the people might be, in turn, to them. When one first hears the voice of Espada's poems, the determined dignity, the intense, quiet care, when the cadence of the language makes a movement having no didactic metric, rather a pace, an undulation, a way of intent walking, or feeling, then one recognizes the presence of this power, which no one owns but some may and can have, as does he. One wishes him safe journey.

*Ithaca, New York*
*April 1986*

# IV  ARTISTS

# On the Road: Notes on Artists & Poets, 1950–1965

Coming of age in the forties, in the chaos of the Second World War, one felt the kinds of coherence that might have been fact of other time and place were no longer possible. There seemed no logic, so to speak, that could bring together all the violent disparities of that experience. The arts especially were shaken and the *picture of the world* that might previously have served them had to be reformed. Of course, the underlying information of this circumstance had begun long before the time with which I am involved. Once the containment of a Newtonian imagination of the universe had been forced to yield to one proposing life as continuous, atomistic, and without relief, then discretions possible in the first situation were not only inappropriate but increasingly grotesque. There was no *place*, finally, from which to propose an objectively ordered reality, a world that could be spoken of as *there* in the convenience of expectation or habit.

The cities, insofar as they are intensively conglomerate densities of people, no doubt were forced to recognize the change previous to other kinds of place. The *neighborhood* had been changing endlessly, ever since the onslaught of the Industrial Revolution, and *change,* like it or not, had become so familiar a condition that there was even a dependence on the energy thus occurring. Nothing seemingly held firm and so one was either brought to a depressed and ironically stated pessimism concerning human possibilities, or

*Poets of the Cities New York and San Francisco* [catalog of the exhibition] (New York: E. P. Dutton, 1974).

one worked to gain location in the insistent flux, recognizing the nature of its shifting energies as intimate with one's own.

Put another way, this situation increasingly demanded that the arts, *all* of them—since no matter how disparate their preoccupations may sometimes appear, their roots are always fact of a commonly shared intuition or impulse—that these articulations and perceptions of the nature of human event *yield* the assumption of discrete reality, of objects to be hung on walls merely to be looked at, or words rehearsing agreed to patterns of valuation and order, or sounds maintaining rationally derived systems of coherence; that the human event itself be permitted to enter, again, the most significant of its own self-realizations.

Hindsight makes all such statement far more tidy than it ever in fact was or could be. As a young man trying to get a purchase on what most concerned me—the issue of my own life and its statement in writing—I knew little if anything of what might be *happening*. I had gone through a usual education in the East, had witnessed in shock the terrifying conclusion of humans killing one another, had wobbled back to college, married (mistakenly) in the hope of securing myself emotionally, had wandered into the woods just that I had no competence to keep things together in the city, even left the country itself, with my tolerant wife, hoping that some other culture might have news for me I could at last make use of and peace with. But the world, happily or unhappily, offers only one means of leaving, and I was returned without relief again and again to the initial need: a *means* of making articulate the world in which I and all like me did truly live.

Most stable in these preoccupations was the sense that any *form*, any ordering of reality so implied, had somehow to come from the very condition of the experience demanding it. That is to say, I could not easily use a previous mode of writing that wasn't consequence of my own literal experience. I couldn't write like Eliot, for example, I couldn't even depend upon Stevens, whose work then much attracted me. So it was that I became increasingly drawn to the proposals of Ezra Pound ("We must understand what is happening . . .") and to the work of William Carlos Williams:

> From disorder (a chaos)
> order grows
> —grows fruitful.
> The chaos feeds it. Chaos
> feeds the tree.

> (*Descent*)

Then, in 1950, a chance contact with Charles Olson gained through a mutual friend, Vincent Ferrini, changed my mind entirely and gave me access at last to a way of thinking of the process of writing that made both the thing said and the way of saying it an integral event. More, Olson's relation to Black Mountain College (which led to my own) found me that company I had almost despaired of ever having. So put, my emphasis here seems almost selfishly preoccupied with *me*—but I was, after all, one of many, all of whom had many of these same feelings and dilemmas. I expect that one of the first tests of the artist is his or her ability to maintain attention and activity in an environment having apparently very little concern or interest in what seems so crucial to oneself. *Company*, then, is a particularly dear and productive possibility for anyone so committed. Mine was answer to every wish I had ever had.

Living in Europe, in France and then in Mallorca, I had come to know some painters, like they say. Ezra Pound had generously put me in touch with René Laubiès, the first to translate selections from the *Cantos* into French, and I found him a warm and intelligent friend. However, I felt rather gauche and heavy around his work, which was in some respects an extension of usual School of Paris preoccupations—that is, he did work to realize a thing in mind, a *sign* or *symbol* that had value for him apart from its occasion in the work itself. His dealer was Paul Fachetti, happily, and it was at this gallery I first saw Jackson Pollock's work, a show of small canvasses giving some sense of the *mode* but without the *scale* that finally seems crucial for him. In any case, these paintings stuck in my head very firmly so that even now I can recall them without difficulty. Lawrence Calcagno and Sam Francis were also showing at Fachetti's, but neither made much impression on me at the time, despite I was delighted they were Americans.

Possibly I hadn't as yet realized that a number of American painters had made the shift I was myself so anxious to accomplish, that they had, in fact, already begun to move away from the insistently *pictorial*, whether figurative or non-figurative, to a manifest directly of the *energy* inherent in the materials, literally, and their physical manipulation in the act of painting itself. *Process*, in the sense that Olson had found it in Whitehead, was clearly much on their minds.

Coming to Black Mountain the spring of 1954 was equally gain of that *viability* in writing without which it, of necessity, atrophies and becomes a literature merely. Robert Duncan, in recent conversation, recalled his own intention then, "to transform American literature into a viable *language*—that's what we were trying to do . . ." Speaking of Frank O'Hara, he noted that extraordinary poet's attempt "to keep the *demand* on the language as *operative,* so that something was at issue all the time, and, at the same time, to make it almost like chatter on the telephone that nobody was going to pay attention to before . . . that the language gain what was assumed before to be its *trivial* uses. I'm sort of fascinated that *trivial* means the same thing as *three* (Hecate). Trivial's the *crisis,* where it always blows. So I think that one can build a picture, that in all the arts, especially in America, they are *operative.* We think of art as doing something, taking hold of it as a *process* . . ."

At Black Mountain these preoccupations were insistent. For the painters, the information centered in the work of the Abstract Expressionists, many of whom had been either visitors or teachers there—although their large public approval was yet to come. What fascinated me was that they were entirely centered upon the requalification of the *occasion* of painting or sculpture, the sense of what it was given to *do.* Again, a *literature,* in this case art history and criticism, had grown over the viable condition of the possibility. So, as John Chamberlain put it, "a sculpture is something that if it falls on your foot it will break it," both foot and sculpture. It weighs a lot. It sits on a so-called pediment. In contrast, he wanted a new vocabulary to speak of what a sculpture might be, terms like "fluff" or "glare." When asked why he had used discarded automobile parts for much of his early work, his answer was that Michelangelo had had, apparently, a lot of marble sitting in his backyard, but junked automobiles were what Chamberlain found in his own. *Material* was crucial again, regaining the tensions, the instant-to-instant recognition of the nature of what *was* in hand as mind took hold of it. In contrast, John Altoon saw the School of Paris as so much "polishing of stones," what R. B. Kitaj calls a "patinazation," a concern with decorative texture which prevented perception of the possibilities of the *act* of painting itself.

In like sense, *all* assumptions of what a painting was were being intensively requalified. Hence the lovely definition of that time: *a painting is a two-dimensional surface more or less covered with paint.* Williams' definition of a poem is parallel: *a large or small machine made of words.* In each case there is the marked attempt to be rid of the overlay of a speciously 'historical' 'appreciation,' a 'tradition' which is finally nothing more than congealed 'taste' or 'style'— which, Duncan notes, is distinctly different from art. "No man needs an art unless he himself has to put things together—to find an equilibration . . ." Style is predicated on the habit of discrimination previous to experience of the objects thus defined, whether these be so-called "art objects" or simply the clutter of a dump or city street. Duncan's point is that "the objects are not arriving [in perception or consciousness] that way, nor are the objects of thought arriving that way . . ." The collage or assemblage art of Wallace Berman, George Herms, and Larry Jordan—all working in San Francisco in the fifties—makes use of a *conglomerate,* coming out of what people discard, out of *any* time.

Possibly the attraction the artist had for people like myself—think of O'Hara, Ashbery, Koch, Duncan, McClure, Ginsberg; or Kerouac's wistful claim that he could probably paint better than Kline—was that lovely, uncluttered directness of perception and act we found in so many of them. I sat for hours on end listening to Franz Kline in the Cedar Bar, fascinated by, literally, all that he had to say. I can remember the endless variations he and Earl Kerkham spun on the "It only hurts when I smile" saga, and if that wasn't instance of initial story telling (an *art*), I don't think I'll ever know what is or can be. Kline could locate the most articulate senses of human reality in seemingly casual conversation—as I remember he once did, painfully, moving, by means of the *flowers* in a flower shop a friend had just opened, to the *roses* Kline had once brought to the pier to welcome his bride from England—to find that she had had a breakdown in passage. Those "flowers" gave us both something to hold on to.

It may also have been the *energy* these people generated, which so attracted us, and we may have been there simply to rip it off in a manner Wyndham Lewis warned against long ago. Writers have the true complication of using words as initial material and then depending on them as well for a more reflective agency. It would be absurd to qualify artists as non-verbal if, by that term, one meant they lacked a generative vocabulary wherewith to articulate their so-called feelings and perceptions. The subtlety with which they qualified the possibility of *gesture* was dazzling. So Michael McClure speaks of having "totally bought Abstract Expressionism as spiritual autobiography" and of Pollock as "so integral [to his own life and thought] that his work began immersing my way of thinking in such a subtle way so early I can't tell you when . . ."

The insistent preoccupation among writers of the company I shared was, as Olson puts it in his key essay, "Projective Verse" (1950): "what is the process by which a poet gets in, at all points energy at least the equivalent of the energy which propelled him in the first place, yet an energy which is peculiar to verse alone and which will be, obviously, also different from the energy which the reader, because he is a third term, will take away?" Duncan recalls that painters of his interest were already "trying to have something *happen* in painting" and that painting was "moving away from the inertness of its being on walls and being looked *at* . . ." *Action* painting was the term that fascinated him, and questions such as "to what degree was Still an Action painter?" He recognized "that you see the energy back of the brush as much as you see color, it's as evident and that's what you experience when you're looking." He notes the parallel with his work of this time, "The Venice Poem," which is "shaped by its own energies" rather than by a dependence on the pictorial or descriptive. Most emphatically, it is "not shaped to carry something outside of itself."

In his *Autobiography*, published in 1951, Williams reprints the opening section of "Projective Verse," feeling it "an advance of estimable proportions" insofar as Olson was "looking at the poems as a field rather than an assembly of more or less ankylosed lines." Earlier, seeing the text in manuscript, he had responded enthusiastically, noting that "Everything leans on the verb." *Energy* and *field* are insistently in mind in his attempt to desentimentalize accumulated senses of poetry by asserting its *thingness*. He uses his friend, the painter Charles Sheeler, as context: "The poem (in Charles' case the painting) is the construction in understandable limits of his life. That is Sheeler; that, lucky for him, partial or possible, is also music. It is called also a marriage. All these terms have to be redefined, a marriage has to be seen as a thing. The poem is made of things—on a field."

This necessity—to regain a focus not overlaid with habits of *taste* and the *conveniences* of the past—is found in all the arts at this time. At a retrospective show of his early work (in company with Claes Oldenburg and George Segal) Jim Dine said it constituted his own battle with 'art history,' his specific attempt to test and find alternatives for its assumptions. In like sense I once heard John Cage, speaking to a group of hostile and 'classically' oriented music majors at a New York university, point out that the music with which they were engaged had to do with *concept* and its understanding, whereas the music to which he was committed had to do with *perception* and its arousal. He also made the point that their music occupied only one fourth of the spectrum from a theoretic silence to white noise. Being an American, as he said, he felt that wasteful, and was also particularly interested in the possibilities of what's called *noise* itself. Just as Williams had to fight all his life the curious stigma which labelled him "antipoetic" (a term unintentionally provided by Wallace Stevens in an introduction to his work, which Stevens wanted to separate from saccharine notions of poetry), so we had to fight to gain a specific diction common to lives then being lived. No doubt the implicit *energy* of such language was itself attractive, but the arguments against it, coming primarily from the then powerful New Critics, made its use an exhausting battle. Allen Ginsberg remembers coming offstage after his early readings of *Howl* often so nervously worn out and shocked by the public antagonism, that he'd go to the nearest toilet to vomit. In contrast—and in grotesque parallel indeed to what was the literal condition of the 'world'—we both remembered the authoritative critical works of the time we were in college, books with titles like *The Rage for Order* and *The Well Wrought Urn*. Whatever was meant by *The Armed Vision*, the guns were seemingly pointed at us.

There was also the idea, call it, that poets as Ginsberg or myself were incapable of the formal clarities that poetry, in one way or another, has obviously to do with. Even now, at public readings in which I've read a sequence of poems whose structure has persistently to do with the parallel *sounds* of words having marked recurrence, someone inevitably (and too often one of my colleagues in teaching) will ask me if I've ever considered using rhyme? It blows my mind! I can't for the life of me figure out *where* they are in so-called time and space. As Pound pointed out, we don't all of us occupy the same *experience* of those situations, no matter we may be alive together in the same moment and place.

When my first wife and I decided at last to separate in 1955, we met in New York to discuss the sad responsibilities of that fact. At one point, locked in our argument, I remember we were walking along Eighth Street not far from the Cedar Bar, and suddenly there was Philip Guston, across the street, waving to us. My wife had not met him, and I had but recently, thanks to Kline—and had found him a deeply generous and articulate man. Most flattering was the fact he knew my work, although at that time it would have been hard to find it in any easily public condition. (It's worth noting that de Kooning, Kline, and Guston—the three I knew best—were all of them 'well read,' to put it mildly, and seemingly kept up with the new work of that time as actively as the writers themselves. Guston especially had a great range of 'literary interest.' A poem in *For Love* called "After Mallarmé" is actually a translation of a poem of Jouvet's which Guston quoted to me, having brought me up to his loft, with characteristic kindness, to show me the few paintings still there just previous to his first show with Sidney Janis. My 'translation' is what I could make of the French he quoted, in my scattered recollection of it.) In any case, my wife had become increasingly suspicious of what she felt were the true incompetences of my various heroes, i.e., Kline painted the way he did because he couldn't draw, and Williams wrote in his fashion, because he couldn't rhyme. So here was one she could physically confront, and she didn't waste any time about it. Guston had brought us to a restaurant which had just opened, and so there were free *hors d'oeuvres*—to his and my delight. Once we were seated, she let him have it: *how do you know when a painting is finished* (painting the way you do). He answered very openly and clearly. Given the field of the painting, so to speak, given what might energize it as mass, line, color, etc.—when he came to that point where any further act would be experienced as a diminishment of that tension (when there was nothing more to *do*, in short), that was when he felt the painting was finished. She let the matter rest, but I knew she felt almost complacently dissatisfied. "He doesn't know what he is doing—he's just fooling around." She, like so many others then and now, did feel that there must be an intention factually outside the work itself, something to be symbolized there, some content elsewise in mind there expressed, as they say. But that a *process*— again to emphasize it—might be felt and acted upon as crucial in itself she had not considered. So a statement such as Olson's "We do what we know before we know what we do" would be only a meaningless conundrum at best. I guess she thought we were all dumb.

Far from it, for whatever use it proved. There was, first of all, a dearly held to sense of one's *professionalism*, as Duncan reminded me, and all of us *practiced* the art which involved us as best we could. He spoke of the "upsurge in the comprehension of the language" in each art, and "not only writing, or painting, was going on, but *reading*," a veritable checking out of all the possibilities inherent in the physical situation and associative values pertaining. So painters are working "from a very solid comprehension of the visual language they come from, including anyone who may be looking." They know, as do the poets related, the *state* of the language—in a sense parallel to the scientist's saying something is in a volatile or inert *state*—so that "we do convey what we mean" and there is attention to what is happening in *every* part of the work, to keep "a tension throughout."

The diversity of possibilities gained by such an intensive inquiry is still the dominant condition. At times it may seem almost too

large an invitation to accept, and in any situation where it is used
either for convenience or habit, an expectable bag of tricks, then
whatever it may have generated is at an end. This is to say, more
vaguely, what Ezra Pound emphasized: "You cannot have literature without *curiosity* . . ." Or what Olson's qualification of *attention*
makes clear: "the exaction must be so complete, that the assurance of the ear is purchased at the highest—forty-hour-a-day—
price . . ." There is also the dilemma demonstrated by the story
Chamberlain tells of his first wife: "She said she wanted to be a
singer, but what she really wanted to be was famous." Good luck.

Possibly the complex of circumstances which made the years
1950 to 1965 so decisive in the arts will not easily recur. No one can
make it up, so to speak. But there were clearly years before, equally
decisive, and there will no doubt be those now after. This clothes-
line is at best an invention of pseudo-history, and the arts do not
intend to be history in this way, however much they use the traditions intimate to their practice. When Duncan saw Olson for the
last time, in hospital a few days before his death, he said to him,
"important as history was to you, there are no followers—and as a
matter of fact that isn't what happened in poetry." Olson grinned,
and Duncan added, "It *was* an adventure . . ."

It's always an *adventure*, thank god. When Rauschenberg arrived
at the Art Students League in New York, one of his teachers, Morris
Kantor, felt that his wife, who'd come with him, really had the more
practical competence as a painter. But what Rauschenberg had as
curiosity was fascinating, e.g., he'd put a large piece of butcher
paper just in front of the door by which students came and went,
would leave it there for a day or so, and then would examine it intently, to see the nature of pattern and imprint which had accumulated. Characteristically it is Rauschenberg who questions that an
'art object' should live forever necessarily, or that it should be less
valued than a car which manages to stay in pristine state for a very
few years indeed.

What seems most to have been in mind was not the making
of *models*, nor some hope of saving a world. As Duncan said of
Olson's sense of a city, "You have to confront it and get with it," not
"straighten it out. Optimism and pessimism have nothing to do
with being alive." The question more aptly is, "How much alive-
ness is found in living in a city," as much to the point now as when
Whitman made his own extraordinary catalog. Moral as the arts are
in their literal practice, I do think they abjure such program in
other respects. At least they do not serve easily such confined atten-

tion, however humanly good. I am sure Allen Ginsberg, despite the persistent concern he has shown for the moral state of this country, would nonetheless yield all for that moment of consciousness which might transform him.

But none of this, finally, has anything to do with any such argument at all. As Wittgenstein charmingly says, "A point in space is a place for an argument." You'll have to tell mother we're still on the road.

*Placitas, N.M.*
*August 28, 1974*

# Divers Sentiments

Looking through old manuscripts, I find the following, from a little known *Journal de M. Laubiès* written upon the occasion of his arrival in Paris.

> Ils me chargeoient incessament de mille brocards & de mille injures; je me suis veu en tel estat, que pour ne les aigrir, je passois les jours entiers sans ouvrir la bouche . . .

Hence, perhaps, the kindness of Laubiès to critics, even to myself. Painting these days is the discharge of a rare duty, and the public has of course its usual right of comment—to wit: *La Nature n'a pas les bras assez longs, etc.*

This was the death of romanticism, or better, of those poor painters at the turn of the century, with their *eaux d'essences,* and their hope of competition with appearance—which any woman might have undeceived them concerning. What followed led finally to that peculiar situation:

1. *C'est le naturel des artisans de se plaindre et de gronder.*
2. *La diversité des gages les fait murmurer, etc.*

And/or the jungle of Paris. Against that any man stands a little, at least, helpless. And Laubiès' work has been judged accordingly. I heard recently that his paintings had been much influenced by a visit to Mallorca. The colors, of course, became those of that delightful retreat—although the truth of the matter was, very simply,

Galerie Fachetti, 1953 or 1954.

that he found himself running low on everything but red, brown, and death's head (purple?), and so he made out the best he could. There was also an old lady (*"Ils me répétaient sans cesse: Nous te brûlerons; nous te mangerons; je te mangerai un pied; et moi, une main, etc."*) who wished to hang her tomatoes in the studio in which he was working, and one morning arrived at a little before seven to throw both paintings and Laubiès out.

May I suggest, then, that painting is one thing to a public—and quite another to a man so engaged? I don't think there is any reason to take it much beyond that. It is neither the business of the one nor of the other, to think very much about what each, in turn, thinks. I am tired, as I suppose many others are, of reading of deep, deep symbolism and mutterings of a soul, and so on. These are all, at last, much too far from that very thing we might otherwise notice—the work itself.

At least some such attention might be reasonable. As it is, and no matter "true or false," some sufferings merit acknowledgment:

> . . . *ny le froid, ny le chaud, ny l'incommodité des chiens, ny coucher à l'air, ny dormir sur un lit de terre, ny la posture qu'il faut toujours tenir dans leurs cabanes, se rammassan en peloton, ou se couchans, ou s'asseans sans siège & sans mattelas, ny la faim, ny la soif, ny la pauvreté & saleté de leur boucan, ny la maladie . . .*

Much that we see, we forget.

# René Laubiès: An Introduction

One doesn't have to develop theories to look at anything, all he has to do is open his eyes and look. Or call that the rational minimum for an attitude toward some character of painting which may not have a formal category, or some settled opinion concerning it, which can be appropriated for a guide.

Such guides are in fact deceptive. What the eye sees is also deceptive, but in a more useful sense. Say, for example, that you come into a room, drop your coat on a chair, switch on a light—and there, on the wall, is the shadow of a monster—perhaps. Obviously it is a shadow, and what else could it be. Just as the man who looks like Harry is not Harry, unless he is Harry. But this can wait.

A picture is first a picture, the application of paint or ink or whatever to a given surface—which act shall effect a thing in itself significant, an autonomy. And it may of course be that there has been something seen, a visual impression, which the man painting wishes to record, literally, without distortion, that is, without more change of that impression than his media, and the limits of himself, enforce. So representational painting, as we know it, has partially at least the necessity to overcome, by virtue of technique and media, a disturbance of the object, of the thing, so that its use is in the fact of its transference, from there to here or wherever it is, to the picture—so at last the picture is the thing, without need of further reference.

It is here that nonfigurative art becomes relevant, insofar as it

*Black Mountain Review*, Spring 1954.

can be, in inception, without reference of this usual kind. But that is a vagary, and one which has caused much confusion. Forms are—there are no 'dead' forms; form is the declaration of life. And not at all generally, because what we call life is utterly specific, and must be—to be itself. But the nonfigurative painter does not begin with the bowl of apples, however much he may see it. Or if he does begin there, his process is different from that of the man who would paint it as 'real.' He eats the apple, and then paints the picture. That is the sense of it. So it is a different engagement, a different sense of intent.

But often, wandering through a gallery of contemporary work, one looks up at the walls, and is bored. It is nothing, the painting is not 'real.' A clutter of unspecific forms, without trees or sunsets, proves little.

And this is how it can fail, insofar as such 'forms' may have nothing to declare of themselves—except that they are 'A Painting,' which is very hopeful. Otherwise it could and does happen— no argument can withstand it—that at times we are all of us shaken by forms perhaps unidentified but intimately involved with us, and unmistakably. Can we anticipate that? Or is it ridiculous for me to see the shadow as a thing, a very real thing, which frightens me? Laubiès knows this very deeply, and anticipates it.

It is his art, if you will, to begin here, at this point of things as yet unrecognized, without more reference than themselves. It is his purpose to effect these things as form, as a painting, simply there. So that we are involved unmistakably—like a sound perhaps, which no 'language' has yet found 'words' for, may affect us nonetheless.

# A Note on Franz Kline

There are women who will undress only in the dark, and men who will only surprise them there. One imagines such a context uneasily, having no wish either to be rude or presumptuous. Darkness, in effect, is the ground for light, which seems an old and also sturdy principle. There is nothing quite so abrupt and even pleasant as such "light"—ask any woman. Think of the masses of misunderstanding that come from a betrayal of this. Make a list. Picasso? Much a way of being *about* something, minus night, etc. There are some men for whom it seems never to get dark. As, for example, for Klee it never quite seems to be sun, etc.

But, more interesting, think of it, a woman undressing in broad sunlight, black. What if light were black—is there black light? If there is black light, what is black? In other words, argue to the next man you meet that we are living in a place where everything has the quality of a photographic negative. Take hold of his coat, point to anything. See what happens.

With Kline's work, if the blacks were white, and vice versa, it would make a difference, certainly. It has to be black on white, because there he is, New York, etc. He has no wish to fight senses and all. But he is a savagely exact laugher, call it. I don't know literally if he depends on argument for a means to cohabitation, but I would myself argue that he is a lonely man. Men rarely laugh this precisely, without such a thing for a control. What is 'funnier' than forms which will not go away? If you say this to someone, they will

*Black Mountain Review*, Winter 1954.

laugh at you, but all the time, right behind them, there is a sky-scraper! It's incredible how they can notice it, if they do, and still talk to anyone.

So what is form, if it comes to that. That question I once tried to answer in relation (as they say) to the theater. I was convinced that a man, formally, is no more and certainly no less than a chair. Fool that I was, I took two chairs, placed them either side of me, and sat down on the floor. The answer was, from these friends: Who would go to the theater to see a man be a chair? What would Kline have said, if anything. Is this thing on the page opposite looking at you too? Why do you think that's an eye. Does any round enclosed shape seem to you an eye.

There is no 'answer' to anything. A painter (possibly a musician) can assert this more effectually, more relevantly, than any other 'artist.' He can be present all at one time, which no writer can quite be—because he has to 'go on.' If no one sees a painter, or, rather, what he is doing—finally, not 'doing'—doesn't he still have *things?* At least no man can point at a painting and say it's nothing, he'll be lucky if it doesn't come down off the wall and club him to death for such an impertinence.

God knows we finally enjoy, deeply *enjoy,* wit, the grace, the care, of any thing—how it is. Kline's audience (no doubt in Paradise) will be a group of finely laughing women, plus what men won't be jealous.

# Philip Guston: A Note

For a sense of it, say—I tried to be careful, but the form would not have it. My care was the form I had given to it. How to care, that one does care? *Care*, it seems, comes from several words, among them the Anglo-Saxon *caru, cearu* (anxiety) and the Old Saxon *kara* (sorrow). Is it moving with care through care, that it comes to? I care, certainly.

I think—in that denseness of anxieties, and sorrows, like a nightmare world, of forms which are all exact and there, yet *not* the forms? What *are* the forms, one says. It is not possible that one should not arrive at them. Somehow not to be accidental, not even enough or too much 'accidental.' No one understands, but some know. It is a very articulate determination which can, at last, " . . . take care/by the throat & throttle it . . ." with such care.

*Black Mountain Review*, Spring 1956.

# Harry Callahan: A Note

What the eye is given to see, as image, in any sense, is a curious occasion. What is it, that they point to, for us to see? The new house with the dirt for lawn, the new tooth, the hat that does not fit, etc. And in the eye at last convolutions of precisely the despair, of no new house (not enough), of the tooth of no one at all, hat I never wore. I hate it all—pictures! What can I do with them, except ache to be there—? Or to get away as fast as possible, turning the page.

So that the subtlety (immense) of Callahan's photographs must, of necessity, be already another thing: not 'pointer,' or reminiscence, or even 'experiment,' but fact. In them there is no movement to any image beyond the one, given. We will never see the face of the boy, or of the woman, or will (to remark it), the white pigeon light. It will always be (flat) winter with trees, trampled grass, window curtains and reflections, and paint. These are (as seen) images also of an isolation; that must in fact be almost another 'given,' to not drive the forms home to pasture, to 'where else,' in short. There is no quicker eye to see, nor mind, equally, to seize upon the instant, of chance. All of which (words) here go flaccid against the dry, clear 'eye' of it all.

*Black Mountain Review*, Autumn 1957.

# A Note

*"The Question Answer'd"*

*What is it women do in men require?*
*The lineaments of gratified desire.*
*What is it women do in men require?*
*The lineaments of gratified desire.*

WILLIAM BLAKE

And all the world lies in between, so to speak. Here is a paradox, and pathetic joke, that that which is most given to men and women, as a common occasion, should be also that least shared by them. We make a cult of the beautiful woman because we will never know her, if men, or be her, if women. We would rather look at the coldly suggestive than feel, in any part of our bodies, the substantial fact of our own warmth.

But these are drawings of another order than that which we are accustomed to in that they let us look. It was perhaps the primary heroism of Peeping Tom that let him look at Lady Godiva, no matter the occasion. The man who shuts his eyes at the sight of a lovely woman is a fool, and the woman who is blind to what sight she might be is also a fool. Finally, I like the comfortableness of these drawings, I like love so seen in its place. It is always there.

Alice Garver, *Togetherness* (Albuquerque, 1962).

# Feedback:
# "Contemporary Voices in the Arts"

The whole thing began characteristically enough.* I'd got to the Mohawk terminal at La Guardia, and met the others—Billy Kluver, John Cage, Merce Cunningham, Stan Vanderbeek, Jack Tworkov, and Len Lye. Some were hungry, so went off to find something to eat quickly, leaving Len, myself, and a young friend of Stan's to find some place to be comfortable till the plane was ready to go. Len led us into a rather formal restaurant where a waitress immediately gave us large menus and waited for our orders. We simply wanted to talk and so Len with a lovely avoidance kept the whole scene in confusion. We sat there with all this *function* around us somehow unable to catch up with the fact we were not really there to have dinner or to do anything but that which we were obviously doing.

There is a lag in the situation of the eye's response to projected film image, for example, which Stan reported as about one-tenth of a second, that lets the eye see a continuous image rather than the literal fact of the static frame-by-frame that is the case. Just so in the proposal of the restaurant, the assumption of a *necessary order* let the three of us use it in quite another manner, and we were thus able to enjoy the lag of their adjustment to the fact that we were there to do nothing more than sit comfortably and talk.

At one point—at Albany State—Billy and John were continuing a conversation with students that had started in an almost impos-

*Arts Magazine,* Summer 1967.

*Early in 1967 a group of seven artists toured several universities in New York State as part of the New York State Council on the Arts program "Contemporary Voices in the Arts."

sibly dead ballroom, just that no one could hear anything said even a few feet from them, and now we were all sitting in an anonymous classroom. John had been speaking of what he felt to be the necessity of testing all assumptions of cause and effect. As answer to a student who asked him how that might be done, he said, simply try to make use of any situation in a way that the assumptions proposing it have not dealt with. If you get a grant, say, proposing you study cloud formations, see if you can use it for a trip to Europe, or whatever might interest you in that sense specifically.

We were an odd company without question. Often I felt an awkward distance in my own occasion from that which was clearly the possibility of the others, and I envied the articulation and particularity of Stan's nonverbal 'language.' Reading poems, as I'd known it, with the discreet placement of the audience, the fixed focus, the single term of the reader's voice and image, all seemed to make an impossibly static circumstance. Consequently I never made use of it during any of the eight evenings we had together. Instead I tried to project voice into the simultaneity of the multiple occurrences much as Stan was in fact doing with his battery of projectors and view-o-graphs. I was very curious to discover what *kinds* of hearing were actual in such a multiplicity of event. When some people at Union said they hadn't been able to hear anything back of the first few rows, I couldn't really care, just that I'd heard, as I knew those first few rows had, a fantastic blast of sound into which entered *images* of voices as actual as William Carlos Williams saying, in a suddenly vacant quiet, "Be patient that I address you in a poem . . ." to be bumped abruptly by whatever it was did then occur. The world of my own head, selfishly enough, was changing significantly.

Since there were seven of us, and, in the two weeks of the tour, seven places to be visited, we decided that each one of us in turn would take an evening. He could, if he chose, make use of the others as he saw fit. Since Harpur had an active dance program, Merce was given direction of that evening, and the rest of us were placed at various points on the stage, which was segmented in at least five sections, all of which could be raised or lowered independently. David Vaughan, the tour manager, was back of the stage operating the control panel without being able to see us, so that we went up and down with a lovely randomness. Back of us Merce drew the form of the space into a sequence of extraordinary articulations. There were various microphones placed about which we could use as we wished, either to note senses of dance or to say whatever we wished. Billy read a quietly didactic sequence of proposals with an icy blue-white spot on him. Len, always impatient with any *located* place, was walking around somewhat like a carnival barker, trying to get hold of the audience directly and admonishing them to admit the fact of their own feelings. I felt like Gagarin, saying something like, I'm a bird, I'm a bird! John was making great gnomic sense, but Jack was somehow most articulate of all. He sat there, saying literally nothing, as the section of stage under him raised and lowered the chair he was sitting in, as Stan's images floated all around him and off the walls and ceilings surrounding. The intensity of his attention to the *newness* of this experience was so evident it became more than any of us could say.

Immediately when we had first met, we decided any formal *panel* procedure would be specious. As John said, if we began by talking about where we thought the arts were going, then we'd be stuck with where we thought they had come from—and that was patently an endless dialogue. In the discussions that did often follow the specific activities of the evenings, there were inevitably both faculty and students who felt themselves defrauded by our conduct. I remember one professor in particular at R.P.I. who said he felt us pathetic, coming as we did with what were acceptably defined abilities in the various arts he assumed us to represent, to engage an audience in what he could only recognize as a primitive randomness. John answered him sharply, pointing out that he was imposing a decision of taste and habit upon a situation that was literally a process of exploration. There were no assumptions there to be insisted upon other than the one which might feel possibility to be more interesting than the limits of habit.

Much that was said continues to be very active for me. For example, in an afternoon conversation with students, John said: "Distinguish between that 'old' music you speak of which has to do with *conceptions* and their *communication,* and this new music, which has to do with *perception* and the arousing of it in us. You don't have to fear from this new music that something is bad about your liking your own music."

He made use of a simple diagram on the board: conceptions/fixed—perceptions/fluid. He suggested: Likes and dislikes are associated with the ego not on its dream side but on its daytime side in connection with what it receives through the senses. Now if you divide your sense perceptions into what you like and dislike, you might just be cheating yourself. As far as we know for sure, you're only alive once. Your sense perceptions are in good working order. They will not necessarily remain in good working order. Beethoven, for instance, growing deaf . . . While your ears are in good working order, and while your eyes are in good working order, it seems to me that you would want, rather than shutting your eyes and ears to available experience, rather to open them . . .

Stan put frequent emphasis on the very evident fact of *process* as condition of contemporary environment, noting that colleges and universities, as airports, were always being built, rarely completed. Again, it was in the exploration of this situation that we found a common vocabulary. Billy Kluver made a unique contribution to the company in that, being an engineer, process is an unequivocal attention for him, happily apart from a conceptual 'aesthetics.' At R.P.I. he and Robbie Robinson, another engineer from Bell who had participated in the "Nine Evenings," created a sound system that permitted the audience to tune FM radios to particular 'broadcasts' of live activity, so that one had 'campfire' situations of various groups in the audience so tuned in as all the other activity went on around them. He had wanted a kind of trade fair environment, with each of us in 'booth' locations that the audience might move freely around, again tuning in what interested them. But once there, the limits of the equipment and the auditorium, with its fixed seats, which he had to work with, caused a modification—proving again that what happens is more relevant than what doesn't.

Toward the end a kind of feedback gained in the continuity began to be a problem, I felt. Inevitably we gained a sophistication in dealing with the kinds of questions we were asked. Yet the habits, in that sense, of the audience were the most continual limit. It is interesting to remember how the idea of the last evening, the "TV Dinner" eaten literally at the Y in New York, came about. We were in Albany, having dinner, guests of Mr. Hightower, and Jack said, why don't we do this—and immediately John was thinking of contact mikes, Stan of the possibility of closed circuit TV, Billy of the obvious engineering problems, and Len of his lovely fish. When the actual evening came, I found I'd learned one very useful thing— to trust the fact of any literal condition I am in. But the fairly discreet rage of the audience—neither students nor faculty this time, and very sophisticated indeed as to its judgments—was something else, and the screaming feedback, and the projected pleasure of that meal and ourselves eating it, seems to have met with active qualifications.

I don't think I've ever eaten a better piece of meat, and the company was especially pleasant. There was a very happy air of being together again. At one point apparently the Y's stage manager came up to Robinson and said, "You've got to do something, the crowd is getting very restless." Robinson continued with his own preoccupations. They were literally more interesting.

# John Chamberlain

There is a handle to the world that is looked for, a way of taking it in hand. But not as something familiar, nor as some reference to something else. Senses of Chamberlain's sculptures that want to return them to "crushed automobiles" seem to me as absurd as trying to put mother back together again. Surely what has happened is something too.

Things, then, are large or small objects, having the fact of space in whatever dimension becomes them. Space—such as we are given to conceive—is already the dimension of our own. We measure by what we are, as things, in what relations are possible to us. The small man sees the door as large, the large man as small, etc. But what things move more complexly in how they are, come forward insistently, disobliging all such scale, and will be other than big or small—as if we stood finally on our hands, and the so-called bottom disappeared at our feet.

"A new world is only a new mind," says Williams, and equally a new world is not only but wholly a new thing. Our sense of history looks for conformities of acts and effects, and in that respect does us poor service in the arts. Skills are accumulated but the effects of those skills have at each moment to be recognized. There are such things now present that the sciences have no vocabulary wherewith to describe them. They are confronted as facts of literal presence.

You will not live long if you look always for what was there, assuming the world to be no more than the time track of your

*Recent American Sculpture* (New York: The Jewish Museum, 1964).

particularities. A sudden crash, a disfigurement, the loss of any-thing not simply a pencil or some wish, and all becomes a present so huge it falls on you, crushing you more than that automobile you thought so neatly to remember. It was there, but now you are con-tained in a thing already changing, bringing you into its terms—and your house shrinks, far off, and things are bright and twisted.

But what things are is, again, more complex, and more distinct than some incidental violence done you. In that sense they used to say, stand back—but these things neither invite nor reject. It is the virtue of a mountain not to care—or not, at least, in such words as we use. Here as well to be liked is not an issue.

One wants a world wherein all that is possible occurs, neither as *good* nor *bad*—however terrifying. It must happen. These things have come from such time that no one remembers it, and from such space they assert their own. It is all here.

# Frank Stella: A Way to Go

One of the most insistent gains of abstract expressionism is that it gets rid of the frame as limiting factor. It regains the canvas as surface—or literally imposes as significant surface anything on which the painting occurs. Instead of making the canvas, as it were, a view box or screen where something is then to happen, painters of this group forced the sense of limiting edge to give place to what was happening in the painting itself. Equally, accumulated senses of composition—for example, the Renaissance use of perspective as a vanishing point—were largely displaced. The senses of balance, of 'tops' and 'bottoms' in relation to 'weight,' were also revised. It would now seem inevitable that, in contrast to a nonfigurative painting that wants only to disguise the nature of its figuration, painting of this kind was most absorbed in that activity momently confronted as it, quite literally, occurred. What could be seen then and there was dominant, and if all the forms so discovered had counterparts in other visual contexts, they were nonetheless decisively found in the primary act of painting.

One aspect of this insistence is that painting loses its historical sense of *picture*, insofar as our sense of a picture seems to imply something which is referential. It is very hard to think of a picture without wondering, of what. So, again, abstract expressionism rids painting of having to be pictures of things, symbols, mirrors of some otherwhere present reality.

But what follows directly from these painters, both as mystique

*Lugano Review,* no. 1, 1965.

and example, is more confused. As Robert Duncan has usefully
made clear, abstract expressionism has to do with energy embodied
in the painting ( *felt*) rather than energy referred to (*seen*). This fact
makes the energy implicit in the character of the brush stroke, of
the forms which it asserts by its activity, a dominant qualification of
the painting itself. It explains Pollock's situation when he says,
"When I am *in* my painting I'm not aware of what I'm doing . . . I
try to let it come through . . ."

It is impossible to qualify what, then, will be significant about
such 'being in the painting' except by looking at what comes of it.
However, a sense of painting that wants to make itself significant by
a random occasion of such energies—or looks for accidental dis-
coveries of 'balance'—leads finally to an implicit chaos, which, in
turn, yields only to taste and fashion. In other words, what follows
from abstract expressionism, in direct imitation, too often depends
upon an arbitrary process of discrimination, one that wants the
thing to look like it looks like nothing.

It is interesting that it should be in what seems the antithetically
disciplined formalism of Frank Stella, and those akin to him as Neil
Williams and Larry Poons, that the gains of abstract expressionism
are most used. For example, the interest in the materials possible to
painting is continued, whereas the contemporary Action painters
depend on those defined by the older men. Equally, the sense of
the canvas, or whatever surface is used, is for Stella and the others
noted a major preoccupation. Most relevant, the painting is not a
reference to another reality—not even another painter's reality—
but remains unequivocally its own occasion.

There are several senses of Frank Stella's work that seem to me
useful. John Chamberlain speaks of him as having painted one line
without stopping for the past ten years. What he finds interesting is
that Stella has found in that apparent repetition the possibility of
maintaining that line's activity. He is after it, like they say, and will
not let go.

Neil Williams, on the other hand, told me of Stella's first use of
Motherwell-like forms. As he said, there is this early parallel, but
that then something began to happen. The forms became more
formal, and in turn led to a linear context, so that—in Klee's vocabulary—the planar effect yielded to linear. But there must be a
simpler way to put it. Suppose, for instance, one first sees a set of
things as mass, e.g., bulky hills, large clouds, things occupying substantial senses of space. But then, as one goes on looking, that way
we have of relating any such group of things, as occupying places

together, leads us to senses of their position, in such relationship. The hill's top is roughly the apex of a triangle which points to the cloud, itself an awkward rectangle—and so on, because all that I am trying to note here, is that *lines* are an adamant assumption in any reference to space. Therefore, it is simple enough to recognize how the movement from preoccupation with shapes, or mass, to line occurs. It is not really the out-line, or the 'edge' of the mass, that is the point here—but rather, that what one calls a shape is primarily an activity of line.

So then, as Williams spoke of it, there begins to be an increasing interest in the linear relation of forms—of how they develop into (for the example he gave) a sequence of rectangles moving from right to left, parallel, but each in turn of less length than that to its right, but with a common balance in their point of possible intersection supposing a line drawn through the middle of the canvas on the horizontal axis—and, again, so on, because this is to say, much more simply, that these rectangles begin to assert the lines of a triangle, and that those lines, in turn, begin to determine the possibility of what 'forms' they can take.

Suppose a square, or rather, make one, as Stella now does, and taking the canvas as its possibility, a square canvas in turn, what is implicit in the linear fact of that square that can continue to happen throughout the area which the canvas offers? What is a square, in fact, that it can be drawn with line, or that a line can draw one? And, having drawn one, is a second square enclosing it another line or—despite the apparent fact that it happens in another place, and of another size—the same one?

These are curious questions, and worth the emphasis simply that a first impression of Stella's work may lead one to think that color, and more specifically, the bands of color which he uses to locate line (itself to my knowledge never painted, but left as the surface of the canvas itself), are the significant activity. This same factor leads, at times, to senses of depth or volume which lend the painting the possible effect of an optical illusion. It may be that this aspect is relevant—akin to Op painting more generally—but I have, finally, the impression that it is rather how the line follows through such a variable, that is the point. In "Sharpeville" (1962) there can be a sense of 'looking in,' although it seems soon embarrassed by my own feeling that the *line* of the squares is always on the same plane.

Squares, as a formal possibility for the line, lead to a number of variations. However, these terms seem left as constant: first, the bands, or intervening colored areas between the lines, are left equal in width—so that whatever occurs as qualification of that space is managed by color; and, secondly, the diagonals are insistent, very often implicitly as those lines which would pass through the angle of each square to meet at center, and also explicitly, as in "Meknes" (1964). The effect of this last is to emphasize the four triangles which the diagonals define.

Two forms are therefore present, which now move to a complex of relationships. These in turn seem to me to follow two distinct patterns, which are difficult to describe—but briefly, they seem as follows. Either the squares occur as they do in "Line Up" (1962), so that one of the diagonals will originate from a point the width of one band in from the edge of the canvas; or else they begin as a development from a central point, itself the intersection of the diagonals from the edges of the squared canvas, as in "Sharpeville." The situation of the triangles is modified in each case in a distinct manner. Either they seem to set up alternative positions and/or to displace the presence of the squares (as in "Line Up")—or else lead to an intensification of them (as in "Sharpeville" and others of like kind). Then there are further possibilities in the 'double image' of "Jasper's Dilemma" (1962), with its negativized, tonal parallels in the right-hand square balanced against the 'positive' of the left.

At this point the fact of the square canvas is itself a concern I think, in the sense that although it is a limit, the structure of the painting works to include that fact in the activity of the painting. I mean, simply, that the sense of backwall, or edge, is played against, and used at times to return one to the intensity of the center. But what is happening in the painting forces further qualifications; and the forms which are there become increasingly active, clearly, and are demonstrating other possibilities in turn.

The triangle, and the angles involved by it, lead the line to qualify not only the context of shape within the painting, but as well its actual circumstance in the actual shape of the canvas. There are a number of variations which lead to this—increasing play on the activity of the diagonals for one thing—in "Fez (2)" (1964)—, so that they are shifted to pass through the center at a point midway on each side of the painting, making in that way four squares within it, and the sequence of expanding squares, familiar from the earlier work, is here shifted on its axis to make an increased emphasis on the triangular, chevron-like pattern the squares effect as they move to the outer edge. The bands of color, limited to an orange and green, alternate from one to the other as they meet at each diagonal, and the whole effect of the painting is an expanding pressure against that limit of edge, but one which also, paradoxically, returns to a balance as these bands grow shorter, approaching each of the outside angles of the canvas.

The frustration is really that it is a little specious to write of something which is so active when seen. Speaking now of what happens when the line begins to define the shape of the canvas itself, is even more so. But it is nonetheless what one has to do, simply that so much is so loosely assumed. The sense that 'function defines form' is familiar enough to people who have used hammers, or any so-called tool that has a specific thing to do. But that information does stay, oddly, an abstraction in that people reasonably don't want to be bothered when doing something, with how it happens they have something to do it with, etc. If one speaks of lines having similar possibilities, even necessities, it seems all the more vague. But there are so many simple instances. One, for example, that has always fascinated me, is that of moving the center white line, on a road, so that it goes off the road, and all the cars smash up in the ditch. Or take the friend who got a job once painting the stripe down the center of a village street, past a bar he was drawn to as he painted toward it, and finally the line hit the sidewalk—and the street likewise. Because where the line goes is where it is, and what locates itself with reference to that line goes too.

Line begins to have this unequivocal presence in "Haines City" (1964) in that the shape of the canvas is directly the form given it by the activity of the line, and the form it defines. The diagonals are, again, a center for this activity, but now the parts of the canvas which cannot be used are removed. In other words, not only has the activity broken free of the physical situation of a canvas within a frame—as abstract expressionism managed to do, insisting that the coherence of what was happening in the painting was quite enough—it has managed to affect all that context of surface qua 'picture' to such an extent that only such surface as is actively engaged by the painting will be admitted as a physical object. It has done this with line.

Last fall I was able to see Stella's show at Kasmin in London, and it was an extraordinary experience—for these reasons. First, line in these paintings not only determines the context of the canvas' shape; it further allows no other possible sense of such shape to begin with. It is moving on a ground that can only be felt as its activity. It does another thing as well. I was there with a friend, and as I was sitting on that bench seen in the illustration, she walked in front of the painting on the far wall. It was as if she reoccurred,

momently, i.e., her own size shifted and changed with reference to
the lines she moved in front of—the painting was as much a defining *object* as she was.

But the lines, in any case, were going elsewhere, and it is not only
the point, that they had this effect. Nor that they created 'architectural' effects (as she said) and seemed to make a volume. I think
the fact that they had gained their own articulation, that they
found shape as they moved—rather than as 'it' might—is the primary one.

What Stella himself secured seems to me a large possibility indeed. In his show at the Ferus Gallery in February relationships
of triangular forms reoccur, and the shape of the canvas follows
them, with a quiet, intense wit and care. After the more variable
'open' shapes of the Kasmin show, he comes to these with a line so
sure he has only to follow it.

# "Mehr Licht . . ."

Not so very long ago it was characteristic to associate film with dramatic or with narrative art. We *saw* the images, so to speak, but we tended to place them as a story, a continuity necessarily involved with a message that either a novel or a play might otherwise convey. Something flashing, or stuttering in a myriad of colors, might alter our attention, but it was at best, we thought, an effect used in support of the actual purpose: to get on with the story itself.

In contrast to this presumption, a film by Stan Brakhage wants to push us out, to force us, in fact, to *see* as the activity of light itself permits us to. One mutual friend may object that he is "ruining our eyes" but I would emphasize that it is in the defense of those eyes, and their possibility, that his work takes on its most real and singular character. Therefore I interrupt myself and these notes to look again at a beautifully simple and precise instance, *Mothlight*. What do I see?

> pulsing—
>> kinetic—flicker
> tones brown, green
>> details of [moth] wing, other parts—
> occurring between light source—and
>> the light now on the wall—
>> scale—as detail of "size"
> the presence (present-s as he would say)
> of what occurs *in* the light.

*Arts Canada,* December 1968.

> And I find myself seeing the "blank" film
> at the end as particularized now—dust bits,
> scratches, something *in* the light.

My understanding is that this film was made by placing fragments of mothwings and parts between strips of scotchtape—and of making from that a print capable of projection. To see, in short, what is in the light—as dust motes in the air might be so seen.

His early films are, effectually, "psychodramas" but his work moves intensively, and quickly, into the literality of light as the eye is given to experience it. A significant film of this experience is *Anticipation of the Night*, which he has spoken of as follows:

> The daylight shadow of a man in its movement evokes lights in the night. A rose bowl held in hand reflects both sun and moon like illumination. The opening of a doorway onto trees anticipates the twilight into the night. A child is born on the lawn, born of water with its promissory rainbow, and the wild rose. It becomes the source of all light. Lights of the night become young children playing a circular game. The moon moves over a pillared temple to which all lights return. There is seen the sleep of innocents in their animal dreams, becoming the amusement, their circular game, becoming the morning. The trees change color and lose their leaves for the morn, they become the complexity of branches in which the shadow man hangs himself . . .

What I find interesting here is the apparent melding of a vocabulary involved with symbolic action ("a circular game") and with the phenomenal character of light itself ("anticipates the twilight into the night").

His notes for beginning film-makers are relevant in that he proposes one take film into a light-free room and there expose it to specific activity of light—for example, the flare of a match or the beam of a penlight. Equally, he suggests scratching on black filmstrip, so that this qualification of light may be experienced. He wants to emphasize that what the film will evoke or more accurately make manifest is the *activity* of light as the eye is given to experience it by means of its action on the "light sensitive" film.

Consider how explicit the activity of light is to film in all senses. We see the movie by virtue of the fact that light is being projected from a source, through a material variously prepared (e.g., by camera, painting, scratching, direct exposure, alternate chemical action, etc.)—and here of course the point is that light may be used not only to "create" the initial condition of the film, but is itself "created" and/or brought to reveal the multiple condition of its nature by its passage through the film.

In fact, it is *light* and the *eye* which experiences it that seem to me the two insistent terms of Brakhage's activity as a film-maker. I know that he has also deep concern with "what things mean" and with basic human relationships—but light, in all its modality, as "seeing sees it," is much more to my own mind his insistent preoccupation. So it is that perhaps the most ambitious of his masterworks is called *The Art of Vision*. No doubt he thinks as well of that kind of vision which is called "visionary" and he without question possesses it. Yet I love that teasing, nonsense wisdom of, "Where was Moses when the lights went out . . ." It must be part of all that says, "Let there be light . . ."—or that calls one into the light, asks that light be shed on this, lightens the load well as the heart.

Not long ago I sat with friends watching a number of the 8mm films which comprise the lovely *Songs* sequence, and because we were in the living room of an adobe house, and senses of earth in that way all around us, and because there were the occasional lights of passing cars, like firelight flickering on the walls—I felt an oldtime invocation of *possibility*. Pound says, "Damn your taste! I'd like if possible to sharpen your perceptions after which your taste can take care of itself . . ." John Cage has spoken of that previous music, as he might put it, which had to do with concept and its demonstration, and of that music he himself has had so much to do with, which concerns perceptions and their arousal. The center of what we were seeing was the very possibility of sight itself. We saw the light.

To return then . . . I have been looking at a recent issue of *Scientific American* (September 1968) devoted to "Light," and much of it I can't follow. Still much of it and/or what its subject concerns is familiar to me because of conversations with Brakhage. For example—that what we see as color is due to the failure of the material from which light is being reflected to absorb that color. But more to the point here: the experience offered by his films is initial, and has to do with the primary fact of sight, as light creates it.

*October 29, 1968*

# Ecce Homo

One evening last year in San Francisco, a number of people came together to hear discussion of a nonhuman concept of *beauty*, e.g., what a butterfly or blue whale or a three-toed sloth might 'define' as beautiful in another member of its group. The zoologist Peter Warshall emphasized that it was, seemingly, those functions or physical attributes which permitted the most appropriate (secure and productive) rapport with environment that were chosen. I was interested that the other participant that evening was Diane di Prima, whose *Revolutionary Letters* constitute a basic 'how-to' manual for social-political survival. The series itself, of which this evening was one instance, had been arranged by the physicist Frank Oppenheimer, who, with his brother, Robert, had faced a severely imposed 'question' as to legal conditions of human interest and commitment during the fifties.

Whether the art be painting, music or writing, one may note its overwhelming preoccupation with *process* during the periods of the Modern and, now, the Post Modern. Also echoing in mind is William Burroughs' somewhat sardonic remark in *Naked Lunch*, "Where do they go when they leave the body. . . ." One may presume that the substantially collective *human* body was left toward the end of the nineteenth century, and that, in the Western world, the faintness of an intellectual humanism, having no physical authority for its ruminations, went down also, as increasingly sophisticated fragmentations of the human event took over. The point

Introduction to the exhibition catalog *R.B. Kitaj: Pictures/Bilder* (London: Marlborough Fine Art, 1977, with German translation by Ursule von Wiese).

here can be made simply by noting some of the primary names of that time, Freud, Einstein, Marx, et al.—each of whom, be it said, thought to speak for a collective situation of the human, but, nonetheless, presents primarily a singular plane of its event. *Schizophrenia*, as Surrealism or Cubism, is a term invented about the time of World War I, and Ezra Pound's great cry *de profundis*, "I cannot make it cohere . . . ," has obvious parallel with Yeats—"The centre cannot hold. . . ."

What had been lost, to put it so, was an *image of man*, some order of and in experience, both collective and singular, that could propose itself as constituting *something*, in whatever dimension or context of practical fact was elsewise the case. The insistent, whining question of our time is, "Who am I?"—and that *I* is not the one which is of necessity the many, plural and communal as given. Quite the contrary, it is Descartes' proof of existence, swollen with paranoia and frustration to a *me* of irreconcilable abstraction. Marlowe's Faustus—possibly the first significant instance of this crisis in our literature—now becomes Everyman. "O, I'll leap up to my God! Who pulls me down?" Be it said that there are a remarkable number of cultures and persons surviving who do not share in our specifically Western dilemma, but our equally specific use of the world since 1900 has resulted in a horrifying reduction of such cultural units and the language groups relating.

In his notes concerning "The Human Clay," an exhibition he selected for the Arts Council of Great Britain (1976), Kitaj says, with disarming simplicity, "The single human figure is a swell thing to draw . . . I'm talking about skill and imagination that can be *seen to be done*. It is, to my way of thinking and in my own experience, the most difficult thing to do really well in the whole art. . . . It is there that the artist truly 'shows his hand' for me. It is then that I can share in the virtue of failed ambition and the downright revelation of skill. . . ." This preoccupation has nothing to do with a 'documentary' art or with 'photorealism'—each seems too simply an exploitation of a one-sided 'reality.' Rather, it's what that single footprint meant to Robinson Crusoe, in Defoe's mind. It's *there*, physically, without question. What Defoe then realizes, by means of Crusoe, is the *informational* crisis it provokes in another human. So James Joll and John Golding, extraordinary humans indeed, look out 'From London' to see Europe, their own information surrounding—as Kitaj, in turn, sees them, and remembers both the Europe of their insight and his own determining sense of it, all present in such resonant, echoing detail, from such a range of human preoccupation and vocabulary, one cannot simply list its occasions. For one instance, however, see that Mr. Joll's head has been 'repaired' in the manner of certain frescoes of Giotto—which recalls, in turn, that charming Modernist tenet, "a painting is a two-dimensional surface," etc. As Kitaj might say, *of course.*

More complex possibly, as its title, *If Not, Not,* can be felt to signal,* are the multiple dimensions of this painting, 'measures' of an insistent variety of human information and feeling about 'things,' a curious soft welter of 'dreams.' Here the physical order of sight shifts and turns in 'perspective,' informed by diversities of human artifact, presence, and memory. Color leads and coordinates, a deliberating act, insisting on the primacy of the painting as a human decision.

*The Jew Etc.*—as the earlier *Bill*—begins a 'character' (like those one might find in a novel, Kitaj said in conversation, who come and go in various possible books) found also in *If Not, Not.* Here he is singular, in progress—as a 'history' in a shifting 'place.' The other figures thus—as *Catalan Christ (Pretending to Be Dead)*—are historic increment and prototype, but in situations which have their own decisive echoes and accumulations. The physical dimensions of the 'single figure' paintings themselves are frequently the literal measure of a human space.

If anything stands presently in need of definition, like they say, more demandingly than the word *person,* I don't myself know what it is or can be. Whether the preoccupations be social, political, psychological, legal, economic, or biological, there seems no commonly satisfying resolution of meaning, either in or among the concepts variously attached. When the zoologist pointed out that particular markings of the Monarch butterfly are apparently considered to be 'beautiful' to others of that species, he presumed that the 'reason' was the camouflage they afforded—and that the Monarch's bitter 'taste' was also 'beautiful' insofar as it protected it thus from the interest of possible predators. Another species of butterfly, in fact,

---

*As instance of Kitaj's own social and political context, and the complexity of its resolution here, consider the following from a book found in his library: "'We who are as good as you swear to you who are no better than we, to accept you as our king, provided you observe all our liberties and laws; but if not, not'—this formula of the ancient coronation oath of Aragon defines the relations of the sovereigns to their noble subjects in all the kingdoms of medieval Spain." F. D. Klingender, *Goya in the Democratic Tradition,* 2nd ed. (London, 1968), p. 18. *All* these elements, e.g., Klingender, Goya, etc., can be present, albeit transformed by Kitaj's use of them in the painting itself.

mimics the Monarch's color pattern for this very reason. It may be late in the day to invoke such utilitarian concerns, but I wonder, finally, if we've ever truly had done with them. Certainly I hope not. Put simply, I want to *know* something—I want to know how and why and what it is, to be *human*—and I believe, as did Konrad Lorenz, that the arts give any of us the most specific, intensive information of those questions possible in the given world. If Kitaj were only a 'genius' insofar as painting was concerned—if he could not otherwise count beyond five or read a newspaper with a literate comprehension—delight me he well might, but it would be as the wind in the evening or the water's deep present blue. *I* am human, and I am restless, unsure, insistently questioning as to how *you* are feeling, what it is *you* know, and what do *they* mean. In Kitaj's art there is such a driven amplitude of attention, so many articulate layers of information and care. The axes of possible directions at times seem infinite—as if one might 'go anywhere'—and yet the preoccupation seems to me always rooted in the fact of the human: the singular, the communal, the one, the many, in the places of its history, in the presence of our lives. As he says, "No one can promise that a love of mankind will promote a great art but the need feels saintly and new and somehow poetic to me and we shall see. . . ." Here I believe that we do.

# Three Films

for Gary Doberman

My layman's sense of this art finds a diversity of connections. Most generally, the nostalgic fact of first permission to be 'entertained' or, more truly, to see *things* which otherwise could not be felt as 'real.' Hence—as with Jack Kerouac's lovely evocations of Saturday childhood afternoons in wonder of local movie house—it was that miraculous 'outside' coming into one's sight, scrunched down in seat, stuffed with popcorn, kids again in that insistent impulse of, "what's going to happen *now?*" I think of how peculiarly rare is that occasion, in a common life, when "the house lights dim" and there is no question of the legitimacy of specific anticipation, no judgment other than one's *pleasure.*

An art, any art, would seem to me to have to be *interesting,* so to speak. And what, among other things, would seem so is that fact of a revelation, that an *information* occur—again, that *something happen.*

I've never felt that the arts had to be taken care of, in some charitable way, and I've loathed the often pretentious context of interest, primarily social, which used the activity for a badge of its own taste and/or its authority. Ezra Pound years ago made a very simple statement in contradiction: "Damn your taste! I want if possible to sharpen your perceptions, after which your taste can take care of itself . . ." We surely will not all have the same "taste" but the arts

Robert Creeley, *Was That a Real Poem & Other Essays,* ed. Donald Allen (Bolinas, Calif.: Four Seasons Foundation, 1979).

are not 'about' 'reality,' nor are they merely instances of possible social agreement. No doubt they all make manifest factors of specific social habit and history—and that is interesting. But for *me*, selfishly enough, they begin at the beginning, which is to say, they constitute physically real acts, things, and occur in the world as objects of that order, to find use, effect, as all else in possible human experience will or will not.

As a writer I have been endlessly fascinated by the apparent fact that words, language, constitute a particularly human creation. I don't at all mean that we each one 'made it up,' that is, thought of an apple and then searched around for the appropriate 'word.' As Wittgenstein suggests, it is very difficult to think of thinking apart from the functions of language. However obvious it is to remark it, a dog does not 'talk' in the same way that we humanly do. Its barks, yelps, whines, etc., are not demonstrably an abstraction of something 'out there' into something 'in here,' my head, call it, where *indefatigable, shoe string,* and *water* may all find *a place* with no immediate necessity to be *here* otherwise at all. Sigfried Gideon in his book *The Eternal Present* proposes early on that the arts have a significant initial relation to the human ability *to abstract* and therefore *to symbolize*—and that, humanly, this power has both its obvious wonders and, equally, its distortions and evils. He would point to a crisis thus gathering in the Renaissance and coming to culmination with Descartes' famous statement: "I think, therefore I am . . ." Many ways now active in thinking, feeling, proposing, *using* 'the world' can contest his assurance, and the ego, the castle of this proposition, has long since been made to yield.

But, you see, there was never a "castle," certainly not here, in this room—and though I might track it as "castellum" or as some memory of King Arthur and his knights—did he even have, to speak precisely, an actual *castle*—or how shall we now realize this *thing* which will in turn help us, apparently, to make actual "ego" . . . A metaphor? Symbol? *A figure of speech*—which instantly I translate to the shadowy formation of some charming body, tentatively, shyly, approaching—"a fine figure of a woman"—which in turn provokes instant memory of a crony's accounting of Hardy's somewhat peculiar fascination with hangings, in this case of a woman: "She was a fine figure of a woman, against the morning sky . . ." Death invites, day invites—which D shall we follow?

Because—which word itself is only, dearly, *language* "because" there is no 'because' other than in mind—it seemed to me (and *seem* is the passive form of *see*) that *we*, which is to say, no longer only *I*, had been wandering in a seeming field of flowering possibilities which words precisely *make* actual to human attention and delight.

So my pleasure, as an artist, has had an abiding interest in that fact. Louis Zukofsky—extraordinary poet of our mutual lives in the habits of the English-speaking world—picked up Wittgenstein's: "A point in space is a place for an argument . . ." But do I quote either correctly? Is it possible to make an 'incorrect' statement, or is virtue, forever and ever, its own irreducible reward? That is, in language, what *is* said is always the case—at least, for *what* is said, if not for what is *not*.

But sitting again in the Maynard, Mass., movie house—the Colonial, as I recall, as opposed to the People's Theater—we are waiting for the movie to begin, presumably a western, and are we to think of it as a 'future' which will or won't be 'correct'? I emphasize this aspect of 'correctness' for many reasons—some personal, e.g., I dislike intensely right people who tell me I am wrong; some rather shabbily philosophic—"is this for real?"—and some quasi-scientific—I would like to know if there might be ultimately a *correct* way of living in the world, etc., etc. In poetry there has been, I think, a marked respect for Coleridge's having called for "a willing suspension of disbelief." Shakespeare well before that—and I am sure many, many others in parallel situation—had asked that of his audiences, simply to admit the power of human gesture and language to transform an otherwise crunky approximation of the coast of Bohemia to affective, actualizing 'reality.'

I don't see—my thinking has so occluded my sight—how I'm now to enjoy anything at all in this situation. The movie seems hours in beginning, preoccupations proliferate and I'm again literally in this room, which is not 'this one' but another where I sit writing these words. Behind me, flat on a small cabinet-table, there is the severed muzzle of a literal bear's head, with intensely affecting eyes, although they are not 'real,' whose patience in that situation provokes and touches me. Where is the rest of his sad body? What was his life? He is a mute 'speaking' head no longer in time but as object—a whole world somehow attendant but never to be entered except by speculation: when was he otherwise? Where?

In some grotesque way, then, this part can manifestly stand for that whole—whether one means the 'all of it' or the gap, the space, the proposed 'rest of him' would imply. The interest for me here is in the fact that what's here can so clearly include all that apparently isn't. In fact, there is finally nothing else to be here at all, but what is here. One is amazed that, humanly, so much value can be given to what is absent as against what's present. Too, the root of that word, *absent,* would seem to be literally, *to be away*—which is presumably impossible, if one is anywhere at all.

Enough of this, so to speak. Clearly I like talking—I love the *places* words are, the things, the goings on, the mistakes and the accuracies. Writing is not, finally, some limited situation of dogmatic intentions. You must remember that film-making also wants to play, pun, echo, mistake, start over—and always is, at each point, only where it is, and all else that might be is there too. *Bear with me,* like they say.

Walking down streets daily, have you noticed that what's there is somehow true enough, i.e., it really seems to be there before anything else? I'd suppose that people who came upon the escaped hippo in that pond south of Los Angeles, assuming they knew nothing of its escape, would feel consternation, but its being there primarily would be their first impression one would think. Now if they didn't find it particularly interesting, to see such a thing, they are surely acting legitimately if they simply walk on by. But it doesn't seem so acceptable if they say, "Why isn't it a giraffe, or the jolly Green Giant, or President Roosevelt?"

Film, as poetry, as the language arts more generally, is a serial art. One thing 'comes after' another: words, images. Often it's thought that artists in these mediums are extraordinarily conscious of specific intentions. No doubt some, even many, are. They have something to say. They think of the various possibilities open to them of saying it. They make resolution, and then they make the so-called art. Franz Kline said, "If I paint what I know, I bore myself. If I paint what you know, I bore you. Therefore I paint what I don't know." He isn't saying that he paints what he doesn't know *how* to paint—but that he paints what he cannot conceptually enclose as intention. *And* he is doing it with consummate intelligence of the possibilities inherent in such an 'open' situation—where what happens takes precedence over what 'should' happen—and with most alert perceptions. That's the point, for me at least, that the world be let in, that all the range of the art's powers of revelation, of doing something, be admitted. William Carlos Williams had a lovely qualification of the alternative: "Minds like beds, always made up . . ."

So—*one thing after another,* and what that factor has as powers . . . Have you ever played that game with others, where a piece of paper is folded, then one of the company begins a drawing, leaving a little bit of its line visible on another face of the fold adjacent, so that the next person continues the drawing with only those edges of line as a locus—and so on, till the paper is exhausted? Then the paper is opened up to show the whole 'image'—and it is provocative because no one could anticipate what the image so constructed would be. The congruence, rather the *contiguity* there used seems to me a very sturdy element in either film or poetry, and in human life as it is consciously experienced: "One day after another./ Perfect./ They all fit."

One would like to say, with respect to a poem, *read the words*— don't limit yourself to a preoccupation with what *isn't* being said. Again Pound is most useful: "You can't blame a man for not doing what he isn't trying to do." I tend always to take things literally, for whatever reason—that is, it took me some years to recognize that the name of a cafe in Santa Fe, LY 'N BRAGG, was not, specifically, the two names of its owners. So, in seeing anything, whether metaphorically or physically, I tend always to begin at that beginning of what it is that *is* there. Thus I'd want to say, look first, think later— and of course I want it to the ends of the world.

Williams—possibly in a somewhat defensive sense—said of a poem, that it was "a small or large machine made of words." The Abstract Expressionists insisted, with delight, that a painting was "a two-dimensional surface covered (or not) with paint"—and presumably the factual, physical situation of a film is equally to be insisted upon. I know that Brakhage likes to remind us that a 'moving picture' is a sequence of rapidly changing single, static images. If presently we are flooded with preoccupations of this kind, seemingly—I am thinking of the didactic, actually self-dramatic, insistence on process and its physical occasions—do recall that Brakhage is revealing the *means* of the film (much as Méliès asked Pathé to do), not the *ends* possible, which he has also so brilliantly shown us. I do believe, to say it, that life *is* its own reward—but I get absolutely irritable if it has always to be a situation of, "look, Ma, I'm dancing!" I never did like dentists who explained what they were 'going to do' to me.

*System* . . . One time in college a friend, an Englishman, John Hunter, discovered a 'system' wherewith to win at the races. We all put in what we had, so that he could go to the racetrack in Providence, R.I., and win us a bundle. We put him on the train, and waited. Late that night comes a call from John, that he has indeed won—but in the celebration of that fact, has now spent all the money, etc. All these years later—I think my share would have

been something like $78.27, not very much but surely *something*—
that system really impresses me, and I finally had or have no argument with John's spending the money—but that's not the 'system'
you understand. I mean, it's John, that pleasant, flush-faced sober-
seeming bright English friend then, and that he *won*, you dig it? We
*beat* the System! Terrific! Which is the only comment on structur-
alism I'd like to make at this time.

*Personal* . . . "and art is art because of you . . ." We are a *personal*
so-called society, brothers and sisters. Don't get *personal* with me,
was what she said. I think *persons* are some of the nicest people I
know. "To tell what subsequently I saw and what heard . . ." Speak
for yourself, John.

And so—to work!


## 1. *Western History*, Stan Brakhage

As Archie Moore once put it, via Melville, "The eyes are the gateway
to the soul . . ." And another useful point, that Charles Olson was
wont to emphasize, is that for primates the eyes constitute the most
crucial sensory agency. What's called 'image,' then, means for us a
most significant information, whether we consider it as an *interior*
condition, that is, the *image* in the word *imagination*, or else the outside, those *images* we will momently see. If an imposition of necessary exterior 'meaning' anticipates our experience, clearly we'll see
what we'll have of whatever necessity to see; for example, a driver's
test will require us to see the forms of triangle, square, rectangle,
and circle as significant bits of information concerned with "stop,"
"caution," speed limit, etc. It would be impossible, I think, to discover anyone who did not have a habit of "seeing things" in particular patterns of received and/or habituated idea, as in "seeing
red," for one instance. If the usual situation of literary narrative is
then imposed on the activity of film, expectably the visual activity
becomes a support of the story otherwise the case—as in a play or
usual movie.

Brakhage tells a story without exception, but my point is that it is
a story of visual information, not of literary details. In his earlier
work, *Desistfilm*, for example, there was the grid of this other order,
a narrative that might have been told in words. One might say that
also of *Anticipation of Night*—but by this time the narrative is moving primarily as a visually defined activity, although the 'story' is
still very clear in other possible terms.

As you see this film, you might think too of its title—although far better to put such preoccupations out of your mind. They are appropriately left to the occasion of afterthoughts in this case. But the film is, nonetheless, a particular experience of "history" and of "Western history" in particular. Since this is not a test, you will not be expected to tell me or anyone else why.

You will certainly see many things that you'll recognize very simply. Colors, surely—forms, movements, even places and things. You'll be interested, I hope, by the *pace* of their interaction and by their divers contents more singularly. In short, you'll be seeing a specific rhythm of visual activity which is itself an obviously definite information. Much as in the case of poetry, these rhythms and the pace thus defined will have a very significant role. The parallel with constructs in music is useful also.

I remember asking Robert Duncan one time to identify for me all the ways in which *rhyme* might occur in poetry. So he rehearsed the familiar situation of sounds, e.g., full rhyme, *go blow;* assonantal rhyme, *get gain;* rhymes of rhythm, *until outside;* rhymes of parallel constructs, *in the box, up the hill*—and so on. Again you might consider how visual instances of rhyming are used here.

Finally, this is, simply, a *beautiful* film—which constitutes the possibility of that literal pleasure I'd earlier spoken of. It delights the eyes with an intensive proposition of their very literal function: *to see.*


## 2. *Domicile,* Gary Doberman

Think of a couple of things, like they say: "Limits are what any of us are inside of . . ."; "Verse consists of a constant and a variant . . ." Already the world is here, truly, and anyone who has ever had experience of actual confinement—jail, hospital, body, army— common to human state can't really be patient with any assumption that we need to do it to ourselves. "The way out is via the door . . ."

Equally *measure* is a human preoccupation, even a responsibility, recalling Robert Duncan's "Responsibility is the ability to respond . . ." William Carlos Williams said in his humanly dear epic *Paterson,* "To measure is all we know . . ."

The artist has specific responsibility in that he or she is often in a territory of hitherto unacknowledged significance. As Pound put it, "Artists are the antennae of the race," and grand though that statement may seem to some of you, recall that artists in our present society have significantly made us aware of crises in our human world otherwise unattended. I am thinking, for example, of Allen Ginsberg's *Howl.*

In this film there is a simply accessible *constant* which you will have no difficulty in recognizing. There is an equally apparent *variable.* So your question—to phrase it poorly—might be, what is it that is being measured here? I know, intuitively and quite otherwise, that something, some factor, some common event, of human life is here manifest in a most literal way. Well, if you saw a person walking toward you, would you presume it to be a table? There is the circumstance, of course, when the inoffensive hat stand, in the dark, becomes the inexplicably malign monster. And the monster is as "real" as the hat rack. But first things first, so to speak—so consider, literally, again, what you are seeing.

The materials of this film are personal, comfortably so. Nothing in that way distorted or untoward. But the *choices* of the artist are both crucial and defining, and there is evident attention to what he has called *boundaries.* One is also impressed that there is such confident articulation of resources particular to film, marked technical skill—"without which nothing."

To contradict, in a way, what I've been thinking about here, I recall a friend of years ago, Tim Lafarge, who used to dance with Merce Cunningham. He told me at one point he used to work out by putting a dime on the floor of a closet, then getting in, locating himself on it, the dime, and seeing what bodily rhythms and articulations were then possible. So at various times and in various needs, there is great interest and use in devising the limits which increase perception of the resources also present nonetheless. "How to dance sitting down . . . ," for example, which is my own preoccupation as I try to write these words—not at all metaphorically, because it *is* an absolutely physical event for me.

This too is a beautiful film, factually, with a lovely shifting counterpoint in the pacing. Like an old slow blues, after some up-tempo number—so, read it and think.


## 3. *Short Films 1975,* Stan Brakhage

Being myself a very *personal* writer—which is to say, one who speaks always for himself despite the hopeful community I'd also insist upon in that fact—I'm dismayed, and often irritated, that the *personal* as a situation in experience of otherwise content comes now under attack. I grew up in a time which used to propose a kind of contest between the objective and subjective. That should really date me for all of you. Anyhow, people used to say things like, "let's take an objective look at the facts" or, "you're getting too subjective." For the true scholars present, there's a piece I then wrote called "A Note on the Objective," *Goad*, Summer 1951, collected in *A Quick Graph*—and I really haven't changed a bit apparently in the twenty-seven years since. It isn't that I love myself in some overbearing way, or that I think I have some privileged and authoritative information of the world. But for me it *is* true that this complex piece of meat, *me*, is factually the author of that 'world' the also present 'I' has as experience. Did you know, for example, that the word *world* comes from a root in *wiros* (Germanic), which means "life or age of man . . ." I presume they left the article out, because there never was "man" without one or the other. Ok. So much for 'objectivity,' though a heavy *humanism* would bore me equally.

But as Allen Ginsberg has it in "Wales Visitation": "Particulars!" Or, Williams, "To tell what subsequently I saw and what heard . . ." I am amazed that people can think there is either information or record without the agency of the human—that is, *for* humans, no matter what the birds may be saying to one another otherwise.

So this last film is certainly *personal*, and I love it. I take a lot of trips, I get stuck in drear motels, I dream of home. There are two lovely instances of language in this film which are really *right on*, like they say. Be it also said that Brakhage is very aware of the powers of language, and thank god he is *not* here tonight to hear me lay it on his valuable creations. So—enough of that.

*But*—which is truly a great word, isn't it?—you know, like, it never is the last word no matter what happens, death included. But—don't we care what others feel in this life, how they literally *have* a life? This film is so wisely, gracefully, *real* to that demand. I could never so actualize my feelings in those places where these images were collected, never substantiate those moments of true consternation, yearning, witness, love as he does here.

"With your eyes alone / with your eyes / with your eyes. . . ," Ginsberg wrote in his never to be forgotten masterpiece "Kaddish." Hear it. We are all related, we are all *here*. *See* this world we live in.

*Placitas, N.M.*
*June 19–20, 1978*

# Bill the King

It's important that we have some place we come from, and another we get to. For if it is true that no one is going anywhere, like they say, ultimately, nonetheless we do literally come into this world and finally we leave it—and, in the meantime, live a life. So what's to be done. Who's going to tell you what you've got to know about anything, how you move at all, for example, or why you move, or even when. This country needs heroes possibly more than any other, just that there's still no time we can count on, and no backwall of history we can take as intimately our own. We're still the immigrants we started with, and we've killed almost everything else that was here.

But our heroes have to be men and women, as the poet Ed Dorn put it—the classical measure, the dry, the particular. In short, they can't be the accumulated gods or the spirits of mountains and rivers. They've got to be the staggering, bemused, grotesquely but inevitably appropriate persons of that instant of act or insight makes the whole damn world a possible splendor. Or have wooden false teeth like George Washington—or say not much at all like Daniel Boone. Above all, they have to stick, both with what they do and what they do for us as their people.

It isn't easy to be an American, and one of the great pleasures of de Kooning is that he really chose to be one of this great country's bedraggled company despite he might have had all of Europe at his feet, I like to think. He really believed in that old American folksong, that our streets were paved with gold. But, even more, he dug the cowboys and Indians, and the heraldic look of our flag. It took

Previously unpublished.

him six tries to get here, *and* he made it—*and* three days later had a
job in Hoboken as a house painter. New York was it from the first.

Not long ago, looking at a large book of reproductions of
de Kooning's work with the painter Jorge Fick (whose book it
was), he kept insisting I should really look at the recent photos of
de Kooning in his studio, at the literal *things* he had there—like the
bowls for the paint, the safflower oil, the large pail for the slops—
like, nothing wasted, nothing other than common, but for the
brushes which, again, had absolute functional utility, they could
hold a lot of paint, etc. Because this fact is also paradoxically heroic,
American—you don't depend on solutions that are privileged, isolating, expensive. You find your means in the common. Like going
to work, like living in New York with millions of other people.

It used to be said of William Carlos Williams that the literal fact
of his being there gave us one *clean* man we could utterly depend
upon, that nothing could buy his integrity. We had the same feeling
and respect for de Kooning, who, in those days, we'd see most
every night in the Cedar Bar, usually in company with Franz Kline,
another of our absolute heroes. De Kooning, characteristically, was
good to us, but he didn't let us off the hook—as, for example, the
night Kline got stomped and lost a tooth on his way back downtown
from a party at Motherwell's in our company. De Kooning's question, very simply: "And where were you guys?" Likewise he could
demolish the whole Black Mountain *mystique* with an equally quiet
comment: "The only trouble with Black Mountain is that if you go
there, they want to give it to you." So the sense that the Beat poets,
as Gregory Corso, were just trying to hitch on to a star is too simple
in that it forgets the fact and use of *heroes*, which we were desperately in need of to offset the awesome weight of *social* authority in
our art, poetry. Here was this man, then, living in a common walk-
up apartment on 10th Street, who was also, by all our conceptions
of the possibility, a *great* artist, who had, often, a wad of bills in his
pocket would choke a horse but did not seem to be overly concerned about it, who would sneak us into an opening at Janis' our
very state of dereliction would offend, and who, at the same time,
would *not* let us off the hook of our pretensions, bullshit, faking,
laziness, you name it.

In hindsight, and with this country's apparent dominance in the
arts, it's all too simple to forget how harsh the battle then was to
force a recognition that *here* was a place of equal possibility and authority. The European habit of symbolization and patina, the intensive intellectualization of *idea*, the incremental power of tradition, all seemed a *weight* beyond anyone's ability to change, much

less to move. So Soulages and Hans Hartung were thought to be doing what Kline was doing—but better. And Fautrier wondered how *any* painter could presume to be seriously "prepared" if he'd not had the resources of a $40,000 a year income, presumably, from birth. It was *snobbisme*, clearly enough, but it found a significant favor here as well as in Europe.

If one might rephrase Williams' famous battle cry to accommodate de Kooning's, it would become, "No ideas but in *paint*"—no symbols, no concepts but those actualized, no styles or groups or schools of any generalizing order. At the same time one can hardly be dumb about it, or think that just because one is born into this world for the first time, that's the first time it ever was. Much has been made, usefully, of de Kooning's extraordinary information of the traditions of painting and of his intimate relation with the master works of the past. But never forget how *he* says it: "Flesh was the reason why oil painting was invented . . ." That's the Renaissance—think of it. "The drawing started to tremble because it wanted to go places . . ."

All dressed up and no place to go is a familiar dilemma in this country. Sometimes it all seems elsewhere, *over there*, as it were. Or else you can get cosily familiar, make those baked beans a veritable caviar. But images, *things*, call them, if you determine to *look* at them, not just cover them up with some glaucous gravy of great thoughts, have an active demand to make—that you change, in that seeing, and that they also change, in that sight. So it is that two persistent themes in de Kooning's work, landscapes and women, are not the simple fact of a 'subject matter' but, rather, the insistently provocative demand of *place* and *person*, as most humanly obvious facts. In whatever he has said of his art, the emphasis is always upon the directness of the engagement, literally—and "abstraction," for example, would be most usefully understood as the endlessly complex task of making 'there' *here*, not the possibility of a part of something's being taken away from it, either to 'symbolize' it or to become, merely, something else. "Form ought to have the emotion of a concrete experience."

Because, otherwise, what have you got—some snaps of Betty the day of the wedding? Mother smiling from the porch? Neither of which, humanly, can be so simply rejected—but *Betty? Mother?* And you can't just make them pretty, or comforting, or just another 'abstraction.' It's got to be as good as the German de Kooning tells of, with all the international breads, in Hoboken yet, who let them get "good and hard and then he crumpled [mark you, *not* crum*b*led] it and spread it on the floor in his flat and walked on it as on a soft carpet . . ." As on some summer day, as 'twere in dream, as if it were once and for all. "I could never figure him out, but now when I think of him, all that I can remember is that he had a very abstract look on his face."

I guess, finally, what I so respect in this dear man's work is that he does stay in there, that he comes on with everything that's in him, all the mind, all the heart, and that it all moves with such intensity. I'm fascinated by where his line goes, and with what consummate *human* grace. How all the colors, particularly those one was told years ago weren't nice, get a chance. How like it all is to a physically *lived* world—but more, how much *in* that world it is. And the *humor*—thank god! Subtle, droll, persistently relieving—just that it *is* the last resource for any one of us. I remember years ago now, having been given the honorable task of keeping him company in his place on 10th Street—he'd been drinking, as the saying goes, and usual friends had told me, a kid!, to mind the store—anyhow he'd lain down on his bed, in this meticulously shipshape apartment entirely occupied by his stuff for painting except for the cot and small place to cook, and I backed off and gawked at the actual work there, one painting on the easel, several others hung on the walls. It felt like being where we were all first made, so to speak. And then I must have figured he'd gone to sleep because he was now fully out on the bed, but one extraordinarily valuable leg had not made it, and was off the near side, looking very uncomfortable. So with intensively deliberate care, I got a hold on it, and tried to lift it so as to place it alongside the other, on the bed. Then, for whatever reason, I looked up at his face—to find that he'd been watching me all the time, with a lovely, wry smile. So—what's left to say that he hasn't? Surely you'll see that point. Therefore—"it's a personal thing . . ."—these few last words:

*The World*

>    *for Bill*

Never to be wrong, mama—
and never to be right either.
Just to eat as I was able
everything they put on the table.

>    *Placitas, N.M.*
>    *February 24, 1979*

# "Some Place Enormously Moveable": The Collaboration of Arakawa and Madeline H. Gins

*We wanted some place enormously moveable, started from that.*
*I cannot make a map for you but . . .*

ARAKAWA, in conversation

There seem endlessly those situations of particular experience wherein one knows and doesn't know, all at the same instant— which is to say, the information is inherent, actual, in the given system, *but* (itself a word of this qualification) we cannot step out of its context to see "what it is" we thus "know." As it happened then, Arakawa had been asked by the city of Hannover to design some ennobling "monument," an artifact which would dignify that city, enhance its self-respect, etc. His first question, of course, concerned the seriousness of the city's commitment to their choice of artist and whether or not they would permit him to exercise a determining choice of artifact. Therefore, at an early meeting with the city officials, he took a large sheet of drawing paper, signed it, and said, that's it—pay me. And as one of the officials began, in fact, to make out the check in payment, Arakawa stopped him, asking for two months' time to complete the design, etc., etc.

So far, so good—one wants to say. That is, "who they are" and "who he is" would seem to have come to some sort of resolution and/or reassurance. But a person, no less (or more) a city, is not so simply to be known or, more accurately, to be presumed as a "this" or "that." So in two months the same people regathered, to consider the now completed design. First there was the question

*Artforum*, Summer 1980.

of materials, which in this case was a sizeable amount of Carrara marble—in short, the most precious marble we, as a history of peoples, have actualized. Somewhat abashed but amenable, the city officials agreed to its purchase; it would be used to make a block of impressive steps within the city's park, an approach to the crucial "point" of information. But what then would "it" say? Very simply, on the face of the top step, incised with appropriate care, this: the words, in German, *Welcome to Berlin*. . . . But this is *not* Berlin, said the officials. This is *Hannover*. In fact, Berlin was their rival and in all respects a most odious object of comparison. All of which one might presume Arakawa to have known. Or not to have known— since he is Japanese, an artist living primarily in New York, whose factually indispensable collaborator comes from the Bronx, is a poet, etc., etc., etc. So that was the end of that.

If it were only a question of some misappropriation of names, we could no doubt move to resolve any number of human conflicts by the mere shifting of names themselves, e.g., calling New York *Moscow*, and vice versa. And men *women*, women *men*. That would certainly be a step in the "right" direction (or left, up, down, backwards, forwards). Consider the heart-breaking wistfulness of Hart Crane's "A Name for All":

> Moonmoth and grasshopper that flee our page
> And still wing on, untarnished of the name
> We pinion to your bodies to assuage
> Our envy of your freedom—we must maim
>
> Because we are usurpers, and chagrined—
> And take the wing and scar it in the hand.
> Names we have, even, to clap on the wind;
> But we must die, as you, to understand . . .¹

Such dependence on nominalism, sadly enough, leads only to the least attractive possibilities regarding *Hannover/Berlin*, whichever is which. And more, it cannot be that living has as its primary definition only the physical resolution of death. I know that Arakawa and Madeline Gins met at a time when both felt a harshly flat despair, hardly uncommon in this world as we presently think it. Yet (to paraphrase Arakawa's recent conversation) *Life has to have choice . . . Yes, an extreme beginning . . . There were hard times in the war . . . dreary . . .*

1. Hart Crane, *The Complete Poems and Selected Letters and Prose of Hart Crane*, ed. Brom Weber, New York, Doubleday, 1966, p. 164.

*having to check the physical body all the time . . . like a potato . . . cut, slice, disappear . . . so, above all, first we must study how not to die . . .*[2]

In the preface to their collaboration, *The Mechanism of Meaning: Work in Progress (1963–1971, 1978)*, Arakawa and Madeline Gins write:

If we had not been so desperate at that time, we might not have chosen such an ambitious title for this work. Yet what else would we have called it? After all, the phenomena we were studying were not simply images, percepts, or thoughts alone. Our subject is more nearly all given conditions brought together in one place.

Death is old-fashioned. We had come to think this way, strangely enough. Essentially, the human condition remains prehistoric as long as such a change from the Given, a distinction as fundamental as this, has not yet been firmly established.

If thought were meant to accomplish anything, surely it was meant to do this. Yet why had history been so slow? Was there something wrong with the way the problem was being pictured? What if thinking had been vitiated by having become lost in thought, for example? What is emitted point-blank at a moment of thought anyway? Let's take a second look at these comic figures, we decided. There did not yet exist even the most rudimentary compendium of what takes place or of the elements involved when anything is "thought through." Why not picture some of these moments ourselves, we thought, just a few?[3]

In like sense Arakawa said, *we don't know what it is that is mind, what it could look like. From Plato to the present so many different maps have been tried, but we still don't have a model. This is because probably all our language is one-sided. Nothing is left to hold the "form." We have not yet formed even a profile. So far, using only one or two senses at a time mind has been felt out a bit, but that's all, so, so far only it has been a question of singing a song.*

One dilemma apparent is that "mind" has been used primarily as

2. Arakawa and Madeline Gins were principal speakers at a seminar, "Imaginations of Person," sponsored by the Gray Chair of Poetry and Letters, State University of New York at Buffalo, November 29, 1979. Their film, *For Example (A Critique of Never)*, 1971—itself a part of their collaboration, *The Mechanism of Meaning*, as noted in the publication of the text with still photographs under the same title, Milan, Alessandra Castelli Press, 1974—had been shown the previous evening. Quotations and/or paraphrases of their conversation, unless otherwise noted, come from this occasion with some subsequent textual changes by agreement.

3. Arakawa and Madeline H. Gins, *The Mechanism of Meaning*, New York, Abrams, 1979, p. 4.

a means of significant association, humanly, and that the usual scientific understanding of the term *meaning* would be the context described by "association" itself. One can recognize the resourceful power of this mode of "tracking"—and also the inherent confounding of phenomena that cannot be "associated," for which a "ratio" or reason cannot be found. Therefore, these are "meaningless," however determinant they prove in the actual fact of living. Moreover, a present commonplace would be the fact that "facts accumulate at a far higher rate than does the understanding of them," which "understanding" or "rational thought" ". . . depends literally on ratio, on the proportions and relations between things. As facts are collected, the number of possible relations between them increases at an enormous rate."[4] A small instance of this would be the present monitoring of "signals" from "outer space" (or "inner," for that matter), which constitute such an immense bulk of possibly significant data that the mind boggles at the idea of "containment" or "subject" implied.

Thinking elsewhere, here is a sequence of "things said" by Arakawa and Madeline Gins (roughly, directly), noted during conversation:

A:  First, Leibniz's proposal for an amusement park to be based on scientific principles may be considered a coherent precursor to what we are preparing to do. Yes, as you suggest, also, Hegel's absolute world is of course related. . . . But language, any language, always runs parallel to the world, so is consequently a representation of only one side. With such a tool you cannot pinpoint, always only point out generally. What you arrive at is always only some sort of agreement. All art depends on agreement, of course. If you don't play the game of this agreement it all becomes abstraction.

G:  About fifteen years to do the book—how to do art without being seduced by doing it. Through desperation, we chose: 19 subdivisions [cf. *The Mechanism of Meaning*, p. 3].

A:  Forget about meaning after all. . . .

G:  Old book requires you use everything you have as you have before—(interesting, but no new moves . . .).

[reads preface, *The Mechanism of Meaning*]

4. W. Grey Walter, *The Living Brain*, Harmondsworth, England, Penguin, 1961, p. 126. The "mechanical" construct of the brain is much emphasized in this discussion as is its "value" humanly. Cf. Chapter 7, "The Seven Steps from Chance to Meaning," pp. 139–70.

A:   In 1971, our book was published in Munich. At that time
we were lucky enough to meet some physicists, some of
whom were using our book in their work—in a very strange
way, I guess. At an international, but informal, meeting of
29 quantum physicists, we were the only non-physicists.
We are working on something so small, beyond description, they told us. But, we said, we know something smaller
than that. These particles are so split, there is nothing
whatsoever to see, they are that small, we can't even imagine how small they are, we were told. After we heard that
we said: But your thought about that (or this) is a quantum which is even smaller. To which they replied: What is
your field? The answer was: Nonsense.

By the way, later on in his life, Heisenberg, interestingly
enough, began to write what on the surface appear to be
rather high-school-like poems, yet I find these to be often
ingenious descriptions of what cannot be seen or said in
ordinary physics. To paraphrase one of these:

> When I wake up at 7
> I drink coffee
> I look at the window
> I see blue, brown, grey
> Then after lunch
> The next time I look
> There is light blue, light brown, light grey
> At night
> At the window
> Dark grey is modulated.

One window changes that much "in time." He's trying to
say to us, *don't* focus, if you want to see anything. As for
intention, you have to *spread* intention—a single 'I' does
not exist . . .

G:   Thought itself is a blind spot . . . Have to look at that again.

A:   'I' is always forming something, disembodied. . . . Rimbaud's "I is an other"—but *how* so? is the question—this
peculiar distance from and within time. . . .
   Alchemists, very much looking for/had intentions very
close to ours (present). . . . When research is divided into
subjects such as art, philosophy and science, at that moment we tend to lose the Subject. The Subject such as: *we
are here.* . . .

G:   Lenin: Best title I know for a book is, Lenin's *What Is to
Be Done.* . . .

A:   We have to go as far as possible. Shakespeare's "To be
     or not to be" is no longer the question—in our time
     we must only consider *to be!* Nothing is too much in
     this world.

     Remember always to consider more than 360 degrees.
     One more thing is that for all our talk of "there" and
     "here" it is always in the same place.

G:   Localization and Transference [cf. *The Mechanism of Mean-
     ing*, pp. 11–14]—how would you make any interchange-
     able point or location into something?—this is demon-
     strated here. And then, once we know we do that, we can
     relax and just know we do it—and *not* rely on it and be-
     lieve into it, mindlessly for 100 years.

     So many conveniences we don't have, that we should
     have—such as a helium belt. . . . We wanted to make a
     helium belt that everyone could wear, so that whenever
     you'd walk, you'd be just a few inches off the ground all
     the time.

A:   Wearing this would alter your sense of balance, you might
     find a new kind of center. . . .

     We are not talking about "artificial intelligence"—far
     from it—I should say—a new nature (nature, I hate this
     word!)—a new *given.* . . .

G:   And to develop a new nature. . . .

A:   How will you recognize a new nature anyway? That's an-
     other problem. That problem is not a problem.

Albeit a layman in all respects, I am impressed by these preoccupations as increasingly, often brilliantly, explored in a diversity of informational "fields." For example, Paul Kugler, himself a
Jungian analyst particularly involved with consciousness and language structure, had previously given me information of Ilya Prigogine, the Belgian physical chemist who was awarded the Nobel
prize in chemistry in 1977 for his theory of *dissipative* structures.
Simply put, Prigogine's theory demonstrates that order "emerges
*because* of entropy, not *despite* it. . . . The new state occurs as a sudden shift, much as a kaleidoscope shifts into a new pattern. It is
a nonlinear event; that is, multiple factors act on each other at
once. . . . With each new state, there is greater potential for change.
With new levels of complexity, there are new rules." As Prigogine
puts it, "there is a change in the nature of the 'laws' of nature. . . ."[5]

5. *Brain/Mind Bulletin*, vol. 4, no. 13, Los Angeles, 1979, p. 1. This issue is devoted to Prigogine's work and includes a useful bibliography.

The same friend referred me as well to René Thom's *catastrophe* theory as presented in *Stabilité Structurelle et Morphogénèse: Essai d'une théorie générale des modèles* (1972),[6] and here again the parallels are most interesting for an apprehension of the range and significance of *The Mechanism of Meaning* as a continuing collaboration. As Dr. Kugler has suggested, this work too has much to do with semantic "catastrophe," and lest that aspect of it be too simply "understood" as either a convenient surrealism or a speciously engaging humor, one might well consider Dr. Thom's proposal of "les signifiants abusifs": "Le comique apparaît donc comme la *manifestation d'une obstruction à la signification globale d'un message localement signifiant.*"[7]

Further, one must recognize the absolute necessity of collaboration insofar as the information will not resolve itself as a linear and/or "singular" pattern. Prigogine, for example, refers to "a book, a crystal, a cup of cold coffee" as *equilibrium* structure, "closed and finished, not taking in and dissipating energy. . . ."[8] In like sense, William Carlos Williams attacks a presumed "containment" in *Paterson: Book Three, II:*[9]

> We read: not the flames
> but the ruin left
> by the conflagration . . .
>
> Dig in—and you have
> a nothing, surrounded by
> a surface, an inverted
> bell resounding, a

6. René Thom, *Stabilité Structurelle et Morphogénèse*, Reading, Mass., W. A. Benjamin, Inc., 1972. Chapter 13, "Des Catastrophes aux Archetypes; Pensée et Langage," is particularly useful for the layman.

7. *Ibid.*, pp. 314–16. It's to the point, also, to emphasize Arakawa's early (and continuing) relation to Marcel Duchamp, whose gravestone has a characteristic and charming insistence upon semantic catastrophe: "D'ailleurs, c'est toujours les autres qui meurent." Cf. *Marcel Duchamp*, ed. d'Harnoncourt and McShine, New York, Philadelphia, Museum of Modern Art, New York, Philadelphia Museum of Art, 1973, pp. 31, 174–75, 181.

8. *Brain/Mind Bulletin*, p. 4.

9. William Carlos Williams, *Paterson*, New York, New Directions, 1963, pp. 148–49. Williams' own attack as a poet upon the limiting preconceptions of his art is worth noting. Cf. Joseph N. Riddell, *The Inverted Bell: Modernism and the Counterpoetics of William Carlos Williams*, Baton Rouge, Louisiana State University Press, 1974. Also of interest in the present context: Dickran Tasjian, *William Carlos Williams and the American Scene 1920–1940*, New York, Berkeley, Whitney Museum, University of California Press, 1978.

white-hot man become
a book, the emptiness of
a cavern resounding

If presently our world is experienced as a vast and insistently
conflicting spectrum of "special languages," of locked and crippling conceptual patterns, clearly the human need becomes un-
avoidably explicit: *change*. Williams' "The Orchestra":[10]

Say to them:
"Man has survived hitherto because he was too ignorant to
know how to realize his wishes. Now that he can realize them,
he must either change them or perish."

    Now is the time
           in spite of the "wrong note"
                I love you. My heart is
innocent.
           And this the first
                (and last) day of the world.

The intense self-preoccupation of the arts in our time has usually
been thought of as a defensive and socially hostile conduct, insofar
as the presumed audience has been, for the most part, significantly
ignored. In short, there are no publicly evident institutions—either
religious, as in the past, or widely political—that serve as sponsors
or patrons for a collective information. There is, therefore, no
"center" in that respect. Even more to the point, however, is the
intellectual self-consciousness of this period in which "humanness"
would seem not only the most dominant but the altogether determinant factor in its powers to appropriate "reality."

Therefore Arakawa's and Madeline Gins' emphasis upon "escape
routes,"[11] however wryly the term may echo civic plans to evacuate
various urban populations out of cities under nuclear attack, is
entirely appropriate for the "place" our conceptual patterns and
modes of conduct have made. "Meaning" is again the crisis:

The vagueness of the term was suitable. Meaning might be thought of
as the desire to think something—anything—through; the will to
make sense out of the ever-present fog of not-quite-knowing; the recognition of nonsense. As such it may be associated with any human

10. William Carlos Williams, *Pictures from Brueghel*, New York, New Directions,
1962, p. 82.
11. *The Mechanism of Meaning*, p. 5.

faculty. Since each occurrence of meaning takes place along one or another of these paths, we roughly derived our list of subdivisions from them. The list as a whole is not intended to be any less inconsistent, clumsy, or redundant than the original on which it was based, that is, the composite mechanism of meaning in daily living viewed point-blank from moment to moment.[12]

The list itself follows:

1. Neutralization of Subjectivity
2. Localization and Transference
3. Presentation of Ambiguous Zones
4. The Energy of Meaning (Biochemical, Physical, and Psychophysical Aspects)
5. Degrees of Meaning
6. Expansion and Reduction—Meaning of Scale
7. Splitting of Meaning
8. Reassembling
9. Reversibility
10. Texture of Meaning
11. Mapping of Meaning
12. Feeling of Meaning
13. Logic of Meaning
14. Construction of the Memory of Meaning
15. Meaning of Intelligence
16. Review and Self-Criticism[13]

One will note the topological nature of their procedure here, that is, its primary concern with the function of meaning as a process of mind. Presuming meaning to be the crisis of consciousness, whether collective or one's own (if that is possible as a thought), the visual/verbal materials of the text itself effect an intensive *place*, in Wittgenstein's sense that "a point in space is a place for an argument." Because—the experience of the mind's response to verbal imperatives in relation to visual context is a sharp and displacing body of information. Thus one begins to *know*, as a differentiating response, how it is that one has both *presumed to know*, and *is knowing*. Here is the response of one astute "reader," Arthur Danto:

> Here is a panel that commands us to count the lines in a ragged grid. We are not to point. But counting *is* successive pointing, associating the set of numbers with the set of things. There is *no* counting without

12. Ibid., p. 5.
13. Ibid., p. 3.

pointing. But then there, in the next area, is a single line. If it made sense to count a single thing, we could count this easily, there being nothing else to count. But is this counting? If there is one person in the audience, does the discouraged manager inform his actors of the fact and expect them to ask him to count "them" again? Do we see there is one or do we have to count if we are to use the word "one" in its cardinal sense? If there is only one item, is it a list? How many items are then needed before it is a list? Two, three, four, five? So the game continues—or it is a new game, silly and serious, dumb and sharp, inane and profound, at once playful and lethal, a samurai slash at the throat of Reason.[14]

Apropos the situation here evident, Madeline Gins said to another "reader": "We are making a 'text' between you and this text. You're making that text. You are the ostensive 'definition.' It's going to keep going back and forth, echoing . . ."[15]
To which Arakawa added:

Because functions can be repeated, we can say that they are somewhat stable. This is better than to really think of a stable "you" or a stable "I." But the reader is the one who functions according to the subdivisions we propose, so, even if you never get a "right" answer, that's the answer—you're getting it constantly.[16]

At present Arakawa and Madeline Gins are at work upon the invention of a "situation," a construct which will embody (*texturalize*) the modes of mind with which they have been engaged.[17] Obviously

14. Arthur Danto, "The Mechanism of Meaning, etc.," *The Print Collector's Newsletter,* vol. 10, Sept.–Oct. 1979, pp. 135–36. This review is brightly perceptive, and the fact that Danto is Johnsonian Professor of Philosophy at Columbia University gives his comments a useful "point of view."

15. See footnote 2.

16. See footnote 2.

17. A recent catalogue, *Arakawa: Düsseldorf, Städtische Kunsthalle,* 1977, has excellent texts by both Arakawa and Madeline Gins. Her long introduction—"Arakawa's intention (to point, to pinpoint, to model)"—is a most useful survey of their present activity and its basis. Arakawa's "Some Words" includes a "list" of what he feels necessary for the "construction" noted; as well as the following:

"Whenever 'I' or 'We' is pronounced, it feels or seems as though there will follow a full presence of a subject in addition to that of the speaker. But these pronouns are only 'forming intentions.' We are given only shifting space or a field of play. Even the object of these pronouns is unclear, without a determinable presence, so in the shifting about, their subject might be even more moveable, less determinate a presence.

their work thus far has been a remarkable service to anyone whose mind has been somewhat less to him or her than that once proposed "kingdom" of stable assumption. In short, it is not that any one of us is going anywhere. Very simply, we *are* here. Think of that.

---

This presence, a waited for texture, this idea of a subject, controls (feeds) the formulation of *subject matter* and gives it its sense of urgency. There is a sense of urgency or an insistence to understand the nature of these nonsensical presences (self-willed?).

In this way, many aspects of any philosophical inquiry may be seen to be at least partially derived from nonsense or its suggestive presence. Usually sense has been derived from a state of nonsense. For another state of accuracy, to pinpoint, derivation is not enough.

I have begun to consider the construction of a situation for a parallel, reminiscent of the situation of Frankenstein, as a strong way to respond to the nonsensical urgency of subject matter. So, *Moral/Volumes/Verbing/The/Unmind* nos. I and II are examples which point this way. I want to construct for subject and subject matter the presence they have been denied for centuries."

# Introduction to *Larry Bell: New Work*

Thankfully, there is no simple qualification to make of Larry Bell's genius as an artist, nor of his work. There is no static information in the latter, for example, a single thing simply to be seen and, by that act, understood. This art particularly provokes a daily, persistent accommodation of interest, much as a changing sky or river will. There is no one thing it factually is.

The artist is also a variable, both in and of himself. There is a very deliberate intelligence present in the fabrication of the standing glass pieces, a remarkable technical mastery, because a thumb print's smudge, at this stage of the work, can fracture the authority of surface. There is also a brilliant intuition of possibility, which can see the work long before its actual existence. There is, finally, the complex of feelings and relationships, of which the work is product.

Or best put as he does, speaking of the vapour drawings: " . . . these images represent very strong personal feelings. Not anguish, pain or joy but daily mundane drama. The stuff that reality is made of: ambition, personal prejudice, short sightedness, far sightedness, the desire to do something different, most of all they contain my efforts to overcome strict technical discipline, to become spontaneous, intuitive, improvisational and casual in my approach to the visual things that keep me going . . ."

His initial commitment to glass as a material had particularly to do with its surface and the fact that, as he says, "by simply laying thin films of different kinds of metallic and non-metallic com-

*Larry Bell: New Work* (Yonkers, N.Y.: Hudson River Museum, 1980).

pounds onto the surface of the glass, I could change the way the light was reflected and transmitted through the thing . . ." He thought of himself as a sculptor, working with "mass and weight and things that sat on the floor . . ." Preparation might require six months of setting up before anything could actually begin.

The point is that his means of working and the material he has chosen demand of him a singular range of information and skill. Otherwise one would be talking of simple impediments, however interesting. For example, finding that commercial treatment of his pieces is increasingly impractical, he spends a year finding a firm to build the equipment he needs, which in turn takes a year to construct it, and then he takes another year in order to learn how to use it. One thinks of Pound's quoting Brancusi: "All my sculptures take fifteen years . . ." It is a rare and practical definition of responsibility in either case.

Paradoxically, he will say, "At first I wasn't interested in light as a medium, it only came to me after working for a long time on things that I realized—I thought I was working on glass, I thought I was working with structure and stuff like that—it wasn't until I had worked for a long time that I realized that I was actually working with light . . ." In his uniquely subtle registrations of its ambience, and with the power of his own determination to respect both it and himself, he brings *light* to all.

*Buffalo, New York*
*October 27, 1980*

# Memories of John

When John Altoon died in the early spring of 1969, it was brutally
sudden. Kitaj called from Los Angeles to give me the news, and
spoke of having been at a party the night previous at which he'd
met John finally, and then shortly after saw him leaving in a rush
with Billy Al Bengston, apparently in some difficulty. As it happened, they were on their way to see Dr. Asher, John's friend and
collector, to whom he'd previously complained of heartburn, showing up occasionally in the evening with the hope the doctor could
fix him up. Suggestions that he come around to the office for a
complete checkup never got him there. The "massive coronary"
described as cause of death before he had been got to the hospital
was the last thing he'd have thought of—still in his early forties,
with a life at last solid and productive, and a great deal of the past's
psychosis now mitigated, thanks to the help of another friend, Dr.
Wechsler.

He was so particularly L.A. American, so much the determination of this country's conflicting 'images' of itself, that one is forced
willynilly to think of art and artist as one. It was a decisive way of
life as well as all else. More, he was a classic storyteller with a humor
and a wit that kept working in all manner of demands. So I tell you
in large part what he told me without the least interest in whether
or not it is precisely true or accurate, as they say, to the facts. We
don't live facts, we live our imagination of them.

Long before I ever met John he was already instance of that so-
called power of the imagination, and when we did meet, I confess

*New Mexico Studies in the Fine Arts* 6 (1981).

that this one sense of him I had immediately to recognize. When I was a kid in the Depression, given our unstarving but nonetheless modest circumstances, the elders would prod us to finish up our food by saying, "Remember the starving Armenians . . ." At that time I knew no Armenians, but hardly wanted them to starve, so that they became exotic, haunting persons in my head. I wished I could give them the food, rather than eat it only on their behalf. As he later told me the story, John was sure *my* Armenian. I got the sense of a poverty stricken family, three children (he had, as I remember, a sister and brother), a father working in a bakery, lifting the sacks of flour. John said that when he was eighteen his father got him a summer job at the bakery, and he undertook the same labor but couldn't keep it up—whereas his father, now in his sixties, doggedly continued until he at last retired, then lost his sight a very short time after. This same man had for years the dream of returning to the site of where his village had been, previous to the Turks and the slaughter of his family. He was possibly the only survivor and when John himself attempted to locate the place, after his father's death, he found that it was now in Russian territory and effectually nonexistent. Then there was the uncle who lived up in the valley, outside of L.A., whose modest plot of ground blossomed with the proverbial fruit trees like the promised land.

Meanwhile John's mother was dying of cancer all the time he was growing up. He said nights when he was supposed to be sleeping, he'd listen to the adults talking of the situation, rehearsing meager hopes, provisions, the mother painfully and quietly enduring. John said he'd go to the movies, forget for that time his mother was ill and dying, then hit the street and sunlight only to remember it all. He proposed himself as a classic delinquent, always in some trouble or other, cutting school, hanging out, testing the edges. He said often he'd get in the back window of their place just as the police were at the front door, to ask his mother where her son was—and she'd answer, he's up in his room, and then go to get him. And there he blessedly was.

I'm not now sure just when the family began to think of him as the artist. Families with a very tender and legitimate hope have often a person, one of them, who is given such an office and responsibility. What may well have been John's quite usual interest in copying pictures—surely a lot of kids do it—became in any case a family dream, and he got a very useful encouragement. He'd copy the covers of magazines and all would delight in how much these copies looked like the actual picture. He was clearly talented. Their imagination, and his also, was that he would become a successful commercial artist, which is my recollection of what he does in fact get trained to be. Art, in its reflective and aesthetic presence as value, had little to do with either their understanding or needs. You are what you can do.

One of John's stories was how he used to sell newspapers in downtown L.A. and the guy just across the street from him, also selling newspapers, was the subsequently terrific science fiction writer Ray Bradbury. He told of the gang he hung out with at the beach, of great destructive challenges like riding motorcycles no hands at speeds exceeding 100 m.p.h., or driving souped-up cars at like speeds, blindfolded. I was dazzled and a very attentive listener. And I believed him and still do, incidentally. For example, my own favorite was the account of the stunted tree, growing in a more or less vacant lot adjacent to Wilshire Boulevard, some well traffic'd section thereof, which John and his cronies managed to turn into a giant slingshot by hacking off its two spare branches to make a crotch, getting a length of inner tube for the sling itself, putting a substantial boulder therein, and laboriously hauling it back as far as they could, then letting go to have the boulder go sailing up over the battered board fence into the traffic (jesus!), hitting thankfully the hood of a car only, and stopping it dead. The kids are long gone before the dazed onlookers can figure out what's happened. Hardly a nice story—but it satisfied some lurking anger with the part of life that feels like trying to cross an endless street against hordes of indifferent drivers. Or—more honestly—I just like that it worked.

I met John quite unintentionally in 1954, having come back to this country from Mallorca in order to teach at Black Mountain. I'd get to New York as often as I could, crashing variously with friends. One, from college days, a pianist, Race Newton, was living on Spring Street and across the inner court lived an extraordinary lady, Julie Eastman. The novelist Fielding Dawson has given her a succinct immortality in *An Emotional Memoir of Franz Kline* (1967): "Creeley had kept me spellbound about her—the witch from El Paso. Creeley had written a beautiful story about her and the jazz pianist who lived across the courtyard from her, and the jazz trumpeter who lived on the floor below her . . ." So that was Race, and the other man, also from Boston days, was Ty Frolund. My story was called "The Musicians" and it was by fact of these various associations that I came to know John.

Like Fee, I no sooner met Julie than I was remarkably interested, not in her body, as they say or so I told myself, but in the weirdly

pervasive authority she seemed to gather out of the air. Literally I
followed her around and so it was she took me along on some of
her errands, as she said. One was involved with going up to see
Peter Stander, Lionel's bright nephew, then both painter and actor,
and also intrigued by Julie—and very jealous on the instant that I
was the new attraction although, dumbly, I never figured out his
instant hostility until later. And then, that same afternoon, on a
corner round about 27th and 4th, we ran into John, who looked me
over quickly after Julie's introduction, then asked her about getting
his portfolio back. It seems she'd been taking it around for him—
he was getting what straight commercial work he could then—and
had also been living with him it turned out, but that was now over,
but the portfolio hadn't been returned. Dear Julie!

I think I saw John very briefly after that, possibly once or twice. I
know I must have given him my address in Mallorca, to where it
proved I returned very shortly, to try another year with my wife
then (patient woman, but so was I). Anyhow, back in Mallorca, we
one day got a letter that John was coming and would have with him
two other couples, also painters and their wives, Arthur Okamura
(from Los Angeles as was John) and Leon Berkowitz and poet-wife
Ida. Terrific! I loved Americans at that point—I'd had the colonial
battle all by myself far too long, and no matter Robert Graves and
family were most decent to us, and friend then Martin and Jan
Seymour-Smith had both got us out of France and kept us company thereafter, it was just a persistently different world, and I was
sick unto death of trying to make actual my own. In retrospect, the
closest any friend also a painter from that world ever got for me
was René Laubiès, a singular man in all respects whom Pound had
directed me to—and he showed me Fautrier, Hartung, took me to
meet Julien Alvard, etc., but again I was far more interested by a
small show that Pollock had at his gallery, Paul Fachetti's, at that
same time—a veritable letter from home.

We were living in Bonanova, up from El Terreno, the suburb of
Palma where the heavy money tended to settle. There was a trolley
line out from the city and it continued up to the edge of the hills,
where John, Arthur and Liz, and Leon and Ida, all managed to
find houses. I was very homesick for simple conversation, so almost
immediately I began to spend as much time as possible with all the
new arrivals, but particularly, as I recall, with John, just that he was
by himself and was usually free. He'd set himself up in the garage
attached to the house he'd rented, itself packed in against the steep
slope of the hill. It was windy up there, and I remember that John's
easel, which he'd often put outside, would now and then crash with

a sudden gust of wind, dumping the painting on the gravel. I make it sound almost intentionally awkward, on his part, but now recalling, I wonder if he wasn't, in fact, making it as hard on himself as he could. He was working with oils, for example—never a happy means or medium for him, just that the paint physically slowed him in a way ink or air brush didn't—and to further complicate the process, he'd begun to use raw pigments, mixing them on the spot. It was an incredible sight, these piles of dry pigment, then the sizable can of linseed oil, then John, his eyes on the canvas, reaching out with his free hand to get hold of the oil which he'd pour, still without really looking, on one or more of the piles. Then, with his brush he'd sop some of it up, and off he'd go—remarkably, altogether articulate.

His friends back in New York had been people like Gandy Brodie, mavericks, or certainly inconvenient. John spent time at the Arts Club but never felt easy about it. There was an edge of masters and disciples he didn't easily accept, or not in that manner. He felt it no respect of those one did thus revere, to lean on their agency and provision. He'd told me he'd come to New York specifically as a commercial artist, an up and coming one, in the proverbial lightweight suit, straight from L.A., only to find the weather harshly cold and beyond all expectation. He'd been invited to an annual dinner of successful elders, people like Gilbert Bundy (whom it was felt he might one day take the place of). He was shocked by their cynicism, particularly by Alfred Dorn's taking him over to a window of his penthouse, where the celebration was being held, and pointing out an old tenement where he said he'd grown up and his mother still lived. He could spit on it from that very window, and did. John got drunker and more angry, and after being asked to say something, as the newly arrived youngster, gave them veritable hell, or what he hoped was that. They applauded, and said it was just what they needed, someone to keep them awake. I don't finally know how crucial to him, or successful otherwise, John's commercial work was finally. He drew extraordinarily, always, no matter the occasion—I felt him an absolute genius in this respect—and that gift was equal across the board. For one thing, he never used the usual device that projects an image for tracing, but worked always 'free hand'—and did endless studies, in this way, for very mundane drug ads indeed. I don't think it was any question of his perfectionism, call it. He simply felt most active and comfortable working that way.

But because of this training, and the facility he brought to it, he was wary of the pretty, or call it the literally beautiful, in common sense. I remember one time he did a hauntingly lovely sketch of my son, David, looked at it, said, *too pretty*, and tore it up. Often he'd smudge, blur, distort, work over, do anything he could to break up the simple, direct containment of his line. He'd watch our kids draw, and delight in how they could know, intuitively, where the action was, where the line could find it.

He was a very warm, intensely reassuring man during this time. I knew nothing of his periodic depressions, actually the paranoid seizures, that so battered him during those years. My own life was falling apart and it seemed to me as if John had some psychically determined intuition of it all. Then, as my wife drew farther away from me, it happened she was drawn to him, and that could have no simple resolution. I left to come back to the States, and for some years only heard occasionally of how he was.

So some time after, I was living in New Mexico, I must have got word of him through some mutual friend like Tony Landreau, or possibly Stu Perkoff, whom I'd just met at his reading in San Francisco, etc., etc. Those particulars are always hard to get exactly. In any case, we were back in touch by the late fifties and my wife, Bobbie, and I would stay with him now and then when we were on the west coast. I recall one place he had then, a sort of bungalow feel to it, somewhat down Wilshire Boulevard, or off in back. There was a younger man living with him, whom he'd befriended—shy, raw in manner, very loyal to John, I remember he gave Bobbie a little leather purse he'd made, as a compliment. John himself gave us *many* drawings; I was embarrassed but deeply pleased and grateful to have them. He was working in ink, drawing with intensely quick resolution, extraordinary haunting suggestions of people, things, very often animals or birds. I have one of a mournful crow-seeming bird, with a little window of sorts in its breast, with a little man's face in that. I could dig it, like they say. He'd give us piles of them to look through, they were on a mat board, often very large— there was just no way to make a simple choice, or probably one wanted them all.

When John talked of women in the abstract, like they say also, he gave a sense of this utterly blonde, clean, white person, impeccably erotic often, but with no pubic hair, for example, and really no odor nor tone of any specifying kind. She was the American dream, in short, and she was far more a defense, I thought, as an image, than any active desire. I know that John had girl friends who were the classic dumb blondes—but I don't *know* that, I'm only saying they *looked* great, and were always nice to me. I never had a chance to know his first wife, Fay Spain—we talked once on the telephone after they'd separated and her intelligence and care of him was very moving. He had said it was the money that had made it hard, the fact she could go out and buy a Mercedes the way he might a pair of pants. When he went on location with her, he was the awkward, in the way husband. That could never sit well with him, despite how much they shared as people who had made it the hard way.

Then, more years later, after a time out in Santa Monica—I recall a great time on the carousel with John's terrific dog running round and round after us—he was back in a place on Harper. (He did a great series of that name, sadly slashed during a time of breakdown.) But writing, I can't trust my memory of the time pattern. But this I do remember very vividly. I was in L.A. again, another old friend, Neil Williams, was there also, and he knew John well. Neil was telling me about John's *great* new wife, Babs—which proved utterly true. He said she really ate and I should watch her in action. So not long after, as it happens, we all four went out for dinner and I think we had the proverbial steaks, which tend to get filling, after ample drink, so it seems we variously left this and that, the salad, the bread, the steak, etc. All of which Babs politely, quietly, and completely ate up. God knows where it went, she never showed it. I think the fact was she had a factually healthy person, as my mother would say, and the system was working perfectly.

At this point I feel empty that so much hasn't got said here, even arguments I'd like to continue on John's behalf as to why hasn't there been more use of him. Not much is so good or so humanly relieving. Talking to Tibor de Nagy one time at his gallery, being there to see what he had of John's, in fact, he said that possibly people were intimidated, even spooked, by the humor. They didn't know what to do with a picture that was so inescapably funny, and if it was in part laughing at them, it surely could be with them also. John invited me generously into a portfolio once, the first Gemini ever did and the first ever of his lithographs—and we cast about for a title, and ended up with a pretty crunky one, *Of Women*. Not even Picasso ran so many particularizing numbers on that possibility as did John—cowboys and Indians, the works. My own favorite is one of the usual dowdily buxom lady leaning over the fence to attend a gesticulating, squatty, and naked man, who is pontificating in an amiable way whilst his erect and knobby malehood stands forth from him in a charmingly emphasized way, i.e., the head is a singularly yellow rose. Well, one picture is worth a thousand words—but don't tell me art doesn't *mean* something. John Altoon always did and so do I. If you don't mean it, why bother.

# My New Mexico

Whatever the newcomer's disposition toward it all, the place is adamantly a condition in all that she or he can do. But it is as far, finally, from a simple regionalism—some accretion of human place and time—as is the literal moon, despite people have now walked on it. The scale is wrong, so to speak—immense, dry, displacing, vast, inhuman, intently particular. Yet we have been here specifically a long time, thousands upon thousands of years, in fact, and this secularizing aridity was once the ample bed of an ocean as fossils still testify. So who are we—not Indians certainly; hardly the initial *chicanos,* for instance, Cabeza de Vaca, moved by his own wanderings to write to "Your Majesty": "And who is any of us, that without starvation he can go through the kingdoms of starvation?"[1] It would seem we come here in some peculiar moon-driven loneliness to stave off (starve out) the contemporary devils of distraction, who buy and sell our lives in lieu of ever confronting us more particularly. There is no success here, no matter what star of what firmament has briefly come to rest and dazzle. The trade is elsewhere, and clearly those who make a life here either forgo it or else retreat here from its involvements.

Therefore two classic patrons of this way of life, this concentration upon an art, may well be considered as measure for those here presented. D. H. Lawrence had no patience with any aspect of the old world from which he'd come, and in the new he recognized an

*In Place* (Albuquerque: Albuquerque Museum, 1982).

1. Haniel Long, *The Power Within Us: Cabeza de Vaca's Relation of His Journey from Florida to the Pacific, 1528–1536.* New York, 1944, p. 32.

unresolvable contest of beliefs because our old way of seeing and believing put us always at a remove from the thing itself, whereas the peoples indigenous, the "Indians," were at one with all the forms of an existence shared with myriad species thereof—or as he puts it in another context: "Everything is very soft, subtle, delicate. There is none of the hardness of representation. They are not representing something, not even playing. It is a soft, subtle *being* something."[2] Lawrence is prevented from returning to his ranch in Taos (actually in the mountains north of Taos, above a small town called San Cristobal, appropriately enough) because he has tuberculosis and the United States health officials are committed to preventing the admission of anyone so infected with an epidemic disease. So he is recognized as a carrier of plague, physical as well as spiritual, which last he had long known.

More happily, Georgia O'Keeffe, born in Sun Prairie, a small Wisconsin farm town, of Irish, Hungarian and Dutch descent, second child of seven, was always 'local,' and when she comes to live year-round in New Mexico in the late 1940s, she has, in fact, known it since 1917 if only in passing through, but substantially since 1929, when she begins to spend summers in Taos, settling finally near Abiquiu at the Ghost Ranch. But what she says in 1944, in a statement "About Painting Desert Bones," is the point to be recognized:

> "I have picked flowers where I found them—
> Have picked up sea shells and rocks and pieces of wood
>     where there were sea shells and rocks and pieces of wood
>     that I liked
> When I found the beautiful white bones on the desert I
>     picked them up and took them home too
> I have used these things to say what is to me the wideness and
>     wonder of the world as I live in it"[3]

No matter what particular relations may be so involved—even if any of these artists care at all about their elder *loner*, who, as they, will (as she always has) take care of herself—it's *both* the stripping off of particularizing human habit and ego, the investments of life characteristic of an intensive city pattern among others possible, *and* a Blake-like emphasis upon "the wideness and wonder of the world as I live in it . . ." In short, everything is remarkably, even casually, *here*.

2. D. H. Lawrence, *Mornings in Mexico*. London, 1927, p. 110.
3. Lloyd Goodrich and Doris Bry, *Georgia O'Keeffe*. New York, 1970, p. 25.

Just so, then, Terry Conway's insistence that: "Painting is seen, or read, when its intensity forces us to participate in the illusion and in a dialogue with a world where the beautiful and the ugly, the common and absurd are indivisible—a world in which history, fantasy and reality, dream and memory are inseparable . . ."[4] The resonances, echoes of surface, which his paintings can manage with their "incomplete erasures"[5] (as one critic put it)—effects of overpainting or wash, or scrims applied with a dry roller—are neither faint nor recessive in a world itself so sparely present, so intently dry about its own admission of either emotion or others. So this surface, as one says, is ground of extraordinary tension, but without a finally willful human confidence to shout out at its company some demand that it enter, touch, take heart, be accessible in more than an illusional sense. It is as if our dream of community had been pressed between large plates of glass and as it "bled," one saw its forms even as they faded—except that here one side is canvas, and the other a proposedly "open" world of being alive. Let me quote his friend, the writer Gus Blaisdell: "Conway's pictures seem to exclude everything that has not been already absorbed into their interior ardency. We are reminded by them of a mutual contingency—there is no need for either of us to be here—a mood which underscores the evanescence of emotions, causing the depiction to waver; as if a consequence of acknowledgement is discovered in the unravelling of monstrous feeling."[6] There is, of course, no explanation—only what this same friend calls "the intelligible silence that is the heart of painting" and what we enter is what we see before us, to be *there*—when *here* was all we were.

This intent disposition of spatial context may be of necessity the bulwark kept against the "all outdoors" that can bear in so heavily. A critic of Conway, William Peterson, aptly quotes Robert Smithson: "The desert is less 'nature' than a concept, a place that swallows up boundaries."[7] The point is well made for all who live where one can, not uncommonly, see more than one hundred miles in any direction. It proves a curious reduction of objects in their usual places. Therefore Allan Graham goes *into* his painting much as did Pollock, recovering a locus for all the possibility of transformation

4. Terry Conway, Statement for one-man show at Hoshour Gallery, Albuquerque, New Mexico, November 1979.

5. William Peterson, "Terry Conway at Hoshour, Albuquerque," *Artspace*, April 1981, p. 61.

6. Gus Blaisdell, "Terry Conway," *Artspace*, Fall 1979, pp. 41–44. (Quotations taken from p. 43 and p. 44 respectively.)

7. Peterson, "Terry Conway."

and recognition that he, humanly, must have for survival. He finds therein not an idea of his intelligence or person but an accounting of his own perceptions, a track of emotional orders. He leaves one place (the insistent, fragmented, intently textured *herringbone* grids) to find another (the speed of the calligraphy, the incremental echoes of the underpainting)—albeit they are one. He is, in short, what he has defined a painter to be, "a person entirely involved in a two-dimensional surface. He feels it; he loves it; he is sensitive to everything that happens on it. If a person is a painter it doesn't matter what he paints, for the two-dimensional surface is the language he speaks." [8]

In some contrast, the surfaces of Richard Hogan's paintings are apparently more quiet, yet deceptively so, since the gnomic teasing and luminous color of his drawing are fact of an intelligent reduction to that which permits a 'traveling light,' a 'place in mind' discovered in that which *is,* factually the canvas and the means wherewith to mark it. He has lived here a long time and it is, as he puts it, literally home. He is therefore looking out from what others may presume themselves to be looking into, and his is a tradition thereby of being *in* place, blessed with it, stuck with it, cursed with it, either way. He makes line serve as no direction in or out, but far more as oldtime tally sticks or such markings as one meets with in primordially local places, marking the time and presence of human attention to its amusements, its musing with the edges of where it discovers itself 'on edge,' a place apart. There's an old hymn that goes, "Brighten the corner, where you are. . . ," with reference, I believe, to a lighthouse—and these are many lights, then, moving with whimsical care for that "someone" who wants to bring it all home.

Possibly the impulse most common to these artists is that of localizing, in one way or another, whatever the content of their various activity may prove to be. Clearly, they are somewhere and would like to insist upon it as actuating perception rather than mere social appetite. For example, William Masterson writes of recent work ( January 1982): "My latest paintings are derived from figurative, and, lately, landscape sources. Rather than representing these sources, they are a record of a way of looking, as well as a coming to terms with the painting as a unique event. The paintings have become progressively more active with the eye of the viewer

8. Allan Graham, *Fifteen Paintings, 1978 and 1979.* University Art Museum, University of New Mexico, Albuquerque, 1979.

moving about the field. The field color has become more saturated and interacts more with the colored lines. There is an implication of a limited space in these paintings in tension with the actuality of the surface."[9] Again the intentional modesty of the work is significant because it is neither indifferent to the information of a universe, call it, nor inarticulate when so confronted. Rather, it seems the compacting of such information, the sense of "a limited space in these paintings in tension with the actuality of the surface," which clearly knows there is more room, so to speak, yet places "a record of a way of looking" in reductive lines or gestures rather than "representing" an actual or imagined wholeness. One feels a time compacting also, as if there were entirely a pressure to be finished, complete, before all melted into an undifferentiated space forever.

Such preoccupation proves insistent, whether inside the frame of a painting or placed in the box of a room or a yard bounded by fence or edges, however determined. David Anderson speaks of his work as being "within the current movement of the 'new architecturality'"[10] and his sculptures, primarily of steel, are modes of affecting spatial situation much as a wall might, or a table, in short, any *thing* that locates movement in a necessary focus or pattern. However, they are equally iconographic, particularizing images, but faintly so. For example, it is characteristic of him to drill small holes at random into the plate steel so as to echo the situation of stars. As he says, "The night sky is a dominant reference for me" and with that quiet emphasis, one realizes how far the top and bottom of a usual world have been extended. In contrast, the works themselves have a variable scale and character, ranging from massive steel constructs to others one can hold in a hand.

Less apparent, possibly, is Bill Gilbert's extraordinary authority with abstraction, by which one means not so much the power to take away something as to redistribute the habits of its acknowledgment. Because the materials with which he works are often humanly sweet—adobe, juniper—associations will inevitably occur, especially in a place having so long had the common use of such stuff, be it for house or for sheep pen. But there is no argument. As he has said, "I opted for a material that reflected a closer associa-

9. William Masterson, Statement for one-man show at Hoshour Gallery, Albuquerque, New Mexico, January 1982.

10. David Anderson, Statement for one-man show at Linda Durham Gallery, Santa Fe, New Mexico, October 1981.

tion with the earth and the elements in an attempt to open a more humble dialogue with our world. In my development as an artist, this dialogue has led me away from the enclosed forms of pottery [he was initially a ceramicist] toward a more fluid apprehension of matter in space; matter as a combination of particle and wave. I have chosen the format of installation for its ability to invoke the fragility of the massive, and the impermanence of the permanent, implied by this theory of matter."[11]

Still much remains doggedly exterior to any imagination of human world, and especially in this one. If this is the Wild West of Geronimo and Billy the Kid, it's also that of White Sands and the first atomic tests—equally brutal and ahuman. Because there is so much *outside,* such a vast, extraneous skin, such a plethora of virtually useless space, one hands it over to whatever can inhabit it, missile ranges, uranium mines, anything to take it away. So most crucial *and* dear are the persistent, quiet, unaggressive attempts to internalize it, to make the small world of human habits and understanding also undertake it, bring it in. Gloria Graham works in this way, no matter such statement can or can't say what she does. It is her *secrets* that matter, the tightly bound urns, the insides that don't spill out in a vacancy of self-exposure. It's living with what one doesn't know, is never to know—or has to forget ever knowing. So she stacks, ties, places the *things* of her art with their half-echoes of function—but what? But what do any of us *do* here or anywhere. These will keep us good company . . .

Finally, I had not expected our drive to the east of Santa Fe out over the arid mesa to where the condominiums and ersatz town houses are already accumulating as a raw and leaking wealth— to arrive, I say, in such spillage at the particular house of, of all people, a nomadic French photographer who is *not* an 'artist' as he will tell you, simply one who takes photographs with a classic 50 mm lens, neither more nor less. He is the latest arrival, although his people were among the first of our own to come to the 'new world.' *Mon Nouveau-Mexique* . . . So after an excellent lunch with his wife, Kathi, and small son, Shane, Bernard Plossu gave me specific and careful audience, showed me a range of his photographs taken in Africa, Mexico, New Mexico, talked of a mutual friend in Paris, Denis Roche—with Giles Mora and Claude Nori they consti-

11. William Gilbert, Statement for "Clay Alternatives," Aarnum Gallery, Pasadena, California and Fischer Gallery, University of Southern California, Los Angeles, 1981. Exhibition catalog.

tute *Ulysses* and also produce *Les Cahiers de la Photographie,* an excellent journal—and of, as he calls them, "the brown lands": "My photographs reveal what I personally relate to: Place, weather, music, sensuality. I like the desert . . . there's nothing better than to be on top of a hill in the desert and look all around you and it's just space, no noise, no time. You have to be at peace with yourself. That emptiness is very good for the soul. We just wanted to keep that 'brown lands' feeling, to be in the desert, and the American desert is one of the most beautiful in the world . . ." [12]

Insofar as eyes are the most primary of human senses, and what world we make with them will be ours of necessity, the eight people of this place, this still new place "New Mexico," are crucial arbiters of whatever vision, whatever sight, we may still be permitted. They have as yet no fashion or school simply to contain them. But the ground they stand on is the edge.

12. Bernard Plossu, Interview with Lisa Sherman, *Artlines,* March 1981, p. 4.

# Jim Dine/Five Themes

## Hearts

Just as one's self will serve as constant in a world of otherwise shifting reference, a *heart* is sign that one can care, that there is a consistent presence of feeling. In a curious way this heart is neither inside nor outside oneself but, rather, exists in a hieratic determination of its own possibility, and so lives in a place that can be as powerfully singular and remote as the moon or as physically evident and contained as one's own hands, feet, and head.

This heart is an imagination, of course. One knows the actual heart looks not at all like those most familiar from the iconographic slogans of Valentine's Day—which seems itself an invention from faint root except that there must be one day on which, unequivocally, hearts triumph. *Have a heart* . . .

It would be an error, however, to presume that these specific hearts are either symbolic or ultimately abstract. They are far more like weather, a shifting presence that has faces but is not itself a fixed content. More apt then to call them, among other things, a ground or context which serves as means for feeling out the possibilities of what is going on.

The insistent echoes of this image must have been delight to an artist so remarkably open to language and its powers. One can trust the associations here of everything from 'A heart as big as all

*Jim Dine/Five Themes,* ed. Graham W. J. Beal (New York: Abbeville Press, 1983).

outdoors' to 'hardhearted' or 'broken-hearted' or, simply, 'The heart of the matter.' The language of the titles is a useful evidence of how variously this 'heart' can find occasion, whether it prove "I'm Painting with my Animals," where a veritable outside comes in to lean against the heart, or "Nancy and I at Ithaca (Straw Heart)" with its backward pun upon *The Wizard of Oz*. The point is that it does not stand for something else nor has it only a force determined by what it means, or wants to. As a presence it gathers resonance as would a cross or flag, even without information. Playing literalizing objects against it, or determining it as object also (as must be the case with "sheet iron and straw, 60 × 70 × 12½"), leaves it much as a whale on a beach, persistently itself in whatever locus.

Therefore what changes is all else, and that is why one does engage in "Romancing in Late Winter" and "Painting a Fortress for the Heart." It is an elegant, fructifying image, often voluptuous in its provocatively paired French curves. Yet one feels the pain and frustration its emblem has incessantly borne with it, pierced with arrows, split in two, blackened, cracked. It wears its colors bravely.

## Robes

If clothes can make the man, these *robes* exist in a place that is neither quite one nor the other. They stand foursquare through the years, sometimes primarily an outline but always with an intrinsic volume much as if an invisible man were their occupant. In that way they are like houses for a particular imaginal body, a self embodied in a 'self portrait,' which sees always what it is either doing or what is being done to it. The heads are missing because the plane of the painting has no room for them. They would fall off like those ships once were thought to, having come to the edge of the ocean. But more, the torso is under the cloth, not apart from it. There are no necks or hands, for example.

It is also interesting that they are robes, not suits, or coats or other modes of clothing. It seems that a robe, a bathrobe or dressing gown as it may variously be called, makes a dignity possible between a state of usual dress and undress. It is both intimate and intently formal. So too is the repetitive stance, faced to a presumable mirror, taking a clearly determined look.

Initially it all seems playful or at least open to an employment of possibilities which are more fact of the situation resolved on than what's brought to it. "Double Isometric Self-Portrait (Serape)" and "Self-Portrait Next to a Colored Window" each have a double play on any presumed fact of person, not only this one. In short, the same is not the same but always different. It thinks apart from itself, by objectifying mechanical agency in one instance (it holds *itself* together, thank you (twice)) and, in the other, what's alongside so defines it that there's no getting out of it at all (a dotted line no less). Another work of this year (1964) has much the same intrinsic humor, "Charcoal Self-Portrait in Cement Garden," the garden a few fragmented bits of funereal oddment or possibly pedestals for birdbaths—but nothing, in fact, very funny at all as the figure back of them finds its dimension and substance somehow located by these squat, small solidnesses. Its belt, for example, has become curiously persuaded.

A little more than ten years later one finds much changed, although the apparent form has survived. Yet one might say that in this work, all of it, content is never more than an extension of form(s). Paradoxically, that formula can be read either way since the terms prove inseparable, at least in thought. And while this work is not overtly intellectual exercise, any of it, it is deeply thoughtful, thinks through feeling. Now there is nothing in front of the image, no term of inherent reflection. All that happens, or that has happened, is manifest directly on the face of what one sees. There one is, whoever, and again as with the surface of the hearts—or literal person or painting—what happens happens here, and is that information, happy, sad, all the same. And all comes closer.

## Tools

Here associations are more explicit, although that may have only to do with the fact that one's information of the Dine family's involvement with classic hardware *tools*—they had a store in Cincinnati—is both provocative and secure. It was the substantial factor in the family's economy. The young artist worked occasionally in the store relating. Tools are both insistent and functional, suggest a complexly ranging physical environment and also keep the stability of 'home,' are familiar and strange.

He obviously thought about them a good deal and if the hearts were and are the emotional weather of his life, the robes the attempt to see oneself not only as others might see one but as that sight given back, then tools are somehow what one does and can do. Or, perhaps better, one can recognize things are done and these things do them. The occasional presence of a glove in the company, in "Untitled (1973)," for example, makes clear the transitional factor of agency, the who does what with what. The tools are forever. At times they are far more than what their function, taken literally, will provide for and two hammers with immensely elongated handles become "The Hammer Doorway." How can one confidently propose this is simply a metaphor for what hammers can make, or a play on the visual suggestions of a hammer head, or even some threatening possibility there is to be violence 'inside'?

At times the tools are codifying anchor for a reality—the artist's whimsical and perceptive understanding of the powers of order—that includes a solid emphasis upon all manner of literal and abstract thing. "Five Feet of Colorful Tools," crowding in all respects the top of this painting "with board and objects," has as much practical density as people waiting for a subway and as curiously evident a sense of time as old coats hung in a closet. All the echoic layering is, one would think, a good deal more than simple memories. If "a place for everything and everything in its place" were ever to have a chance in this world, this painting would still come to haunt it. The act of hanging things up, putting things back, respecting things the way they were, is all wound in here in a way neither ironic nor pragmatic. Even who hung them up is very much a question.

Still the presence of tools is remarkably particular and common, even when they are in situations of transformation ("The Hammer Doorway") or, in some sense, visually incomplete ("Untitled (Pliers)"). They also take place in the painting, drawing, assemblage, etc., in a very matter-of-fact way, upright, either sitting firmly on bottom margin or plane, or else hung in like manner. Clearly they are the things that do work and can, however various, echoing and unlocated one's own relation to them may sometimes be.

## Gates

There seems some change in preoccupations here. For one thing, the *gates*—or more truly the gate, since the images come from one factual gate, as the titles make clear—are a new presence in the ico-

nography. Too, they, along with the trees (which are also new arrivals), are referred to as "forms to hang paintings on." But that
is nothing so remarkably new, thinking of the robes and hearts.
Often the image has been used as a constant, repetitively, to permit
the painting to move as freely in its experience as impulse and recognitions might permit. Insofar as the phrase refers to gates and
trees, that sense of "to hang paintings on" is inevitably interesting.
One is sure it was no casually determined expression.

"The Crommelynck Gate" can be found at 172 rue de Grenelle,
Paris, which is the address of Aldo Crommelynck, master engraver
and printer, who with his brother has collaborated in a singular
range of etchings, from those of Picasso and Matisse to Jasper
Johns and Dine himself, with whom he has worked on several
projects in recent years. This gate is the entrance to the atelier and
residence. The place has a grand and imposing air, somewhat like a
hospital or official residence. Dine must have passed through this
particular gate many times, to sit at an immaculate work bench, at-
tended by very specific provision and respect, to *make art*, as is said.
So these gates (or gate) have an unexpected parallel to those gates
most common in American habit possibly, those of a factory. The
other gates one thinks of quickly are the cemetery's (or heaven's).

Whatever might prove the case, the fact that this image has a literal source is useful. One supposes that most of Dine's images are
so founded, but again the accessible fact of this one gives means to
recognize the particular modes of investment and change he works
with. It is interesting that the image is intently centered, that one
sees that much of it which would be commonly seen walking toward
it from some short distance away. One is reminded of a cinematic
device or focus, curiously, as though one were the 'eye' of a camera.

In quite another sense, a poem of Thomas Hardy's recounts the
awesome terror of approaching such a gate—the gate to death itself—to see on its other side the ghoulish objects of despair and
terminus beckoning. Then he asks, were it simpler to pass through
and have done, rather than to live knowing one will one day come
again? These images depend on an almost elegant insistence of
tracery upon a vast emptiness of opened space. The formal fasci-
nates because it is all that is there to hold any concept, any possibility, of place. But there is nothing seemingly behind it, but "Fog,"
but blackness. Even at home ("Vermont") it remains ambiguously
inviting.

Is one to stop here? All art would wish to remain at one with its human limit, to be so contained. Clearly there is to be an end. But here one cannot know whether this is its sign, or simply the thing *we* see, waiting.

## Trees

There seems always an emphasis upon the singular, the one. Even in a cluster, of tools, for example, it is their particularity as single objects that determines the nature of their company. It is a feeling that they have come together, as people might in some public situation, each from some specific circumstance or use.

There is, in fact, an anthropomorphic disposition in many of the images but it is not an enlargement of their proposed value, by presumption of human attributes. Rather they are seen intently, intensely, in ways that make of them precise human contexts and evocations.

Of all the themes variously engaged, only the *trees* might be said to have no necessarily human origin or invention. Certainly the tools and the hearts are each artifacts that have no meaning apart from how one may use them. Again, the image of the heart has finally little to do with that physical organ it so faintly represents, however closely it may relate to an imagined heart's crucial significance to human life itself. So too with the robes and gates.

However, the language of the titles insists equally upon this relation for the trees: "Painting as Summer Ends"; "Red Tree, Flesh Tree"; "A Tree in the Shadow of Our Intimacy"; "A Tiger Lies at the Bottom of Our Garden." Much as a figure approaching or else loomingly present, the trees are central in each image. Either one looks up to them, or sees them directly ahead, so to speak, in a scale significantly larger than one's own. In that respect they are as dense with imminent human information as might be any actual human figure.

Very probably this fact invests the appearance of these trees, this tree (one would feel them to be a single tree, in shifting perspectives but always forefront), with echoes of a human torso or, more aptly, the look of the robe images with open space of the neck a marked parallel to the effect of the tree's crotch. It is particularly evident in "Desire," with its three panels of robe, tree, and heart respectively. Someone is insistently *here*, one wants to say, whether it be the artist, the onlooker, or the image found in the work itself.

One feels witness to a presence which will momently say much more than its brooding silence will now permit.

To see the trunks of trees, the entangled, twisted branches, as a myriad of human detail (hair, arms, fingers, bodies) would be a familiar nightmare of children, for whom the thing must be the thing as one sees it, without relief. "A Tiger Lies at the Bottom of Our Garden" plays complexly on a diversity of text, both in language and in image, confronting any possibility of securing resolution or containment with unremitting ambivalence. So does a reflecting 'tree of life' become the life itself.

*For J. D.*

Pass on by, love,
wait by that garden gate.
Swing on, up
on heaven's gate.

The confounding, confronted
pictures of world
brought to signs
of its persistent self

are here in all colors, sizes—
and hearts as big as all outdoors,
a weather of spaces,
intervals between silences.

# Face It

It's hard to think of any human world without the insistent measure of others in it, what and how they've done things—and what that meant. Like it or not, there's finally no one here but us people, or certainly nothing that gives a damn about that fact other than those we have a life with, either as past or present. It's a long time, however, since anyone's had the chutzpah to say, "Lives of great men all remind us, etc., etc." Those "great men" have long since fallen with the revelations of Watergate or else the bleakly persistent appetites of such as brought us the casual nightmare of Love Canal. We despair in trust, so to speak, we no longer believe much. High school kids surveyed as to their contemporary heroes recently came back with not one human being, living or dead. They had literally all gone to the stars, of *Star Wars*.

So were there nothing else here but this dear human care for what there is and has been, to go by, it would be immensely moving in itself. That someone can still say he wants to "Pay homage to people whose world and/or life has touched and influenced mine—people I think are important human beings . . ." is unexpectedly reassuring because it's so often felt as square, somehow mark of an innocence, a lack of hipness, a simply naive disposition toward the world that hasn't as yet suffered its own comedown. But this painter is no kid nor are the figures of his proposal a comfortable pop topography. So-called public persons here are as real as

Foreword to *"Man Is the Metaphor"*: *Paintings by Philip Behymer, 1981–1983* (El Paso, Tex.: El Paso Museum of Art, 1983).

anyone else, often as faded and certainly as vulnerable. As one of them, Ed Dorn, once said, *my heroes have been men and women* . . . It is a dry, classical specificness, a toughness of human needs— including that something matter—that wants to look and be looked at. Because otherwise it's too much like an eighteen-year-old seen with dog walking down sidewalk a few days ago, here in this small still backwater Maine town, and on the back of his T-shirt was: "It doesn't matter." Terrifying.

Even so there's finally not enough mileage in saying anything, if the art itself can't bring one to *sight,* to seeing it without any words at all. Therefore all the resources of the painter are on the line, and all the echoes, resources, distractions of the business of the so-called art world are there to blow him away, as and when he falters. Again the strength is the artist's heart, remarkably enough, that in making these complexly personal icons, he can "Attempt to record the sense of the presence of that person as well as simply the image . . ." Impeccably he manages a detail of a photographically determined reality together with a far more subtly actualized experience of the qualities of person inherent. He *digs* these people, he feels their presence as his own.

Back of all of this is that funny word, *face*—and here are many faces, all full face, looking at you. Funny that it comes from a Latin word you find also in *factory: facere,* to make, do. The face was always something you were making, whether it was make-up or simply funny faces. In any case, it's your turn now.

*Bristol, Me.*
*July 21, 1983*

# Seeing Things: Preface to *Scopophilia,* by Gerard Malanga

It is expectable, even reassuring, that a term so quaintly suggestive as "voyeurism" should be taken from the French, like they say, and that it should only become at home in our language as recently as the late '20s. (The OED gives as date 1929.) This peeking, taking looks at, beholding unaware, even spying (as in "spyglass") has old associations with the sexual informing of our humanness. Thus Adam and Eve first "see" their nakedness in the Garden of Eden and it becomes the burden of self-consciousness ever after. Just as they saw themselves, we see others, with that insistent presence of the sexual in any recognition of those ones, whoever they are, out there, apart from ourselves. So it is our habit to respond to this dimension, this potential and presence, of person primarily; and if we are cautious, shy ourselves of observation, possibly we are fearful we will forfeit authority and become equal game.

In the intriguing range and particularity of this book—its *persons* in all respects—the act of looking is the necessary center insofar as the art of photography so depends upon and defines how it is we see, and think we see. Because each image is specific, outside the time or circumstance in which it occurred, a determined possession has already been accomplished, something taken from the otherwise seemingly random and hardly to be recollected flux. So even the most chaste instance of such seeing—the impromptu wedding photograph, the children, the girl or boy friend, even or particu-

Gerard Malanga, *Scopophilia* (New York: Alfred van der Marck, 1985).

larly one's dog—would be counterpart of those here, made to serve
a far more intensive ambition possibly, the will to possess beyond
any moment of time the scene of one's proposed pleasure and its
increasingly pathetic artifacts, the fading subject.

I know the parallel in writing. Despite what the rhyme says,
names do indeed "hurt" and possess equally, and one may make of
any innocent bystander a means to a complex end just by saying,
"you *are* here. . . ." That is, one says so, and so it is. One takes them
unawares.

Because those here collected speak with such apt instance, and
are also masters of their authority, better to let this brief note and
introduction move even more personally. What is it one feels so
questionable in peeking—as if to look before a permission, without
requisite provision, acknowledgment, much like opening a Christmas present too soon? I am sure that the occasions are far more
invested, again as those making so much clear here make very evident as well. I've certainly looked when I wasn't meant to, with or
without discovery, or with an invitation I of course presumed.
Often I was simply afraid to, was displaced, wanted myself to be
seen, seen to, taken apart as a part. The enclosure of such obvious
grounds of human interest by dictates of propriety and good taste
may be legitimate—"legit" feels more accurate —but the illegiti-
mate, that which has only its singular existence for birthright, so
echoes and persuades. Feelings can be made to seem characteristic
improprieties, at least with respect to rational intent. Yet they must
have our attention too, want all that may insist upon response to
be acknowledged, admitted. They preempt thinking, by making it
think twice.

Therefore *Dig this*, as they say, what's so hidden from us, buried,
so covered over with whatever clothing, that we of necessity must
gain means to get to it despite the "no-man's-land" we are forced to
traverse or the fact that we will have no one to speak for us, if discovered. Unforgettable, sad story woman told me years ago, she
was a New Zealander, of her English mother-in-law who had never
seen her husband naked, until at last, when he was old and dying,
she had the job of bathing him. Were eyes, then, hostile to sight
(sex?) so that they were better cast down or removed? There is
D. H. Lawrence's story of the blind man who touches with the
power of seeing.

W. C. Williams had the repeated phrase, "No ideas but in things," to which one wants to add, "nor people either. . . ." One has to look, whatever the cost. The ingenuous diversity of means here evident makes clear that *to look* is not the end in view simply. To see *something* is where it's always at.

*Ithaca, N.Y.*
*April 28, 1985*

# Foreword to *The Poet Exposed,* Portraits by Christopher Felver

How hard it seems, finally, to see another, to apprehend who it is *is* there, and how constantly fragile the whole exchange, even at best. I had been thinking of Robert Burns' wry emphasis, "to see ourselves as others see us . . ." But that's not the point here. Nor is Eliot's: "To prepare a face to meet the faces that you meet . . ."

> There will be time to murder and create,
> And time for all the works and days of hands
> That lift and drop a question on your plate . . .

To define a quick context—faces are *appearances,* the visage, the countenance, the expression of the countenance, the outward aspect, the determined dignity, self-respect, what's manifest as *face value.* Face has a function involved with making (*facere*) as *make-up* would testify. It looks like.

To make a portrait of that subtle, manipulative occasion is complexly demanding. I'm struck that *portrait* has a root sense of "to draw forth," which in turn provokes a sense of "draw" I'd never before thought of. The painter Kitaj called the act of drawing another human being the sum and measure of the art. It is an entirely human one in all respects. No other relation can so define imagination or the power of seeing literally. Photography proves a consummate instance.

The old-time portraiture, like that of Bachrach, in the northeast, had the clear purpose of social investment. My Uncle Hap worked

*The Poet Exposed,* Portraits by Christopher Felver (New York: Alfred van der Marck, 1986).

for their company in the thirties and contrived to have portraits done of his mother and father. Their faces are backed by some curious indeterminacy of lit cloud or smoke; they look solidly secure, bemusedly accommodating—and are in no way my grandparents. There is certainly nothing wrong with that fact. There are other values at work, and image serves by its contrivance to hoist these two commoners into the apparent ranks of the financially blest. We might have some questions, and I don't know what they thought of it all. (The same uncle had battered together an extremely tentative "family tree," which gave us remarkable affiliations—again all bankrupt, in fact.) We did see someone, however, of our relation, in a place we had heard about but never known, and that gave some added dimension to our otherwise mundane lives. Yet the ploy is the same as the undertaker's exceptional use of rouge, the suit bought just for that final occasion, the hair curled at last. Such "drawing forth" as that can be has little to do with its subjects.

Chris Felver's concerns are intensely otherwise, and here one sees writers, *poets*—those most blest by an art but also made most vulnerable. There's no money in it, like they say, or at best very, very little. And so the casual interest fades. (Had any a lingering doubt concerning Cardenal, to see him so comfortable here must banish it forever.) The photographer is a friend, the faces are remarkably open, and a reflective small grin echoes from page to page. I think it is that, for the most part, all are at home in the world, and this person come to call, with his camera, is there in like manner, equally open. What drama there is is muted, faces are extremely without artifice, look for the most part straight forward. So the man looking at them is by that defined.

W. C. Williams makes clear his anger at the cost of Man Ray's portrait of him, if flattered, possibly, by the occasion. He looks alert, raw, vulnerable. Without question Man Ray has put him in his place (in contrast with the portrait by Charles Sheeler). Berenice Abbott's portraits of the same period—of Djuna Barnes or Joyce, for example—show a far more intimate sense of the person sitting there. It isn't just that she cares, but that she knows, explicitly, where she is and in what relation. She honors the subject with her clarity. Otherwise, a lot can be made of a camera, as a defensive weapon, for instance, or a means to manipulate the look—to divide and conquer, as it were. I can't think a photograph any less of a determined artifact than a painting, and to say "the camera never lies" is to be complacently ingenuous. Everything lies, with or without art, cameras included.

Therefore I much respect Felver's own integrity in this work and the commitment shown in the detail and perception his book makes evident. He has given it a significant dimension in the notes and compact poems that accompany each photograph in the person's own script. These are useful, authenticating signatures, again a substantiation of person—that someone is here, that another bears witness.

Oh haunting witness—
you've seen me again
without my knowing it.

Will my face dissolve
in my hands, will I
still remember you?

*Ithaca, New York*
*March 9, 1986*

# V Autobiography and Poetics

# A Note on the Objective

Whether from an altogether 'scientific' attitude, or from some wish to disassociate, only, by way of the surface of language, one idea from another, *objectivity* has become the apparent trademark of the careful mind. Common use would put upon this *objectivity* the air of the cool head, that is, one capable of confronting divers phenomena in their own particulars, rather than as extensions of one's own senses. It was this battle, between the *objective* and the *subjective*, then, which had replaced the looser and more worn fight between classicism and romanticism.

But intentions, as is usual, belie results. Or are belied by them. Because, however actual an intention may be, however well considered, reasoned, etc., its result is not to be found prior to that act which effects it, and altogether useless to assume the intended victory before it's come to pass. In this case, *objectivity* is, in intention, the prime aspect of a method which plans to deal with the 'things around' as characters in themselves, having as their first claim on the attention, their own actuality. In matters of poetry, it amounts to the wish to transmit, free of imprecise 'feeling,' the nature of 'that' which has moved one to write in the first place. As such, this wish intends as complete a break as possible with the *subjective*.

In effect, this break is not actual, since the writing comes to (1) using this 'that' as a character for use (as content in the poem); and (2) using 'that' as an impetus for the act of writing itself—simply what's pushing. In short, while the first is concerned with

*Goad*, Summer 1951.

abstracting the experience as *objective* data, the second is equally concerned with keeping it as *subjective* impulse. And pointless to comment: it's a fight.

A useless fight. However right it may be to damn the use of the *subjective* method as an excuse for emotional claptrap, it's apt to push us away from any understanding of the *subjective* in a more basic character, i.e., "belonging to, or of, or due to, the consciousness . . ." Impossible to write anything, lacking this relation of its content to oneself. Put another way: things have to come in before they can go out.

Perhaps best to junk both terms, or at least to understand this necessary balance, one with the other. We can't stand outside our content and at the same time we can't eat it like an apple, etc. And perhaps, finally, more to the point than either of these two stances is that one which maintains: a man and his objects must both be presences in this field of force we call a poem.

# Notes for a New Prose

*"Language is not reality but another of the* instruments *by which man engages reality . . ."*

It is, certainly, reasonable to comment that Joyce's earlier work presents no such divergence from normality as does, now, even the mention of his name. There is, to be got at, a straight line of impact, search, through the early work, the poems, the play (which is all 'idea') to the fact of *Ulysses* and then *Finnegans Wake*. It is useless to avoid it, or to mistake its point. Which must be: it is not the content which is changed. It is the extension of the content into form that has been tempered, made strong.

To go back. We had been led to believe that connotation was this: the suggestions of 'meaning' beyond the supposedly exact, denotative meaning which custom of usage had put upon the phrase or word in question. Then, by way of the opening created by 'associational' content of phrase, gesture, practice, ways, in short, METHOD—connotation became meaning versus meaning, became the fight for sense, in shorthand. (Some call this 'symbol.') "It isn't what the words mean. It's what they mean to you . . ."

Just so, with Joyce. That is, the possible suggestions (which can now be called: manifestations) of sense (which was about to become: value) became the criteria for an ultimate 'sense' (though no millennium). Because this was done with language, or, more strictly, within the words themselves, there we took our sight, a

*Origin,* no. 2, 1951.

bead on: what might be up. Wrong from the start, since it was not words for the sake of words, but, for the sake of what content, possible, might shape them, into sense. Taken as such, Joyce is the craftsman, casting about for a model, for the model—what is in the head. Not to make himself, but to make, what is in himself.

Form is the extension of content. This was the first rule.


2

*"A man must create himself, if he is an artist, instrument also IN ORDER THAT his work be not expression but illumination . . ."*

Possible arguments for the supposition that poetry is, now, more able than prose, or more able to make itself an extension of the present context, this life, etc., have first to do with the fact of its ability, (1) to compress, and (2) to project supposition, as fact. In prose, the lean toward a 'solution' or a stasis of idea most usually marks the book as a failure; I mean, insofar as a writer of prose is willing to give space to this fixing of idea as the logical 'end' of movement, etc., just so far we usually won't go along with him. And I would figure that we are right. But we deny him, even so, the way out of it, this fix, or what could get him beyond these 'logics.' Take the idea of a man running alongside a train, taking notes yet. He would be about it, what is now expected—while the poet, at home, can project this iron monster to any place which may please him. It is, then, that we are still confused by the idea of 'reality' in prose. We do not as yet get the basic fact, that reality is just that which is believed, just as long as it is, believed. Poets are more used to this thing: reality as variants round the center, or, simply, what has been left us.

So how could a prose catch up? Difficult to make the competition actual. It isn't. Elsewhere, it had been pointed out that "poetry insists upon or suggests a quite different 'Universe': a universe of reciprocal relations . . ." The swing of idea, in stasis—is still poetry. But prose is the *projection* of ideas, in time. This does not mean that the projection must be an 'actual' one, date by date, etc. The word is law, is the creator, and what it can do, is what any prose can do. There is nothing more real, in essence, about a possible prose than there is about any possible poetry. The ordering of *conjecture* will remain as 'real' as the ordering of fact, given the right hand.

More to the point, to note the difference, again, between poetry and prose, one of the differences, since there are others as well. Poetry, as the formulation of content, in stasis; prose, as the formulation of content, in a progression, like that of time. This is a simple way of putting it. But sufficient to show that while poetry depends on the *flux contained,* held within the form, in stasis, prose may intend such a limiting but cannot justify one. It has no beginning or end. It has only the length it happens to have. "Might be continued . . ." Just here is the key to its possible reach, that, in spite of itself, it has to continue, keep going—cannot stop.

So, in some sense, the usual idea of beginning and end has put upon prose an order alien to its nature. This is not to imply a 'necessary chaos.' It means only that it is, by nature, against conclusions—or is (as nature is) intent only on its present. It is the breaking out, of context, of form, and down or back, always to the progression, enforced by the nature of its content, and so determined.

It has neither beginning nor end.

3

> *"Are we not automatic, to think that because prose—and— the—novel did, since the 18th, & conspicuously, in the 19th, & dyingly, in the 20th, do a major job, that it need now be fruitful?"*

As soon as the novel, as soon as prose, generally, supposed for itself, a context other than what it might, on each occasion make, it had done itself the greatest possible disservice. And this is not to be mistaken. We can note, perhaps, that while poetry may have combined itself in several, to mean, one thing worked in the hands of several men, at certain times with success, prose has never been effectual so taken, as a job, or so treated. I can remember the notes that Kafka had written about his attempt to write a novel with Brod—or the more amusing attempts of Dylan Thomas, etc. Certainly, the novelist hates his neighbor, hates him for writing, to begin with, and hates him doubly, for writing prose. Perhaps this is a false lead. It matters little except that it can clear the sense of the necessary singleness of the man who writes prose. And that any constriction, is too much.

The suggestion that record-making can now be taken as one of the major jobs of those that make prose is wrong only in its supposition that there exists any occupation for prose, prior to its coming. It is wrong in the same way that positing any 'frame' for prose

is wrong. Prose is a plausible and profitable instrument for making records. But stories? Novels? One wonders if it is to the point to
set them an end before they have demonstrated their own. "As
Rousset, e.g., wrote *L'Univers concentrationnaire (not Les Jours de notre
mort)*—and, over a weekend, because he figured to die the next
week of the Causes; or Martin-Chauffier, who has been a novelist,
& who chose in *L'Homme et la bête,* to tell not even what he had
heard others say (the last vestige of the novelist!) but only & precisely what had happened to him; vide Joe Gould . . ."

Joe Gould's HISTORY. One wonders. Or, who put him to such
work? Joe Gould.

Pointless to argue such a thing. It is not that prose cannot be put
to such work, that it hasn't that capability, that it couldn't deal with
that end of things. Rather, like nothing else, it must be new. And if,
say, tradition concerns itself with these frames, then prose has no
tradition. None whatsoever. It should demand that it has none.
More than we, or they, may have spoken.

It could be, has been, the collection of ideas. And nothing better,
for such documentation. But records? It was the fact of its perspective, that made what it gave, of such, reliable. That it is without,
frame. What makes it reliable. That it owns to no master, that it
can't. Its terminals, ends, are fictitious. Someone dies. "It was the
end of THAT period . . ." But continual, that it repeats, goes over
and under, around. Has form, frame, only as it is such a going. As
someone had said of Stendhal—it all fell into exact place, exact.

It stands by itself.


4

> *"The reason why, at this juncture of time, one fights so hard for
> prose is that it enables him to get in, to go by, that head of his, to
> let it play over his things, outside objects . . ."*

To go back to Joyce. To that mistaking we have made of him; and
you may document this for yourselves or look to find who has made
of those books something beyond the man who may have written
them. Oddly enough, the most exact criticism of these things appeared at the same time that the books themselves did. At least,
that first interest prevented the fatal preoccupations with the 'purpose,' of Joyce, with his own use, as symbol. At least for a time.

Speaking of James, Pound had written that the logic of the pieces the former had written for the *Yellow Book* group was that need to push beyond the curve, in order to establish it. So, generally, position is established in prose, and intention. Hence, this idea of the assumed obliquity, itself a way of placing something, in the context. Is prose roundabout? It's not that question which should be asked. Any way could be the right one. What is got to, what is placed, would be the better thing to be asking, after it's done.

Again—de Gourmont's sentence, " . . . *d'écrire franchement ce qu'ils pensent—seul plaisir d'un écrivain* . . ." And could it be less, granting it must be more?

A new prose . . . Better to think of this, only, as what may now come. I think we can hang on to those who have left us something strong enough to carry over into this time. Prose cannot exist free of its ability to apply; it can't be faked. So it would be that Stendhal can still give us the sense, or one sense, of the order, the 'form,' not to be taken as the form of poetry, nor as we come back to it, that more basic form of prose. There is the fact that the more correct translation of Dostoevsky's *Notes from Underground* must be—"Notes from Under the Floor," or, "Out from the Cracks Like Any Roach."

Perhaps it will still be necessary to point to the fact that, while poetry will be the clear, the fact of the head, prose will be the coming, and going. Around. It is there that it can hit, beyond poetry. It is not a matter of better, or worse. There is no competition. The drift, in prose, and the way, of the swing, the reach—we have the necessary evidence, or I must believe we have.

> I am very old today, the sky is grey, I am not very well.
> Nothing can prevent madness.
> As an honourable man who abhors exaggeration, I do not know what to do . . .

We begin, or end, there.

# How to Write a Novel

*The Beetle Leg,* by John Hawkes. New York: New Directions, 1951.

The rules have been obvious enough—mainly the injunction to hold to 'character and action,' and one novelist, of at least some reputation, has said he was constitutionally in favor of 'plot.' But it means very little.

Otherwise, one can go back to even the hackneyed examples. *"The Life and Opinions of Tristram Shandy, Gent* . . . appeared on the 1st of January 1760." A simple fact; and from that time, hence, like they say, at least one major evidence, against the above rote, was there to be dealt with.

I am speaking, in short, of *time*—of what that is in a prose narrative, and of what it has done there. As frame, as the main means to a coherent order.

It is certainly very attractive. That is, it is a line, a very solid one, for the hoisting up of anything which may interest the novelist; his characters, etc., his apprehension of 'the meaning of life,' etc. And, more than that, what other continuum is possible; how else effect a reasonable series, how project, by language, the incident reality, say that it is there, and prove it?

At least that, for a clear sense of the problem. By some means or other, this demanded, a man must make of his narrative a cohesion of the things there occurring, must give them demonstrable rela-

*New Mexico Quarterly,* Summer 1952.

tion. Which is order of a kind; and we've gone wrong, only, in believing it to be of one kind, no other to be admitted.

Beyond humor, *Tristram Shandy* is the narrative of one man's attentions, of what they found to fasten on. That is a defensible comment—there is very clear writing in this book.

"The lines were very natural—for they were nothing at all to the purpose, says *Slawkenbergius*, and 'tis a pity there were no more of them; but whether it was the Seig. *Diego* was slow in composing verses—or the hostler quick in saddling mules—is not averred . . ."

Go at it another way. Take it as your own headache, and think, then, if what counts is that the day goes by, etc., etc.; or that something in it, precisely in, was of interest, and that made it all otherwise. This is the contrary—if one can fasten on there.

Similarly, one thing leads to another—with or without *time*. An instant is a precise formulation, even of a universe. It doesn't finally matter much whether it lead to another; it has its own logic. Or say, perhaps better, that there are two ways of evoking a reality: that it has place in *time*, or that it is existent in *space*. There is some choice between them, at least for the novelist.

"Early in 1880, in spite of a well-founded suspicion as to the advisability of perpetuating that race which has the sanction of the Lord and the disapproval of the people . . ." Whereas this present table, with the typewriter on it, two books, milk bottle, is something else again. Or clearly a different *field*. It is that sense I am intent on making clear.

To write of one is not to write of the other. There is the escape of *time*, that escape which *time* affords; so that the man dies, too soon, or the book ends.

What else. ("Is this a fit time, said my father to himself, to talk of PENSIONS and GRENADIERS?")

The divers techniques used to confront *time*, in the long narrative, are ultimately makeshift; they solve very little. Flashback, recall by certain of the characters, juxtaposition (too simply) of 'time' sequences—none of much use. Because, to be in that passage, to make that the sequence (that the days go by), is a definite commitment, and not to be dodged easily.

But put the weight on the other sense, of things shifting, among themselves—and *time* there to be a qualification among many—it is a release.

A release, immediately, of the very things themselves—not gratuitously, since relation is aimed at—why they all keep together.

And to the extent that *time* bears on that, all right, i.e., all right to make use of it. But not as the main line.

The present novel is attack on this ground. Clearly. Unequivocally aimed at that, to break *time* back to a use which isn't crippling. It is of very great interest.

# To Define

The process of definition is the intent of the poem, or is to that sense—"Peace comes of communication." Poetry stands in no need of any sympathy, or even goodwill. One acts from bottom, the root is the purpose quite beyond any kindness.

A poetry can act on this: "A poem is energy transferred from where the poet got it (he will have some several causations), by way of the poem itself to, all the way over to, the reader." One breaks the line of aesthetics, or that outcrop of a general division of knowledge. A sense of the KINETIC impels recognition of force. Force is, and therefore stays.

The means of a poetry are, perhaps, related to Pound's sense of the *increment of association;* usage coheres value. Tradition is an aspect of what anyone is now thinking—not what someone once thought. We make with what we have, and in this way anything is worth looking at. A tradition becomes inept when it blocks the necessary conclusion; it says we have felt nothing, it implies others have felt more.

A poetry denies its end in any *descriptive* act, I mean any act which leaves the attention outside the poem. Our anger cannot exist usefully without its objects, but a description of them is also a perpetuation. There is that confusion—one wants the thing to act on, and yet hates it. *Description* does nothing, it includes the object—it neither hates nor loves.

*Nine American Poets, Artisan* (Liverpool, 1953).

If one can junk these things, of the content which relates only to denial, the negative, the impact of dissolution—act otherwise, on other things. There is no country. Speech is an assertion of one man, by one man. "Therefore each speech having its own character the poetry it engenders will be peculiar to that speech also in its own intrinsic form."

# A Dilemma

Why people don't go out and get better jobs, or finally come to some sense of themselves which might allow a more profitable exploitation . . . On the one hand, there are too many people—you cannot kill them all, you cannot find a logic quite sufficient to do this. And if they will not die quickly enough with sickness, or tiredness, old age and the like, then at least they can be confined to those places where one will not have to, simply, consider them.

A logic is fashioned like this, a logic of impenetrable worthiness. It follows that, between a man and his wife, there must be constantly some means whereby she can spit on him—and he, likewise, on her. Love, at best, will become a question of sensation. And on good days she will sigh, "my lover . . . ," and on bad days she will spit, "my lover . . . ," etc. He will live in a room. With luck, someone will buy him, i.e., someone also bought, and so with means, will buy him—which is the hierarchy of how to live, literally. To make money—at the first, enough to live on, by which I mean, to eat with, to be clothed with, and then, very soon, also to allow that better stance, to be 'better' clothed, and so on.

But some people, if they are still 'people,' have been removed from this by war, by 'depression' areas, by many things finally, in terms of which they are neither very interesting nor important. And let me make very clear that this is *not* a question of any bitterness or sentimentality or whatever. Some people cannot 'live' any-

*Black Mountain Review*, Autumn 1954.

more. There is neither reason for them to nor room nor means nor
values, nor any of those things by which others, certainly more for-
tunate, may still claim 'significance.' And by much the same token,
it is a little hysterical to feel our own securities are endangered by
the specific reality of something like the hydrogen bomb, i.e., suppose one were to install, say, plumbing in a house, a toilet and
all that, and then the toilet is flushed, and, all things being equal—
can it be a surprise, or even the point, that (of course!) the toilet
flushed?

Heretofore our dangers have been of two kinds, the one (big)
metaphoric and the other (contained) literal. So that to trip on a
stone, then, meant, (a) we stubbed a toe (literal) and (b) this pain
was token of the possibility of all pain, accident, and what might
happen (metaphoric). Now enough is accomplished to make an
end to that, i.e., we can have the two as one. We can all die at
one time.

Which is not, really, a relief. It might be, just as for some people
any death not now too painful, not too long, might be. What is
there for an alternative except the dreary love too often exercised
as it is. Belief—in what. And so on. Dead people already, at best.

I am sorry myself not to care anymore, or not to care for much
beyond one or two things. That, say, to love anyone becomes more
impossible. "I did love . . . ," one says, etc. I still want to, etc. Perhaps
against the distortion, lying, deceit, viciousness, horror, cruelty, and
all that, it will still be possible to make that most minimal of defenses—at least the knowledge that there might be others likewise
confronted.

# A Note

I believe in a poetry determined by the language of which it is made. (Williams: "Therefore each speech having its own character the poetry it engenders will be peculiar to that speech also in its own intrinsic form.") I look to words, and nothing else, for my own redemption either as man or poet. Pound, early in the century, teaches the tradition of "man-standing-by-his-word," the problem of *sincerity,* which is never as simple as it may be made to seem. The poet, of all men, has least cause and least excuse to pervert his language, since what he markets is so little in demand. He must find his living elsewhere. His aim must never be deflected by anterior commitment, even to those whom he loves. Words cannot serve responsibly as an apology for those who may wish to make them one.

I mean then *words*—as opposed to content. I care what the poem says, only as a poem—I am no longer interested in the exterior attitude to which the poem may well point, as signboard. That concern I have found it best to settle elsewhere. I will not be misled by the "niceness" of any sentiment, or its converse, malevolence. I do not think a poet is necessarily a nice person. I think the poem's morality is contained as a term of its structure, and is there to be determined and nowhere else. (Pound: "Prosody is the total articulation of the sound in a poem.") Only craft determines the morality of a poem.

Louis Zukofsky offers *A Test of Poetry* as "the range of pleasure it offers as sight, sound, and intellection." I am pleased by that poem

*Nomad*, Winter–Spring 1960.

which makes use of myself and my intelligence, as a partner to its declaration. It does not matter what I am told—it matters, very much, how I am there used. Our world has been so delivered to the perversion of language (the word *qua* trick or persuader) that my own soul, such as I know it, comes to life in whatever clarities are offered to it. Poems allow me to go on living, and I am grateful for my life.

# A Note on the Local

The local is not a place but a place in a given man—what part of it he has been compelled or else brought by love to give witness to in his own mind. And that is THE form, that is, the whole thing, as whole as it can get.

I think we will be fools to be embarrassed by it. We know the other neatness possible, the way of the neat pattern, and the dodging which it must call for. Grace has no part in that. At some point reached by us, sooner or later, there is no longer much else but ourselves, in the place given us. To make that present, and actual for other men, is not an embarrassment, but love.

*First Person,* no. 1, 1961.

# A Quick Graph

1. Recent BBC broadcasts of Pound interviews summarize the following:
   a) Writing: "You can't have a literature without curiosity. You cannot have a literature without *curiosity*. And when a writer's curiosity dies out, he is finished. You can do all the tricks you like, but without curiosity you get no literature with any life in it. . . ."
   b) Literacy: "A man has a right to have his ideas examined one at a time. . . ." (This parallels another comment made earlier, to the effect: literacy consists of the ability to recognize the same idea in different formulations. Both relate to Pound's insistence on the need to be able to dissociate ideas, i.e., to separate those living from those dead.)

2. Measure—which Dr. Williams continues to hammer at, as in a recent mimeographed sheet, "The American Idiom":

   "We must go forward uncertainly it may be, but courageously as we may. Be assured that measure in mathematics as in verse is unescapable, so in reply to the fixed foot of the ancient line including the Elizabethans we must have a reply: it is the variable foot which we are beginning to discover after Whitman's advent. . . ."

One academic, Scully Bradley, some years ago made use of a shifting stress concept in an attempt to 'scan' Whitman—prompted quite probably by the need to regularize common to such men; yet he showed understanding of the fact that the stress *may* be variable and yet cohesive in over-all effect. Too, he made the point of the 'rhyming' implicit in parallel or recurrent thought patterns (much as those used by Allen Ginsberg). Our ears tell us, certainly, that syllables may be grouped in a poem in such a way that they defy usual concepts of metric, and yet maintain a decided rhythm. In practice this has long been established. What does need revision is the old practice of 'phrasal' grouping, *qua* line, a loose solution tending to fall apart as the 'idea' the phrase implies exhausts itself and/or reaches its end. Poems of this sort read: The man sat down/ on the chair/ and lifted his foot/ into the air, etc. At no point should the rhythms *peculiar* to the given word, in the context it comes to *define,* be lost track of. *All* rhythm is specific. (Which in turn explains the boredom implicit in *generalized* iambics, etc.)

3. A sense of order—Louis Zukofsky defines one in his essay, "Poetry":*

> "With respect to such action ["utterance," i.e., the movement of spoken words toward poetry] the specialized concern of the poet will be, first, its proper conduct—a concern to avoid clutter no matter how many details outside and in the head are ordered. This does not presume that the style will be the man, but rather that the order of his syllables will define his awareness of order. For his second and major aim is not to show himself but that order that of itself can speak to all men."

Or reading backwards:

> "The choice for science and poetry when symbols or words stop measuring is to stop speaking."

Such order proves as well "the contest any poet has with his art: working toward a perception that is his mind's peace," which Zukofsky has spoken of in *Bottom: On Shakespeare.*

4. Range—which can be variously characterized:
   a) Zukofsky: " . . . the scientific definition of poetry can be based on nothing less than the world, the entire humanly known world."

*Kulchur, no. 8, 1962.

b) Olson's *Maximus* has built from a like premise, with the
   corollary:

> He left him naked
> the man said, and
> nakedness
> is what one means
>
> that all start up
> to the eye and soul
> as though it had never
> happened before

c) It is equally Duncan's:

> that foot   informed
> by the weight of all things
>         that can be elusive
> no more than a nearness to the mind
>         of a single image

Range implies both what there is to deal with, and the wherewithal we can bring to that activity. Range describes the world in
the limits of perception. It is the "field" in the old Pythagorean
sense that "terms," as John Burnet says, are "boundary stones"
and the place they so describe the "field" itself.

# "Statement" for the Paterson Society

A poem is a peculiar instance of language's uses, and goes well beyond the man writing—finally to the anonymity of any song. In this sense it may be that a poet works toward a final obliteration of himself, making that all the song—at last free of his own time and place. It is curious that this can be most true of that most personal, wherein the man leaves the environment of years and faces, to make his own the poem. But he can only do this, it seems to me, by the most scrupulous localism—because only the particular instance proves free in this way.

Again and again I find myself saved, in words—helped, allowed, returned to possibility and hope. In the dilemma of some literal context a way is found in the words which may speak of it.

*Guatemala*
*January 31, 1961*

*Floating Bear,* no. 6, 1961.

# Why Bother?

An art begins prior to its conclusion—which is why there can be, with great use, an occasion offering that sense of means which conclusions per se deny. It can be put more simply. A magazine, not interested in being either the last word apropos some function, or taste, or simply a reflection of what is already 'valued' speciously or not—such a magazine may define the new possibility by being, quite literally, the place where it can be formulated.

No matter what becomes of it, art is local, local to a place and to a person, or group of persons, or just what's in the air despite how vague that sounds. It happens somewhere, not everywhere. When it does so happen everywhere, it has become a consequence of taste purely, a vogue or fashion, and/or what Pound calls 'style of the period,' and definition has given way to a reflection of a given effect.

No man can work free of the influence of those whom he may respect in his own art, and why 'originality' should imply, in any sense, that he should, is hard to follow. The light moves, so to speak, and those who see it have secured an 'originality' quite beyond that qualified by terms of personality or intent. In poetry, as in other arts, what is learned is first learned by the example, that is, by what exists in the art as a complex definition of possibilities: literally, this or that poem. Taste operates here as well, of course, but again Pound is relevant in that he said, damn your taste, I would

*Tish*, September 14, 1962.

like first to sharpen your perceptions, after which your taste can take care of itself.

May I submit that when the poem, or the opinion, or the taste, has come to that security of whatever large magazine—friendly or not—one may point to, then all has become primarily taste, an approval of taste, and that the actual work of definition which allowed taste its turn has gone?

A friend said once of his wife, that she said she wanted to be a singer, but what she really wanted to be was famous. One can be famous in many magazines, but not in those given to the definition of what a poem, right now, can be. There are no readers, and there are, even, few writers, who will care to be bothered by what may be an attention alien to their own. Can you blame a German, French, English poet for not caring specifically about what you face, here and now, as problems? But can you care for his, if all your mind is centered on the peculiar structure of that language given you, to effect, by its forms and its sounds, what it is, precisely, that you feel only as a poem? With nothing at all sentimental about it, and "Only the poem / only the made poem, to get said what must / be said . . ." as Williams writes all his life.

It is very possible that what one defines, as means, as possibilities, will prove only a temporary instance, a place soon effaced by other use, as when a whole city block is leveled to make a parking lot, or park. But that is the risk. One cannot avoid it, or do otherwise.

I believe in a magazine which is the specific issue of a few men, facing similar problems, places, things. They may, given ability, find the next step all must take if only because they are forced to take each such step with their own feet.

# A Sense of Measure

I am wary of any didactic program for the arts and yet I cannot ignore the fact that poetry, in my own terms of experience, obtains to an unequivocal order. What I deny, then, is any assumption that that order can be either acknowledged or gained by intellectual assertion, or will, or some like intention to shape language to a purpose which the literal act of writing does not itself discover. Such senses of pattern as I would admit are those having to do with a preparatory ritual, and however vague it may sound, I mean simply that character of invocation common to both prayer and children's games.

But it is more relevant here to make understood that I do not feel the usual sense of *subject* in poetry to be of much use. My generation has a particular qualification to make of this factor because it came of age at a time when a man's writing was either admitted or denied in point of its agreement with the then fashionable concerns of 'poetic' comment. William Carlos Williams was, in this way, as much criticized for the things he said as for the way in which he said them. I feel that 'subject' is at best a material of the poem, and that poems finally derive from some deeper complex of activity.

I am interested, for example, to find that "automatic or inspirational speech tends everywhere to fall into metrical patterns" as E. R. Dodds notes in *The Greeks and the Irrational*. Blake's "Hear the voice of the Bard" demands realization of a human phenomenon, not recognition of some social type. If we think of the orders of

*Times Literary Supplement,* August 6, 1964.

experience commonly now acknowledged, and of the incidence of what we call *chance*, it must be seen that no merely intellectual program can find reality, much less admit it, in a world so complexly various as ours has proved.

Recent studies in this country involved with defining the so-called creative personality have defined very little indeed and yet one of their proposals interests me. It is that men and women engaged in the arts have a much higher tolerance for disorder than is the usual case. This means, to me, that poets among others involved in comparable acts have an intuitive apprehension of a coherence which permits them a much greater admission of the real, the phenomenal world, than those otherwise placed can allow. Perhaps this is little more than what Otto Rank said some time ago in *Art and Artist* concerning the fact that an artist does die with each thing he does, insofar as he depends upon the conclusion of what possibilities do exist for him. Paradoxically, nothing can follow from that which is altogether successful. But again this risk is overcome—in the imagination—by trust of that coherence which no other means can discover. It would seem to me that occasional parallels between the arts and religion may well come from this coincidence of attitude, at least at times when neither philosophy nor psychology is the measure of either.

Lest I be misunderstood—by 'religion' I mean a basic *visionary* experience, not a social order or commitment, still less a moral one. Gary Snyder tells me that the Indians consider the experience of visions a requisite for attaining manhood. So they felt their enemy, the whites, not men, simply that so few of the latter had ever gained this measure of their own phenomenality. In this sense I am more interested, at present, in what is *given* to me to write apart from what I might intend. I have never explicitly known—before writing—what it was that I would say. For myself, articulation is the intelligent ability to recognize the experience of what is so given, in words. I do not feel that such a sense of writing is 'mindless' or 'automatic' in a pejorative way. At the end of *Paterson V* Williams writes:

> —Learning with age to sleep my life away:
> saying      .
>
> The measure intervenes, to measure is all we know . . .

I am deeply interested in the act of such *measure*, and I feel it to involve much more than an academic sense of metric. There can no longer be a significant discussion of the meter of a poem in relation to iambs and like terms because linguistics has offered a much more detailed and sensitive register of this part of a poem's activity. Nor do I feel measure to involve the humanistic attempt to relate all phenomena to the scale of human appreciation thereof. And systems of language—the world of discourse which so contained Sartre et al.—are also for me a false situation if it is assumed they offer a modality for being, apart from description. I am not at all interested in describing anything.

I want to give witness not to the thought of myself—that specious concept of identity—but, rather, to what I am as simple agency, a thing evidently alive by virtue of such activity. I want, as Charles Olson says, to come into the world. Measure, then, is my testament. What uses me is what I use and in that complex measure is the issue. I cannot cut down trees with my bare hand, which is measure of both tree and hand. In that way I feel that poetry, in the very subtlety of its relation to image and rhythm, offers an intensely various record of such facts. It is equally one of them.

# "Poems are a complex"

Poems are a complex, and exist by virtue of many things. First, they are a structure of sounds and rhythms which cohere to inform the reader (whether he listen aloud or in silence) with a recognition of their order. In this respect, I much agree with Louis Zukofsky's note of his own poetics, which, as he says, comprise a function having as lower limit speech, and upper limit music. Pound's note, that "Prosody is the articulation of the total sound of a poem," has equal relevance.

Since words are the material, and words have meanings in other senses, that fact also has pertinence. But I do not feel that *thing* in the language we call a poem has to do with a literal issue of semantic meaning. Yet that aspect of meaning is a material also, and clearly enters into the issue of image, or statement—or all such effects of something said.

I think for myself the primary term is that words can move in the measure of song, although I do not wish to confuse poetry with music. But in a poem I tend to hear whatever can be called its melody long before I have reached an understanding of all that it might mean.

Finally, I use several measures though never with much literal consciousness. Two further statements of Pound's long ago attracted me: "Only emotion endures . . ." and "Nothing counts save the quality of the emotion. . . ." I have used that sense with respect to all instances of writing, but I would feel, as he, that poetry is that

*A Nosegay in Black*, Autumn 1966.

most fully charged with meaning. To that I would now add a recent emphasis of Olson's: "That which exists through itself is what is called meaning."

In other words, poems are not referential, or at least not importantly so. They have 'meaning' in that they do 'exist through themselves.' I have no very clear sense of where they may come from, but I have felt them most evident when least assumed. Lorca's "Theory and Function of the *Duende*" is interesting to me, although I would not so simply discredit either the Angel or the Muse to gain the "dark sounds" only. But I do feel poems to involve an occasion to which a man pays obedience, and which intentions alone never yield.

There are many ways indeed to say any of this, and I can't feel any one to be sufficient. I think I first felt a poem to be what might exist in words as primarily the fact of its own activity. Later, of course, I did see that poems might comment on many things, and reveal many attitudes and qualifications. Still, it was never what they said *about* things that interested me. I wanted the poem itself to exist and that could never be possible as long as some subject significantly elsewhere was involved. There had to be an independence derived from the very fact that words are *things* too. Poems gave me access to this fact more than any other possibility in language.

*July 30, 1965*

# A Statement about the Poem "The Name"

My own centers of feeling have much to do with my family—literally my wife, and my three daughters. Feeling, or perhaps best to call it *emotion,* is for me the most significant content of a poem. I don't always or even often care what a poem is talking *about,* but I do care very markedly about the senses and the intensity of the emotion thus engendered. This poem, then, was and is a way of feeling about the fact of my daughter—a way of making that feeling evident for a time when, perhaps, it will be a pleasure and reassurance for her to know both how she came to be, and how then that fact was felt. It is equally for all my daughters.

Too, I like the way this poem moves, in its lines, in the way certain words pick up echoes of rhyme in others, sometimes very clearly, sometimes only as a shading. I like the syncopation of the rhythms—most evident if you will make a distinct pause (called a *terminal juncture!*) at the end of each line, and will read the words relaxedly yet clearly, one by one. I feel poetry as a complex of sounds and rhythms, which move in a parallel to music. In fact, I believe it is just this complex that makes poetry be the very singular *fact* of words which it is.

*Poems for Young Readers,* National Council of Teachers of English, November 24–26, 1966.

# Notes Apropos "Free Verse"

I think the term "free verse" proves awkward just now in that it seems anchored in an opposition to a sense of traditional verse patterns, which are, because of their situation as history, more trusted. "Free" has such a width of associations—"free man," "free fall," "free prizes," etc. Too, it seems relevant that this sense of verse comes largely from American practice and that its primary figure is Whitman.

It nonetheless provokes a real situation. For example, Yvor Winters' tracking of "impulse" as informing principle in Emerson's discussions of poetry, as equally in Whitman's, and then in Crane's, cites the significance of this way of stating oneself in poetry as well as the historical range of its occasion. If one thinks of the literal root of the word verse, "a line, furrow, turning—*vertere,* to turn . . . ," he will come to a sense of "free verse" as that instance of writing in poetry which "turns" upon an occasion intimate with, in fact, the issue of, its own nature rather than to an abstract decision of "form" taken from a prior instance.

The point is, simply enough, why does the "line" thus "turn" and what does inform it in that movement? Clearly to say that it is "free" or equally that it is "unfree" is to say nothing of much interest. I was impressed a few years ago, reading Joshua Whatmough's *Language,* to find him saying, as a linguist, that there was no explicit understanding as to why poetry "turns" in any instance at the precise moment it does—that is, no device of measure then defined

*Naked Poetry,* ed. Stephen Berg and Robert Mezey (Indianapolis, Ind.: Bobbs-Merrill, 1969).

could anticipate the precise articulations of this shifting in verse, no matter the verse be "traditional" or "free." Linguistics has, in other respects, qualified usefully the assumptions of traditional metrical systems in making evident the varying "weights" observable in "stress" (at least four in number) which had previously been dealt with in patterns which qualified syllables as "stressed" or "un-stressed"—in short, a very imprecise and clumsy approximation of the activity.

I am myself hopeful that linguistic studies will bring to contemporary criticism a vocabulary and method more sensitive to the basic *activity* of poetry and less dependent upon assumed senses of literary style. Jakobson's use of "contiguity" and "parallelism" as two primary modes of linguistic coherence interests me. Too, I would like to see a more viable attention paid to syntactical environment, to what I can call crudely "grammartology."

However, these are senses of things still far from my own experience in writing. So, briefly, as to that. I feel, as Robert Duncan put it, "a kind of readiness," much like that makes one feel like taking a walk, some imminence of occasion that has not as yet become literal. I have never, to my own recollection, anticipated the situation of my own writing in the sense of what I was about to say. It is certain enough that preoccupations recur—"themes," as Duncan has called them—but how these might gain statement as writing could not be proposed except as the literal writing then found means. I was struck by a comment Franz Kline once made: "If I paint what I know, I bore myself. If I paint what you know, I bore you. So I paint what I don't know. . . ." I write what I don't know. I feel the situation parallel to what Pollock suggests by his statement, "when I am in my painting. . . ." This, I feel, to be the condition Charles Olson defines in the key essay, "Projective Verse":

> From the moment he [a poet] ventures into FIELD COMPOSI-
> TION—put himself in the open—he can go by no track other than
> the one the poem under hand declares, for itself. Thus he has to be-
> have, and be, instant by instant, aware of some several forces just now
> beginning to be examined. . . .

Pound notes Yeats' dependence upon "a chune in his head"—and it is that equally, an ordering that is taking place as one writes, which one follows much as he might the melodic line of some song.

The simplest way I have found to make clear my own sense of writing in this respect is to use the analogy of driving. The road, as it were, is creating itself momently in one's attention to it, there, visibly, in front of the car. There is no reason it should go on forever, and if one does so assume it, it very often disappears all too actually. When Pound says, "we must understand what is happening," one sense of his meaning I take to be this necessary attention to what is happening in the writing (the road) one is, in the sense suggested, following. In that way there is nothing mindless about the procedure. It is, rather, a respect for the possibilities of such attention that brings Allen Ginsberg to say, "Mind is shapely." Mind, thus engaged, permits experience of "order" far more various and intensive than habituated and programmed limits of its subtleties can recognize.

I think each man writing will have some way, so to speak, intimate with his own condition. That is, I feel there will be an inherent condition for an ordering intimate to the fact of himself as literal organism. Again, one of the several virtues of Olson's "Projective Verse" was that of returning to poetry its relation with *physiological* condition.

For my own part I feel a rhythmic possibility, an inherent periodicity in the weights and durations of words, to occur in the first few words, or first line, or lines, of what it is I am writing. Because I am the man I am, and think in the patterns I do, I tend to posit intuitively a balance of *four,* a foursquare circumstance, be it walls of a room or legs of a table, that reassures me in the movement otherwise to be dealt with. I have, at times, made reference to my own interest when younger (and continuingly) in the music of Charlie Parker—an intensive variation on 'foursquare' patterns such as "I've Got Rhythm." Listening to him play, I found he lengthened the experience of time, or shortened it, gained a very subtle experience of 'weight,' all by some decision made within the context of what was called "improvisation"—but what I should rather call the experience of possibility within the limits of his materials (sounds and durations) and their environment (all that they had as what Pound calls "increment of association" but equally all they had as literal condition, their phenomenological fact). There is an interview with Dizzy Gillespie (in the *Paris Review,* No. 35) in which he speaks of rhythm particularly in a way I very much respect. If *time* is measure of *change,* our sense of it becomes what we can apprehend as significant condition of *change*—in poetry as well as in music.

In any case, Williams showed me early on that rhythm was a very subtle experience, and that words might share equivalent duration even though "formally" they seemed in no way to do so. Pound said, "LISTEN to the sound that it makes," and Olson, in like emphasis, made it evident that we could only go "By ear."

Finally, there was and is the fact of, what it was one had to say— in Louis Zukofsky's sense, "Out of deep need. . . ." I never spoke easily and had to write, for the most part, just as adamantly. There is a section of Williams' "The Desert Music" which might be my own:

> You seem quite normal. Can you tell me? Why
> does one want to write a poem?
>
>           Because it's there to be written.
>
> Oh. A matter of inspiration then?
>
>                Of necessity.
>
> Oh. But what sets it off?
>
>      I am that he whose brains
>      are scattered
>        aimlessly . . .

Why after all say any of this—but for some fear one is not "doing it right" and isn't that, even, the occasion for such argument as still can exist on the subject of "free verse," which is at best some "historical" label. Williams, at the end of "The Desert Music," says all that anyone can:

>           I *am* a poet! I
> am. I am. I am a poet, I reaffirmed, ashamed
>
> Now the music volleys through as in
> a lonely moment I hear it. Now it is all
> about me. The dance! The verb detaches itself
> seeking to become articulate
>
>      And I could not help thinking
>      of the wonders of the brain that
>      hears that music and of our
>      skill sometimes to record it.

*December 11, 1966*

# "I'm given to write poems"

I'm *given* to write poems. I cannot anticipate their occasion. I have used all the intelligence that I can muster to follow the possibilities that the poem "under hand," as Olson would say, is declaring, but I cannot anticipate the necessary conclusions of the activity, nor can I judge in any sense, in moments of writing, the significance of that writing more than to recognize that it is being *permitted* to continue. I'm trying to say that, in writing, at least as I have experienced it, one is *in* the activity, and that fact itself is what I feel so deeply the significance of anything that we call poetry.

For some sense, then, of how it was I came to be involved with poetry, at the outset I was much more interested in *writing* apart from its designated modes, and perhaps I am characteristically American in that respect. To begin with, I was shy of the word "poet" and all its associations in a world I was then intimate with. It was not, in short, a fit attention for a young man raised in the New England manner, compact of puritanically deprived senses of speech and sensuality. Life was real and life was earnest, and one had best get on with it. The insistent preoccupation with words did begin for me early, just that I did want so much to know what people were saying, and what, more precisely, they meant by it.

I think the most significant encounter for me as a young man trying to write was that found in the work of William Carlos Williams.

Lecture delivered at the Literarisches Colloquium, Berlin, January 1967; published in *Ein Gedicht und sein Autor / Lyrik und Essay*, Herausgegeben und mit Einleitungen versehen von Walter Höllerer (Berlin, 1967), and in *Harper's Bazaar*, July 1967.

He engaged language at a level both familiar and active to my own senses, and made of his poems an intensively *emotional* perception, however evident his intelligence. Despite his insistence on his Mediterranean connections, so to speak, he was as Puritan as I—or Lawrence, or Thoreau or the Melville of *Pierre*.

Otherwise, the forties—the time in which I came of age—were complicated in many bitter ways indeed. Not the least of the problems then evident for someone trying to realize him or herself in the world was the confusion about the very nature of "literature" itself. Coming from New England, I felt awkwardness about books to begin with, because they were for me often instances of social mark or measure, even at times a privilege of intellectual order— just as Hardy speaks of them in *Jude the Obscure*. I was very shy about communicating my own commitments in reading, and yet I used books as a very real *place* to be. Not merely an escape from the world—the difficulty was how to get *into* it, not away—books proved a place very deeply open to me, at moments of reading, in a sense few others were ever to be.

Thinking of that, let me note kinship with another writer— Robert Duncan—who has played a very important role in my life, both as mentor, very often, and as one whom I feel to share with me this particular sense of world, and writing, and poetry, which I most deeply respect. In a collection of his called *The Opening of the Field*, significantly enough, the first poem begins:

*OFTEN I AM PERMITTED TO RETURN TO A MEADOW*

Then continues:

> as if it were a scene made-up by the mind,
> that is not mine, but is a made place,
> that is mine, it is so near to the heart,
> an eternal pasture folded in all thought
> so that there is a hall therein
>
> that is a made place, created by light
> wherefrom the shadows that are forms fall.

This sense of a poem—that *place*, that *meadow*—has echoes of so many things that are intimate to my own sense of the reality experienced in writing. One would find that field or "meadow" in Whitman also, and it would be equally the sense of place I feel Allen Ginsberg many times to be entering, to be speaking of or longing for. Charles Olson too possesses its occasion in his sense of "open" verse or that *open field*, as he insists upon it, in composition.

I have found it deeply in H.D.'s writing: "I go where I love and am loved. . . ." And in Pound's "What thou lovest well remains,/ the rest is dross. . . ."

> What thou lov'st well shall not be reft from thee
> What thou lov'st well is thy true heritage
> Whose world, or mine or theirs
>                         or is it of none?
> First came the seen, then thus the palpable
>     Elysium, though it were in the halls of hell,
> What thou lovest well is thy true heritage. . . .

All of these are, to my own mind, not only tokens but evidences of a place, a very distinct and definite *place*, that poetry not only creates but itself issues from—and one in writing is, as Duncan says, "permitted to return," to go there, to be in that reality. There is a poem by Allen Ginsberg which has always moved me deeply. He calls it simply "Song" and it is included in the first collection of his poetry, *Howl*. The closing lines of this poem are:

> yes, yes,
>             that's what
> I wanted,
>             I always wanted,
> I always wanted,
>             to return
> to the body
>             where I was born.

That body is the "field" and is equally the experience of it. It is, then, to "return" not to oneself as some egocentric center, but to experience oneself as *in* the world, thus, through this agency or fact we call, variously, "poetry."

In the same passage quoted from Duncan, there is another sense of much interest to me in the emphasis he puts upon "made": "a scene," as he says, "made-up by the mind,/ that is not mine, but is a made place,/ that is mine. . . ." And again, two lines following: "there is a hall therein/ that is a made place. . . ." This emphasis takes its occasion from the sense of poet as maker, going back to the Greek root, *poiein*, "to make."

One of the few books I've ever had that was stolen—not by me, as it happened, but by a girl I persuaded to steal it for me—was William Carlos Williams' *The Wedge*. It proved *fire* of a very real order, and, for the record, was subsequently stolen from me in turn when I was teaching at Black Mountain in the mid-fifties. In

1944, when it was first published and shortly after which I got hold of it, its content was a revelation to me. In the preface Williams makes this statement:

> When a man makes a poem, makes it, mind you, he takes words as he finds them interrelated about him and composes them—without distortion which would mar their exact significances—into an intense expression of his perceptions and ardors that they may constitute a revelation in the speech that he uses. It isn't what he *says* that counts as a work of art, it's what he makes, with such intensity of perception that it lives with an intrinsic movement of its own to verify its authenticity.

I think this is very much the way Americans are given to speak—not in some dismay that they haven't another way to speak, but, rather, that they feel that they, perhaps more than any other group of people upon the earth at this moment, have had both to imagine and thereby to *make* that reality which they are then given to live in. It is as though they had to *realize* the world anew. They are, as Charles Olson says, "the last first people." Now, in contemporary fact, they are also the oldest issue of that imagination—even in some ways bitterly so, because they have thus inherited the world as not only a place to live in, but also as that reality for which they are responsible in every possible sense.

However, I would mistake my own experience of poetry if I were to propose it as something merely *intentional,* and what men may imagine, either as worlds or poems, is not simply a *purpose* either may satisfy. Williams also had no sense of patness in the making of a poem, or of a world—but felt, as he says in one of his own poems:

<pre>
        Be patient that I address you in a poem,
                there is no other
                        fit medium.
    The mind
                lives there. It is uncertain,
                        can trick us and leave us
        agonized. But for resources
                what can equal it?
                        There is nothing. We
        should be lost
                without its wings to
                        fly off upon.
    The mind is the cause of our distresses
                but of it we can build anew.
                        Oh something more than
</pre>

it flies off to:
        a woman's world,
                of crossed sticks, stopping
thought. A new world
      is only a new mind.
           And the mind and the poem
are all apiece.

To put it simply indeed, it is not the intention to write that matters, but that one *can*—that such a possibility *can* exist in which the mind may make evident its resources apart from the limits of intention and purpose.

In "The Desert Music"—for myself the loveliest form he left us—Williams makes further qualification of the poem in its peculiar and singular function of *making real:*

                        Only the poem
only the made poem, to get said what must
be said, not to copy nature, sticks
in our throats

The law? The law gives us nothing
but a corpse, wrapped in a dirty mantle.
The law is based on murder and confinement,
long delayed,
but this, following the insensate music,
is based on the dance:

                 an agony of self-realization
bound into a whole
by that which surrounds us

                I cannot escape

I cannot vomit it up

Only the poem!

Only the made poem, the verb calls it
                into being.

*Act* becomes the primary issue of "verb," or *verbum,* a word. "In the beginning was the Word"—and the word was the *reality of the imagination.* The "music," which the poem's title emphasizes and which becomes so central a content in the poem's activity, is that which vivifies, the *anima mundi,* lifeness and/or life itself. Our response to it or what it creates, its effects in the reality we are given, is the "dance."

Now the music volleys through as in
a lonely moment I hear it. Now it is all

about me. The dance! The verb detaches itself
seeking to become articulate

Poems are very specific kinds of *dancing*, because language is that
possibility most specific to our condition as human beings. But I do
not speak easily of these things because I feel, always, a timidity and
confusion trying to isolate a sense that can only be experienced in
the literal fact of the poem itself. It is as though I were trying to
make actual a sense of wetness apart from water itself.

It is possible, nonetheless, to continue now to use those men I
have used so much, to make evident what senses of poetry have
been for me insistent. In "Maximus, to Gloucester" Charles Olson
gives measure of the occasion in a way that informs my own:

> He left him naked,
> the man said, and
> nakedness
> is what one means
>
> that all start up
> to the eye and soul
> as though it had never
> happened before

My sense of his statement is this: in the fact of our lives we are
brought to primary situations, primary terms of experience—what
they might have meant by "first things first" but probably didn't.
"Nakedness" is to stand manifestly in one's own condition, in that
necessary *freshness*, however exposed, because all things are particular and reality itself is the specific content of an instant's possibility. In poems we realize, not in discursive or secondary manner,
but with this implicit and absolutely consequential fact of *firstness*,
terms of our own life, manifestations of that life which, otherwise,
are most awkwardly acknowledged. It is, again, that "field" that
Robert Duncan speaks of as being "permitted" to enter. First things.
We arrive in poems at the condition of life most viable and most
primal in our own lives.

I've said that I feel myself to be a poet who is *given* to write. And
I'm even awkward about using that designation, that is, to call myself so, a poet—because I do not feel I have that decision in it. Yet
the complexity of the dilemma seems to me a very real one. How
shall we understand Williams' painfully marked insistence just before the close of "The Desert Music":

I *am* a poet! I
am. I am. I am a poet, I reaffirmed, ashamed

In America, we are certainly not poets simply, nor much of the time.

The saints of my own calendar are saints of this exposure, beginning with Columbus and like men whose imagination realized, *reified,* one might say, the world I live in. They are Poe—who, as Williams makes clear, forced the *local* to yield him a world apart from the habits of English manner; Whitman—for the *permission* of life he insisted upon; Melville—the primary *imagination* of the isolation of our condition; Pound—who, like any Yankee, makes *intelligence* an invention of necessity; Hart Crane—whose "failure" regained the *possibility* of our response to what we are given to feel. It may well be that in the absence of such allusive society as European literature, in its own condition, has necessarily developed, the American in contrast must so realize each specific thing of his own— "as though it had never/ happened before." I think of Williams' sharply contemptuous answer to the British English professor, met with in Seattle, Washington, of all places, who asked him after a reading, "where he got his language"—to which Williams replied, "Out of the mouths of Polish mothers"—meaning not Polish, but the harsh, crude, blocked "poor English" of those immigrant women he had as patients in his profession as a doctor. My "saints," then, are those men who defined for me an explicit possibility in the speech that I was given to use, who made the condition of being American not something chauvinistically national but the intimate fact of one life in one place at one time.

To speak then of the writing itself, which I can do only tentatively—just that I am persuaded by Heisenberg that "observation impedes function"—I have again much depended upon senses of procedure and examples (which are, of course, the point) given me by such men. In the forties there was so much talk *about* the poem, about levels of meaning, ambiguities, symbols, allusions. It was even felt that criticism itself would prove the most significant literary activity of the time.

Pound, in contrast, spoke of the literal condition of the writing, and it was he I used as guide—and continue to now, twenty years later, because his advice proved facts of perception as active to my mind now as when I first came to them. For example, his quotation from Remy de Gourmont, "Freely to write what one chooses is the sole pleasure of a writer," continues for me the only actual measure of the occasion I am aware of. He gave me the experience of integrity as "Man standing by his word." More, he spoke so clearly of the explicit situation of writing:

> In making a line of verse (and thence building the lines into passages) you have certain primal elements:
> That is to say, you have the various 'articulate sounds' of the language, of its alphabet, that is, and the various groups of letters in syllables.
> These syllables have differing weights and durations
>> A. original weights and durations
>> B. weights and durations that seem naturally imposed on them by the other syllable groups around them.
> Those are the medium wherewith the poet cuts his design in TIME.

Against the arguments of taste and opinion which criticism so largely depends upon, Pound called attention to the character of the activity:

> Rhythm is a form cut into TIME, as a design is determined SPACE. . . .
> LISTEN to the sound that it makes . . .

However, it is really Charles Olson I must thank for whatever *freedom* I have as a poet, and I would value him equally with Pound and Williams and those others I have mentioned. *Freedom* has always been for me a difficult experience in that, when younger, I felt it had to propose senses of experience and of the world I was necessarily *not* in possession of—something in that way one might escape to. I mistook, I think, the meaning of "freely to write what one chooses," which both de Gourmont and Pound may well have had in mind, because I took "freely" to mean "without significant limit" and "chooses" to be an act of will. I therefore was slow in realizing the nature of Olson's proposal, that "Limits/ are what any of us/ are inside of," just that I had taken such "limits" to be a frustration of possibility rather than the literal possibility they in fact must provoke. Despite Pound—or rather, because I could not hope to gain such means as he had—I had to find my own way, and at first I was completely ignorant of what it might be.

In consequence, what Olson made clear to me during the late forties and early fifties was of very great use. I am speaking of the *kind* of thinking that is evident in his essay, "Projective Verse," written during the same time. Let me quote an instance:

The objects which occur at every given moment of composition (of recognition, we can call it) are, can be, must be treated exactly as they do occur therein and not by any ideas or preconceptions from outside the poem, must be handled as a series of objects in field in such a way that a series of tensions (which they also are) are made to *hold*, and to hold exactly inside the content and the context of the poem which has forced itself, through the poet and them, into being.

Not long ago, in conversation, Robert Duncan qualified his sense of *choice* as being *recognition*, that is, choice is significantly the act of recognition, and I believe it. What one "chooses" in writing is importantly of this nature, for me, and composition is the fact and effect of such activity. One isn't putting things *into* poems, then, at least not as my own experience of writing informs me. There is never a "subject" *about* which one constructs an activity called "poetry." Nor can one, as Williams says, "copy nature," take from that which is elsewise informed some felicitious appearance, whether a rhyme or a so-called sentiment.

However best it might be put, what Olson made evident to me was that writing could be an intensely specific revelation of one's own content, and of the world the fact of any life must engage. It has nothing to do with "personalism"—which, like personality, is a mirror or reflective image sense, a cosmetic of intentions. To the contrary, what emerges in the writing I most value is a content which cannot be anticipated, which "tells you what you don't know," which you subvert, twist, or misrepresent only on peril of death.

What I have written I knew little of until I had written it. If at times I have said that I enjoy what I write, I mean that writing is for me the most viable and open condition of possibility in the world. Things have happened there, as they have happened nowhere else—and I am not speaking of "make-believe," which, be it said, is "as real as real can be." In poems I have both discovered and borne testament to my life in ways no other possibility has given me. Can I *like* all that I may prove to be, or does it matter? Am I merely living for my own approval? In writing it has seemed to me that such small senses of existence were altogether gone, and that, at last, the world "came true." Far from being its limit or director, the wonder is that I have found myself to be there also.

# The Black Mountain Review

In hindsight it is almost too simple to note the reasons for the publication of *The Black Mountain Review*. Toward the end of 1953 Black Mountain College—a decisive experimental school started in the early thirties by John Rice and others in Black Mountain, North Carolina—was trying to solve a persistent and most awkward problem. In order to survive it needed a much larger student enrollment, and the usual bulletins and announcements of summer programs seemed to have little effect. Either they failed to reach people who might well prove interested, or else the nature of the college itself was so little known that no one quite trusted its proposals. In consequence a summer workshop in pottery, which had among its faculty Hamada, Bernard Leach, and Peter Voulkos, found itself with some six rather dazzled persons for students. Whatever the cause—and no doubt it involves too the fact that all experimental colleges faced a very marked apathy during the fifties—some other means of finding and interesting prospective students had to be managed, and so it was that Charles Olson, then rector of the college, proposed to the other faculty members that a magazine might prove a more active advertisement for the nature and form of the college's program than the kind of announcement they had been depending upon.

This, at least, is a brief sense of how the college itself came to be involved in the funding of the magazine's publication. The costs, if I remember rightly, were about $500 an issue, so that the budget

Introduction to *Black Mountain Review*, 3 vols. (New York: AMS Press, 1969), a reprint of the original magazine issues.

for a year's publication would be about $2000—hardly a large fig-
ure. But the college was in such tight financial condition that it
could not easily find any money for any purpose, and so its support
of the magazine, most accurately the decision of the faculty to commit such an amount to that purpose, was a deeply generous and
characteristic act. Too, it's to be acknowledged that Olson's powers
of persuasion were considerable.

The nature of the magazine itself, however, and the actual means
of its publication, that is, literally its printing, are of another story
which is really quite separate from the college itself. In the late forties, while living in Littleton, N.H., I had tried to start a magazine
with the help of a college friend, Jacob Leed. He was living in Lititz,
Pennsylvania, and had an old George Washington handpress. It
was on that that we proposed to print the magazine. Then, at an
unhappily critical moment, he broke his arm. I came running from
New Hampshire—but after a full day's labor we found we had set
two pages only, each with a single poem. So that was that.

What then to do with the material we had collected? Thanks to
the occasion, I had found excuse to write to both Ezra Pound and
William Carlos Williams. I didn't know what I really wanted of
them but was of course deeply honored that they took me in any
sense seriously. Pound very quickly seized on the possibility of our
magazine's becoming in some sense a *feeder* for his own commitments, but was clearly a little questioning of our *modus operandi.*
What he did give me, with quick generosity and clarity, was a kind
of *rule book* for the editing of any magazine. For example, he suggested I think of the magazine as a center around which, "not a box
within which/ any item." He proposed that verse consisted of a constant and a variant, and then told me to think from that to the context of a magazine. He suggested I get at least four others, on
whom I could depend unequivocally for material, and to make
their work the mainstay of the magazine's form. But then, he said,
let the rest of it, roughly half, be as various and hogwild as possible,
"so that any idiot thinks he has a chance of getting in." He cited
instances of what he considered effective editing, *The Little Review*
and the *Nouvelle Revue Française* when its editor gave complete license to the nucleus of writers on whom he depended 'to write
freely what they chose.' Williams in like sense gave us active support and tried to put us in touch with other young writers, as
Pound also did, who might help us find a company. But with our
failure to find a means to print the magazine, it all came to an
abrupt end. I remember Pound's consoling me with the comment

that perhaps it was wise for "the Creel" to wait for a while before "he highflyz as editor," but things seemed bleak indeed.

Happily, there was what proved to be a very significant alternative. Cid Corman, then living in Boston and having also a weekly radio program there called "This Is Poetry," had come to be a friend. I had heard the program, by some fluke, in New Hampshire, wrote him, was not long after invited by him to read on the program, and soon after we were corresponding frequently, much involved with senses of contemporary writers and writing. It was Cid, in fact, who got me in touch with Olson, by way of their mutual friend, Vincent Ferrini—who sent me some of Olson's poems, with his own, for possible use in the magazine that had not yet collapsed. In returning Olson's poems to Vincent, I made the somewhat glib remark that he seemed to be "looking for a language," and got thereby my first letter from Olson himself, not particularly pleased by my comment and wanting to discuss it further, like they say. The letters thus resulting were really my education just that their range and articulation took me into terms of writing and many other areas indeed which I otherwise might never have entered. But the point now is that Cid, once Jake Leed's and my magazine was clearly dead, undertook himself to publish a magazine called *Origin*. Significantly enough, its first issue includes some of the material I had collected— for example, Paul Blackburn's, whom I had come to know through Pound's agency—and features the work of Charles Olson, specifically the first of the *Maximus* sequence, as well as other poems and prose.

*Origin* was, in fact, the meeting place for many of the writers who subsequently became the active nucleus for *The Black Mountain Review*. More than any other magazine of that period, it undertook to make place for the particular poets who later come to be called the "Black Mountain School." In its issues prior to 1954, and continuingly, it gave first significant American publication to Denise Levertov, Irving Layton, Robert Duncan, Paul Carroll, Paul Blackburn, Larry Eigner, myself, and a number of others as well. Although I had, for example, published stories in the *Kenyon Review* and the *New Directions Annual,* neither place could afford me the actual company nor the range of my own work that *Origin's* second issue provided. For me it was an acknowledgment I had almost begun to think impossible, and I am sure that Cid's consistent support of our writing has much to do with what became of it.

The point is that we felt, all of us, a great distance from the more conventional magazines of that time. Either they were dominated

by the New Critics, with whom we could have no relation, or else
they were so general in character, that no active center of coherence was possible. There were exceptions certainly. *Golden Goose*,
edited by Frederick Eckman and Richard Wirtz Emerson, was
clearly partisan to myself and also to Olson, and published my first
book, *Le Fou*, and would have published a collection of Olson's, *The
Praises*, but for a misunderstanding between him and the editors,
when the book was already in proof. Both men were much involved
with Williams, and made his example and commitment the center
for their own. There were also other, more occasional magazines,
as *Goad*—whose editor, Horace Schwartz, involved me in a useful
defense of my interest in Ezra Pound, just that it helped clarify my
own terms of value.

But, with the exception of *Origin*, and possibly *Golden Goose* also,
only two magazines of that time, the early fifties, had finally either
the occasion or the sense of procedure, which served as my own
measure of the possibility. One, *Fragmente*, edited and published in
Freiburg, Germany, by Rainer Gerhardt—whose acquaintance I
was also to make through Pound's help—was a heroically ambitious
attempt to bring back into the German literary canon all that writing which the years of the Third Reich had absented from it.
Rainer and his wife, living in great poverty with two young sons,
were nonetheless able to introduce to the German context an incredible range of work, including that of Olson, Williams, Pound,
Bunting, and myself. I was its American editor but its literal activity
was completely the efforts of Rainer and Renate. Their conception
of what such a magazine *might* accomplish was a deep lesson to me.
They saw the possibility of *changing* the context of writing, and I
think myself that this magazine, and also the small paperbacks they
were able to publish, effectually accomplished this for present German poetry—despite the bitter fact of Rainer's early death.

In like sense, a group of young writers of various nationalities
centered in Paris was of great interest to me. They were led by
a lovely, obdurate and resourceful Scot, Alexander Trocchi, and
included the British poet, Christopher Logue, and the brilliant
American translator, Austryn Wainhouse. Others too were of equal
interest, Patrick Bowles, for example, who translated the first of
Beckett's French novels into English—and Richard Seaver, who
was later to become a decisive editor for Grove Press. Again, what
these men proposed to do with their magazine, *Merlin*, and the
books which they also published with the help of the Olympia Press
as Collection Merlin, was to change the situation of literary context

and evaluation. I've given a brief, personal sense of my relation to
Trocchi in a novel, *The Island,* where he figures as "Manus." I was
also invited by them to be an associate editor on the magazine—but
by that time the funds necessary to continue publication of the
magazine were not obtainable. But their translation of Genet and
Beckett's work as well as their brilliant critical writing, which extended to political thinking as well as literary, made them an exceptional example of what a group of writers might do.

By 1954 my wife and I were already much involved with a small
press called the Divers Press. We had moved from France to Mallorca, and had become close friends with a young English couple,
Martin Seymour-Smith and his wife, Janet. It was Martin who first
interested us in publishing books, since, as he pointed out, printing
costs were exceptionally cheap on the island and so much might be
done on a shoestring. But our initial venture together, the Roebuck
Press, came a cropper because Martin's interests were not really decisively my own nor mine his. We did publish a selection of his
poems, *All Devils Fading,* but our center was finally in writers like
Olson (*Mayan Letters*), Paul Blackburn (*Proensa* and *The Dissolving
Fabric*), Irving Layton (*In the Midst of My Fever*), Douglas Woolf (*The
Hypocritic Days*), Larry Eigner (*From the Sustaining Air*), and, though
he comes a bit later, Robert Duncan (*Caesar's Gate*). We also published Katue Kitasono's *Black Rain,* and it is a design of his that is
used for the covers of the first four issues of *The Black Mountain
Review* and the credits page. What I felt was the purpose of the
press has much to do with my initial sense of the magazine also. For
me, and the other writers who came to be involved, it was a place
defined by our own activity and accomplished altogether by ourselves—a *place* wherein we might make evident what we, as writers,
had found to be significant, both for ourselves and for that world—
no doubt often vague to us indeed—we hoped our writing might
enter. To be published in the *Kenyon Review* was too much like
being "tapped" for a fraternity. It was too often all over before one
got there, and few if any of one's own fellow writers came too.
Therefore there had to be both a press and a magazine absolutely
specific to one's own commitments and possibilities. Nothing short
of that was good enough.

*Origin* had already done, in some sense, as much as one could
hope for, and I remember having doubts about either the use or
the practicality of simply another magazine more or less "like" it. I
certainly didn't want to compete with Cid. But one possibility did
seem to me lacking in *Origin,* despite occasional notes and reviews,

and that was the *ground* that an active, ranging critical section might effect. I wasn't thinking of criticism finally as judgment of whether or no this or that book might be deemed "good" or "bad." What I hoped for, and happily did get, was critical writing that would break down habits of "subject" and gain a new experience of context generally. If I have any disappointment in the magazine in retrospect, it's only that this part of it does not extend as far as I had hoped. Still, Jung's "The Mass & the Individuation Process" (in the fifth issue)—which I remember he sent to "The Black Mount Review," which pun, unintentional I assume, was a delight—and Borges' "Three Versions of Judas" (in the seventh issue)—which I read with absolute seriousness, not realizing it was a "fiction"—are some instance of what I was after. But, and here I was much influenced by Olson, the possible *range* of such writing as we conceived of it was never fully demonstrated.

There have been various comments and summaries published with respect to *The Black Mountain Review*'s activity as a little magazine. Most lively and helpful, I think, is Paul Blackburn's account which appears in *Kulchur* (Vol. 3, No. 10, Summer 1963), called "The Grinding Down." Among other things, he identifies the initials used by reviewers in the first four issues, and also the pseudonyms used for signature in some other instances. Too, Kent State University Library, in one of its bulletins, provides an accurate and useful bibliography together with a brief note by myself. But now I think it best that the pseudonyms stay pseudonyms, and that initials, if not recognized (I used three sets, for example), be part of the present reader's experience. Often I, or some friend I could quickly get hold of, had to fill blank pages, to manage our length of sixty-four pages, or subsequently the longer format of two hundred and twenty plus. I at times had nightmares of having to write the whole thing myself.

The contributing editors listed in the first issue conform to that sense Pound had earlier made clear: get a center of people you can depend on for consistently active contributions, elsewise you'll have nothing to build with. Olson was to prove that center almost single-handedly, but Blackburn was also very helpful, with all manner of support including legwork around New York to get the magazine into stores as well as much sympathetic and practical handholding. Layton I had come to know through a Canadian mimeographed magazine, *Contact*, which many of us had been involved with as its contents will show. He had an intensive energy and obviously was restless with what was then the Canadian literary milieu. His brother-in-law, John Sutherland, editor of the *Northern Review,* no longer invited him to literary parties because Irving's conduct was too irascible. So he was an unequivocal cohort and wrote, happily, voluminous amounts of verse. If I remember rightly, I also asked others as well—in particular Paul Goodman, who answered he'd prefer being just a contributor, since his other commitments very possibly would not give him time to do more. Rexroth generously agreed although we had little information of each other beyond his own public figure. Less happily, by the time he'd read the first issue, he had realized his error and his withdrawal (as well as that of Paul Blackburn, whose reasons were happily less adamant) is noted at the back of the Fall 1954 issue along with a defensive comment by myself.

Many of the writers who became very decisive to the magazine are not so listed, however. Robert Duncan is very much one of these. His first contribution, sent at Olson's suggestion, was a poem I in turn suggested we print a section of—and Duncan's response was to the effect that if he *had* wanted a section of the poem printed, he *would* have sent it—and I learned much from him also. There was one very amusing confusion involved with a poem of his I did print, in the Fall 1954 issue, "Letters for Denise Levertov: For A Muse Ment." Apparently Denise, for some reason, took it as a parody on her own way of writing, and was thus hurt. And Olson too thought it was some kind of attack on him. I think that poor Duncan and myself were the only ones unequivocally to enjoy it, and it remains for me an extraordinary summary and exemplum of contemporary possibilities in poetry.

Denise herself, Louis Zukofsky (whom I found thanks to Edward Dahlberg and also Duncan), Jonathan Williams, and Robert Hellman (a close friend first in France, who subsequently came to teach briefly at Black Mountain), all were of great help to me in that they were there to be depended on, for specific writing but equally, for a very real sense of the whole act's not being merely a whistling in the dark but something making a way. God knows one often doubted it. Holding to Pound's sense of letting at least part of the magazine seem wide open, I know I printed work at times that any of them must have been puzzled by. Some things I just liked, for example, Gautier's "The Hippopotamus," which appears in the fifth issue. I still do. However, I've never found anyone to share my pleasure in "The Goat Man," by Harold Lee Drake, in the sixth issue. He wrote, to put it mildly, extraordinary prose—including one piece involved with masturbating by the seashore, which the condition of censorship in the fifties never permitted me to print. He was one of the contributors who came out of nowhere, and unhappily seems to have returned there, since I've never seen his work printed again.

Of contributors generally, I've defined, I think, the character of one group clearly evident throughout the magazine's publication. These are writers who have either come together earlier, in *Origin*, or who are "found" by the same nature of attention that *Origin's* preoccupations had effected. Louis Zukofsky would be one of these latter as would be also Edward Dahlberg. There are also "occasional" contributors, like Paul Goodman, and those who simply appear with no previous or necessarily continuing sense of relationship, like James Purdy. I think we were, possibly, the first magazine to print his work in America, and that was surely a pleasure. He had found us somehow, submitted the story, and I printed it. The same is true of Sherry Mangan's story (a curious echo from the twenties) in the seventh issue, or of Alfred Kreymborg's "Metaphysical Ballad" printed there as well.

But two other kinds of contributor were particularly significant. Thus far the relation to the college itself must seem the fact that it was paying for the magazine's publication, and that Olson was the rector of the college. Although Hellman, Duncan, and myself were briefly on the faculty, this was somewhat after the fact because the nature of the magazine was determined otherwise and really prior to that fact. But if those contributors are noted who were either students at the college at the time, or had recently been so, then a relation of the college to the magazine, and particularly to Olson's influence as a teacher, becomes very clear. First there is Jonathan Williams—who is certainly not a "student" at this point, but who is much interested in the college and in Olson particularly, as his own publishing (*Jargon*) makes clear. Look at the advertisements for his press in the various issues of the magazine, for further instance. Then there is Joel Oppenheimer, who had left the college not long before the publication of the first issue and so comes into its activity by that fact. Then Fielding Dawson—also absent at this point from the college, in the army in Stuttgart, but again much involved by relation to the college and so to the magazine also. Then there are those literally there: Edward Dorn, Michael Rumaker, and Tom Field. Dorn had published one poem in *Origin*, in an issue edited by Denise Levertov, and his story in *The Black Mountain Review* is, I think, his first published prose—and clear example of what is to be his extraordinary ability in that mode as well as in poetry. Michael

Rumaker has his first publication of any kind in the magazine, with two stories I feel to be as fine as ever were published—in fact, "The Pipe" I think as exceptional a piece of writing as any of any time. Then, finally, Tom Field—actually a painter, but whose writing struck me usefully, though it has not proven of major interest to himself. But think of it—that a college having an enrollment of about *twenty* people as average during the time the magazine is published should have such gifted men as Dorn, Rumaker, Dawson, Oppenheimer, and Williams have so proven themselves to be. Hopefully, it makes excuse for the kind of eulogy these comments must now seem.

The college closed in the spring of 1956 and at that point Jonathan Williams became the ostensible publisher of the last issue—on the cover of which he put a little sticker to make this fact clear. There was hope we might continue. Some material for the next issue was in hand, some photos of Frederick Sommer's for one thing, and some essays of Edward Dahlberg's. But the last issue itself was almost impossible to manage. I had left Black Mountain, had been briefly in San Francisco, and was now living in New Mexico. The printer, of course, was still in Spain, and the delays in proofing, or even getting the initial printing begun, were almost impossible to manage. However, the last issue—with the addition of Allen Ginsberg as contributing editor—defines the last group of contributors who have particular relevance. Ed Dorn had moved to San Francisco with his family after leaving Black Mountain the year previous. I was in restless state, having separated from my wife, and being really at odds with much in my life. I wanted a new condition and so went west, where I'd never been, to see if that might be an answer. So I was also in San Francisco, in the spring of 1956— and for a writer there was really no place that could have been quite like it, just at that time. The contents pages of the seventh issue will make this much clearer than I can—Ginsberg, Kerouac, Whalen, McClure, Burroughs (Lee), Snyder—and another man I was deeply pleased to include, albeit from the East, Hubert Selby, Jr. It was unequivocally a shift and opening of the previous center, and finally as good a place as any to end. Other magazines had appeared as well, with much the same concerns, among them *Big Table* and the *Evergreen Review*. Whatever battle had been the case did seem effectually won.

A last note, briefly, about the divers reproductions and photographs that appear in the various issues, as well as the covers for the last three. . . . I valued these especially, in that they freshened

everything when otherwise things seemed almost too dense. It was
a particular honor to include Franz Kline, Philip Guston, Aaron
Siskind, and Harry Callahan, because all had been teachers at the
college, and, even more than that, had each made so actively clear a
new way of seeing in their art. John Altoon I can never thank
enough for so much it would be specious to try to list it—and he
also had made very evident how extraordinary a painter he is. Dan
Rice, a close friend of those days and first met at the college—the
same. Edward Corbett I met while I was editing the last issue in
New Mexico, and though I'm sure he thought I was simply hysterical, his cover as well as other generosities is a lovely fact of his
concern. As for Laubiès—he saw it all.

So it's finally all well in the past, either as one's own experience of
something, or else the communal fact of what the writers of that
situation and time seemed to have had in mind. I don't think it can
ever be very different. You want to do something, to see it happen,
and apparently it can't, or at least can't with what then exists as possibility. So you try to change it, and you do or don't as proves the
case. What really now delights me is that a magazine having a usual
printing of some five hundred to seven hundred fifty copies, about
two hundred of which ever got distributed, could have made any
dent whatsoever. That should cheer us all.

> *Placitas, N.M.*
> *December 15, 1968*

# The Writer's Situation

*1. Why do you continue to write? What purpose does your work serve? Do you feel yourself part of a rear-guard action in the service of a declining tradition? Has your sense of vocation altered significantly in recent years?*

"Because it's there to be written," as William Carlos Williams said. I don't really know if there is more reason than that, in relation to some sense of purpose or intent. There are clearly things I've wanted to do in writing—specific forms I've wanted to try, as a novel, for example, or diverse ways in which an active *seriality* might be manifest. But the primary occasion in writing is a situation I've never been able to design, even when I've much wanted to.

Thinking then of why one continues—that's equally inexplicable, except that it is, literally, an active possibility for me, in my life. It keeps happening and the way the world then enters, or how I'm also then known to myself, is a deeply fascinating circumstance. Charles Olson makes a lovely point, that "we do what we know before we know what we do," and that really is the delight in writing, that much happens one has no conscious information of until it is there, in the words. I'm not thinking here of some sort of do-it-yourself psychoanalysis—that's of no interest to me—but a deeper fact of revelation I feel very actual in writing, a realization, reification, of *what is*.

The tradition to which I relate comes, as Robert Duncan would say, "from a well deeper than time." It's not yesterday's news one is concerned with. However one thinks to qualify it, the fact of being a poet teaches one that it is not an ego-centered occupation but a

*New American Review,* December 21, 1969.

*trust* one had really no thought to undertake. But there it was. Suddenly. One morning. With the birds. I'm trying to say that poetry comes from a *tradition* far more complex and rooted in the human condition than any one 'time' can define. Better to consider Konrad Lorenz's sense of tradition as he speaks to it in his book *On Aggression*—the intuitive economy of human experience, biological and environmental in this case.

As to my sense of vocation—for a long time I was very tentative about saying in any forthright manner that *I* was a poet. It seemed extraordinarily presumptuous. But again, it's not a vocation one can earn, however one respects the responsibility of this literal 'calling.' In any case, being a poet is something I can acknowledge more clearly in my own nature at this point. It seems a consistently present reality, although I respect a qualification a friend, Max Finstein, once made: that one is a poet in the act of writing, not otherwise.

However, I realize the nature of this question has really to do with a sense of *literary* tradition, and vocation as some form of *professional* occupation, etc. I've always been an amateur insofar as I loved what I did. Olson said that Melville had over his work table the statement: "Be true to the dreams of thy youth." I respect that commitment deeply. If anything, I feel a deep blessing and good fortune in what my 'vocation' has given me as a sense of my life. Saying that—it seems suddenly a little convenient, in a way, but I do feel blessed by life, no matter that at times it is difficult and painful.

*2. Do you believe that art and politics should be kept apart? Has this belief changed or grown more complicated during the past decade? What influence has the politicization of life during this period had on your work?*

Having come of age in the forties (I started college the summer of 1943), 'politicization' was, it then seemed, so much a part of that time I don't know that it seems more so now. Perhaps it's some sort of weird sandwich one is experiencing, with the blandness of the fifties intervening, the bread being the forties and sixties. But having been in some ways active in the Henry Wallace party, also having been taught politics by the YCL while still in college—it doesn't seem to me that life is now more political. It certainly isn't quite as didactic, let's say, as was the membership of the PAC—or any friends then involved with post-war Marxism. I don't think there is quite the same insistence on the 'right' and 'wrong' ways that there was then.

Possibly political agency is regaining an active contest. But really the advanced younger people of this moment are, if anything, *post-political*, just that the available political agencies seem to them so bankrupt. The militant part of the black community might be the one active revolutionary group still intent on political possibilities. I know that many of the young showed an active commitment to Eugene McCarthy's leadership in the circumstances of the 1968 election, but I question, even with reluctance, that that had initially to do with political occasion or possibility. More, I think, they wanted renewal of a kind of *presence*, in public life, possessed of a demonstrable integrity, even one apart from the usual conditions of political activity. They wanted someone to be literally there—and this was, curiously, not the case either with Kennedy or Nixon. Both were finally part of a system the young have every reason to distrust, as, God knows, the elders might equally.

Obviously the disaster of the national commitment to the war in Vietnam is the largest 'political' counter of the past few years, and it served to energize political agencies in every sense. But again, I'm very intrigued by the hippie culture, so to speak, and its decisively apolitical character. It's as though a very deep shift in the conception of human relations and use of the environment were taking place—and indeed I very much believe that it is. We've come to that time when, as Williams said, we must either change our 'wishes' or perish. I don't feel that present insistence on ecological problems is simply a new game. We have literally to change our minds. In this respect, drugs in the culture have really two, among other, clear possibilities: (1) either to reveal a oneness in all manifestations of life-form of whatever order and thus change the mind by that revelation (certainly the most useful information to be gained from taking LSD); or (2) to kill anxiety, to lull intuitive perception of inherent peril, to simply get out of the 'world' one is actually in—and in this respect the elders are as committed to this use of chemical agency as any of the young.

In any case, I don't see that art and politics, or that order of present experience involved with the post-political, should all be kept separate. I don't see how they can be. One can't, perhaps, entirely respect an art committed to propagandizing or to a use of life not clearly initiated in its own activity. But when men and women are outraged by political malfeasance, it's hardly likely that their art will not make that quite clear.

As far as my own work is concerned—I've not been able to write directly to a purpose of political involvement. It's not given me in my own nature to be able to do so, but I hope that I've made clear where I stood nonetheless. I hate the outrage of human beings that present political acts now effect. One must protest them—they are literally against life itself.


*3. What are the main creative opportunities and problems that attract and beset you in your work? Which movements, tendencies, writers, if any, do you find yourself identifying with or supporting? Which ones do you oppose?*

It's difficult to qualify just what 'creative opportunities and problems' are primary. Just that something does come to be said, is an opportunity of very great magnitude. Too, poetry as I've had experience of it is not, finally, at the service of other conditions or orders of information, however much it may serve them once it exists. Olson says that art is the only true twin life has—in that neither is to a 'purpose' apart from the fact of themselves. They don't *refer*, so to speak. There's no *excuse*.

The 'problems' occur when one gets lost in such possibility, muffs or misuses the nature of what's given. It is, again as Olson says, something as actual as wood, or fish, that one has to do with. It's not in the mind in some sense that one can now exercise a discretion upon it—thinking about it in some privileged way. On the contrary, there is a feeling that adamantly does insist one is being told something and had better get it right the first time, else there won't be another chance. One is told *once*. For this reason I find it hard ever to revise—'re-see'—just because the initial seeing has to be responded to with all the ability possible because I'm not given another chance. It's very like seeing someone you do respond to in the instant and having thus the choice of going home and thinking about it, or making that response a manifest act. I agree with Robert Duncan that choice is recognition—not a debate between alternatives. So if one doesn't know 'what to do,' given such circumstances, clearly there's nothing really to do.

Otherwise I'm not much concerned with either creative opportunities or problems. I love a particular poem by Kenneth Koch, beginning something like, "Thank you for giving me this battleship to wash . . ."

'Movements, tendencies, writers . . .' There is a *company*, a kind of leaderless Robin Hood's band, which I dearly love. I'm sure there is even a horn to summon us all. There is no company dearer, more phenomenal, closer to my heart. A few weeks ago I happened to spend the night at Allen Ginsberg's farm and coming down to the kitchen in the morning, met with Allen's charming remark, "All the poets are up!" Which very truly we were, Lawrence Ferlinghetti, Gregory Corso, Allen and myself—while five others also there slept on.

Whether learned by intuition or by act, one comes to respect and to love that company of writers for whom poetry is, in Bob Rose's phrase, "active transformation," not a purpose, not discretion, not even craft—but *revelation*, initial and eternal, whatever that last word can mean to one whose life is finite. Consequently I both identify with and support—and hope I might be permitted the company of—any man or woman whose experience of writing transcends some sense of its value as money in the bank, or edifying addition to one's identity, etc. None of the so-called Black Mountain writers wrote in a literally similar manner. That is, Olson's modes of statement are certainly not mine, nor are they Duncan's, nor Denise Levertov's—and so on. What was, then, the basis for our company? I think, simply the insistent feeling we were *given* something to write, that it wasn't something we could 'think' to write, that it was an obedience we were undertaking to an actual possibility of revelation. Which to say one might own would be absurd.

What I find abhorrent is any assumption that one has gained the *use* of writing as a private convenience, to me the ugliest of all attitudes.

*4. Has writing entered a 'post-modern' era, in which the relevance of the great modern writers (Joyce, Eliot, Mann, Faulkner, et al.) has declined? If so, what seem to be the literary principles of the post-modern age? If not, what principles of modernism are still dominant and valuable?*

Supposing 'modern' to define the primary consciousness of a decisive shift in the conception of *reality*, which becomes increasingly clear toward the end of the nineteenth century, then one may feel that that consciousness is now a general condition in human experience. The world cannot be 'known' entirely. Certainly it cannot, in the way men are given to live in it and to know it, be 'perfected.' In all disciplines of human attention and act, the possibilities inherent in the previous conception of a Newtonian universe—with its containment and thus the possibility of being known—have been yielded. We do not know the world in that way, nor will we. Reality is continuous, not separable, and cannot be objectified. We cannot stand aside to see it.

Writing, and all of the arts as well, have entered the altered consciousness of our situation in the world. One might speak, possibly, of 'the modern' as the first impact of that realization in the arts: Eliot expressing both regret for previously possible order and recognition of the new experience of how the world happens—simply what takes place. Yeats, in a late note on modern poetry, understandably with frustration, speaks of modern poets as asking us to "accept [a] worthless present." If one thinks then quickly of Samuel Beckett's use of that 'present,' "where to be lasts but an instant where every instant/spills in the void the ignorance of having been," a measure of the change involved is apparent.

Much that the modern writers got said seems to me still of great relevance. Both Williams and Pound—or Lawrence, Stein, H.D., and many others also—point up the dilemma of what may be called individual sensibility in an environment insistently generalizing all circumstances of apprehension and decision. That problem hardly seems solved. However, what is at first feared as a loss of coherence—felt most in the loss of history's authority—starts to become less that as other situations of experience occur. High and low art begin to melt as historical valuations blur. All being *now*, all that *is* there has possibility.

The ego's authority tends to relax and conceptions involved with proposals of 'good, better, best' also lose ground. Most interesting to me is the insistent presence of what has been called the *chance factor* in the activity of all the arts of the past several years. Whether in 'happenings' or in the music of younger composers like Cornelius Cardew, one sees that a discipline, so to speak, is being gained to discover a *formal* possibility in a highly variable context of activity. It may well be that 'beauty' is simply being returned to 'the eye of the beholder,' but what the eye expects to see is nonetheless much altered.

Still it does seem that terms such as 'modern' and 'post-modern' are habits of art history. One tends to use all that he can get hold of and I don't know that one 'time' is thus distinct from another, in the actual practice. *Here* is where one seems to be.

*5. Has there been a general collapse of literary standards in recent years? Are you conscious of a conflict between your past standards and your present ones?*

I remember an incident, like they say, involving a critic I much respect, Warren Tallman, and an Englishman, in a radio discussion of Jack Kerouac's *Big Sur* for CBC. Warren was plugging for Kerouac's genius in being able to make so articulate and substantial all the data of the senses. What impressed Warren was the fact that when some thing or activity was spoken of, one's experience of it was extraordinarily vivid. The Englishman, however, felt that some canon of literary form had been broken. When Warren pushed him to qualify just what 'standard' he was referring to, the man hedged, unable actually to state it—then said, "Well, we know enough to know these standards exist, even if we don't know what they are."

Kind of a wistfully moving point, actually. But I'm extraordinarily wary of *any* 'standard' not the direct result of an active experience in the practice of the art involved. Or as Olson puts it, "telling me what in the instant I knew better of," and this is not by any means an egocentric response to 'rules' imposed by taste and opinion, that have nothing to do with the nature of the language and all the possibilities therein. Pound quotes Remy de Gourmont, "Freely to write what he chooses is the sole pleasure of a writer"—and I agree with that utterly. 'Standards' are only interesting in relation to the possibilities they recognize. In the forties I felt them arbitrarily restrictive and dominated by the practice of criticism apart from the practice of poetry itself.

So far from feeling there has been a collapse of literary standards, I feel there has been a reconstitution of them in the practice of writing itself. Think of the victories actually won: relaxation of censorship in the use of specific words, admission of serial order as a complex and diversely organized phenomenon, a riddance to all senses of 'poetic subject,' poems *bien fait* to some dull mold, and so on. The list is happily a long one. In short, I think that such standards as poetry involves, and they exist unequivocally, are again the issue of the practice—not a viciously parasitic *addendum* put on the practice of poetry by people in no wise committed to it.

My past standards continue to be my present ones. I permit myself possibly more freedom now—not by a relaxation, but in the broader range of perception I am able to respond to in writing, in the degrees of emotional condition I find I can speak. *Man standing by his word*—Pound's translation of the Chinese ideogram for *sincerity*—stays as my own measure, but I have begun to apprehend too the complexity of that situation. It's not a simple honesty, etc.


*6. Have literary criticism and journalism kept pace with, and faith with, the best fiction, poetry, and drama produced in the sixties?*

A lovely novelist we know, world-famous no less, writes on a Christmas card just received: "For Christ's sake keep up the good work and don't be sidetracked by Christmas or the goddam reviewers who are ugly people . . ." As far as I'm concerned, and speaking particularly of the situation of poetry, there is *no* correspondence of any interest to me between the activities in contemporary criticism and that poetry I am myself most engaged with. Even if one considers a particular critic of intelligence, Richard Howard, who is also a writer of poems, the score is still lousy. In his book, *Alone with America: Essays on the Art of Poetry in the United States Since 1950*, there are gaps I so deeply question that the book itself becomes a fine instance of *mandarin* writing—i.e., an 'entertainment' of 'sensibility.' And he is, in my own estimation, perhaps the best. Where 'journalism' may be in any of this, I simply don't know. Reviewers are either so tardy or so absent one can hardly consider them as 'keeping pace.' A fellow wrote recently to tell me he'd been asked by *The Nation* to review my collection *Words* for one of their coming issues. The book was published in 1967. *Pieces,* a subsequent collection of poems, was published last August, and possibly that might be reviewed in the far, far distant future. But really, one hardly depends on it.

The point is, if one meets with an exceptional critical intelligence—e.g., Kenneth Burke, D. H. Lawrence, Edward Dahlberg, Ezra Pound—then *that's* the point, not 'literary criticism.' Joshua Whatmough says, in a book called *Language,* that literary criticism is just an exchange of opinion and has no authority in relation to the activities it criticizes. That cheers me up. When younger, I was not 'criticized' at all. Now older, it seems I rarely do things right, or five years ago I did them right, not now. As for literary criticism 'keeping faith'—I didn't know it had faith to keep. If one is thinking of people active in the arts making notes, etc., then the whole question obviously changes.

# Writing

## I

Some years ago I was trying to buy a truck in Boston, and the salesman after some conversation asked me if I might be available to tutor him, to "improve his English," as he put it, so that he might secure a better job. I think that habit of attitude toward the fact of speaking, and writing and reading equally, is deeply ingrained in anyone who passes through our usual system of education. There is a sense adamantly present that a "right" way and "wrong" way exist and what one is trying to teach and/or learn is the *correct* approach. But writing, insofar as I've had to do with it, is absolutely hostile to such an assumption. There can be examples obviously, facts of writing one responds to and respects, and these become the literal measure of one's own practice. Such measures are, however, inevitably personal, no matter how much they may seem instances of general or topical interest. Millions of people may be involved by what Bob Dylan is saying, but the more significant point, for me, is that each one hears him as a singular occasion.

That, in fact, is one of the delights of writing, that it involves such a one-to-one relationship. At least its most active possibility lies for me in that fact. I know that many people may reach college with a marked resistance to writing, but again, assuming that they have been subject to the *right* and *wrong* emphasis, it seems very evident

Jonathan Baumbach, ed., *Writers as Teachers/Teachers as Writers* (New York: Holt, Rinehart, and Winston, 1970).

that writing as a discipline has been used primarily against them. Even when they've done it *correctly*, the effect is most often a complete generalization of their own concerns, and what hopefully they began with—some explicit fact and their own relation to it—has become "correct usage" only.

Of course language, *a* language, is a system, and acquaintance with the nature of that condition is most useful. But what a difference there is between the usual college grammar text and such a book as Ernest Fenollosa's *The Chinese Written Character as a Medium for Poetry*—or Gertrude Stein's notes on parts of speech in "Poetry and Grammar"—or Edward Sapir's *Language.* Clearly these represent my interests, and I cannot assume their relevance for another—but the point is, I would like to, and in teaching I would absolutely depend on texts having explicit involvement with language as a system rather than the generalized "rule books" all too frequent.

But this gets the cart before the horse, just that in teaching writing, or any other possibility, one begins with the students themselves. If I speak French and they speak Chinese, no communication occurs. It's not indulgence that argues the use of knowing the terms and active content of those one proposes to teach. So, then, "why write?"—and is any possibility to be found in it that they themselves value? What do they read, if they read? What uses do they find in writing, if any? Is it an activity merely demanded by their various courses—reports, analyses, explanations, etc.

Don't be discouraged if, at first, nothing much happens at all. I was once in a writing class taught by Delmore Schwartz, who began with the reasonable assumption that there must be *one* writer that all of us respected in common. Unhappily there wasn't—and the class sat in that dilemma for the full length of the semester. It isn't that he was wrong or right, but rather that *any* assumption about what can or should happen must yield to the actual situation. Most frequently the people one is trying to teach will have been habituated to feel that reading and writing are activities having as necessary purpose the gaining of a didactic information, and in a class which, hopefully, is not intended to center upon a "subject," or to make known specific content of such order, a significant number may well be disgruntled, feeling that the course is a waste of time. Others, proposing more sympathetic interest, will want immediately to know what ways of writing will be most useful to their intentions and will expect to be taught these in a rather literal manner—with appropriate notes as to adequate and inadequate "performance." I'd suggest that both attitudes be balked—there is nowhere one is necessarily going, there is really nothing more to say than what seems of interest to them at the moment, and if no one has such interest, then that's true—for themselves as well as for you.

If such a way of beginning appears to be extraordinarily lax— granted that writing is, in one sense, a discipline of very complex and actual particularity—do remember that one's own interests and commitments in no way involve the possibility of others until those others have entered their condition. My excitement will only be an irritation for anyone who finds himself sharing neither my situation of experience nor my own commitment to the terms of the activity involved. How, then, engender such circumstance as makes a common ground?

First of all, begin with what's there—by which I mean, the literal fact of the people. You can ask them "what they want to do" and may well get the answer, "nothing"—but that's enough, i.e., push that, "what is that state of activity," or literally *do* nothing, if that is chosen as the state of possibility. In such a situation the one thing most dulling seems to me to insist that such and such is a "great" book or that this or that way of writing is most "effective" and to argue consequently, but only with oneself, all the possible justifications.

You may choose to impose upon them the necessity of writing something—there is obviously no reason not to—but don't limit it too didactically to a "subject" and don't look for what you think it *should* say. The dreary habit of parroting so prevalent in contemporary education comes of such insistence, and profits no one at all. Take what *is* said as the context and use that as the means of exchange. You cannot apply to an alternative or to a rule you may respect, which the writer himself has not experienced. In other words, make known to him that what he is saying has the possibility of this or that extension—*not* that what is unknown to him is a constant and frustrating limit.

Having once taught the first grade, I can remember that lovely experience of witnessing someone's coming into the possibility of reading and writing, so that the literal fact of speech gains extension in time and space in immeasurable senses. It is an absolutely *human* delight, and if people have forgotten that, it may well be due to the fact that this incredible agency has been so hedged in by impositions of *purpose*, and necessary *meaning*, and all manner of didactic insistence. As if the only point in learning how to swim were to get from A to B . . . Poets were once called "makers" and the word *poetry* comes from a root meaning "to make." But *what* to make—despite all insistences to the contrary—is as viable as language and human condition can make manifest. It's hardly permissive to want to return some of that possibility to senses of teaching and learning.

In fact, that seems finally the point—that unless writing does become that pleasure, it remains a drudgery and only an occasion prompting more criticism, more "doing it wrong." How to make it such pleasure no one can easily tell another, nor can one assume that all people will share equally in its delights. But you don't have to kill it. You don't have to humiliate and ignore and find contemptible what may be the very possibility you are committed to foster. I am sick to death of "taste" which wants to convert all experience to terms of fashion and the social. Rather, respect Pound's "Damn your taste! I want if possible to sharpen your perceptions, after which your taste can take care of itself." Your own are involved as well as those of your students.

How you do what you do remains your own possibility, and invention. It may or may not involve books, newspapers, films, television—or any fact of activity possible to your life and that of your students. Writing is an activity, not a subject. You cannot propose an isolated area of its relevance.

What follows, then, is an instance of my own involvement with teaching and writing, specifically with poetry—although writing is, for me, all that is made with words and written down.


## II. Contexts of Poetry*

What Allen suggested, and what I thought would be a good idea, would be to begin with some sense of writing in the most literal of possible contexts. Now the supposition, I suppose, on the part of some of you who've come, is that we write poetry; in other words, this is what we do. And we, in effect, have been given a definition publicly as poets. We've published books and all the rest. But that kind of qualification is something I'd not like to take on, in this or any other context. So I would like to take up the issue of writing as a physical act. What I will tell you is how I write, and Allen, then you take it from there, you do the same. In other words, I want to speak of what is involved in writing for me.

*This text has been transcribed by George F. Butterick from a tape made by Fred Wah at the Vancouver Poetry Conference, Wednesday morning, July 24, 1963, and was first published by *Audit* (1968). The speaker of the italicized portions is Allen Ginsberg. I am the other speaker.

When I first met William Carlos Williams, for instance, I remember he took me upstairs to\show me where the bathroom was, and as we went by the—I think the bedroom—he showed me the desk that had been in his office when he was in active practice; and he showed me his typewriter, which was a large old office machine, and the way it fitted under the desk; and he showed me the prescription pads that he used to use. And again, Allen and I were thinking of how the qualification of the size of the paper, for example, will often have an effect on what you're writing, or whether or not you're using a pencil or a pen. Habits of this kind are almost always considered immaterial or secondary. And yet, for my own reality, there is obviously a great connection between what I physically do as a writer in this sense, and what comes then out of it. So I want briefly to qualify it. I was curious to know how I do it myself, in the sense of what really do I do. Well, say, first of all, I write always with a typewriter. I get very nervous about using a pen, because pens run out of ink in a way . . . ball points are what I would use, as and when I do write that way . . . pencils have to be sharpened, I get so involved with the sharpening of the pencil. Also, I think it goes back to a sense I had when younger, that typewriters, typewriting, implied a "professional" context. If you were going to be serious, or going to *claim* seriousness for yourself, the instrument that you used in writing had to be particular to what the act of writing was. So that I had, I think, a basically naive sense of this kind. I wanted to be able to do it with a typewriter. Now, equally, I never learned to type. So I mean my typing is a habit that's developed, with two fingers. I never took a class in high school or any other place that taught me how to use the full, you know, all your fingers when you're typing. Think again, that begins to be a qualification of how *fast* I can write. In other words, I find that the pace of my writing is concerned with the speed with which I can type. Now, I can type actually about as fast as I can talk, with two fingers. I find, for example, if I have to work on somebody else's typewriter, I'm displaced, because there may be a slight variation in the space between keys. I find that now I can use the typewriter I do use without looking at it, so that I can be thinking of something without consciously wondering where my fingers are. I find . . . let's see, I want to keep on a little bit in this sense of what the physical conditions are . . . because again, I started writing in a context where I was embarrassed. I didn't want to bother anybody. I didn't want, you know, like, don't mind me, but just go right ahead with what you're doing, with your *serious business,* with your serious preoccupation. This was primarily in a former marriage, and the problems thereof . . . I didn't want to call attention to myself, because doing that might force me to define what I was trying to do—which is obviously impossible. So, the next thing I would do would be to create a context in which there was a residuum of noise, constantly present, so that my own noise wouldn't be intrusive. And so I find often I turn on the radio. I used to—back in New Hampshire, where I think I really sat down to think of how to write or what to write—I used to play records all the time. We had at that time, I remember, one of these big Jensen speakers and all, and amplifier, and I'd put on the records that I then much valued, as Charlie Parker and what not—but just because that rhythmic insistence, I think, kept pushing me, I kept hearing it. And lately for example, in the last year, I finished a long prose work, a novel, and I found that what I was writing could be actually stimulated by playing particular kinds of music. In other words, I don't know . . . I'm not a psychologist or even interested in this aspect, what I'm . . .

    *What kind of music?*

        Well, for example, the whole first part is written primarily to an old Bud Powell tape, a record, where you get these great kinds of almost concert style . . . let's say a poor man's concept of beauty, you know, where you get these great crescendoes of sound, and where you get actually a basically simple melody, as "I Got Rhythm" or anything, playing through this, and then you get this involvement that constantly comes back to the simple statement because it's embarrassed actually with its own hope. So this first part of the novel is written in that sense. Then the whole middle section is written primarily to John Coltrane, where you get deliberate dissonance and you get fragmentation—I wasn't conscious of this—and then the last part is written to a kind of Nancy Wilson, you know, where you get a "where love is gone," dig? And you get a *real slick* pretension. In other words, where she's singing, in effect, the memory of some authenticity which she no longer even . . . she never meant it. I saw her on television and . . . she's no slicker than any professional, but she's singing in a manner which is now a *manner.* She's not an innovator, as was Sarah Vaughan, or, more particularly, Billie Holiday. Again, the middle section involves Billie Holiday. But what I'm trying to say is: so, that's a physical requirement for me. I find it very useful . . .

    *Even in poems?*

Even in doing anything. It gives me something to focus on or to relax back into as a place where I feel safe. Anyhow: the typewriter, the insistence of music, rhythm, something with a strong rhythmic character, not *too* loud, subtle enough so that you can always go back to it . . . and paper. Usually an 8 × 11 sheet. I best like, most like, the yellow copy paper that's not spongy, but has a softness to it, so that when you type, the letter goes in, embeds a little. I hate a hard paper. When you erase this paper you take a layer off. And I remember again—now this is why I want to point out, this is not ridiculous—because I remember one time when living in Spain, there was none of this particular size copy paper that I was used to using. So I got a legal size sheet. And it was suddenly a terror, because I would finish what was normally my habit of dealing with the paper and realize that I had about six inches left at the bottom that was blank. This set up a whole different feeling. I remember writing a story actually using this paper, and it seemed to me that things were taking an awfully long time. In other words, the whole balance or pattern of the way of working with the thing was being changed. So the paper is significant. Again, Allen and I were talking about the way Jack Kerouac . . . the qualification of his writing that occurs when he is working in small notebooks. Or could I say the same of Robert Duncan, for example, who uses a notebook and writes in ink, and the composition of his books is obviously done as he's writing. There is, for example, an actual instance of a book of this kind that he did, called *Fragments of a Disordered Devotion,* in which it's reproduced from the actual . . . well, actually he wrote it as a copy of his own manner. It's an imitation of his manner by himself, so it has that. . . . But you realize that it's all happening visually as well as intellectually or mentally. Olson, in his letters . . . you begin to realize Olson's spacing, the ordering of where things occur in his thought. He'll begin a letter like, "dear so and so," and then start with the information, and before he's, say, halfway through the page you've got these things jumping all around . . . the movement, is moving, trying to locate like, let's put that there . . . no don't, now this goes there, oh but you can't forget that . . . but you can't forget this too . . . you can't put them like that, because it's a lie, they don't exist that way, you've got to . . . He's trying in effect to give the *orders* of thought—in no pretentious sense—and a typewriter for him, for example, is something that has much defined his habits of writing, as he said himself in *Projective Verse.* But equally, he has a speed in handwriting that's fast, a very fast style of writing. . . .

But positions and textures of papers, envelopes and what not . . .
I find again that in order to be taken seriously by myself that I
again had to create a context in which I could exhibit the instance
of professionalism. I remember some friend, for example, who
said he always washed his hands before he started to write, because
he wanted to be clean, he didn't want to get anything dirty. I can
remember equally, when I had run out of paper . . . the circumstances of living at some remote place . . . I would really get . . . it
would be awful. And then you'd start to improvise paper from envelopes—but very carefully folding them and all but ironing them
out to get the right feeling. What I'm trying to say with all this rambling, is that the particular habits of writing that you begin to develop will have, curiously, a great significance for what you write. If
you think I'm fooling, you might for example try to see what happens if you write with different kinds of media. In other words, try
writing with large crayons, or—I wish we had access to this—it
would be interesting to see what happens if you try to write on
something the size of this blackboard. I taught first grade also . . . I
remember this . . . where you're writing things like [moves to black-
board] . . . I could do this, in teaching handwriting. . . . Now, I
can't write like this, I get so absorbed, involved with the voluptu-
ousness, the sensuous . . . it's distracting to me. Because what I'm
trying to do, if I'm successful . . . I am not anticipating what I'm
thinking, I am not anticipating any content before it occurs. At the
same time, I'm trying to recognize, or rather, I'm awfully bewildered by confusions between certain terms—the states of consciousness—e.g., the difference between recognition, understanding, realization, knowing. I'm trying to describe a state in which one
primarily feels what is happening as a fit balance. If you do things
like ski or swim or drive, for example, you know that sense of feeling when the car is operating smoothly, when the balance of the
steering and the movement of the car is coinciding with an intention of your own and is following with a sense of grace, an appro-
priateness. Everything is, in effect, falling into place. You're not
intentionally putting it there, but you're recognizing the feeling of
its occurring there. So that when I'm writing myself, if something
becomes dissonant or something becomes jarred, arbitrarily, then I
have to stop. One other thing I should note, also about the sense of
the physical act of writing, is that the same habit of wanting it to be
"perfect" in its appearance, means that if I'm writing and I make a
mistake, I take the paper out and copy it down to that point, correct

the mistake, and then throw the paper away. In other words, I have a great difficulty writing on the paper. For example, I can never write in books. And I get awfully upset if other people write in my book . . . writing in my book . . . seeing dirty hands all over my book . . . Because I don't really think that I can own a book. I don't think that I have the *right*, to write.

In college itself . . . now let's go back there, because that's where we are again . . . I was in the context of other younger men of that time who wanted to be writers also . . . Donald Hall, for example— that was in Harvard in 1946, a group which then centered around *Wake*—Seymour Lawrence, now editor for Atlantic Monthly Press, Kenneth Koch. I remember, say, Kenneth Koch one time invited me up to his rooms for, I think it was sherry, and to listen to records, like Bach and what not, and to read me a few poems. Well, I can remember going up to his room, and it was, you know, it was a very comfortable room. Kenneth comes from a family that has money, and so that was evident in his room. It had very tasteful reproductions, there was furniture that he'd bought . . . I couldn't do that. At that time I wasn't writing anything that I felt was that significant. I mean I was desperate to understand what would actually be a poem. Again, as Allen and I were talking yesterday—you've really come at a good time!—because I think each of us in our own circumstances has come to that point where the very definition of a poem as a possibility, not as a possibility perhaps, but as an actual construct, is something we are very unable to state like that. In other words, I cannot define a poem. It's a curious state of mind to have arrived at. I cannot tell you what I think a poem is. I think that has to do with the fact that all the terms of consciousness are, at the moment, undergoing tremendous terms of change. We were again talking, thinking of the context now in the States. There is an alteration of a very deep order going on in the whole thrust or push of the consciousness, literally the Negro consciousness, that has been for years relegated to a kind of underside or underworld. As Duncan says, "I see always the underside turning . . ." Well, see, the Negro personality in the States has been forced to live in this underside world, except in contexts which he could control. LeRoi Jones, for example, grew up in a fairly secure middle-class background that had, let's say, the securities of that status. But you see, there was always a limit to it. You could always take one step beyond the control of the neighborhood and you were suddenly in a world which was utterly unresponsive to your reality. Now this reality,

which has become *the* dominant reality in the States today, is the
Negro reality, it is not the white reality, it's the Negro reality. You
may want to interpret the activities of the Kennedys as large, liberal
recognitions that have been long overdue, but I think it would be
utterly naive to do so. I think that the Kennedys are being washed
along in a shift that is not only located in the States but—now Allen
can tell you much more accurately these terms—but is coming
from a whole shift of controls and communication terms that are
actually centered in Africa and Asia.

I don't want to take us too far afield, but my point is that the very
premise on which consciousness operates is undergoing modifica-
tions that none of us I think are at the moment capable of defining.
We can only recognize them. Let's say, that if Pound says artists are
the antennae of the race, I think that any of us here is in a position
to be responsive to this feeling that's so immense, so definite, and so
insistent. Not because we can *do* anything with it. It simply is, it's a
big change, it's a deep change in consciousness, and I'm curious to
see what's going to happen—which is a mild way of putting it. Indeed! But you have a poem, Allen, in which you say, "Where all
Manhattan that I've seen must disappear." And this for me is what
is happening in the States in a different relationship, in a different
context—where all the terms of consciousness that I grew up with
must disappear, are disappearing momently, daily. The terms of reality are changing. Even the terms of this course are changing . . . by
which I mean, this course would have been impossible ten years
ago, by definition. Senses of writing would have been impossible to
present in this fashion ten years ago. We were, happily, involved
with a reorganization of premise that gave us our particular occasion. Yours is going to be perhaps even more a mess. I mean that
I think that the change which is occurring now is more significant than the Second World War by far, because it's the residue of
that war in reference to the atom bomb and, equally, the shift
in *all* terms of human relationship that have been habitualized
since, oh God, thousands of years. This goes back to correct, not to
correct, but to reorganize premises that have existed for thousands
of years, concepts of person. . . . Look, I'd like you to talk for a
while . . .

         . . . *the last time I wrote was on a train to Kyoto and Tokyo. I
suddenly had a great seizure of realization, on a whole bunch of levels. I
was thinking of a poetic problem which is not along lines. . . . It's another
matter. Also, about an emotional problem which was just resolving itself.
And I was suddenly having feelings for the first time, certain kinds of feel-*

*ings for the first time in about a half year. I was feeling something that had been growing and growing and growing and all of a sudden appeared to me on the train. So I had to get it then because I knew in an hour when I got to Tokyo I'd be all hung up in Tokyo—you know, looking for a room in Tokyo—and I'd be having other feelings, or going back to material problems of arranging things. But here I had that moment and. . . . That's what I don't understand about your writing, what happens to you if you suddenly realize something—do you have to, arrange your paper? What do you do then, you lose it!*

You're right! No, I was just thinking as you were saying this, that the limit of my ability to write, at the moment, and has been for the last two years, is that I have to secure a physical context in which I can "work." It not only has to be qualified by having paper and the rest of the paraphernalia, but it has to have equally a social qualification. I remember, for example, friends walking in when I'm working. I literally stop. I cannot work when someone's looking at me. So that, I *envy* you. I remember . . . again this experience of knowing both you and Jack in San Francisco, and Jack equally will walk always with a notebook and be writing away. Or Robert Duncan, again. . . . That's why I suppose I always end up living in these circumstances that are very isolate, in other words, where I won't be disturbed. Yet I don't think it's a pretentious thing. It's frankly a need I . . .

*. . . what you set up . . . does that actually catalyze feelings?*

It seems to create a context in which those feelings can occur. The thing is that I'm so shy—in no specious or stupid sense—but I'm so worried about keeping myself together when I'm in public, so to speak, as even now. I mean these habits of speaking are, after all, the habits that I got from teaching. But when I'm writing, you see, that business of Olson's, "He left him naked, / the man said, and / nakedness / is what one means . . ." In order to be in that state of nakedness, I have to be where—it isn't so much distraction—but where I can open up this equally small thing, and feel it with the intensity of all the perception that I . . . that the ego bit can recognize, and then destroy the ego by its own insistence. It's shy in other words . . .

*Situated where there is no threat.*

Well, equally, it's an . . . see, I would be embarrassed for years. I remember when I got to the Southwest, the people there have a very easy and pleasant habit of embracing one another when they meet; that is, in-laws or friends.

It took me *years!* I was, frankly, when I saw you for example, I was so pleased that I could put my arms around you as an old friend and hold on to you. It took me years to be able to do that, and maybe one day I'll be able to do this too. I'm not satisfied with the habits of limit that I've created for myself, because not only have I given myself a million excuses for doing nothing nine-tenths of the time, but I've created a context in which only—I realize now—only certain kinds of feeling can come. In other words, after all, when you've got the fort, like all the guns mounted and ready to blast until you're utterly safe, and you let out this little agonized thing . . . it skips around the room, you know, and you're embarrassed, you hear someone move in the kitchen, think O my God they're *coming* . . . no wonder the poems are short! I'm amazed that there are any at all! At the same time, you see, one is stuck with one's actuality, at the same time this is the only point I can begin, this is the place where my feelings are most present. I mean that in the sense of I have a horrible training. . . . Olson speaks of being trained to speak, you know. He said that when he was a younger man—he's a very large man—and as a younger man he was . . . obviously must have been awkward, and his presence was a problem. He'd walk in, people would, like, duck, or they'd *respond* to him in ways that were not *particular* to his feelings at that moment. I equally had somewhat the same thing. I found that my feelings had an awfully bothersome quality for people I wanted to get to. God I'd, you know, I'd do anything to please them, and I found that I couldn't. I mean I couldn't in a way that I could depend upon. So that the poems anyhow began to be a way of dealing with things that I was otherwise prevented from having. Well anyhow a sense of security . . . I don't mean security in the sense of insurance or not being afraid. I think in those instances within that room all hell breaks out, as you well know, in the sense that everything is possible there in a way that . . . Again and equally, if I walk on, if I'm sitting on the train with a notebook, I'm so self-conscious about it. Again this habit of my environment. I think what we're trying to do with all this is to insist to you that these aspects of what we're talking about are not immaterial. In other words these are the . . . I don't mean to give them undue significance or to . . . I don't want to qualify this way at all. What I'm trying to say is don't start thinking of writing as some particular activity leading to some particular effect for some particular purpose. It is just as relevant what size paper you use, as whether or not you think you're writing a sonnet. In fact, it's more relevant. And this aspect of your activity ought to be, you ought to be aware of it, simply that you should begin to feel as rangingly all that is issuing as a possibility and as a qualification of that possibility. In other words, if you want to write with a paper like this, please *do!* If you find yourself stuck with habits of articulation, try doing something else, try shifting the physical context. . . .

## A Postscript

The preoccupations here evident were, in fact, more decisive than I could then have realized. I had trusted so much to *thinking,* apparently, and had gained for myself such an adamant sense of what a poem could be for me, that here I must have been signaling to myself both a warning and the hope of an alternative.

Not too long after I began to try deliberately to break out of the habits described. I wrote in different states of so-called consciousness, e.g., when high, and at those times would write in pen or pencil, contrary to habit, and I would also try to avoid any immediate decision as to whether or not the effects of such writing were "good." Some of the poems so written are to be found in *Words,* among them "A Piece," "The Box," "They (2)," and "The Farm." These were, however, still written on the customary 8 × 11 sheets and in the security of my usual home. But nonetheless they began to gain for me the possibility of *scribbling,* of writing for the immediacy of the pleasure and without having to pay attention to some final code of significance.

When *Words* was published, I was interested to see that one of the poems most irritating to reviewers was "A Piece"—and yet I knew that for me it was central to all possibilities of statement. One might think of "counting sheep"—and I am here reminded of Williams' poem, which Pound chooses to include in *Confucius to Cummings,* "The High Bridge Above the River Tagus at Toledo":

> In old age they walk in the old man's dreams
>  and will still walk in his dreams, peacefully
>  continuing in his verse forever.

To count, or give account, tell or tally, continuingly seems to me the occasion. But again I had found myself limited by the nature of the adding machine I had unwittingly forced upon myself.

Slowly, then, I came to write without the mechanic of the typewriter. I also began to use notebooks, first very small ones indeed, and then larger—and I found many senses of possibility in writing

began consequently to open. For one, such notebooks accumulated
the writing, and they made no decisions about it—it was all there,
in whatever state it occurred, everything from addresses to moral-
istic self-advising, to such notes as I now find in the smallest and
first of them:

> This size page forces the
> damn speciously gnomic
> sans need for same—
>    —it
>     it—

There was no hustle to argue the virtue of any possibility instantly,
nor to do more than write, which same "freely" to do, as Remy de
Gourmont in Pound's quotation of him insists, "is the sole pleasure
of a writer." How long it took me to realize that in my own life.

It would be impossible to thank Allen Ginsberg enough for what
he was somehow able to reassure me of—or to thank those other
friends whose way of writing was of like order: Robert Duncan,
Charles Olson, Denise Levertov, and the many others, who were
wise, like they say, long before myself. It's lovely to do something
with your bare hands and mind, in the instant it *is* possible, and
finally I know it.

# On the New Cultural Conservatism

Some years ago an elder friend was much disturbed by "campus unrest," although any instance of its literal effects was very unlikely to reach her. It seemed her fears were really the fact of her being increasingly unable, physically, to defend herself or to "get out of the way," should some "violence" occur in her environment. There must be a large number of people indeed who, biologically, one wants to say, find themselves unable to respond to any change of this order and who want it "as it was," just that that stasis, they feel, secures them in their own increasing limits of possible activity.

I find that attitude deeply human. I remember Pound's saying somewhere, that "after fifty one can't keep one's eye on all the sprouting corn," that one has to get one's own work done if it ever is to be got done. Hopefully, one learns something about the possibilities of an art, be it sewing or singing, and having done so, one wants the center of that information and the possibilities of working with it to stay put.

Perhaps even more to the point, art is by nature conservative—which is to say, it pays a strict and constant attention to the materials and modalities wherewith it comes to make a thing. In that sense I remember Charles Olson's insistence that "we are the last conservatives," those who were given to care, in John Winthrop's phrase, about the kind of world we live in.

Politics, sadly, does not seem to care about that world except in small, preferential segments of its existence. The only political

*Partisan Review* 39, no. 3 (Summer 1972).

group I find myself consistently attracted to is, paradoxically, that of the black community. They would seem to be engaged in both gaining and saving the possibilities of distinct human life. That their actions are often "radical" only emphasizes for me the precise conservatism of their intent. They are not fooling, so to speak, and their action tends to follow the literal pattern of their commitment. The farm workers are another, if smaller, instance of the same nature of action.

As a poet I will do anything to secure my own realization of what the possibilities of imagination are. Obviously such a commitment can be at times a destructive and isolating phenomenon. But the *conservatism* of my own nature—that endlessly insistent "save the baby" demand I feel—will not let me act otherwise. I am a literalist. I am confused by what seems to be, yet when actually approached or met with, proves not to be at all. To recognize that another artist is painfully and arbitrarily limited in what he or she feels possible because some group "doesn't like it" strikes me as outrageous. In that sense I have tended to be far more open to other artists in their work than I have been to their critics, radical or conservative.

# The Creative

One seems to begin at a beginning, and then, after a time as difficult to recognize the actual measure of as any other *thing* that may or may not happen, one comes to an end. In that literal situation of what one calls experience, the *outward,* call it, of the content of perception, a life is lived in the explicit package of meat one calls the body. A mind thinks of it, at first so intrinsically the organism itself that there is, apparently, no separation experienced. The eyes see, the mouth tastes, the nose smells, the ears hear, the hands touch and hold, the legs stretch and walk. Hair, skin, bone, the body fills, voids, heats, cools, sleeps, wakes. An interminable one of many, the thought of life apart from itself is vague, impossible to consider. There is no one but instantly proves all, *people* some vast horizontal of seemingly similar size, a growth then of precisely repetitive proportions.

I want to speak of *creative* in the simply complex situation of: what creative means to me. Ezra Pound wrote of the deceptive syntactical simplicity of the request, "Buy me the kind of Rembrandt I like"—as complex in actuality as the numbers of people who might make it. Speaking now, it must be that this factual person, *me,* is familiar, so like so many, in fact, his hair, teeth, pants, etc. But the *I,* as Wittgenstein put it, is what is "deeply mysterious." In a world

Black Sparrow Press, *Sparrow* 6 (1973).

of objects, *me*s, this is the one manifestation of existence that cannot so see itself as literal *thing*. It is my experience that what I feel to be the creative has location in this place of personal identity.

A friend recently here told me of a book he'd been reading wherein the creative as a concept is attributed to Renaissance art and its artists, although they felt their notion to have in turn roots in their own sense of historical past. This fact—as it instantly, 'creatively,' became one in my thinking—coincided with another I had got from Giedion's discussion of *abstraction* in the first volume of *The Eternal Present*. As he says, "Like the symbol, abstraction came into being with the beginning of art. It existed: nameless. It was simply there . . ." Certainly these two agencies, symbol and abstraction, have a powerful resonance in any situation we speak of as 'creative,' or surely they have had. To take from this that, to make another—this must, in thinking, be an extraordinary act of mind— to have of another a one, itself thus thing of the other, symbolic, and yet apart, abstract—so becomes the magic we feel in all transformation. Initially, as Giedion assumes it, there were two possibilities in abstraction: the ability to make of all the seemingly endless divergency and occasion of thing a general agreement, a *one* in which the *all* of its situation might come to rest and be recognized; but also, the impulse to have the one be a part of the whole, in a way which overrode it, became specific more intensely than all the other 'parts' otherwise equally present, an 'I' that wants so much more than to be merely 'human' or 'people' or, simply, 'like them.' Giedion notes that there is an increasing social egocentricity in that time between the Middle Ages and the Renaissance, although it is myself who calls it 'social'—a feeling that what the elders of our own time felt as 'individual sensibility,' an insistence on the intrinsic value of what each one of us may feel, think, or value as singular persons, was growing in multiple social senses at this time. Giedion also emphasizes that it is this same dominance of egocentricity that permits Descartes to say, "I think, therefore I am," and to make thus separation of emotion and intellect in the context of human experience. The *abstraction* here accomplished is of the second kind.

We may feel as common persons of the world a terror we will not be given specific witness, that no one will ever know our actual lives have been lived at all. But why, I wonder, do we so imagine our lives *not* to have their own inherent orders, as Charles Olson might say—or why do we so wish to extend ourselves beyond the literal, the usual, even the casual circumstances of any day we do so live? As such persons we yearn for the possibility, as we would say, of doing something truly 'creative,' 'different,' not at all like anything anyone has ever done before. It is as if that sadly insistent 'humanism' of Descartes, that intensely flat and drab *rationalism*, had taken us to pure possibility—We think!—and then left us there to ponder: What can we think of now? Unhappily there is an automatism just as actual in processes of thought as might be felt to be in processes of digestion. My own irritation with the notion of creativity, as it has to do with writing, and, frankly, with living as well, is that it has been so given this place of the will—as though an act of thought resolved as an intention became thereby instanter revelation.

I had hoped, ignorantly, that *create* and *credible* might share some root, thinking of the Spanish *creo (I believe)*—because it would be lovely indeed if creation and belief were joined at some initial point in their experience. However, that is not the case, but 'create' is issue of such lovely company I see no reason to be disappointed: "*ker-*. To grow. Suffixed form *\*ker-es-* in Latin *Ceres*, goddess of agriculture, especially the growth of fruits," whence our *cereal*. Or in the Latin *creare*, "to cause to grow." Or the o-grade forms in "*\*kor-wo-*, 'growing,' adolescent, in Greek *kouros, koros*, boy, son" and in *\*kor-wa*, "in Greek *kore*, girl, maiden, pupil of the eye." Or that most lovely, possibly: "Compound *\*sm-kero-*, 'of one growth' (*\*sem-*, same, one . . .), in Latin *sincerus*, pure, clean": whence our *sincere*. "Only the most absolute sincerity under heaven can effect any change."

One should, after all, have danced more, under the moon, and been a farmer, instead of a man given to thought. At least one has been father and teacher, giving such care as one knew how to, sincerely, to that growth of persons, in places very possibly not the most suitable. One had created them—hearing sometimes as blessing, sometimes as snigger, *fruit of my loins. Fruit of the loom, loam. You fruit. First fruits. The fruit of their labor.* I remember that early *create* meant *make*, for me, insofar as I had apparently created a disturbance, had made a mess. Woodenly, I could see no very clear difference in the fact and stubbornly set out to make a poem, a man, of myself. I thought you could think of it, and, having plans, follow them till the thing appeared, gloriously, complete. In like sense the creation of the world seemed to me a specific labor of God's in the same way this building seems the specific labor of carpenters. My company in this dilemma was obviously a number of my nineteenth-century countrymen, who seem to have made love, money, and monsters, all with the same convictions. One can hear even now, for example, that anguished voice shouting, "I have created a monster!" The possible 'disturbance' was unquestionably the real point in mind.

Our contemporary 'creations' are somewhat drabber: dresses, new styles, sad brittle poems written in sterile surroundings to mechanical senses of the possibility. But why should one be so hostile to what is, after all, a very human hope that something might thus change, might come to be said—*be new*? What does one know of creation except that insistent "Make it new," which Pound so emphasized? But he says also, "I have brought the great ball of crystal; / who can lift it? / Can you enter the great acorn of light?"

It is possible we live entirely in that act we so call 'creative,' that that is, in fact, the place of our possibility and recognition of life—that that fact of *place* is a mind, that *body* is equally the idea of it which possesses us. I am struck by the situation of schizophrenia wherein the experience of body may so place the hands or feet or anus in the consciousness so affected, that no communal agreement as to their location is possible. A *self-created* reality in that way dominates and isolates the one who has become, even without intention or agreement, its world.

In like sense, one of the human dilemmas of artists, particularly of writers who are participant in a kind of image-making that has as agency that most powerful, possibly, of human abstractions, *language*, is megalomania, delusions of greatness, of exceeding power or omnipotence. There is persistent impatience with those unwilling or unable to enter the world so proposed, and its obviousness to the one who has served as its creator makes him appear *fascistically*, in the political sense, determined upon its actuality and harmonious economy. One can think instantly of a diversity of writers who exhibit that situation in greater or lesser degree: Knut Hamsun, Céline, Wyndham Lewis, D. H. Lawrence, and Ezra Pound himself. The world, so to speak, depends upon them for its own realization, but as they work to accomplish this reality, another world, equally present, insists upon those limits, which they, humanly, must accept.

To say of someone, that his or her appearance is *pleasant*, or *ugly*—each is a creative act. A 'world' in each case occurs in which that person takes place, whether or no his or her agreement is given. "Give a dog a bad name . . ." is not a specious homily but recognition, however casual, of the power of naming. "A rose by

any other name . . ." might well smell as sweet, but not the *rose*—
that would no longer exist, and an odor only would be the point.
For years I have been intrigued by a quotation of Louis Zukofsky's
from Wittgenstein: "A point in space is a [the?] place for an argument . . ." Think of it. Is that the point? What point? What has
come to it? Who is present and realizes that to be the case? When?
Is there the possibility of agreement in any such situation? "How
many angels can dance on the head of a pin?" True questions of a
reality experienced as *created*—that is to say, in this case, something
said. "I didn't mean to hurt you. I loved, love, will love—you. Here.
There. Then. Now." "The indefinite period of time yet to be . . ."

It is that *spell* of words that now comes to mind, and one had forgotten, thinking back all those years, to fusty smells of oiled corridors and boots and wet coats, sitting, trying to think, to remember, how does one spell 'patient' . . . Spelling! So obviously and so
simply evident—and the grammar, the *glamour,* is instantly present, the patient 'patient,' and the heavy dead odor of the sickroom,
roses in a vase beside the bed, because roses, not dandelions, cost
explicit money and betoken care and tender concern. So you do
have me 'under your spell,' and it is 'that old black magic,' again.

But quickly that other 'world' I had mentioned asserts itself, demanding time, demanding one be in it, physically *actual.* Robert
Duncan, with characteristic clarity, posits the situation of these two
'worlds' as *reality* and *actuality.* The real is what we value in *real*
estate, and has to do with things of this life: *res, rei*—possession,
thing. *R*epublic—dig it . . . One for all and all for one. But the actual has got that 'act' in it: "actus, an ACT." It's moving, causing
things to skitter and bump, get on with it in some actual sense. One
can return to reality by way of the *actuarial,* having to do with the
computing of insurance risks and premiums, etc., etc., but it will
never be the same. Which is to say, the tree is real, but when you hit
it, it's actual.

"Don't you poets get tired of living in a world of your own imagination and want to get back to reality?" Whose reality? Who owns
all this? The Swedish poet Lars Gustafsson pointed out to me that
marriage, like the car, is an invention. It is not actual, although for
many people indeed it may be real. But one doesn't drink it, or
stumble over it, throw it on the fire. It isn't flesh or fur or fin. You'll
remember the story of the sad fisherman who was given three
wishes, who was both married and caught in reality, so that the demand upon him was to get more and more of that substance. Things
upon things upon things—and no place to be. No one actually

home at all, no matter it was all too real. It's an equally sad mistake
to think that what is called 'creative' in poetry seeks a bargain in
space and time, wants to exchange this for that, hike up the prices,
so to speak. When Robert Graves writes, "There is one story, and
one story only, that is worth your telling . . . ," he claims for poet
that power of *revelation*, that care specific to this gift that the elemental nature of existence *not* be lost in the thought of it.

At the funeral of Jackson Pollock, Wednesday, August 15, 1956,
the minister, the Reverend George Nicholson, read from St. Paul's
statement, Romans, Chapter 8: "The world of creation cannot as
yet see reality, not because it chooses to be blind, but because in
God's purpose it has been so limited—yet it has been given hope."
Later he said, not really having known Pollock but in a very certain
sense cognizant of the occasion: "It seemed to me that at that moment when the art world had collected around that grave, on that
beautiful day, all our skills & philosophies added up to a fragmen-
tary & sorry collection. Like Plato's cave we were men living in a
shadowy illusory world of sounds & sights—like dogs in an art gallery—sniffing around at corners.

"No, I didn't know J. Pollock. But in the Epistle to the Romans
Chapter 8 there is more than a hint of glory and greatness—always
in short supply."

Charles Olson's response to 'creative' social thinking was a muted
sneer, "Oh, change it altogether . . ."—much like Pound's, "you
who think you will/ get through hell in a hurry . . ." The point is:
"Who even dead, yet hath his mind entire!/ This sound came in the
dark/ First must thou go the road/ to hell . . ." "First came the seen,
then thus the palpable/ Elysium, though it were in the halls of hell,/
What thou lovest well is thy true heritage/ What thou lov'st well
shall not be reft from thee . . ."

Pound's respect for Confucius, for that "sound given off by the
heart's core," the possibility of things said, is measure of the *sincerity*
I had earlier invoked. Whitman insisted, "The theme is creative
and has vista," and in his sincerity, the heart of the matter, an imagination found the literal body of its impulse realized, made substantive, transformed. For it is *imagination*, only, which has this possibility. Hear it. "Only the imagination is real!/ I have declared it/ time
without end . . ." "Light, the imagination/ and love,/ in our age,/ by
natural law,/ which we worship,/ maintain/ all of a piece/ their dominance." Realize that you *have been* told, by the myriad men and
women for whom *creation* is the literal place we live in, under sky,
on ground, by water, in air. Pollock said, "When I am *in* my paint-

ing, I am not aware of what I'm doing. It is only after a sort of 'get acquainted' period that I see what I have been about. I have no fears about making changes, destroying the image, etc., because the painting has a life of its own. I try to let it come through. It is only when I lose contact with the painting that the result is a mess. Otherwise there is pure harmony, an easy give and take, and the painting comes out well."

What is here to discover is neither new nor significantly esoteric. Henry Corbin, in the introduction to *Creative Imagination in the Sufism of Ibn 'Arabi*, makes this useful point: "Today, with the help of phenomenology, we are able to examine the way in which man experiences his relationship to the world without reducing the objective data of this experience to data of sense perception or limiting the field of true and meaningful knowledge to the mere operations of the rational understanding. Freed from an old impasse, we have learned to register and to make use of the intentions implicit in all the acts of consciousness or transconsciousness. To say that the Imagination (or love, or sympathy, or any other sentiment) *induces knowledge,* and knowledge of an 'object' which is proper to it, no longer smacks of paradox." Thus you will recognize the sadly familiar, and *useless,* difficulty William Carlos Williams meets with in "The Desert Music": "You seem quite normal. Can you tell me? Why / does one want to write a poem?// Because it's there to be written.// Oh. A matter of inspiration then?// Of necessity.// Oh. But what sets it off?// I am that he whose brains/ are scattered/ aimlessly . . ." At the close of this extraordinary poem the moment of revelation is literally accomplished: "I *am* a poet! I/ am. I am a poet, I reaffirmed, ashamed// Now the music volleys through as in/ a lonely moment I hear it. Now it is all/ about me. The dance! The verb detaches itself/ seeking to become articulate . . ." The word *dances,* in the literal garden of *desire.*

Louis Zukofsky wrote, "Out of deep need . . ." But what nature of *need* is it? To eat, to sleep, to find a form merely? I question that. In Berlin I am delighted to discover that the eminent scientist Heisenberg, himself in Munich, has fallen upon the arts as though upon a blissful bed of flowers, *knowing,* in his age, as Gregory Corso would say, that the *conceptual* dilemma of the sciences leads them round and around the careful maze of their various *contexts,* true Bottoms but alas no Shakespeares to love them and get them home. Zukofsky also writes of these *things made,* these *poems,* as being source of profound solace—where the heart finds rest. It is the need to *enter* what we loosely call the vision, to be one with the

Imago Mundi, that image of the world we each of us carry within us as possibility itself. What can we say otherwise? Peace, brother. It's going to be all right. It's soon over and it won't hurt.

But the heart *aches*—"Out of deep need . . ." Corbin: "This power of the heart is what is especially designated by the word *himma*, a word whose content is perhaps best suggested by the Greek word *enthymesis*, which signifies the act of meditating, conceiving, imagining, projecting, ardently desiring—in other words, of having (something) present in the *thymos*, which is vital force, soul, heart, intention, thought, desire . . . The force of an *intention* so powerful as to project and realize ('essentiate') a being external to the being who conceives the intention, corresponds perfectly to the character of the mysterious power that Ibn 'Arabi designates as *himma* . . . Thanks to his representational faculty . . . every man creates in his Active Imagination things having existence only in this faculty. This is the general rule. But by his *himma* the gnostic *creates* something which exists outside the seat of this faculty . . . In the first case, as it is exercised by most men, its function is representational; it produces images which are merely part of the conjoined Imagination . . . , inseparable from the subject. But even here, pure representation does not, *eo ipso*, mean 'illusion,' these images really 'exist,' illusion occurs when we misunderstand their mode of being. In the case of the gnostic . . . , the Active Imagination serves the *himma* which, by its concentration, is capable of *creating* objects, of producing changes in the outside world . . . When in contemplating an image, an icon, others recognize and perceive as a divine image the vision beheld by the artist who created the image, it is because of the spiritual creativity, the *himma* which the artist put into his work. Here we have a compelling term of comparison, by which to measure the decadence of our dreams and of our arts . . ."

Well, no use no way, *and* comparisons *are* odious—and the plan we had was that all this was going to get it together and be a happy place to be *in*, like. But that *himma* shit, man, that's *really* my kind of people. Heart-felt. I really mean it, this time, this place, this—. He forgot the word, walking around, was momently in Bolinas, Berlin, Oslo, Bergen, London, Bolinas—time's like that, sometimes. Days spent watching surfers, days spend time like there was no end to it, forever. "He wants impossible liveforever . . ." "Capsules wherein we wrap up our punishable secrets . . ." You going to read us a *poem*, Bob? "Who even dead, yet hath his mind entire!"

You really have to believe in it, as Coleridge said, all those years ago, so gently, "the willing suspension of disbelief . . ." Like that lovely, 'once upon a time . . .' I knew a man once who had a lovely team of horses, this was in West Acton, Mass., and one of them kneeled on a nail was in the planking of the stall, and the knee got infected—Mr. Green was his name—and Mr. Green, who lived alone with his wife, both about in their seventies, he used to, literally, take the blankets off their bed, this was in winter, and go out into the stall and wrap up that horse and put poultices on her knee, to draw out the poison, and he'd sit there with her, all the night, and finally the old horse, old in its own way as him, got well.

Take it from there, cut through. Breaks in time, head. Allen Ginsberg feels poems to be 'time capsules,' messages you don't really get the fact of till later. Have those bones begun to sprout—Eliot? True poet, not at all that he wanted to be—so rational, so Augustan in that old elegance. Let's create a spectacle! The sixties had 'happenings': "I painted 'I love what I'm doing' in orange and blue. When I got to 'what I'm doing,' it was going very fast, and I picked up one of the jars and drank the paint, and then I poured the other two jars of paint over my head, quickly, and dove . . . through the canvas . . ."

Such report as I had of studies done some years ago at the University of California at Berkeley, and at Stanford, of the situation of 'creative' behavior and personality with respect to specific persons, seemed to indicate a rather low return of information. Who can be anticipated as being in a situation with a high potential for creative behavior? No one apparently, with any surety. One may be born into a family of ten children, or one, have both parents actively present, or none, have a high degree of affluence present, or none, be black, white, yellow, red—without much proving the case. In like sense specific training in areas deemed creative, as music, dance, art, writing, may or may not effect anything. The composer Morton Subotnik pointed out that by far the greater number of eminently competent classical musicians, call them, in this country were the children of Russian Jews, simply that no other group could so unremarkably oblige their children to practice their instrument for six to eight hours daily, from the tender age of three onward. He himself was an exceptional clarinetist and had lovely wish fulfillment dreams in which both his arms were removed from his body, blissfully. He even joined the army, hoping to break the spell—but was instantly put into Special Services, to play the clarinet. Finally, in his early twenties, he managed, of his own will, to put it down. What he had *wanted* to play, aged three, was the trombone, but he could not name it for his parents, and when they showed him endless pictures of musical instruments, in consternation and fatigue he pointed to the clarinet as being most like that thing he had seen in nursery school.

We must respect the fact that what we call the creative cannot be simplistically 'included' in a rationalistically based 'program.' Art schools do not of necessity make painters, although a significant number of them may, variously, come to be there. But that is not *why* they are painters—if they are. We must respect equally the fact that we do *not* know why people are painters, or composers, or poets. In usual, mundane reality, to be any of those 'things' is not a simple, nor even desirable, situation of experience. My mother, with very gentle discretion, used to say, "I like to think that Bob *could* get a job if he had to." Olson's advice, "Poets, you should get a job . . ." makes clear the other side of this vacancy, if by 'poet' one proposes some idealistic creature who is too tender to manage the harsh buffetings of 'real life.' There must be *some* place to live in, together, and if poets tend to get people overexcited, emotionally, as Plato felt, then we simply have to take that chance. We must know by this time that reason, often, can only excuse itself, and it really doesn't seem to be an *initial*—by which I mean a 'first time'— situation in experience. Gregory Corso used to say to people who invited him up to their penthouses for a closer look, "Why don't you just give me the money and let me go home." The creative is frequently a situation of that order, but it isn't a question of, "Give me the tools and I will do the job." Poets have got the tools. They just want to live a little.

So there is this world one thinks of, and another, no doubt, that seems to be there no matter. Jung called them the *creatura*, significantly enough, and the *pleroma*, the first being the mind's world, the world of ideas, differences, distinctions, thought, and the second, the world of physical event purely, having no 'idea' of itself, no 'imagination,' no this or that. Having *two* things, worlds or whatever, the mind wants to ask immediately, which one is *better*—or rather, the *Western* mind does. But you have to give up that 'better,' it just doesn't work—or of course you can go on being a sternly humanistic rationalist, but it won't get you *here*. Because *there* will always be here too, to really drive you out of your head.

One wants to keep growing. One looks for whatever signs seem the issue of that possibility. The plans are to secure that situation, but the hope may be a sad one. I don't want to say that there's no use in living in whatever imagination of the universe is your own. Democracy is literal and will tell you where you are inexorably. You know the people and they know you. Each day, night, you are alive will be specific, even if you are in some body state that seems altogether inaccessible to the others. 'Creative,' as actuality, is here always, never elsewhere in any sense.

I think that where my own confusion lies, in trying to think of 'creative' as an adjective, as some *descriptive* term, is in the fact that I cannot conceive of 'creative' as something available to an attitude of discreet choice—as though one were able to agree or not, as its interest quickened or waned in one's thought of it. Life continues as it makes more life? Is that the self-growth principle? Are we a circumstance of cells having as limit the ability to exhaust the environment in which we find ourselves? "Well met by moonlight . . ." A dream of universe that has affections, qualities, and kinds. How did we get here, like they say. I was born some years ago and I have paid attention as I was able, to all that came to attention. I'm an honest man, I pay what I owe. He was speaking in some heat, irritated that those who listened to him were not apparently impressed. "How can we tell the dancer from the dance . . ." Who was it that wanted to. Olson's sense, that art is the only true twin life has—it 'means nothing,' it doesn't have a point. The painter Arakawa's delight in *zero set*, the real nitty gritty for any head-trip. Or—wanted to forget it, get out of the whole demand. On automatic pilot. Is that 'the creative.'

Basil Bunting said his own recognition, that he was to be a poet, *was*, in fact, came to him while sitting on the hearth at the age of four or so, listening to his parents talk about the Russian-Japanese conflict. It was only hard, he said, because he didn't know clearly what a *poet* was. Does one only say that later. I don't think so. I don't think it's really any different than the recognition that D. D. T. has such harsh effect on the environment—an *idea* become substantial, something's really having happened. Richard Alpert told of a man's jumping off a four-story building, then dying, smiling through blood, in the street. He said the man must have been happy—*smiling*. Is it discreet, this life. It is discrete. The *growth* must have multiple phase, like water boiling or freezing, must have multiple condition, transfer—transformed to other energy, agency. Eat it up—is eaten. The farmer feeds the horse a little less each day until he arrives at that point where the horse is subsisting on nothing at all. Succeeds, then—but the horse dies. There is no *reason* why the idea should not be successful, with or without the horse. It only depends on what you want.

Seeds dormant thousands of years, given chance, luck, might—

could—did grow. They eat the flesh of the mammoth frozen millennia, in ice. Hold it! They got the picture. Article in old *Reader's
Digest:* "New Hope for the Dead." Simple-minded con trip deigns
to speak of 'the rest of us.'

If I could just create the kind of world I'd really like to live in . . .
*I* wouldn't be there. 'I' is an experience of creation, which puts up
with it no matter. There's a lot to get done. You've been born and
that's the first and last ticket. Already he changes his mind, makes
the necessary adjustments, picks up his suitcase and getting into his
car, drives slowly home. He lives with people whom he has the experience of loving. It all works out. He says. It has to. One to a cus-
tomer. It's late. But they'll be there. He relaxes. He has an active mind.

*For My Mother: Genevieve Jules Creeley*

*April 9, 1887–October 7, 1972*

> Tender, semi-
> articulate flickers
> of your
>
> presence, all
> those years
> past
>
> now, eighty-
> five, impossible to
> count them
>
> one by one, like
> addition, sub-
> traction, missing
>
> not one. The last
> curled up, in
> on yourself,
>
> position you take
> in the bed, hair
> wisped up
>
> on your head, a
> top knot, body
> skeletal, eyes
>
> closed against,
> it must be,

further disturbance—

breathing a skim
of time, lightly
kicks the intervals

days, days and
years of it,
work, changes,

sweet flesh caught
at the edges,
dignity's faded

dilemma. It
is *your* life, oh
no one's

forgotten anything
ever. They want
to make you

happy when
they remember. Walk
a little, get

up, now, die
safely,
easily, into

singleness, too
tired with it
to keep

on and on.
Waves break at
the darkness

under the road, sounds
in the faint
night's softness. Look

at them, catching
the light, white
edge as they turn—

always again
and again. Dead
one, two,

three hours—
all these minutes

pass. Is it,

was it, ever
you alone
again, how

long you kept
at it, your
pride, your

lovely, confusing
discretion. Mother, I
love you—for

whatever that
means,
meant—more

than I know, body
gave me my
own, generous,

inexorable place
of you. I feel
the mouth's sluggish-

ness, slips on
turns of things
said, to you,

too soon, too late,
wants to
go back to beginning,

smells of the hospital
room, the doctor
she responds

to now, the
order—get me
there. "Death's

let you out—"
comes true,
this, that,

endlessly circular
life, and we
came back

to see you one

last
time, this

time? Your head
shuddered,
it seemed, your

eyes wanted,
I thought,
to see

who it was.
I am here,
and will follow.

*Bolinas, California*
*October 15, 1972*

# Inside Out

## Notes on the Autobiographical Mode

for Jane Brakhage

> *I'm telling you a*
> *story to let myself*
> *think about it. All*
>
> *day I've been*
> *here, and yesterday.*
> *The months, years,*
>
> *enclose me as*
> *this thing with arms*
> *and legs. And if*
>
> *it* is *time*
> *to talk about it*
> *who knows better*
>
> *than I?*

There was a time—primary but not primitive—when experience
of consciousness did not separate it from the sensory and perceptive as an agency somehow isolated from those other situations of
experience. I mean, the concept and location of *mind* is relatively
'new' to us as people. Some obviously felt it a significant step forward, as Bruno Snell in his book *The Discovery of the Mind*. Others
were less happy, feeling that the isolation, thus, of the mind in

Black Sparrow Press, *Sparrow* 14 (1973).

body, and its use as a *decision,* call it, for all that otherwise constitutes body information, overweighted the *mental* as against what I'll
call the *physical.*

*Mental* and *physical* are aspects, clearly, of one primary unit or organism called a human. But, curious now to realize, there was a
time when the eye saw, the hand held, the skin felt, ear heard, nose
smelled, etc., each in a primary input to the body as total organism.
There was no debate, so to speak—the thought occurred in the experience: Bang! Once mind could think of itself, and so propose an
extensive condition of its own function, these primary inputs—and
they must remain so, no matter what's 'thought'—seemingly yielded
to the mind's activity. Thus, if one were cold, the trick was 'not to
think of it' or else 'to think one was not *very* cold,' hence warmer
than one was apparently feeling.

I love these tricks of the mind, yet feel increasingly uneasy concerning the impact upon us of their authority. A few years ago Tuli
Kupferberg promoted a lovely, if terrifying, slogan: Kill For Peace.
How could that be? Well, you had these bad guys, that is, one
*thought* they were 'bad,' and these good guys, similarly created, and
if you killed all the bad guys, then of course the good guys were
'free'—as they had been to kill—to live in peace. Get the appropriate context and anything in the world can be very simply thought
of as 'true.' I smoke, for example, not because it may give me cancer and kill me, but because I like to, or I have it as a habit, or I
think it gives my hands and mouth something to do. I—what I experience as *my mind* thinking of *me*—have no problem in removing
the causes of possible distress. After all, it's only my body that dies
in any case. My mind never will, etc.

*Auto-bio-graphy* I translate as a life tracking itself. One interesting
factor here is that *bios* (life) did not initially extend to *animal* life but
was involved with human only. Later, in compounds, its meaning is
made to cover organic life in general: biology. It would seem that
even at this point life had something very significantly to do with
life thinking of itself. What is my life to me? Is it a good life? Organic or animal life *happened.* It could be acted upon, even obliter-
ated—like the dodo bird, but its occasion seemed inextricably involved with its event. There's a large lion in the forest, said the man
to his wife whom he had thought of one night in April and thus
married. It's me, she said, looking at him. What does it mean:
there's a large lion, anywhere, and has anybody told the lion?

I want to think for a while, of anything. Say birds—I like them.
People—terrific, if they like me. What a great life we're having, if

comfortable in our seats and minds and hearts. Or horrible,—rejected, unloved, in pain. I want to think it over. And over and over and over. Will thinking get me anywhere? To Detroit, possibly. Or here, for those of us who came from elsewhere, truly another abstraction.

In fact, it was that we could haul *it* away, like some ultimate garbage crew, that we came to be here at all, in this place with heads alert to learn, aching for information: The New-s. Abstraction, that yanking from one thing—call it organic life—just enough of it to let it still be there somehow, like the Venus de Milo, and then to use the arms to indicate the whole, so to speak. Obviously she was a lovely woman and her arms were really great to have around you. Once home, with them safely tucked into bed beside you, it possibly occurred to us, as to you, that something precisely to be desired had been left behind.

So what happened? That's where one possibility of the autobiographical can clearly enter. Try to remember. Statue. Arms. You. What did you do with them? What day was it, or night? Think. We'll give you all the time you need. "Lives of great men all remind us/ we can make our lives sublime/ and departing leave behind us/ footsteps (prints?) on (in?) the sands of time . . ." I can't remember. Simply write as clearly as you can what you think was the situation. It's *your* life.

Or, paradoxically, it may have little at all to do with memory. Or let's say, memory is a source of material, fantasy as well as fact. I remember! "I remember, I remember/ the house where I was born . . ." Like a movie my wife told me of in the old days, of doctor coming home in carriage with horse through driving rain, finally pushing his way through door into house, wife all excited and waiting for his first words, which are: Tonight history was made. I have just delivered Louis Pasteur!

You begin at any point, and move from that point forward or backward, up or down—or in a direction you yourself choose. In and out of the system, as Buckminster Fuller would say. It's a system—of valuation, habit, complex organic data, the weather, and so on. Usually the choice is to track it backward, that is, most autobiographical impulse tends to follow this course. One can think of one's life as not worth remembering, in fact one can want to forget it—but if what has constituted it, the things "of which it was made up," as William Carlos Williams says, are dear to your memory and experience of them, then it may well be a record of them, a graph of their activity as 'your life,' is an act you would like to perform.

This mode of autobiography is close to our usual senses of history, *his story* as we said in the fourth grade, and it is also useful here to note *history* comes from a Greek root, *historein:* to go find out for yourself. This was Charles Olson's clear point of emphasis in his own procedures, that *self-action*—the middle voice—was crucial in human existence. Why he so insisted, I think, comes of his belief that humans get truly lost in thought and language insofar as no substantiating act, particularly from and of and to the human itself, takes place. You can't be taught if you won't learn—just like the horse who won't for whatever reason drink.

So here then is possibly a motive, as well as a mode, for a kind of autobiography that might well be interesting to any of us. Olson also said, we do what we know before we know what we do. That's deeply interesting to me—it's where our bodies return to our minds, among other things. I feel a threat, not a pleasure, in Descartes' statement: I think, therefore I am—*if* that experience is felt to be somehow the most significant thing we can do. Again it's the situation of the abstract that I am uneasy about, that we can be here as *thought,* and that we will so *be,* with primary reality—which of course we also have thought—no matter what else may prove our actual state of being. Or it may be that he was just defining the word 'I'— that *I* thinks, and *me* is otherwise the case.

*Me* leaves many traces. Diter Rot made works of art the accumulation of what *me*-ness in the physical world is: rooms or apartments which slowly filled with casual input, bags, papers, garbage, junk, and when they were no longer habitable, being simply too full, he sealed them, then left, deeming them actual in a way another record of his existence within them could not accomplish. Another man suggested taking daily pictures of one's physical self, face or whatever, at a photomat, say, so that a 'track' of that aspect of one's life might be documented for referral. In each case it would seem that the point is not the *thought* of one's life but rather the *fact* which no situation of 'I' can gainsay.

Autobiography in this circumstance might be very interesting indeed. You know the way people say, we all have a story within us—something specific in our lives that would, could we only get it said, be something worth hearing. That may well be true but I don't think art is particularly involved by it. Writing, for example, is an activity dependent on words as material. It may be *felt* that it matters what they 'say' but far more decisive is the energy gained in the field or system they are used to create. *Small hambones* versus *big beef cutlets.* That is, you may *see* literal things thus suggested, but you are hearing also a system of sounds and rhythms that these materials are effectually creating. In like sense, the "Chef's Special" may sound good to you—but it may be awful to literally eat, and you won't know what it is until someone who does know tells you.

Again—stop it all. The boat's left, it's gone, nothing comes back from that place. You can run the film backward but it won't be the same. E.g., Ken Mikolowski has a lovely poem simply of the fact you can reverse linear patterns: *Oh say can you see* becoming *See you can say oh.* Time is either an imagination or else a phasing inherent in the system, organic or inert (including abstractions). What *is* your life that you're going to write it down, or make films of it, or whatever it is you had in mind. The one thing clear about your life is that you are living it. You're here—wherever that is. Whitman was quick about it, saying, "Who touches this book touches a man." He knew that whoever was holding the book to read it would physically be there. And that, believe it or not, is really fast thinking. I write *these words*, muttering, thinking, to myself. Cross fingers *and* I may well be dead before I ever chance to read them to you—a powerful and dangerous thing ever to say even to oneself. Witness what the words have done to *me* as *I* gains locus.

We—that unimaginable *plural* of I!—want our lives to be known to us, we don't want it all a seeming dream, back to Plato's cave again. We want the *light*—even a rock band or particularly a rock band *called* Plato's Cave, if nothing else seems to get it on. We don't want to hang around waiting to be x'ed out at some 'later date.' Henry M. Yaker writes: "Certain primitive cultures have no past or future tense in their language, and express all events of life, real or mythological, in an 'eternal now' . . ." That sounds fair enough. Everybody's here at this point, and they always were—despite the lack of communication. Of course a 'we' will still be found to flood thousands of acres of forest at the headwater of the Amazon, regretting they haven't means to inform the divers people living in those forests of the impending 'event.' That's another mode of autobiography, 'think big.' This will really get them in Des Moines. And so I tell you, friends and neighbors, although I come from humble origins, early in life I took the big chances—and won. You want to work for someone like that? Don't—even if you have to. Fuck him up, like they say. He's taken everything else.

Is autobiography, at least the written, just a means of self-justification, the 'facts' that excuse you? A few days ago in New York I got five parking tickets in forty-eight hours. When I put that

into my linear patterning, it fair broke my mind—and I felt like
leaving for California that very night. The car, happily, was already
there, viz. California license plates—so, *I'll* be back. But not always
to say, gee, I'm sorry, or, wasn't it nice yesterday. Shucks.

Too often we are told to generalize ourselves in the pattern of an
idea that may or may not have specific relevance for what we feel as
persons otherwise. The *imagination* of a commonwealth must make
that sharing literal—there cannot be an invested partiality hidden
from the participants. When the New York Police Department has
persons within it who will literally threaten to run other persons
down with trucks in order to gain their compliance, no matter how
'guilty' those threatened may be, one cannot accept the agency.
Realize that the *general*, the *we-ness* proposed in various realities,
may well prove to be this kind. Obviously any 'we' must, willynilly,
submit to the organic orders of its existence: must sleep, must eat,
must drink, must move, must die. But that is very nearly the totality
of the actual demand. Elsewise, the "geography leans in," as Olson
put it. Place is a real event—where you are is a law equal to what
you are.

To discover a precision in this situation, to act in the specific context, takes all the wit and alertness any one of us can bring to it.
You'll recognize that people tend to check one another out, coming
from divers places. With hitchhikers a few nights ago, I had an extraordinary information of routes that can move us across this
country, bypasses, numbers, weather, places—and the people to be
met with in every major nexus of persons from here to L.A. Time
as well was particular—as it is insistently for the Guatemalan Indians, who have a precise vocabulary of explicit measures for the
way in which you are moving—on foot, say, or on horseback, truck,
etc. And these are *not* interchangeable, only translatable.

What the autobiographic does, primarily, is to specify *person*—at
least it has that capability. Reading, for example, Mandelstam's
widow's book, *Hope Against Hope*, persons become actual—there is
no generality of impression such as, Russia is hostile to the Jews. A
literal man is demonstrated as experiencing a viciously insistent
persecution, finally resulting in his death. One can, of course, feel
the report exaggerated, simply that it is his widow who relates the
story. But *her* words are again, literally, a *person* saying them. You,
as person also, can make up your own mind—and the question isn't
one inviting you to feel that poetry in Russia should be more respected. The fact is, it *is* respected—so much so that Mandelstam
dies *because* the power of his gift is so feared. Think: scrawled on

the wall of a death camp by someone waiting to die, a *line* of Mandelstam's, one not even to be found in a so-called book but carried in the ear, mind and mouth, person to person, all that bitter distance.

One time, years ago now, Allen Ginsberg was at a party in New York talking with a young woman about the apparent hostility publishers then felt toward the younger American poets, myself in particular. She was, as it happens, a junior editor at Harper's, and listened patiently to his irritation. Then she said, we've been in business for over eighty years and I think we know what we're doing. At which point Ginsberg naturally flipped—You? *You've* been in business for over eighty years? Why you're only twenty-two years old!

Why not speak for yourself. Sooner or later you'll have to. There are no sure investments. Watch the dollar do the dirty float—like a mind, a dead idea, fading out.

I'm tired and I want to stop this mumbling. But I've made a commitment, and I want to respect it. That's true. What other experience of 'I' is interesting, except that which manifests its patterning, the laws of its own imagination and possible experience. Tell me who I am. Amnesia, but the person continues eating, sleeping, begins again. In group therapy investments of the experience of 'I' are relinquished, even forced out. Richard Alpert recalled his first experience of LSD as being a loss of all ego support—his sense of himself as a brilliant young psychologist, a professor at Harvard, a successful son, and much more, melted like ice in hot sun. Can you melt yourself, 'autobiographically,' can you stand, literally, not to be some absent dream of glory, just what your mother always wanted.

Or consider Gregory Corso's reaction to people talking about the joys of ego loss: lose your egos? You're not even good enough to *have* egos. Agh.

So keep on tracking—life. "To measure is all we know . . ." You want to use somebody else's ruler, that's your business. I don't know that all the emphasis upon individual sensibility isn't some simple con game, simply 'divide and conquer.' But who *are* you, and why does your life propose itself as a collective. Is it a premise got from the fact we constitute a species, 'we are many'—which is certainly attractive to any *me* of myself I can experience as *I*. There's no pleasure in being by yourself finally, always alone.

I love the possibly apocryphal account of nineteenth century people in Russia going up to absolute strangers in the street, grabbing them by the knees, and then confessing to them some incred-

ible act. Like Dostoyevsky's account of the rape of a child with
which he had been involved. Or Ginsberg saying to the old poet in
Peru, I want to know your dirtiest secrets. We've had a lot to do
with those 'secrets,' lately. In the My Lai inquiry soldiers told humanly awful stories in seemingly unquestioning tones of voice—
such as giving a pesty kid a spam sandwich with a thermal device
inside it, which then flared in the kid's throat and stomach, killing
him. What gave them containment was the *general*—the United
States Army in this instance. You give each of the six men of the
firing squad a gun, only one of which has a live bullet. You shuffle
the guns first of all, so that even you can't identify the lethal weapon.
Then you check your own commands, and then you give the order
to shoot. No one has killed anyone, specifically—he's just dropped
dead. Suddenly I think of the *general* of an army, old Mr. Abstraction himself. Ours not to reason why—ours just to do it, and let
those mothers die.

Autobiography might be thought of, then, as some sense of a life
*responsive* to its own experience of itself. This is the 'inside out,' so to
speak—somehow reminiscent of, It ain't no sin/ to take off your
skin/ and dance around in your boh-hones . . . Trying to take a
look, see what it was all about, why Mary never came home and Joe
was, after all, your best friend. Not to explain—that is, not to lay a
trip on them—rather an *evidence* seems what one is trying to get
hold of, to have use of oneself specifically as something that *does*
something, and in so doing leaves a record, a consequence, intentionally or not.

The sculptor Marisol speaks of using herself, over and over, in
her work. "When I show myself as I am I return to reality." When
one wears a uniform or otherwise generalizes the condition of one's
experience of oneself, that "reality" is most difficult to enter. There
was, sadly, a professor employed at the University of New Mexico
who one time began a lecture with the statement: As I was shav-
ing this morning, seeing myself in the mirror, Professor Jones, I
said . . . That is the end of the story, just another professor, no one
otherwise home. There can be a different experience of that situation as one of the earliest discovered occasions of written language
makes clear: I, John, foreman of Pit 7, hereby testify . . . Or words
to that effect. This is the responsibility of identity, not its specious
investment. Do you *know* how to drive the car, *can* you stop this
bleeding, *are* you a competent doctor, lawyer, teacher, father—or
are you just out to lunch.

There must be times when the experience of being oneself is almost unendurable—by which I mean, something has happened, oneself being the agency, and it is unspeakably difficult to accept *what* one has thus done. Williams, a markedly autobiographical writer, spoke of poems as "capsules wherein we wrap up our punishable secrets." That is a Puritan sense certainly, but Puritans have been great practitioners of autobiography—Thoreau, D. H. Lawrence and Edward Dahlberg among them. Any context which makes one feel singular in life, a specific isolated consciousness in the universe, intensifies the attraction of this situation of statement. Camus' first draft of *The Stranger* uses an *I* which is markedly himself, I am told, and certainly 'existentialism' is a Puritan stance.

No doubt there are clear signs of a kind of paranoia in this mode, just that the *I* feels itself surrounded by a *they* to which its experience of itself cannot easily refer. Paranoia in the arts is by no means unfamiliar. The artist must often feel that he or she has been deliberately cut off from some generality of social grouping, and so must both state, and implicitly justify, the fact of his or her 'life.' Since no one else apparently cares, I will speak of myself to myself. I know that I, as an artist, have never dared to imagine in working that an actual audience might be literally attentive to what I have to say. Therefore my primary experience of an audience has been my own eye, or ear, listening to what it was that was being said. My wife tells me that I often mutter when writing, and also frequently laugh—both instances of the situation I am describing. Now, older, when I am at times asked to say something specifically to an audience, I am still dependent primarily on what I hear in saying it, not what the audience may hear. In that respect I am very thick-skinned, and can take a good deal of abuse, as long as that which is getting said is of interest to me. Another situation of statement would obviously stop, confounded, when it found that response, apart from its own experience of itself, was hostile.

When Angus Fletcher speaks of the change in the *imagination* of how persons may experience the world, from Marlowe to Bunyan, say, he is emphasizing the shift in consciousness from a communal locus to a singular one, to an *I* that has discovered the possibility of its own assumption of the *right*, self-defined and self-asserted, to be an *I* co-present and equal in that sense to all other possibilities of reality. It is a giddy moment, and perhaps a deeply tragic one. Bunyan, despite the fact that *Pilgrim's Progress* uses the *form* of autobiography, is far indeed from its literal experience as we would now define it. He is a deeply communal man and cannot speak as *one*. Marlowe, on the other hand, seems very present in *Dr. Faustus*—we think of *his* literal life, witnessing that play. With Goethe, we are in a different 'place' entirely, far closer to social 'mythology.'

It is Castaneda who 'autobiographically' tells us of Don Juan's teachings. Don Juan is not interested in 'himself' in that way, as those teachings, even so filtered, make clear. I think it wise to be aware of this problem, so to speak, insofar as any autobiographical mode can seem to be significant *in itself*—just as the *I* of its creation has assumed, *ipso facto*, that what he or she has to say is significant. If, by *significant*, one means that the statement signifies something, no matter what, then all seems well and good. Anything that happens 'signifies.' But if there is otherwise an intention, an ulterior motive as it's called, then the problem is very much more complex. Is that great man's life, which reminds us, *in itself* directed to do so? That is, did he literally live it for that purpose? Possibly yes. But what he *thought* he was doing, no matter how directed, can never to my mind be as actual or as significant as what he *was*, literally, doing. Which is to say nothing more than that Hitler must have been no less possessed by an *idea* than was Jesus, *and* we know that what affects us is the *event* of that fact in each case.

When people are very old, and there is the consciousness of death coming upon them, a very marked impulse to tell what their lives have been occurs. I don't think it is simply loneliness in that situation, or that they have lost otherwise a *place*. The grandfathers, and grandmothers, are the great storytellers—and in societies alert to that human need they are of course so used. They tell a life of *I* that becomes more than singular consciousness in isolations of intent or assertive energy. They are, as it were, taking the *I* back to its center. Olson once told me that the initial sign for the pronoun *I* was a boat. Insofar as *I* is a vehicle of passage or transformation, its powers are clear. Realized as will or personality, that 'mealy seal' as Olson called it, the power vitiates as soon as the energy necessary to sustain it exhausts itself. "L'état, c'est moi" is truly the end of a period.

Those of us who came of age in the forties remember the extraordinary turmoil within human consciousness, which was, on the one hand, the Second World War, and, on the other, existentialism. We saw what Jung might call the 'individuation process' enter the nightmare of 'divided creation,' torn from centers of physical reality. The heroism of Allen Ginsberg in the fifties cannot be overemphasized: "*I saw the best minds of my generation destroyed by madness, starving, hysterical . . .*" Come *back* into the body. We do not go 'backward' or 'forward' in the mind—we live and die. Olson, dying, was relieved, almost to delight, that the *fundament*, that physical *thing* we are, had not been lost in the *firmament*, that *mind* world of stars and extensions.

What can one do? "Tell the story." "To tell / what subsequently I saw and what heard / —to place myself (in / my nature) beside nature / to imitate nature (for to copy nature would be a / shameful thing) / I lay myself down . . ."

To bear witness. To be here, to hear. To tell.

*Buffalo, N.Y.*
*March 22, 1973*

# Foreword to *Robert Creeley: An Inventory, 1945–1970,* by Mary Novik

I came to writing with some awkwardness, just that nothing in the situation in which I grew up seemed particularly involved with that possibility. My sister Helen, however, four years older than I, was an intensive reader, and it was she who gave me both Conrad and Dostoyevsky to read when I must have been about twelve or thirteen. She also wrote poems which had gained the approval of Robert P. Tristram Coffin among others. At school I had several exceptional teachers, all of whom increased my articulation and also my perception of what "saying things" could accomplish. One, for example, had us translate sections of Joyce's *Dubliners* into Basic English, an exercise which made very literal the actual agency that the words in Joyce's text were making. When it came time to go to college, I sent applications to Amherst, the University of Pennsylvania, and Harvard. The first two offered excellent preparation for veterinary medicine, which I then hoped would be my profession, and both offered me substantial scholarships. Harvard's acceptance, however, despite the lack of any financial assistance, must have turned my head, coming from a small town in Massachusetts as I did. In any case, the decision to go to Harvard was also a decision to commit myself to writing, no matter that I was probably not that certain of it at the time. My friends there quickly expanded senses of writing I had had to include Pound and Stein among others. They were also the first to publish me and to invite me, generously, to be one of the editors of the Cummings issue of the Har-

Mary Novik, *Robert Creeley: An Inventory, 1945–1970* (Kent, Ohio: Kent State University Press, 1973).

vard *Wake*. Willy Gaddis, Jake Bean, Bernie Weinbaum, and Bill
Lieberman also had myself and Gordon Rollins elected to the Harvard *Advocate*, but our subsequent conduct caused the university to
expunge all record of that fact.

The rest of it, so to speak, is to be found here. It's a very strange
feeling now looking through the various entries, much like seeing
the rings on a tree stump. I have never had the sense that I was
getting very much done, and so it's a particular pleasure to see how
much has accumulated no matter. I'm grateful, of course, that it
has mattered to others, those readers who I've never dared assume might be there. I felt I was doing something very like tossing
pebbles in a pool. The way the rings have gone out is a very deep
pleasure.

I must say I have very few of the books, pamphlets, magazines,
etc., that are here listed. We have moved so frequently in past
years—twenty-two times in the past fourteen—that it was impossible to keep any such backlog in hand, even had I wanted to. So I
thank Mary Novik very much indeed for recalling all of them to me.
Her conscientiousness has been an act of extraordinary generosity.

*Bolinas, California*
*December 31, 1971*

# Last Night

## Random Thoughts on San Francisco, March–June 1956

There are lovely moments in the world when persons and place "burn with a like heat," as Olson would say. Who knows why, finally, except that some intuition or habit or simply coincidence has arranged that this shall be the case—and all those to be blessed, truly, will be present.

I felt that way, arriving in San Francisco in March of 1956. The city was humanly so beautiful, but that fact would not have changed my mind in itself. I'd left Black Mountain just at the turn of the year, in real despair, with a marriage finally ended, separated from my three children, very confused as to how to support myself—and so I had headed west, for the first time, thinking to be rid of all the 'easternisms' of my New England upbringing and habit. I had friends living in New Mexico—a phenomenal *place* in its own right—and thought to settle there, but after a month or so I found myself restless, dependent, and in no sense clearer as to what might be my next move. An old friend and student from Black Mountain, Ed Dorn, was living in San Francisco, so that's where I headed—to see the Pacific Ocean, if nothing else.

I got there mid-afternoon, if I remember correctly. Ed and Helene gave me a whirlwind tour of the city, in their tiny Morris Minor, and we drank a lot in celebration. Ed told me that Rexroth had generously invited us to dinner but that he had to go to work at the Greyhound Bus Terminal at six. I in the meantime was getting

First published in French as "Hier Soir: Au Hasard de Mes Souvenirs de San Francisco (mars–juin 1956)," *Entretiens* 34 (1975). Translated from English by Etienne de Planchard.

drunker and drunker, and recall vomiting heavily in the street before going up to Rexroth's apartment. People had already eaten,
but tactfully made no point of my late arrival. Later that same night,
returning to the Dorns' apartment, I was charmed by the arrival
of Allen Ginsberg at midnight (he got off work at the Greyhound
Terminal at that hour), and we talked much of the night about
writing and "Projective Verse" and his own interest in Kerouac
and Burroughs. My information of the former was meager, but
fascinating, i.e., Robert Duncan had told me that Kerouac was the
man who had written a thousand pages in which the only apparent
*physical* action was a neon sign, over a storefront, flashing off and
on. Burroughs, in a story that had him confused with Jack, was said
to have been asked at a party to demonstrate his expertise with re-
volvers by shooting an apple off the head of his wife. A gun was
given him, he took aim and fired—and sadly killed her. His apocryphal remark was: I should never have used a 45. They always
undershoot . . .

Rexroth's weekly *evenings* proved an intensive meeting ground.
The Place, a great bar with genial host Leo and sometime bartender John Ryan, was another. One night Allen asked the Dorns
and myself to meet him there after he got off work, so he could
introduce us to Jack Kerouac, now back in the city. We got there
early, and sat at a small table in the front of that small space—and
waited, peering about to try to figure out which one of the others
might be Jack. I was particularly drawn to a man who was sitting up
against the back wall, on the way to the toilet, seemingly alone, sort
of musing, with extraordinary eyes and a head that had somehow
larger than 'life size' intensity. When Allen came in, he asked us if
we'd seen Jack, and we said, no—and then he pointed to this man
I'd been watching, and said, there he is. But we had little conversation that night, unhappily. Jack was pretty comatose from drinking,
and when we all got back to the apartment he was sharing with Al
Sublette to eat—the large steak, I remember, kept getting dropped
on the floor in the process of being cooked—Jack passed out on a
bed, and when I was delegated to wake him up, he regarded me
with those extraordinary eyes and I felt like a didactic idiot.

Remembering now, it all tends to swirl. Great parties at Locke
McCorkle's house out in Mill Valley—Allen and Peter charmingly
dancing naked among a dense pack of clothed bodies, flowers at
the prom! Jack and I sitting on the sidelines, shy, banging on up-
ended pots and pans, 'keeping the beat.' Gary Snyder's wise old-
young eyes, his centeredness and shyness also. Phil Whalen's, "Well,

Creeley, I *hope* you know what you're doing . . ." Visits to Mike Mc-
Clure's with Ed—Ronnie Bladen upstairs in their undesignated
commune. Mike practicing the trumpet (in the cellar?)—anyhow,
blasts of sound, and talk of Pollock, *energy.* Lawrence Ferlinghetti,
standing outside his great and initial City Lights Bookstore, asking
me what living was like in Mallorca—cheap? He'd had the care to
review *The Gold Diggers* for the *San Francisco Chronicle,* and that was
surely a first. Walking around the city with Allen and Phil, Allen
reading us *Howl,* which he had in a big black binder notebook, each
time we'd stop at a curb or in a cafe (Mike's—great Italian food) or
just on a bench in a park. Later I typed the stencils for a small 'edition' of that transforming poem—I was trying to get work and
Marthe Rexroth gave me the job, as I remember, Allen had given
her—prior to the City Lights publication.

There were other dear friends of that time, James Broughton
(an old friend of Duncan's), Kermit Sheets, Madeline Gleason.
(Duncan himself was in Black Mountain, but his care that I should
be at home in the city was so kind.) I'd go to them when I was exhausted, and that was frequently. I finally managed to get an apartment on Montgomery Street, though I never succeeded in living
there. I did write some poems, though—on a huge typewriter Marthe had got me: "Please," "The Bed," "Just Friends" (old Charlie
Parker favorite), "She Went to Stay," "A Folk Song," and "Jack's
Blues" among them. One night I invited the gang over, like they
say, and one of the company was a particularly ominous *heavy,*
whose pleasure was turning school girls on (there were two with
him) to heroin, and finally I got freaked. Peter Orlovsky, true angel, somehow managed to clear the whole room of people, then
paused himself at the door before leaving, to say, would you like
me to turn off the light?

We talked endlessly, day and night. We rehearsed our senses of
writing, possible publication, shop talk. Jack was *not* going to let the
editors cut up *On the Road* the way they had *The Town and the City*—
he was getting himself ready for Malcolm Cowley's impending visit,
'to talk it over,' which Jack rightly feared might be heavy-handed
'advice.' Both Ed and I were asked a lot of questions about Olson
and his "Projective Verse"—was it just more razzle-dazzle intellec-
tualism? McClure and Whalen were particularly intrigued, and
were at this time already in correspondence with him. Allen, as always, was alert to any information of *process* that might be of use.

So time went by—and it was so packed with things *happening,* it
seems now strange to me it was such a short time—only three

months. Came June, and I was restless again, and so headed back
to New Mexico, with huge rucksack (I managed to get all my stuff
*and* Marthe's typewriter into somehow) and sleeping bag Jack had
helped me locate in an army surplus store on Market Street. I still
have them. The sleeping bag, in fact, is presently on the bed in the
next room.

Why does that matter. At times it seems all we have of the human
possibility, *to keep the faith*—though why an old sleeping bag and a
primordial army issue rucksack now looking like a faded grey ghost
should be the tokens, one must figure for oneself. Each time I drive
cross country, in the underpowered battered VW I likewise hold on
to, hitting those Kansas spaces (where Burroughs rightly remarked,
one gets the *fear*), I think of Neal Cassady and that Pontiac he could
wheel round corners as if on a turntable. Pure burning energy. Listening to fantastic "Bombay Express" Indian record of Locke's,
Neal flagging the train on through . . .

People give you life in that way. Things you didn't think you
knew or could do. Suddenly it's possible. Answers you never expected to come out of your own mouth. One time—after a night-
long party at Locke's—people had variously come to rest either in
the house at the bottom of the hill, great sloping ground of musky
eucalyptus and grass, or else in the small cabin toward the top, kids
and big people all together in one heap—Jack proposed he and I
sleep outside just to dig that wild soft air and tender darkness. I
woke in bright dazzling morning light, with Jack's face inches from
mine, asking in mock sternness: *Are you pure?* To which I replied, as
if for that moment in *his* mind, *that's like asking water to be wet.*

*Buffalo, N.Y.*
*September 13, 1974*

# Was That a Real Poem or Did You Just Make It Up Yourself?

As I get older, I recognize that my thinking about poetry may or may not have anything actively to do with my actual work as a poet. This strikes me as no thing cynically awry, but rather seems again instance of that hapless or possibly happy fact, we do not as humans seem necessarily aware of what we are physically or psychically doing at all. One thing, therefore, that does stay put in my head, as something said in youth, is "we live as we can, each day another—there is no use in counting. Nor more, say, to live than what there is, to live. . . ." I did not feel that a pessimistically argued reality back then, nor do I now. It is very hard for me to live in any projection of reality, in a plan or arrangement of the present moment that uses it primarily as a 'future' term. I have long experience of my own restlessness and impatience, and have managed quiet and a feeling of centeredness only when the *here and now* literally discovered it for me. Elsewise I have battered myself and the surroundings with seemingly useless energy, pleased only that something at least was 'happening.'

My writing seems to me no different. Of course I learned as much as I could about the *how* of its occasion. Like many of my contemporaries I felt myself obliged to be an explicit craftsman so as to have defense against the authoritative poetry of my youth—whose persons I'd like now not to recall just that it's taken me so long to forget them. So, from that initial, crotchety purview, I've continued, finding and choosing as heroes men and women who must

Black Sparrow Press, *Sparrow*, 40 (1976).

at this point be familiar to anyone who has read me at all: Williams, Pound, H. D., Stein, Zukofsky, Olson, Duncan, Levertov, Ginsberg, Dorn, Bunting, Wieners, McClure, Whalen, Snyder, Berrigan— and so on, being those I can almost see out the window if I look. Put more simply, there's been a way of doing things which found company with others, and in that company one has found a particular life of insistent and sustaining kind.

That has been part of the situation of 'what poetry means to me,' but dear as it is, it has not been either the largest part nor the most significant. A few months ago I was sitting with friends in a lovely house on a lovely afternoon, and we began a collaborative poem, on impulse, using an electric typewriter that was on a nearby table. It took me real time to get to it because it intimidated me— I've never used one particularly—and also intrigued me, and so my feelings and thoughts began to singularize me, isolate me in relation to the others. But I've always been able to do that, so to speak. But is it some necessity of my own working? In any case, my contribution to the poem stood painfully clear in its twisted, compressed statement—even the spacing of lines shrank to a small fist of words, defensive and altogether by itself.

No wonder that I've never forgotten Williams' contention that "the poet thinks with his poem, in that lies his thought, and that in itself is the profundity . . ." Poems have always had this nature of revelation for me, becoming apparently objective manifestations of feelings and thoughts otherwise inaccessible. Did I love Mary—a poem or story would quite usually make the answer clear, no matter it might take years to know it. A pleasant woman met this spring pointed out, for example, that "For love—I would/ split open your head and put/ a candle in/ behind the eyes . . ." was a literally violent proposal that was not demonstrably involved with usual senses of 'loving' the recipient. Yet I had always felt that poem a true measure of an ability to love, and possibly it is.

As a young man, then, moved by poetry, feeling its possibilities as inclusive, bringing all the world to one instant of otherwise meaningless 'time,' I wanted, not unexpectedly, to participate in that wonder. We struggle with them a good deal, mutter, mistake, but *words* seem even so significantly common and in that respect accessible. My own commitment to them was not easily understood. Was it that nothing else was open to me? Did I turn to them simply that no other act or substance permitted me such occasion? I know that I felt in those years now past very often useless in other attempts to find place in the world. As so many of that time, I married primarily to reify what might be called my existence. The fact of wanting to be a social person, as well as a private one, seemingly demanded it. Again, there was nothing I otherwise 'did' that argued my relevance to a general world.

In short, I was markedly self-preoccupied, lonely, inarticulate at crucial points in my relationships, and again, and again, restless. If they did nothing else, words gave instant reality to this insistent flux, which otherwise blurred, faded, was gone before another might in any sense witness it. That poems, stories, fed on this experience of reality was of great use initially. Just as I had used reading as a place to be, a world of volatile and active nature yet also 'unreal,' not 'flesh and blood'—and yet that surely, how else could it be—so now the possibilities that words might engender became a deep preoccupation.

At various times I've put emphasis on the fact that I was raised in New England, in Massachusetts for the most part. So placing myself, I've argued that that fact clarifies my apparently laconic way of saying things, especially so in my early poems. But might that use of words not come also of feeling tentative with them, unsure of their appropriate significations—as though there were a *right* way that was being distorted, lost, by fact of one's ignorance? I sense an aspect of this dilemma in Williams' plaint, "many years of reading have not made you wise. . . ." I know that he did share with me a tacit fear of the well-trained, academically secure *good English* he felt the comfortable equipment of various of his contemporaries. We both depended, it would seem, on enthusiasms, rushes of insight or impulse, read only to a purpose if the appetite underlying would settle for nothing else. I was delighted, for example, to realize that Williams did not spend long hours researching *Paterson* in the library but rather, as Michael Weaver first told me, got his information from a lovely, old time *local* historian. To this day I am so intimidated by the *nature* of libraries, the feel of them, the authority of their ordering of books on shelves, etc., that I rarely if ever go into them. I feel toward them much as I feel toward telephones, that their function is disastrously limited by their form, no matter what efficiencies are also clearly the case.

But why worry about that? If one has spent close to thirty years writing books, in effect, why be so fearful of this one place they may come to rest? Why be afraid of *poems*, for that matter? Thinking of that world 'out there,' and recalling my own tentativeness in trying to find my own use in it, always the *general* measure of reality can hurt me, can say, in short, 'of course *you* like it, you wrote it—but what about other people, don't you care what they think or feel or want?' More specifically, why not write poems the way they are supposed to be written—as simple acquaintance with poetry as a *subject* would easily define. Thus, if you seriously want to be a poet, you study the prevailing models of its activity and you set yourself to their imitation as diligently as you can. And slowly you acquire, or do not, the requisite ability.

I don't believe it. I *know* that attention to what has been written, what is being written, is a dearly rewarding experience. Nonetheless, it is *not* the primary fact. Far closer would be having a horse, say, however nebulous or lumpy, and, seeing other people with horses, using their occasion with said horses as some instance of the possibility involved. In short, I would never buy a horse or write a poem simply that others had done so—although I would go swimming on those terms or eat snails. Stuck with the horse, or blessed with it, I have to work out that relation as best I can.

Posit that music exists despite the possibility that no one might be consciously able to make it, that what we call *poems* are an intrinsic fact in the human world whether or no there be poets at this moment capable of their creation. That would characterize my belief—which gives me no rest, which, too often, causes a despairing sense of uselessness and ineptitude. Why can't *I* write them, fall in love, reveal the actual world, and be the hero in it? Isn't it *mine*. No. Yours? No. Theirs? No. Ours? No.

Days, weeks, months and sometimes years can pass in that sad place. Nothing gets done, nothing really gets even started. A vague, persistent echo of possibility seems all that is there to depend upon. Perhaps tomorrow, or later today—or even right now. To work. Useless paper, useless pen. Scribbles of habit and egocentric dependence. But you did it once, didn't you—they said so, you thought so too. Try again.

Sometime in the mid-sixties I grew inexorably bored with the tidy containment of clusters of words on single pieces of paper called 'poems'—"this will really get them, wrap it up. . . ." I could see nothing in my life nor those of others adjacent that supported this single hits theory. Dishonest to say I hadn't myself liked it, haiku, for example, or such of my own poems that unwittingly opened like seeds. But my own life, I felt increasingly, was a *continuance,* from wherever it had started to wherever it might end—of course I felt it as linear in time—and here were these quite small *things* I was tossing out from time to time, in the hope that they might survive my own being hauled on toward terminus. Time to start over, afresh, began to be felt at first as increasingly limited, finally as nonexistent. The intensive, singularly made poems of my youth faded as, hopefully, the anguish that was used in the writing of so many of them also did. I was happier? Truly pointless to answer insofar as I lived now in another body and with an altered mind.

More, what specific use to continue the writing of such poems if the need therefor be only the maintenance of some ego state, the so-called *me*-ness of that imaginary person. Lost in some confusion of integrity, I had to tell the truth, however unreal, and persisted toward its realization, even though unthinkable. So writing, in this sense, began to lose its specific edges, its singleness of occurrence, and I worked to be open to the casual, the commonplace, that which collected itself. The world transformed to bits of paper, torn words, 'it/it.' Its continuity became again physical. I had no idea of its purpose, nor mine, more than a need to include all that might so come to mind and survive to be written.

My tidinesses, however, are insistent. Thus forms of things said moved through accumulated habits of order, and I felt neither ease nor possibility in the jumbled or blurred contexts of language. No doubt I will repeat the manners of small kid with mother town nurse and oider sister most articulate in West Acton, Mass., 1930 to 1935 forever. Only the town is changed, to protect the innocent.

*If* one were a musician, the delight might be sounding again and again all that composite of articulation had preceded one, the old songs truly. In poetry, the dilemma of the circumstance is simply that some *one* is supposed to write some *thing*, and it becomes a possessive and distracting point of view. It is interesting to remember that Archilochus and Sappho are known to us because literacy comes to 'write them down,' no necessary concern of theirs nor of lyric poetry more generally. Yet I am very much a person of my time in wanting to leave a record, a composite fact of the experience of living in time and space. It was Charles Olson's hope to make an *image of man* in writing *The Maximus Poems*—not at all to write some autobiographical memoir. I use all poetry to write anything, and only wish I might know more of its vast body, which is seemingly as various as the earth itself.

What *is* poetry? In a dictionary I've hauled around for almost as long as I've been writing (*The Pocket Oxford Dictionary of Current English*, Fowler and Fowler, in a "New and Enlarged Edition revised by George Van Santvoord," 1935), it says to my horror: "elevated expression of elevated thought or feeling, esp. in metrical form. . . ." If I turn to a more recent dictionary, *The American Heritage Dictio-*

*nary of the English Language,* 1969, I'm told that poetry is "the art or work of a poet," which has got to be a cop-out. So all these years people have been screaming that one was not writing *real* poetry— and it turns out nobody, certainly no one in that crowd, knew what it was to begin with. No wonder they insisted on those *forms!* They wouldn't know it *was* a woman unless she was wearing a dress.

So now I will make up poetry, as I always have, one word after another, becoming something, as sounds, call them, as beats, *tum tum.* All very familiar. But each time I take the bus I do see something new, somehow. Eyes possibly? Certainly a turning world. Verse turns, and takes turns in turning—which are called *verses,* in my book, like changes—and not those *stanzas* or stops, standstills. *Onward then, multiple men, women too, will go with you*—boohoo. Which is a poem because I say so, it *rhymes.* That was a primary requisite for years and years. But so lovely when such rhyming, that congruence of sounds which occur in time with sufficient closeness, to resound, echo, and so recall, when *that* moves to delight and intensity, feeling the physical quality of the words' movement with a grace that distorts nothing. To *say* things—and to say them with such articulation can bring them physical character in the words which have become them—is *wonder.*

It is equal wonder when the rhythms which words can embody move to like echo and congruence. It is a *place,* in short, one has come to, where words dance truly in an information of one another, drawing in the attention, provoking feelings to participate.

Poems have involved an extraordinary range of human and non-human event, so to discuss that fact seems pointless. We will talk of everything sooner or later. Americans have had the especial virtue in the last hundred years of opening both content and form in an extraordinary manner, and the energy inherent continues without apparent end.

But again, one lives a life, and so, personally, one speaks of it, and of the people and places it was given to find. I cannot say that my children particularly respect or find other interest in my being a poet, and, at first, that bothered me because I wanted them moved by what moved me. False hope, I now think—although it might otherwise come to be the case. At times I hear the niggard comment that poets seem only to have other poets as an audience. It is certainly true that the dearest company I've had in reading has been so. But many people otherwise have heard too, through no intent of mine. I couldn't predicate they would, in writing. As a young man I questioned that anyone would ever hear at all, although it did not occur to me that I might therefore stop writing.

The tacit lament in this way of speaking strikes me as pathetic. Getting a purchase on writing, so to speak, was for me a one-way ticket to bliss. I've never really come back. In those long, lonely nights I've wailed the sweetest songs, possibly, certainly those most designed for my own pleasure. Years back, again, Williams said, why don't we make clear we write for our pleasure, that we *like* doing it? It's a fair question. Nobody wants their pleasures criticized, and that fact no doubt explains why nobody really wants to be explained, nor wants to explain either. And I suppose that's why one uses either a tendentiously 'critical' vocabulary in speaking of 'his work' or else pushes clear with a, gee whiz, fellers, it's really nothing.

At first I was intent upon getting *anything* to hold, so that the experience in reading had the same qualities as the impulse in writing. But then I don't really know, nor have I ever, what's being said until it comes to some close, and it's now there to be read through, as one thing. Elsewise I trust the location implicit in feeling it's going well, opening, moving without a sense of hesitance or forced intention. I don't want to write what is only an idea, particularly my own. If the world can't come true in that place, flooding all terms of my thought and experience, then it's not enough, either for me or, equally, for anyone else. It must be somehow *revelation*, no matter how modest that transformation can sometimes be. Or vast, truly— "the world in a grain of sand."

The title for these divers thoughts comes from a lovely story told me about 1960 by John Frederick Nims in Chicago as he afforded us a charming lunch in his role as editor of *Poetry*. It concerned a friend of his, another poet, who had been on a tour of readings in the Middle West. And, as was his wont, he invited questions from the audience at one particular college, on completion of his reading. And a guy puts up his hand and says, tell me, that next to last poem you read—was that a real poem or did you just make it up yourself? Terrific. That's stuck in my head so lucently so long! Much as the phenomenon of another friend and student at Black Mountain in the middle fifties, who in truth could perceive no demonstrable difference between a cluster of words called *poem* and a cluster of words called *prose*. She felt the typographical form of the poem was all that apparently defined it—and that of course was a very arbitrary gimmick, to her mind. I tried everything, "Mary had a little lamb," tum te tum, clapped my hands with the beat, pulled out the vowels à la Yeats, probably even sang. Still it stayed flat and arbitrary. She felt the beat and texture of the sound was imposed by will of the reader and was not initial in the words themselves. All the usual critical terms were of course useless, far too abstract. Finally I truly despaired of gaining more than her sympathy and patience. Then one day, we were reading Edward Marshall's "Leave the Word Alone," and for some immaculate and utterly unanticipated "reason" she *got* it, she heard all the play of rhythms and sounds bringing that extraordinary statement of primary humanness into such a density of feeling and song.

Would that all had such a happy ending—and 'American poetry,' like they say, soared on to the stars. Senses of progress, also familiar, really want that in the worst way. Meantime one's brothers and sisters are out there somewhere wailing on, to make the night a little lighter, the day a little brighter, like. Bringing that sun up and bringing it down again, every time. I don't know where it's supposed to 'get to' in that sense, more than to persist in the clarity of human recognitions and wonder. Poetry, as Duncan says, comes "from a well deeper than time." It's 'contemporary' in the way that fire, air, water, or earth might be said to be particularly involved in any apprehension of present existence. Sadly it can, as these, go away, be lost to other appetites and acts. Talking to Michael McClure a few days ago, thinking of the primary *stances* in the arts, to the three most familiar (Classicism, Romanticism, and Surrealism) he felt a fourth might be added: the Beat, which, distinct from the other three, does not propose 'the world' as a stable, physical *given* but, in ecological terms, realizes its fragility and thus the need for human attention and care.

As a poet, at this moment—half listening as I am to the House Judiciary Committee's deliberations—I am angered, contemptuous, impatient, and possibly even cynical concerning the situation of our lives in this 'national' place. Language has, publicly, become such an instrument of coercion, persuasion, and deceit. The power thus collected is ugly beyond description—it is truly *evil*. And it will not go away.

*Trust to good verses then* . . . Trust to the clarity instant in being human, that knows and wants no other place.

*Bolinas, California*
*July 31, 1974*

# A Note for *Hello*

Coming to New Zealand in our spring (your fall) of 1976 (momently to be my fiftieth year)—I knew, intuitively, a time in myself had come for change. I don't mean simply clothes, or houses, or even cities or countries or habits. I mean, *all* of it—what *it* ever is or can be. No doubt one's a poor tourist, so preoccupied—but one needs specific *places* for specific acts, and if the demand be that one step out into space, that life as we say we presume to live, then best it be a giant step, as far from what's known as one can manage.

Thank God you speak English, however—no American is quite that daring. My invitation to come was, in fact, from a dear fellow-poet, Alistair Paterson, and it was our common concern for what could be done with the English language in New Zealand or American poems, that resulted in the divers lectures and readings I gave, either alone or in generous company, the length and breadth of your pleasant land.

But you know that, as I do—and what seems far more to the point is to cite, here, such senses of New Zealand as stay put for me. For example, the *clouds* of your country—especially in Wellington—are so active and so lovely. I know the wind blows too, often harshly, but those clouds are such a cosmos of possibility. Then there's New Zealand *light*—intense, clear, particularizing, ruthless, unlike any I've ever previously known. In my own concerns, it brought all things factually to *stand in the light*, and that's where finally one wants to see them.

Robert Creeley, *Hello* (Christchurch, New Zealand: Hawk Press, 1976).

Coming from a mainland, with three thousand miles between its eastern and western coasts, your two islands seemed fragile and vulnerable. In humor, but also in a curious seriousness, I wondered if one might not extend oars from either side of each, and row them about in celebration of some appropriate festival. Thus you are *out there*, humanly, in the vastness of the Pacific, truly a human dream in a seeming eternity of endlessly moving *water*. I realized that no one of you ever lives so far from it that it is not a daily, substantive reality.

So, too, your mountains. I'd ask, at times, in the company of classrooms and the like, if anyone had ever lived out of sight of them. Apparently not. Mountains are one of the two primary dimensions, and you will know, as few others, the human accuracy of, *I will lift mine eyes unto the hills whence cometh my strength . . .* They too abide.

Finally, people—so good to me, so often. As now, sitting here, I'd particularly like to thank the patient persons of a pub in Wellington who, gamely, attempted to sing with me *Breaking Up Is Hard To Do* and that other, even more deeply instructive old time hymn, *Farther Along*. Hopefully I'll be back, and we can continue from where we left off.

Thanks to all, in short—to the dear households who accommodated me, to the persons and agencies of the QE II Arts Council and the NZUSA Arts Council who put it all together—to those friends of my heart now forever.

*Buffalo, New York*
*May 31, 1976*

# Letter from Berlin

It's now some years since one had wandered in various states of mind Berlin's present main drag, the Kurfürstendamm, along whose two-mile stretch, as the Berlin Tourist Office's very useful guidebook tells us, are "1,100 shops, department stores, boutiques and art-galleries . . ." Whatever it is or was that accounts for the scaffolding surrounding the Kaiser Wilhelm Memorial Church, adjacent to the Europe Center, the heart of the city's swirling consumerism, this blasted remnant of World War II bombings still echoes without apparent change the world that did, in fact, end here.

I am classically new in town, a writer who speaks only one language, and that with remarkably little confidence. I share what has been my country's persistent and statistically determined lack of interest in a language other than English. Yet I have been brought here by an intensively active academic sponsor, the Deutscher Akademischer Austauschdienst or more exactly, its Berlin Artists Program—which interestingly, provides for foreign artists to be brought to no city other than Berlin. DAAD, as it's called (*"Day-Ah-Ah-Day"*), provides most usually for a year's residence without duties except for the presumption that one will have company with local artists, hardly very much to ask. So, shortly after my arrival, Ted Joans, also American and a poet, gets me out to Wannsee on a bus that takes us through a substantial patch of the Grünewald to the edge of a lake where the Berliners go in the summer to enjoy

*Washington Post Book World,* December 18, 1983.

"the white sandy beach . . . one mile long and 250 feet wide . . . ,"
again as the guidebook says.

Our fellows are met at the Literarisches Colloquium, whose fact
and influence has much to do with the poet-professor Walter Höl-
lerer, now in his sixties. Through such magazines as *Akzente* and
*Sprache im technischen Zeitalter,* and in the landmark anthology *Neue
Amerikanische Lyrik (Young American Poetry),* edited with Gregory
Corso here in Germany in the early '60s, he has argued for a free-
ing of German diction, particularly in poetry, and so had much to
do with the authority which American poets such as William Carlos
Williams (through Enzensberger's excellent translations) and Frank
O'Hara (possibly the most presently valued) have had. The Collo-
quium has been for years an amiable and far-reaching consensus of
mutual interests beyond the simply national.

Back in the street, I am slightly claustrophobic as I again construct in mind *die Mauer,* the Wall, that literally encloses this city
and has done so now for almost forty years. As I ride on the excellent buses and subways, I watch, furtively, my fellow riders and
wonder if their covert studying of me is only my own paranoia. But
here one is close to all the proposed bogeys of American propa-
ganda. A visit to Berlin's Amerika Haus involves a confrontation
with the security guards our embassy has put there since a bomb
incident of about a year ago. Several stand outside the two-story
building (a block or so from the central Zoo stop on the subway,
where the junkies used to hang out and one can mail a letter
twenty-four hours a day). Inside Amerika Haus are several more
guards, who question those who enter for the art shows, the movies
or lectures, or just for private business as myself. The guards' effect
on public sense of Americans would be interesting to know.

Writers here are of a very particular world. For example, I asked
the poet Karin Kiwus if feminism was an active center for women
writers as it is in the States, and was answered that neither it nor
any similarly determined factor of sexual nature, e.g., gay lib, had
such attention, although they were certainly present and provoked
the usual responses. It was the peace movement that engaged all
articulate women and served as a political base among them. She
gave as instance the East German poet, Christa Wolf, whose first
book, published in the '60s, is aptly called *The Divided Sky* or *Heaven*—the German word *Himmel* translates as either. Her newest
work, *Cassandra,* uses that archaically echoing voice of prophetic
challenge—the artist's only resource against the increasing abstrac-

tion of human presence in the increasingly complex manipulations of power.

In a sense it is curious that writers and artists here generally have insisted upon information from their East German confreres. The first Writers Conference involved with this exchange was held in East Berlin about a year and a half ago, and the most recent was on this side of the Wall, last February, at the Akademie der Kunst, of which Günter Grass is now president, Karin Kiwus head of the department of literature, and K. P. Herbach, one of the city's most significant bookmen and authors, the secretary of press and public affairs. So writers such as Wolf Bierman and Sarah Kirsch have become as significant in West Berlin's literary and social thinking as they have been in the East.

What is harder to convey is the extraordinary spate of public readings, some forty a week at present rate, and all with an audience of some eighty to two-hundred people utterly pleased to be there. I watched, for example, the charmingly elder Berlin author and actor, Robert Wolfgang Schnell, read from his expansive autobiography, *Sind die Bären Glücklicher Geworden?* (which certainly *sounds* good!) and was impressed that a decorous lady to my right was rolling soundlessly in fits of laughter, while a gentleman to my left snorted with Germanly reckless abandon. It must have been funny. Next night I was at another reading, this time with American novelist and playwright Cecil Brown, who got more than a fair hearing from a predominantly young group of night-clubbers, and finally, the third night, at an art gallery where Ted Joans was having a *finissage* of his surrealist and historical artifacts—including a great film of himself in Timbuktu, which the Germans loved, with fine readings by Richard Anders, a poet we should know far better, the younger Ernst Bauerschaum, and Ted himself. By and large such readings are characteristically sponsored by book dealers, art galleries and cafes rather than the academic or institutional sponsors familiar to Americans. They feel local, almost like neighborhood action, and it is quite true that Berlin has its favorites, as the actor Schnell or the inimitable Johannes Schenk, with his great hat and country manners, who may or may not be known beyond the city limits.

So—*es geht ganz gut!* And now to learn some German. . . .

# Berlin, Etc.

For whatever reason, living in Berlin sans any adequate language ability or practical interest in being there, other than the money and domicile provided, opened a flat and unredeemable perspective into the bleak past of one's own public lifetime. It's like an oldtime movie, locked in a vocabulary "we" gave it in 1945, re-emphasized soon after by *die Mauer,* the wall that cuts off the historic center of the city, Unter den Linden and all the rest, from what's now the "Western" half. Then, of course, the city politically "ours" is separated from its own country by some hundred miles of physical distance, and must be arrived at by either a "corridor" which planes use, else carefully monitored rail and freeway systems.

Yet Berlin, *West* Berlin, that is, is Germany's New York, at least in imagination, and the young long, seemingly, for its privileges and dispensations. For example, one is exempt from the draft if one lives in Berlin. A bus costs about half of what it does in comparable cities in other parts of the country. Food, housing, significantly subsidized, are all cheaper. There is much pressure to keep this segment of the old city "alive" by pumping in various cultural action, an energy of synthetic order despite the persons or things so brought may have undeniable integrity. But here they float somehow, just that the appetite is so distracted by expectation, by *not* being where any such possibility has come from. Never was the sense of a city feeding on its surrounding context more vividly illustrated.

It was impossible for me not to have strong memories of my own, of coming of age in the early 40s and all the implications thereof.

*Continental Drifter* 11 (1984).

The first time I came to Berlin, a few years previous, the plane landed at the Tempelhof Airport, and for moments I hadn't the least problem seeing in imagination those incredible gatherings there I'd first witnessed in newsreels. Thankfully one now arrives at Tegel, a less dramatic occasion in all respects. It was early October when we arrived in what's certainly a northern city, grey, frequent rain, cold chill of winds, a flat close sky often, but with monumental clouds and a sense of evening space I was very moved by, almost Eliot-like in its "The winter evening settles down . . ."

I don't know what I'd expected. There were a few friends there, then others unexpectedly met again, as Ted Joans, who lived upstairs in the same building as us. He was very helpful with simple directions, ways one could deal with it. He said Berlin finally bored him despite he kept a social action going of extraordinary range and good-nature. Our family did a lot of daily walking, of taking buses, sitting in parks, going to the zoo, museums—whatever was free and simple of access. We were insistently domestic, went to bed very early, and had little money over and above the cost of our daily living. Therefore, like it or not, we lived in one respect very commonly.

The feel of things seemed depressed and depressing. There was none of the street action I'd known in other cities, for example, no spontaneous emotion such as sudden laughter, playfulness, or even anger. It wasn't that people were careful, discreet. Rather it seemed the habits of their activity were so ingrained they offered no room for willful edges of response. The only time I met with much strength of feeling was when I dumbly broke a rule, tried to get on a bus with my small son before the drivers had finished the very particular exchange of their authority, one coming on duty, one going off. I watched a policeman working a stop-light on the Ku'damm (as it's called) manually, mid-morning one Sunday, no traffic to speak of, a mean sleety rain and a cutting wind. He was timing the action precisely to his watch, ignoring the few cars or persons passing, involved in the peculiar need to be mechanically "accurate" against any alternative of a more perceptive judgment. In like sense, one rarely sees anyone cross a street against a light, despite there may be no traffic. It seemed the whole country was didactically committed to its procedures. On another occasion, given only five minutes to change trains in Frankfurt, I was told that trains are never late and that the time would be sufficient. My train was late, as were several others I took, and I missed that connection. Remarking it later to my hosts, I was told again that German trains are *never* late. I dropped the subject quickly.

Older women of a secure social class are merciless in Berlin, will push, shove, all very discreetly yet firmly, to get their way. A younger German woman told me of two elders trying to crowd into her cab, having to be physically held off, unheeding of the invitation to share the cab, etc. That will is very disquieting. Although there is, I was told, familiar paternalistic emphasis on family, children, there is in fact no clear social room for the former nor much interest or liking for the latter in any respect. My American sentimentalizing of "kids" may blur the evidence but I rarely if ever, not even in children's playgrounds, found much active place for children in their own social needs. The equipment was remarkable, the care all one might imagine possible, no broken glass, dogshit, but equally no humor, no invention (except for very occasional congeries of Cocteau-like adolescents who took over care of their younger siblings). All somehow drab, patient.

I was intrigued by a *Liegewiese* (a lying-place?) which was just in front of the post office I went to in Wilmersdorf, at one end of the park there, a substantial rectangle of public ground landscaped to make curiously planed rectangles, each a little larger than human body, so as to accommodate public sun bathing, the angle of the ground making exposure optimum and permitting shifting as the sun did. A surprising "nude beach" permission, it seemed, in a city of this size—and it was, in fact, met with frequently in parks adjacent, despite the chill weather. There was nothing sexual about the nudity, as one says, rather a doggedly "intelligent" proposal that the sun was very interesting, however faint.

The museums were incredible, all the accumulations of that nineteenth-century bourgeois mercantile appetite. They were good at it and, like all things German, thorough. So one walks through virtual acres of artifacts of all manner of cultural kind, from high Renaissance to Easter Island, whatever, wherever. I spent a lot of afternoons killing time out in Dahlem, where the US Army base is and where we'd managed to get Willy into a drop-in preschool. I hung out with him, till he got settled, talking with the other children, stories of where their grandma lived in Bakersfield, or Bolton, Mass., and where was I from, American talking as the fall came on more, leaves dropped, cold standing waiting for the 60 bus. I'd walk, once Willy was settled, to a museum a couple of miles away. I liked simply cruising in that sense, nothing in mind. Just watching traffic, people I'd pass, kids coming out of school about three, the crowd in the museum. They were very polite about coats and stuff, at the check-stand, toilets were good, food not hopeless. For an average of six marks (something under three dollars) one could get a big poster of this or that show from extensive stock. They helped brighten our walls, like they say.

But a contemporary show at the National Museum seemed drab echo, almost a mannered "street" harshness, cozy political gesturing. Sad. It was at the time of the protest against the missile deployments, a solidly massive gathering in many cities all over the country. As I was landing in Hanover, for instance, the plane's company was alerted to avoid the downtown sections of the city, else one might be engaged by the demonstration. Many older people, settled and middle class, were involved, which seemed good news. I asked Walter Höllerer in Berlin what might be the effect of the numbers of the protesters, and their clear seriousness, on political thinking. Sadly, he felt it would be little, just that the political/economic patterns of the country were so locked into American program. It was therefore impossible to think of an accommodation, given the relation. In like sense the general political tone moves increasingly to the right, and neo-Nazi elements that ten years ago would have been judged criminally liable are now looked to as the firm, no-nonsense guarantors of public welfare and sane thinking. Some of the Literarisches Colloquium's funding, remarkably, is now taken to pay for a commitment to an MIT project with military overtones. The small fact is, the arts fare poorly. The large fact, it's very much one world, this side of the wall at least.

Hard to leave Berlin without more positive a disposition, but in truth we fled, provoked by fears for my wife's pregnancy, but also just plain running. Too much there was locked echo of my life's failed symbols and political, social despair. I grew up in New England where people occasionally do go to their graves without speaking to one another, the dumb result of an argument, whatever—just the will left, locked in abstract place. In Berlin that sense one could die, live and die, in such an abstract manipulation of one's literal world, the neighbors, the days and nights spent, the job, children, all of it so determined by attitudes that didn't even deign to look at you, just looked over and past at the designed enemy . . . It is awful to live with that sullenness, the truculence, righteousness, sophistication, appetite so prolonged. No matter the young get there, and long to, it's a classic place of the middle-aged, the middle-class, the variously self-conscious dispositions of that limited privilege. In short, a use found in habit that long ago lost impulse. I thought of Fassbinder a lot, also of Günter Grass—who no longer lives there, though he comes often to the city and is head of the Akademie der Kunst significantly. He's a very useful man. (Then Kafka also spent time in Wilmersdorf, etc.).

I met Richard Anders early on, one evening at the Colloquium's monthly gathering in Wannsee. Ted had taken me out on the bus, a long trip through what seemed young forest of straight-rowed fir, all very picked up, small in scale, long horizontal as bus kept going. Place we were in was faded old baronial hall. Someone said Goebbels (?) had had it during the war. Something. (There is always an echo of the past. The Hanovers at Göttingen, Richard Wordsworth at Heidelberg, aptly enough.) Anders proved tall, lanky, shy-mannered contemporary, from part of Germany now in the East, teacher, translator, writer, poet. Surrealist of quiet order. A week later I went up to see him at his place, old apartment top of building, lined with books as they say, wife sadly dead, son comes in with cake for us, sit drinking tea in late afternoon.

So, what's poetry doing in Germany? Not very much. Return to more conservative, classical determination after time of active experiment—like Maoists move abruptly to Buddhism, served by fact both don't like "talking about it," as disciplines so-called. We ate cake in pleasure, musing. He tells me of time he is, as soldier, condemned to death, is in group to be x'd, and war collapsing about them, officer says, oh, go on, get out of here. He is now off to India, for the first time, somewhat in pursuit of love he hopes possible there, a girl, but to be moving, I think, just somewhere else. But not to America, for whatever reason, however many there may be.

*"Ich Bin . . ."*
*for Richard Anders*

Ich Bin
2 Öl-tank

yellow squat
by railroad

shed train's
zapped past

round peculiar
empty small

town's ownership
fields' flat

(Note: An earlier and shorter report was published in the Washington Post's *Book World*, Dec. 18, 1983, p. 15: "Letter from Berlin" (see pp. 581–83). Of the poems, "Ich Bin . . ." was written on a train just before getting to Frankfurt and takes off from yellow *bomba* or "oil tank" that was on the platform of small town train station we went through, with advertising on it as quoted, viz., "I Am 2 Oil Tank(s)." Only

production towered
by obsolescent hill-

side memory echoing
old wornout castle.

### Den Alten

Then to old Uncle Emil,
*den du immer mimst,*
you always

missed,
missed most,
*häng einem alten Haus*

in fear, hung
from a rafter, a
beam old

Uncle Emil you
*immer mimst*
over the logical river

*Fluss* in the
truly really
*feuchten* clay, fucked finished clay.

### Late Love

Stuck in her stone hut,
he fights to get the window up.

Her loopy Dachshunds
have made off with pupils

of his eyes, like, or else
now from summit to summit

of whatever mountains against which
he thinks he hears the stars crash,

sounds truly *nada*
in all the sad facade.

---

words really understood, of that morning (11/4/83). Then "Late Love" and "Den
Alten" are both parodies, of a sort, of two poems by Richard Anders, "Rat" (from
whence "Den Alten") and "In Seiner Mauerhaut" ("Late Love"), *Preussische Zimmer*
(1975). They are *not* translations, nor even adaptations—rather free play on sounds
and occasionally understood words of those texts—in homage to his own patient
clarity.)

# Form

*The Whip*

I spent a night turning in bed,
my love was a feather, a flat

sleeping thing. She was
very white

and quiet, and above us on
the roof, there was another woman I

also loved, had
addressed myself to in

a fit she
returned. That

encompasses it. But now I was
lonely, I yelled,

but what is that? Ugh,
she said, beside me, she put

her hand on
my back, for which act

I think to say this
wrongly.

David Lehman, ed., *Ecstatic Occasions, Expedient Forms* (New York: Macmillan, 1987).

Form has such a diversity of associations and it seems obvious enough that it would have—like *like*. Like a girl of my generation used to get a formal for the big dance, or else it could be someone's formalizing the situation, which was a little more serious. Form a circle, etc.

It was something one intended, clearly, that came of defined terms. But in what respect, of course, made a great difference. As advice for editing a magazine, Pound wrote, "Verse consists of a constant and a variant . . ." His point was that any element might be made the stable, recurrent event, and that any other might be let to go "hog wild," as he put it, and such a form could prove "a center around which, not a box within which, every item . . ."

Pound was of great use to me as a young writer, as were also Williams and Stevens. I recall the latter's saying there were those who thought of form as a variant of plastic shape. Pound's point was that poetry is a form cut in time as sculpture is a form cut in space. Williams' introduction to *The Wedge* (1944) I took as absolute credo.

"The Whip" was written in the middle fifties, and now reading it I can vividly remember the bleak confusion from which it moves emotionally. There is a parallel, a story called "The Musicians," and if one wants to know more of the implied narrative of the poem, it's in this sad story. The title is to the point, because it is music, specifically jazz, that informs the poem's manner in large part. Not that it's jazzy, or about jazz—rather, it's trying to use a rhythmic base much as jazz of this time would—or what was especially characteristic of Charlie Parker's playing, or Miles Davis', Thelonious Monk's, or Milt Jackson's. That is, the beat is used to delay, detail, prompt, define the content of the statement or, more aptly, the emotional field of the statement. It's trying to do this while moving in time to a set periodicity—durational units, call them. It will say as much as it can, or as little, in the "time" given. So each line is figured as taking the same time, like they say, and each line ending works as a distinct pause. I used to listen to Parker's endless variations on "I Got Rhythm" and all the various times in which he'd play it, all the tempi, up, down, you name it. What fascinated me was that he'd write silences as actively as sounds, which of course they were. Just so in poetry.

So it isn't writing like jazz, trying to be some curious social edge of that imagined permission. It's a time one's keeping, which could be the variations of hopscotch, or clapping, or just traffic's blurred racket. It was what you could do with what you got, or words to that effect.

Being shy as a young man, I was very formal, and still am. I make my moves fast but very self-consciously. I would say that from "Ugh . . ." on the poem moves as cannily and as solidly as whatever. "Listen to the sound that it makes," said Pound. Fair enough.

# Index

Compositor: G & S Typesetters, Inc.
Text: 10/12 Baskerville
Display: Baskerville
Printer: Maple-Vail Book Mfg. Group
Binder: Maple-Vail Book Mfg. Group